School-Community Connections

Leo C. Rigsby, Maynard C. Reynolds, and Margaret C. Wang, Editors

School-Community Connections

Exploring Issues for Research and Practice

Jossey-Bass Publishers • San Francisco

Substantial discounts on bulk quantities of Jossey-Bass books are available to corporations, professional associations, and other organizations. For details and discount information, contact the special sales department at Jossey-Bass Inc., Publishers. (415) 433-1740; Fax (800) 605-2665.

For sales outside the United States, please contact your local Paramount Publishing International Office.

▲
TCF Manufactured in the United States of America on Lyons Falls Pathfinder Tradebook. This paper is acid-free and 100 percent totally chlorine-free.

Library of Congress Cataloging-in-Publication Data

School-community connections: exploring issues for research and
   practice / Leo C. Rigsby, Maynard C. Reynolds, and Margaret C.
   Wang, editors. — 1st ed.
      p.   cm. — (The Jossey-Bass education series)
   Includes bibliographical references and index.
   ISBN 0-7879-0099-0 (alk. paper)
      1. Community and school—United States—Congresses.
2. Education and state—United States—Congresses. 3. Education—
Social aspects—Congresses. I. Rigsby, Leo C. II. Reynolds, Maynard
Clinton. III. Wang, Margaret C. IV. Series.
LC221.S27   1995
370.19´31´0973–dc20   95-1303
                                                             CIP

FIRST EDITION
HB Printing   10 9 8 7 6 5 4 3 2 1

The Jossey-Bass Education Series

Contents

0016967

Preface

The challenges facing children, youth, families, and schools today stem from a variety of cultural, economic, political, and health problems. These out-of-school problems—with which schools must nonetheless deal—are complex, and their solutions require the application of knowledge and expertise from many disciplines and professions. The impetus for publication of this volume arises from the need to draw insights and practical implications from the research bases of varied disciplines to improve our capacity to educate, particularly in this nation's urban communities. For it is in our cities that a host of perilous circumstances place children and families at risk.

The chapters in this volume were originally presented at an invitational conference on school-linked coordination of services for children and families in urban communities. The conference, entitled "School-Community Connections: Exploring Issues for Research and Practice," was sponsored by the National Center on Education in the Inner Cities (CEIC) in collaboration with the National Center on Families, Communities, Schools, and Children's Learning.

The contributors to this volume represent varied disciplines and professions, including business administration, communications, curriculum and instruction, educational psychology, sociology, urban studies, social work, educational policy, psychology, and other social science–related fields. A common thread throughout their work is their seeking to understand and identify ways that integration of services and collaborative efforts between schools and the communities they serve can enhance the capacity for education in this nation's urban communities.

Participants in the conference included policymakers at federal, state, and local levels, and researchers and practitioners who are nationally recognized for their work on how resources in cities can be utilized effectively to improve the life circumstances of children and youth and, ultimately, to enhance their schooling success. Thus, while some chapters focus on theoretical and research concerns, others are focused expressly on the practical, day-to-day intricacies of service delivery.

A basic issue guiding discussion at the conference, and determining the content of this volume, is the need to draw together theory and research bases from many disciplinary perspectives with the practical knowledge of the various professions to enhance the delivery of educational and related human and health services to children and their families. It is also important to remember that schools are embedded in complex community structures that express, and often represent, varied expectations of parents, local businesses, social agencies, and diverse cultural groups. Understanding and taking account of the often conflicting perspectives of these myriad stakeholders is essential if we are to improve the delivery of support services to children and youth.

This view of the nature of school-community connections raises a number of complex questions, including: What is the nature of the influences of the larger community on processes within schools (both teaching/administering and learning) and on schooling outcomes? Which disciplinary perspectives do we need to examine to gain the necessary understanding of these processes? What knowledge of the different relevant disciplines and their practice is essential to gain the richest understanding of schooling processes? How can dialogue *across disciplines* (such as economics, education, and political science) and *across arenas of service responsibility* (for instance, the criminal justice system, educational research, and health care) be made more efficient?

These questions and the attempt to answer them were the central focus of discussions at the conference. They also define the substantive scope of the chapters included in this book. They aim not only to highlight theoretical and research issues but also to summarize the well-confirmed knowledge base on effective practices. Clearly, schools cannot solve the out-of-school educational problems of students and families through activities that are separate and independent from those of other social agencies. Therefore, an urgent need exists for coherent multiagency support and assistance in servicing children and their families.

This book aims first to understand school-community connections and the most effective ways to mobilize school and community resources in the service of children and youth. Its second aim is to understand the complexities of communication and exchange of information, both across disciplines and across professional boundaries of service responsibilities. Professionals often must work without the benefit of relevant information about the persons to be served or their social context. There are numerous barriers to sharing information and knowledge, including disciplinary specialization and organizational constraints such as privacy of information, incompatible formats of databases, and inaccessible information resources.

The chapters included in this book attempt to address these communication issues, focusing on problems of interprofessional and interagency coordination in attempts to serve highly stressed children and families in inner-city environments. Increasingly, school leaders and educational policymakers seek collaboration with representatives of welfare, health, and corrections agencies to improve service to students and families. Many hurdles arise when such collaboration is sought, including general inefficiency in cross-professional dialogue, legal limitations concerning exchange of "private" information, and bureaucratic limitations on funding joint programs and negotiating accountability requirements. All of these obstacles must be overcome if essential services are to reach those who need them most—children and families in our nation's inner cities whose circumstances place them at risk.

The intended audience for *School-Community Connections* comprises policymakers and researchers focusing on integration of services and collaborative efforts between schools and their larger communities. It is our hope that readers will find the book useful, and that it will stimulate further research on interagency collaboration and help to advance the knowledge base from which practical efforts in the field are now moving forward.

The book is organized into four sections, each including substantive chapters and commentaries that originally were delivered at the conference. The first section provides an overview, the "keynote" paper, and two commentaries on that paper. Three chapters and two commentaries that address key issues raised by efforts to mount collaborative programs make up the second section. The third section, also consisting of three chapters and two commentaries, examines the social context of schools and collaborative programs. The final section contains four chapters (one of which is a meta-analysis of literature) that analyze ongoing programs, followed by a commentary.

Many individuals have made significant contributions to the preparation of this book. We would like especially to express our deep appreciation to Dr. Aquiles Iglesias, associate director of CEIC, for handling the many administrative details at the conference, and for his substantive feedback on the initial drafts of the papers. We also thank Jesse Shafer for his editorial and administrative support, and Erin Corcoran and Don Gordon for their editorial support in ensuring the book's timely completion. Finally, we gratefully acknowledge the guidance and support of Oliver Moles and Jackie Jenkins of the Office of Educational Research and Improvement of the U.S. Department of Education, which provides funding support for CEIC. The opinions expressed in this book, however, do not necessarily reflect the position of the funding agency, and no official endorsement should be inferred.

April 1995   Leo C. Rigsby

                                               Maynard C. Reynolds

                                               Margaret C. Wang

The Editors

Maynard C. Reynolds is professor emeritus of educational psychology (special education programs), University of Minnesota, and senior research associate at the National Center on Education in the Inner Cities and the Temple University Center for Research in Human Development and Education. He received his B.S. degree (1942) from Moorhead State University and his M.A. (1947) and Ph.D. (1950) degrees from the University of Minnesota. He is a past president of the International Council for Exceptional Children and the recipient of that organization's highest award, the J. W. Wallace Wallin Award, in 1971.

Leo C. Rigsby is associate professor of sociology and senior research associate of the Center for Research in Human Development and Education at Temple University. He also serves as senior research associate at the National Center on Education in the Inner Cities. Dr. Rigsby received his Ph.D. degree (1970) in social relations from Johns Hopkins University. As project director of TU–TOR (Temple University–Taking on Responsibility), a program of the Exemplary Schools Project, Dr. Rigsby supervised a pilot project designed to field test a model for enhancing and nurturing young people's basic skills development and their motivation to succeed in school and in their work lives on completion of formal schooling. He organized the National Invitational Conference on School-Community Connections: Exploring Issues for Research and Practice, the proceedings of which serve as the basis for this book.

Margaret C. Wang is professor of educational psychology and the founder and current director of the Temple University Center for Research in Human Development and Education, a broad-based interdisciplinary research and development center focusing on the human development and education-related fields. She also serves as director of the National Center on Education in the Inner Cities, one of the national research and development centers established by the Office of Educational Research and Improvement of the U.S. Department of Education.

Wang is recognized nationally and internationally for her research on learner differences and classroom learning, on student motivation, and on implementation and evaluation of innovative school programs that are responsive to student diversity. A major thrust of her research on student differences is analysis of the role of the learner in school learning contexts and its implications for instructional practices and program development. She received her Ph.D. degree (1968) in child development and educational research from the University of Pittsburgh. Wang was among the first group of recipients of the Spencer Fellowship of the National Academy of Education, in recognition of her early career contributions to the theory and practice of education.

Wang is the developer of two major school programs: the Primary Education Program, an early learning curriculum; and the Adaptive Learning Environments Model, a comprehensive education program designed to support implementation of classroom instruction that provides for individual differences among students. She is the author of twelve books and more than one hundred articles in a variety of researcher- and practitioner-oriented journals and books.

The Contributors

Harriet H. Arvey is assistant superintendent of student services for the Houston Independent School District, the fifth largest public school district in the country. Her responsibilities in the district encompass supervision of the Child Study Bureau, the Guidance and Counseling program, the Drug-Free Schools program, and programs for at-risk students. Arvey holds a B.A. degree (1965) from Occidental College; her M.S. degree (1974) in counseling and Ph.D. degree (1976) in educational and counseling psychology are from the University of Tennessee. She is a licensed psychologist. She serves on several local boards consistent with her interest in children's mental health, community psychology, and public education. Most recently, she chairs the Hogg Foundation "School of the Future" board in Houston and is on the National Advisory Committee for the National Center on Education in the Inner Cities, located at the Temple University Center for Research in Human Development and Education.

David W. Bartelt is professor of geography and urban studies at Temple University, where he is also director of the Institute for Public Policy Studies and a senior research associate at the National Center on Education in the Inner Cities. He received his B.A. degree (1965) in sociology from Temple University, his M.A. degree (1969) in sociology from Ohio State University, and his Ph.D. degree (1979) from Temple University, also in sociology. Bartelt was an assistant professor at Glassboro State College before joining the urban studies program at Temple in 1979. He was a visiting professor at Kings' College, University of London, in 1985–86. His major research interests are racial segregation, urban structure, and the development of underclass communities, particularly as they impact inner-city schools.

William L. Boyd received his Ph.D. degree from the University of Chicago. He holds the title of Distinguished Professor of Education in the College of Education at The Pennsylvania State University. Prior to moving to Penn State, he taught at the University of Rochester. He was a Visiting Fulbright Scholar in Australia in 1984 and in Britain in 1990–91. Boyd has conducted research on education reform efforts in the United States, Australia, Britain, and Sweden, and was a consultant to the Swedish National Agency for Education. He also was president of the Politics of Education Association, and is currently a member of the steering committee for the U.S.–Australia Policy Project. He serves on a number of editorial boards, has published more than eighty articles and chapters in books, and is coeditor of seven books.

Iris Carlton-LaNey is associate professor at the University of North Carolina, Chapel Hill, School of Social Work. She received her B.S. degree (1972) in social work from North Carolina Agricultural and Technical State University, her M.A. degree (1974) in social work from the University of Chicago School of Social Service Administration, and her Ph.D. degree (1981) from the University of Maryland, Baltimore, School of Social Work. Much of her research has been in the areas of gerontological social work and the social welfare history of African Americans. She has served as a member of the board or as a committee member for numerous nonprofit and public organizations, including A Child's Place: A Transitional School for Homeless Children.

Robert L. Crowson is professor of education in the Department of Educational Leadership, Peabody College, Vanderbilt University.

He received his B.A. degree (1961) in economics from Oberlin College and his Ph.D. degree (1974) in educational administration from the University of Chicago. His research has been concentrated on the organization and administration of urban schools, the politics of education, and school-community relationships.

Don Davies is the founder of the Institute for Responsive Education and co-director of the Center on Families, Communities, Schools, and Children's Learning. He has been professor of education at Boston University since 1974. He received his B.A. and M.A. degrees from Stanford University and his doctoral degree from Teachers College, Columbia University. He was a high school teacher of English and journalism, and has taught at San Francisco University and the University of Minnesota. In 1973 he founded the Institute for Responsive Education, a nonprofit public interest organization working to encourage family-community-school partnerships, which resulted in his establishing the League of Schools Reaching Out, a ninety-member international association of schools working toward education reform through parental and community involvement. He is the principal investigator of the first multinational action research study of parent involvement in school reform.

Lawrence J. Dolan received both his B.A. degree (1971) from Boston College and his Ph.D. degree (1980) from the University of Chicago in educational psychology. He was a program officer for the Spencer Foundation and assistant professor at the University of Rochester before coming to Johns Hopkins in 1984 as a faculty member in the Department of Mental Hygiene in the School of Hygiene and Public Health. In 1989 he joined the Center for the Social Organization of Schools as a principal research scientist.

Eric M. Eisenberg is professor of communication and director of graduate studies at the University of South Florida. He is chair of the Organizational Communication Division of the International Communication Association. He received his B.A. degree (1977) in communication from Rutgers University; M.S. degrees in communication (1980) and education (1981) from Michigan State University; and his Ph.D. degree (1982) in communication, also from Michigan State University. Eisenberg has published more than fifty articles and book chapters dealing with communication in interpersonal, organizational, and interorganizational contexts. While on the faculty of the University of Southern California in 1993, he was the recipient of the Burlington Northern Award for Excellence in Teaching. He has twice (in 1984 and 1990) received the annual Speech Communication Association Award for the outstanding publication in organizational communication. Eisenberg advises many major corporations on the subject of organizational communication.

Edmund W. Gordon is the John M. Musser Professor of Psychology, Emeritus, at Yale University. He was formerly the Richard March Hoe Professor of Education and Psychology at Teacher's College, Columbia University. He currently serves as professor of psychology at the City College of New York—where he recently completed one year as interim chairperson of the Department of Black Studies—and as professor of educational psychology at the CUNY Graduate Center. He has served a five-year term as editor of the *American Journal of Orthopsychiatry*, and a three-year term as editor of the *Review of Research in Education*. He is a contributor to the professional and technical literature of education and psychology and has authored more than one hundred journal articles and book chapters. Gordon's research interests include human diversity and pedagogy, human diversity and assessment, the modifiability of cognitive functions, the education of low-status populations, and life-course analysis of persons who defy negative predictions for success. He was one of the founders of Head Start, was its first national director of research, and has been associated with the conceptualization and evaluation of several other of the nation's important experiments in educational reform.

Michael K. Grady has been a senior research associate at the Annie E. Casey Foundation since 1991, helping to design and manage the Foundation's portfolio of research and evaluation studies. His current responsibilities include evaluations of Casey's large-scale systems-reform initiatives in the areas of family foster care, children's mental health, juvenile justice, and teenage pregnancy prevention. Prior to his work at the Foundation, Grady was director of research and evaluation for the Prince George County Public Schools. He received his B.A. degree (1977) from Washington University and his Ed.M. (1983) and Ed.D. (1988) degrees from the Harvard Graduate School of Education.

Barbara Gray is professor of organizational behavior and director of the Center for Research in Conflict and Negotiation in the College of Business Administration at The Pennsylvania State University. Gray received a B.S. degree in chemistry from the University of Dayton and a Ph.D. degree in organizational behavior from Case Western Reserve University. She is author of *Collaborating: Finding Common Ground for Multiparty Problems* (1989) and coauthor of *International Joint Ventures: Economic and Organizational Perspectives* (forthcoming).

Geneva D. Haertel is currently a senior research associate at Temple University's Center for Research in Human Development and Education, where she conducts research syntheses on programs and practices that influence the academic achievement of at-risk children. Haertel is also a research associate at the Center for Research on Educational Accountability and Teacher Evaluation at Western Michigan University, where she reviews literature on models of teacher evaluation. She has published more than forty articles and chapters in educational and psychological journals and books. In 1990, she coedited *The International Encyclopedia of Educational Evaluation* with Herbert J. Walberg. Her recent publications include a research synthesis entitled "Toward a Knowledge Base of School Learning" and a book chapter on educational resilience in inner cities, both coauthored with Margaret C. Wang and Herbert J. Walberg.

Wayne H. Holtzman received his B.S. (1944) and M.S. (1947) degrees from Northwestern University, and his Ph.D. degree (1950) from Stanford University in psychology and statistics. Since 1949, he has been a faculty member in psychology at the University of Texas, Austin. Currently Hogg Professor of Psychology and Education at the university and special counsel of the Hogg Foundation for Mental Health, Holtzman has served as Foundation president, dean of the university's college of education, and associate director of the Foundation's research program. Author of more than 150 articles in scientific journals, he served as editor of the *Journal of Educational Psychology*. Among his books are *Inkblot Perception and Personality*; *Computer-Assisted Instruction, Testing and Guidance*; *Personality Development in Two Cultures*; *Introduction to Psychology*; *Mental Health of Immigrants and Refugees*; and *School of the Future*.

Carolyn Kelley is assistant professor of educational policy and organizational theory in the Department of Educational Administration at the University of Wisconsin, Madison. She received her B.S. degree (1982) in journalism from the University of Illinois, her M.S. degree (1985) in public policy from the University of Michigan, and her Ph.D. degree (1993) in educational administration and policy analysis from Stanford University. Her research interests focus on programs and policies to address the needs of at-risk youth. She has written on school-linked services, parent time investment, and organizational change issues.

Michael W. Kirst has been professor of education and business administration at Stanford University since 1969. Before joining the Stanford University faculty, Kirst served in several capacities with the federal government, including a position as staff director of U.S. Senate Subcommittee on Manpower, Employment, and Poverty. Kirst has authored ten books, including *Schools in Conflict: Political Turbulence in American Education* (with Frederick Wirt, 1992). He is a member of the research staff of the Center for Policy Research in Education, a federally funded center. His most recent book concerns a new role for U.S. school boards, published with his colleagues at the Institute for Educational Leadership.

Roslyn Arlin Mickelson, a former high school social studies teacher, is associate professor of sociology and adjunct associate professor of women's studies at the University of North Carolina, Charlotte. She received her B.A. degree (1965) in anthropology, and her M.A. (1980) and Ph.D. (1984) degrees, in the sociology of education, from the University of California, Los Angeles. Prior to coming to the University of North Carolina in 1985, she completed a postdoctoral fellowship at the University of Michigan, Ann Arbor's Bush Program in Child Development and Social Policy. Her research examines the political economy of schooling, in particular, the ways that race, class, and gender shape educational processes and outcomes. Currently, she is researching the curricular and equity implications of business-led school reforms.

Alan Peshkin is professor of education at the University of Illinois, Urbana-Champaign, where he is also acting director of the Bureau of Educational Research. He received his B.A. (1952) and M.A. (1954) degrees from the University of Illinois, and his Ph.D. (1962) degree in curriculum and comparative education from the University of Chicago. In support of his earlier research on the school-community relationship, he received a Guggenheim Fellowship (1973–1974). Most recently, he was appointed to the Center for Research in the Behavioral Sciences, Palo Alto, California (1992). His books include *Growing Up American* (1978), *The Imperfect*

Union (1982), *God's Choice* (1986), and *The Color of Strangers, The Color of Friends* (1991).

Samuel F. Redding is executive director of the Academic Development Institute in Lincoln, Illinois, where he is also the founding editor of the *School Community Journal*. A former teacher, professor, and college dean, he received his doctorate in education from Illinois State University in 1976. In 1990, he received an Award of Excellence for contributions to education from the Illinois State Board of Education. In 1994, he received the Ben Hubbard Leadership Award from Illinois State University. His Alliance for Achievement model for building school communities is used by a network of schools in Illinois.

Salvatore J. Saporito is a doctoral candidate in Temple University's sociology department. He received his B.A. degree in sociology from Glassboro State College. As part of a collaborative project with William L. Yancey, he is currently studying the influence that urban ecology has on the learning environments of students in Philadelphia and Houston. He is also examining the influence of neighborhood violence on school climate and educational outcomes under a research grant from the National Institute of Justice awarded to Temple University's Center for Public Policy.

Carol B. Truesdell is executive director of the Youth Trust, a Minneapolis-based nonprofit organization dedicated to the development of partnerships and collaborations focused on mentoring and workforce development for Minneapolis youth in kindergarten through twelfth grade. She previously has held positions with the Minneapolis Public Schools, the Pillsbury Company Foundation, and CHART, a career development and employment center for women. Truesdell received her B.A. degree (1958) in psychology from Mount Holyoke College, and has participated in postgraduate programs at Harvard, Stanford, and the University of Minnesota.

Alfredo Tijerina is coordinator of Hispanic Integrative School-Based Services at the Family Service Center in Houston, and of the School of the Future, a joint initiative of the Hogg Foundation for Mental Health at the University of Texas, Austin, and the Houston Independent School District. He is an advanced licensed master social work practitioner and chemical dependency counselor in the State of Texas, and has served as president (1991) of the Hispanic Social Workers of Texas–Houston Chapter, from whom he received the Hispanic Social Worker of the Year award (1992). Since 1990, he has been an adjunct faculty member of the University of Houston, Graduate School of Social Work, and an advisory-board member in 1992 to the children and families concentration at the school. He received his B.A. degrees (1977) in philosophy and sociology from Centenary College, Louisiana; his certification (1976) in Christian education from Centenary School of Church Careers; and his M.S.W. degree (1986) from the University of Georgia School of Social Work.

Herbert J. Walberg is research professor of education at the University of Illinois, Chicago. He also serves as adviser on education and educational research to public and private agencies in several countries. He is chairman of the educational board of the *International Journal of Educational Research*, series editor for McCutchan Publishing and JAI Press, and evaluation editor for the *International Encyclopedia of Education*. Walberg received his B.E. degree (1959) from Chicago State University, his M.E. degree (1960) from the University of Illinois, and his Ph.D. degree (1964) in educational psychology from the University of Chicago.

Maria Grace Yon is assistant professor of education at the University of North Carolina, Charlotte. She received her B.S. degree (1971) in elementary education at Concord College in Athens, West Virginia, and her M.A. degree (1974) in elementary education from West Virginia University. After twelve years as an elementary school teacher, she received her Ed.D. degree (1987) in curriculum and instruction from Virginia Polytechnic Institute and State University. Her research focuses on the process of learning to teach, with a specific interest in student teachers and induction-year teachers. After becoming a member of the board of directors of A Child's Place: A Transitional School for Homeless Children, in Charlotte, North Carolina, she developed a research interest in the education of homeless children and youth.

Andrea Zetlin is professor in the Division of Special Education, School of Education, California State University, Los Angeles. She also serves as senior research associate at the National Center on Education in the Inner Cities. She has extensive teaching experience in special education classrooms in New York and California. She earned her Ed.D. degree (1977) from Teachers College, Columbia University, with a major in exceptional children and a minor in educational psychology.

School-Community Connections

Chapter One

Introduction

The Need for New Strategies

Leo C. Rigsby

The educational literature resonates with laments about how the world has changed; how the children who enter today's schools are not prepared to learn in the same ways as children in earlier eras. While it is not inherently clear that the past was as favorable for educational systems as our historical memory suggests, it is nevertheless apparent that the tasks faced by today's schools are formidable.

We know that U.S. schools have from their beginnings faced difficult tasks (Katz, 1968; Tyack, 1992). On the other hand, even the schools of the early twentieth century faced somewhat different problems from those encountered by schools today. The efficacy of education, for instance, was much less challenged, and the notion that our industrial rivals (countries different from those viewed as "rivals" today) would overtake us simply did not exist. Although the population of the United States exhibited much cultural diversity because of the waves of immigration from Europe, such variation among cultures did not create the extreme sense of crisis that educators and citizens feel from the current surge in migration within specific populations, and particularly within urban environments.

Researchers need only scan the pages of a city newspaper or walk down the halls of an urban school to see that today's generation of inner-city students faces a host of problems that simply were not present, or at least not to such an alarming degree, in previous years. More and more, children come to school bearing the stresses of a seemingly ceaseless upsurge in chaos. Violence by and against our cities' youth is on the rise; weaponry in the schools is a real and frightening concern. Acknowledgment of problems such as poor health; hunger; and physical, mental, or substance abuse has existed for some time, and viable solutions have been outlined. Still, not all solutions help all children. In the midst of threats to their very existence, these children are expected to extend full concentration to such tasks as the mastery of literacy, numeracy, analytic skills, citizenship, and whatever aspects of culture the local context deems appropriate. In light of these criteria, and in the absence of readily available assistance, it is no wonder that so many do not succeed.

Our society has undergone massive changes, leaving families vulnerable. Unemployment; exposure to urban decay where cities have lost their industrial bases; increasing competition for the remaining low-paying jobs from new groups of immigrants; teen pregnancy; substance abuse—each represents a high-risk condition, threatening the well-being and healthy development of all citizens, but especially of children.

Schools in the past never had to deal with such challenges to order; nor were they faced with the daunting task of educating students who suffered so many conditions of risk in their lives. Hence, we must ask ourselves: How can children concentrate on education in the face of such dangers to their very existence? What are the schools to do? How can they carry on business as usual? Unfortunately, schools are themselves lacking in both the professional expertise and the fiscal resources necessary to provide social services on behalf of children. Further, agencies that routinely provide social services for children are not located within the schools. Thus, we are left wondering how we can offer social and health services to children for whom the need exists, and how we can make this accessible in schools.

New strategies for education are essential if schools are to educate our embattled children for the next century. One important focus of research and development in the larger educational arena rests on programs linking social and health services with schools. Such efforts seek to help schools provide or arrange for the services that children need to enable them to undertake the tasks of education. Referred to variously as the "integrated," "collaborative," or "coordinated" services movement, the aim is to bring together existing social service agencies and children in need through the auspices of schools.

Some models depict agency personnel working in schools. Others support having schools send children out to agencies but with joint school and agency monitoring of the services. Further variation exists in models that conceptualize neutral sites (neither school nor agency) in which school referrals and services might be developed and implemented.

The existence of different models suggests in itself that problems are created by these efforts to bring services to children in cooperation with schools. Even the "solutions" raise new questions and concerns. Whose professional expertise determines which children need services and what kinds of services are needed? Should the provision of services take precedence over educating children or should educating children take precedence, with social services being provided at the convenience of educators? What agency should bear the cost of social services to children? What agency is responsible for the welfare and safety of children when they are being educated or provided with services?

Clearly the integration of services for children creates as many dilemmas as it solves. Granted, the problems are of a different nature and surface as enigmatic issues for professionals, schools, and agencies rather than children. In October 1992, Temple University's National Center on Education in the Inner Cities jointly sponsored an invitational conference with the National Center on Families, Communities, and Children's Learning to explore issues of theory and practice related to integrating social services and education for children. The collection of chapters in this book outlines deliberations at that conference and provides a state-of-the-art summary of theory and research on the integration-of-services-for-children movement. In this introductory chapter, a broad framework has been sketched for understanding the integration-of-services movement. Highlighting a new conception of problems and solutions affecting education is the idea that school leaders and educational policymakers increasingly seek collaboration with representatives of welfare, health, and criminal justice agencies in order to better serve students and their families. The innovation explicitly recognizes that many of the important factors that have major impacts on children's readiness and capacity to learn come from the broader environments in which schools reside. School leaders have come to understand more than ever before that they *must* seek collaboration with agencies of the larger society because educators lack both the expertise and the resources to effectively control forces external to schools.

Theoretical Overview

The topics of the chapters and their organization grew out of a keen understanding of both the origins of the educational crises endured by children and the most effective solutions. Kirst and Kelley (Chapter Two) argue in this volume that U.S. policymakers and politicians since the Great Society programs of the 1960s have generally been reluctant to tackle the problems of educating children and youth on any basis other than an instrumental rationale. This rationale asserts that the nation's competitiveness in the global economy depends on developing the human capital skills of its citizenry. That this citizenry increasingly consists of children of minority and third-world origins, whose conditions of life pose severe risks to the levels of educational performance demanded in the global economy, means that schools and their communities must acknowledge the risk conditions. In order to ensure that children and youth are educated to the levels demanded by economic competitiveness, educators and policymakers have begun to address the nonschool problems faced by children and youth. So far the efforts have centered largely on existent problems that interfere with children's educational development instead of looking toward preventive strategies.

Kirst and Kelley explore the possible and likely allies of advocates of integrated-services programs for children and the kinds of appeals that would hold currency with them. Recognizing the multilevel structures that can influence the integration of services for children, they review the roles and strategies appropriate for actors at different levels—from state officials acting to promote holistic views of children's services to local district and building officials acting to participate in or facilitate specific services. Kirst and Kelley end their agenda-setting chapter in an optimistic tone by noting that at all relevant levels public policy is more favorable to integration of services for children than ever before.

Discussion at the conference took issue over whether an instrumental rationale is enough. Can we afford to rely solely on arguments stating that the welfare of children is in the interest of the nation's economy? Is it moral to rely on such arguments when children are hungry, sick, and inadequately housed? Obviously those who are advocates for children must form countless arguments and take many different actions to marshal as much energy as possible in support of the well-being of children. Edmund Gordon (Chapter Three) challenges Kirst and Kelley's rationale for collaborative services, arguing that changes in the world economy and in the nature of family structure and functioning have created new needs for children's services for all children and not just for those whose living circumstances fit traditionally defined conditions of risk. Gordon calls policymakers and researchers to view the problems of children as growing out of new environments that call for redefined familial and societal arrangements and commitments.

Wayne Holtzman (Chapter Four) responds to the chapter by Kirst and Kelley by bringing to bear his vast experience as a foundation president whose focus has been on the social and mental health aspects of the development of children. Holtzman's work has emphasized local partnerships as productive and viable sites of agency-school collaborations. He discusses the perspectives and plans of foundations in supporting these efforts. The building of school-community partnerships with the active collaboration of local business firms and social agencies has shown promise in the work of the Hogg Foundation. Holtzman sees such collaborations as proponents of a new spirit of caring in our society.

Taken together, these introductory chapters focus attention on two facts. First, the social context within which education takes place creates an atmosphere that supplies the broader rationale for providing education—a rationale that has undergone dramatic change over the past century. Stated in such bare terms, this information is hardly revolutionary. On the other hand, it forces us to think about a second fact—that the social context of education is inevitably and continuously in a state of flux. That we must also expect the delivery and content of educational services to change similarly is a conclusion that follows from these facts. We are led to the very poignant implication that models of educational processes must be dynamic and must take account of the changing social context of education. One reason that we face the crises that emerged as a result of attempts to integrate services is that educational policy has a natural tendency to examine the past for models of efficient functioning of education. For example, the policies of the Reagan and Bush administrations and the policy reports of the early and mid-1980s focused on the increasing inadequacies of individuals and families to fit the expectations of schools. Very little attention was given to the need for schools and social service agencies to redefine their work to fit such criteria as the changing patterns of employment and immigration, increasing threats from crime, and the spread of sexually transmitted diseases. Theorizing the ever-changing social context of educational services represents an important advance in our thinking through the present educational crises.

Schools are complex entities that serve varied and at times conflicting purposes. Desired outcomes differ along with representative groups or individuals. Hence, schools simultaneously become places of employment, places of learning, havens from chaotic neighborhood life, brief stops on the road to a different career, and places where a number of children's needs may potentially be met. A fruitful way to think about schools is to see them as structures that are intricately and irrevocably woven into others, all of which serve political, economic, cultural, religious, and social aims. The interrelated nature of such structures makes it almost impossible to plan and implement change in one without affecting the others. For this reason, numerous complex issues are raised by integration-of-services programs.

Schools and public agencies are organizations with professional staffs, with discipline-specific/profession-based discourse for conceptualizing their work, with different types of training, and with models and standards for dealing with "client" populations. Apart from issues of funding and turf protection across organizations, integration-of-services programs require that professionals with different aims and priorities work together, be able to speak about "problems" in languages that foster joint efforts, and be willing to compromise some specific standards or expectations.

How, then, is it possible to create the organizational force that it takes to change the ways in which schools and social service agencies work as separate entities so that they are able to coordinate, cooperate, or collaborate to meet newly defined or recognized needs of children? Each of the remaining chapters deals with this question in some way or another. These chapters are arranged into three sections that focus, respectively, on models and theoretical issues relating to collaboration and integration of services for children; on the embeddedness of schools and other agencies dealing with children in different communities and neighborhoods; and on empirical studies of ongoing integration-of-services programs.

The theoretical chapters consider three broad sets of issues. The first stemmed from concern over delineating critical issues surrounding the construction of effective models for collaboration. Scholars in a number of fields, but particularly in the field of business administration, have studied how to construct organizations and coalitions of organizations to achieve clear-cut goals. This knowledge directly influences how collaborative efforts can become most effectively organized among schools, community agencies, and institutions. Building on her work on collaboration, Barbara Gray (Chapter Five) discusses models of collaboration and applies her framework to the specific case of a failed collaborative attempt among educators, leaders in private industry, and youth employment officials to ease the school-to-work transition for inner-city youth. Gray details how the diverse purposes of individual groups ultimately undermined their joint planning efforts and impeded implementation of plans.

The second theoretical issue was predicated on the idea that different professions and organizations possess unique vocabularies and perspectives appropriate to their work. For example, teachers and schools define their relationships with children differently from the way social workers and agencies define their relationships with children. These variations raise barriers to effective collaborative relationships between schools and agencies. Eric Eisenberg (Chapter Six) brings the perspective of communications to these issues. Pointing out that different kinds of collaborative or integration-of-services efforts require different degrees of organizational or professional change, he questions whether the rational model of organizational planning is the most effective strategy for creating successful collaborative efforts to provide integrated services. Drawing on theory and research in communications, he outlines an alternative scheme.

Our third broad theoretical issue focused on expanding an understanding of how efforts to build collaborative relationships between schools and other community organizations relate to the ongoing efforts to restructure and reform schools. This question brought forth an examination of the political economy of institutions, looking at the variety of interests and conflicts among schools, agencies, and institutions over the control of work, funding, allocation of resources, and organizational change processes. Specifically, Crowson and Boyd (Chapter Seven) present two models of organizational change and explore the effects of the allocation of rewards and the definitions of rules and roles in organizations on such change.

One point stressed in each of these chapters and in the accompanying commentaries is the diversity among ongoing integration-of-services efforts. Programs differ in organizational players, in critical issues, in ultimate goals, in strategies of coordination/cooperation/collaboration, and in the degree to which participants are conscious of the implied mandate for fundamental institutional change. Homing in on this disparity, Michael Grady (Chapter Eight) describes the commitment of the Annie E. Casey Foundation, a major funder of integration-of-services programs, to systematic evaluation of all such efforts so that we can begin to separate more effective strategies from those that are less effective. Grady places strong weight on combining process evaluation with outcome evaluation.

The importance of process evaluation lies in the notion that in general, ultimate goals for outcomes of these programs entail client behaviors in the distant future (such as developing skills for effective lifetime learning, and preparing for unknown job changes in the future). These are outcomes whose accomplishment rests so far in the future that program evaluation cannot logically include their assessment. Grady argues that program evaluators need to incorporate multiple outcomes, including the development of new organizational structures and processes. His rationale is that programs often have as intermediate goals the promotion of organizational change and development to accommodate or anticipate newly emergent problems. Successes or failures in these intermediate stages of programs are more likely to be available for assessment than the long-term outcomes. Likewise, intermediate outcomes for the client targets of programs, such as changes in school attendance, engagement in school, and short-term behaviors and goals are more likely to be available for assessment than long-term changes such as adult employment flexibility.

Carol Truesdell (Chapter Nine) reacts to the theoretical issues from a "brokers of collaboration" perspective. Representing the Minneapolis Youth Trust, an umbrella organization created to foster the development of partnerships to help children and youth from kindergarten through twelfth grade become ready for life and work, Truesdell accentuates the degree to which organizations such as the Minneapolis Youth Trust currently operate in uncharted waters. Generalizations about "what works," she contests, seem empty in a context where one is trying to work with a specific set of players within the boundaries of one particular community. Confirming the readiness for change cited in earlier chapters, Truesdell also corroborates the confusion and resistance generated by organizations when faced with the modification of *their* understandings and practices. Her experience with the Minneapolis Youth Trust further reinforces the delineation of both the abundant opportunities for and the sometimes overwhelming barriers to creating collaborative service-integration programs.

The Social Contexts of Collaborative Efforts

Schools are embedded in complex community structures that provide the resources with which to support education and present the problems and issues with which the embedded educational system must contend. Communities are diverse in economic vitality and growth of new jobs; in ethnic/racial migration and population growth; in age and quality of housing stock, public buildings, and transportation options; and in many other ways that affect the resources available to and the problems faced by educational systems. The community forces affecting educational systems are expressed at many levels—at the differential level of vitality of one city within the national system of cities and towns, at the state level, at the level of the city itself, and even at the level of the neighborhood served by the school.

Schools serve communities that express varied expectations from parents, local business, social agencies, and distinct cultural groups. Viewing the school in its larger community context must incorporate a vision of multilevel causal structures and processes, each of which mediates conflicting interests, polar understandings of interactions within the system, and specific goals for the functioning of schools within the society. In turn, each segment of the school-community system depends on unique kinds of information and resources. Again, to understand the complex interactions among parts of this multilevel nexus (that is, families, businesses, social agencies, schools, churches), we need to draw on the knowledge bases and theoretical perspectives of several disciplines.

The next set of chapters is concerned with the need for integration of services for children in combination with their educational needs among communities. The effects on patterns-of-services needs are explored on three levels: (1) differences among cities in their patterns of industrial development and racial/ethnic composition; (2) differences among neighborhoods and schools within a city; and (3) differences among specific schools and communities.

David Bartelt (Chapter Ten) analyzes city-to-city differences in the kinds of social indicators that others have used to mark the crises of urban education. He shows substantial differences among cities in terms of levels of poverty, percentages of female-headed families, proportionate size of welfare roles, unemployment rates, and proportion of the population not in the labor force (not employed and no longer looking for work). Bartelt argues that these city-to-city differences are linked to the historical development of cities (that is, where they are located and when they developed as cities), the relative loss of industrial base to areas with cheaper labor costs, the shift of middle-class populations to suburbs, and the isolation of the African-American and Latino populations in inner-city areas. Thus, Bartelt reports that the urban crises that have evoked the need for new programs to promote collaborative efforts between schools and community agencies and businesses are themselves caused by larger economic and social policies. To focus, as have the Reagan and Bush administrations, on "family values" and "morality" rather than on decision-making processes that have resulted in the removal of jobs from inner-city areas is to distort our understanding of the causes of (and solutions to) this urgent concern.

William Yancey and Salvatore Saporito (Chapter Eleven) have extended the analysis of social and economic causes of city-to-city differences to a detailed analysis of these processes at the level of schools and neighborhoods within a single urban setting. They show that differentiation of neighborhoods and the increasing segregation of neighborhoods by race and social class have dramatic effects on schools. This conclusion is not at all the same as saying that the staffs of inner-city schools face an insurmountable task because children do not come to school prepared to learn. Rather, these data indicate that the character of schools is affected by the complex social, economic, and ecological processes beyond the population composition of schools and that these larger factors must be brought into play in any solution that calls out to the crises in inner-city education.

Finally, Alan Peshkin (Chapter Twelve), drawing on his earlier ethnographic studies of five vastly different schools, discusses the richly textured and detailed relationships among the stakeholders in communities that must be negotiated for organizational and community change to occur. Reiterating the significant point that schools are embedded and contested institutions, Peshkin analyzes the varied, conflicting interests and perspectives that different stakeholders bring to deliberations about school change. He argues that in our multifaceted society we can neither expect nor desire anything better than the maintenance of embeddedness and contestedness of schools. This means that these qualities must be recognized and respected if they are to be eventually renegotiated and compromised to achieve change.

Samuel Redding's remarks on the social context of education (Chapter Thirteen) raise important theoretical issues surrounding our understanding of the multilayered effects of population composition on educational outcomes. He challenges chapter authors to become more explicit in the theoretical foundations of their models connecting the historical development of cities and neighborhoods to social processes within schools. He poses questions whose answers entail additional theoretical development and the pursuit of different kinds of research, both ethnographic and longitudinal quantitative varieties. He raises the very real issue of the balance between preserving the autonomy and cultural uniqueness of families and the pursuit of efficient education that serves the needs of a dynamic economy.

Don Davies (Chapter Fourteen) responds to issues raised in earlier chapters by stressing that comprehensive approaches to the education and nurturing of children should be our policy goal. He contends that collaborative services and family empowerment are the key strategies to achieving comprehensiveness. More than most other chapters in this volume, Davies persuasively hearkens to family empowerment as a key to collaborative services. His stance anticipates Andrea Zetlin's later commentary in this collection, which indicates that educators, researchers, and agency staff are often unprepared for families to assume serious roles in collaborative ventures. Davies holds that family empowerment is not only a key to comprehensiveness of services for children but is also a significant core value of democracy. That family empowerment remains a point of contention in the development of integrated-services programs and other efforts to restructure existing institutions to better serve the needs of children and families is devastating commentary on the extent to which university researchers, educators, program developers, and funders remain part of the problem as well as the solution.

Empirical Studies of Integrated-Services Programs

The final set of chapters is devoted to studies of existing programs that provide integrated services for children. In the first of these, a meta-analysis of studies of integrated services is presented by Wang, Haertel, and Walberg. The next three report empirical studies that were based at three very different sites: a program that tied together services for children with a middle school and two feeder elementary schools (Arvey and Tijerina); a school for homeless children (Mickelson, Yon, and Carlton-LaNey); and a program of integrated services in three elementary schools within one city (Dolan). Two themes emerge from these chapters: existing programs represent unique accommodations to particular social contexts, and systematic evaluation is extremely difficult to manage in collaborative settings. The difficulty results partly from the distinct qualities of each setting and partly from the conflicting needs, interests, and perspectives of different professions and agencies.

The Wang, Haertel, and Walberg chapter (Chapter Fifteen) is a meta-analysis of the highly disparate literature on the evaluation of programs that can be generally interpreted to be integrated-services and/or collaborative programs. The authors were forced to draw very broad definitions of target programs because few comprehensive evaluations have been published of such holistic programs as New Futures Initiative, School of the Future, and Schools of the 21st Century. Although they were able to document success in some programs in terms of changes in student outcomes and school-related behaviors, they highlight, as well, their inability to report extensively on the effects of social context on program development and outcomes, since few published studies include information on steps of development, organizational or institutional change, or outcomes that go beyond measures of students' performances.

The Houston site of the School of the Future program is featured by Harriet Arvey and Alfredo Tijerina in Chapter Sixteen. As the primary designers, developers, implementers, and evaluators of the Houston site, they are able to provide assessments of both systematic school and agency data and accounts of the social history of the project's implementation. Evaluation processes have been given high priority in the development of the School of the Future program. Arvey and Tijerina share the experience of the program's first year of operation. Their experience well illustrates the truism discussed in other chapters that the rational planning processes, while important, can never anticipate all the day-to-day crises that arise in implementing and evaluating a complex program. One essential quality of successful programs seems to be the built-in capacity for dynamic decision making and adaptation.

Mickelson, Yon, and Carlton-LaNey (Chapter Seventeen) report on their experiences as advisers/evaluators of a newly created institution designed to serve schooling and social service needs of homeless children. In a real sense this institution, called A Child's Place, represents the epitome of radical, deep structure change; its history as documented by these authors represents the apex of conflict/contestedness between existing institutions whose expertise was needed to create the new institution. Conflict over whether the new entity should be a school with agency support or an agency with educational support characterized its creation and early experience. This case study illustrates the many important points about conflict, embeddedness, and the vast range of perspectives discussed earlier. Mickelson, Yon, and Carlton-LaNey have outlined a convincing case for the multilayered, richly contextualized perspective on collaborative efforts developed in earlier chapters of this book. They emphasize the effects of broader societal processes and trends on the educational problems A Child's Place was designed to address.

Lawrence Dolan presents a more quantitative assessment of

three years' experience of the Success for All program in Baltimore elementary schools (Chapter Eighteen). Comparing three Success for All schools with three comparable control schools, Dolan assesses academic, process, and organizational aspects of change. His analysis effectively utilizes academic and social process outcome measures called for in earlier chapters and discusses both the short-term and likely long-term goals/outcomes of the program. His research documents the difficulty in getting agencies outside of schools to share information and in getting schools, even those with university-based research assistance, to carry out systematic process evaluation.

Comments by Zetlin on these empirical studies (Chapter Nineteen) are derived from the perspective of her work in an integrated-services program in a public school in Los Angeles. As a university researcher/practitioner, she emphasizes the pioneering aspects of program development and implementation where the goal is to create what she calls "extended school" programs—programs that "go beyond teaching and learning activities to include family growth and development as a primary aim."

Future Directions for Research and Program Development

The chapters in this book document the relative newness of the collaborative-services or integrated-services trend in U.S. education. Evidence of this infancy is the lack of well-confirmed, extensively documented programs that work (though this is not to deny the likely effectiveness of many programs that exist or are being developed). Another perspective on existing programs and needed innovations is that we are at the beginning stages of a substantial transformation. The transformation centers not only on the delivery of educational services but also on family, religious, and other institutional settings that are the sites of the development and nurturing of humans generally, and especially of children. As we come to understand the importance of differences in cultures, in the experiences of women and men, in the experiences of African-American, Latino, Anglo-American populations and other identifiable groups, we also come to see the infinite complexity of our task: to respect difference, to provide opportunities for the fullest development of individuals, and to prepare our populations for productive citizenship in the next century.

These goals cannot be met in the long run simply through incremental change. Our beginning inevitably will be gradual, as we tinker with existing structures and processes, creating small changes that improve the lives of children. On the other hand, we are part of this larger transformation. We must proceed with dedication to small, immediate change that may produce limited differences and equal dedication to the larger transformation. If the broader scope is left unattended to, our smaller modifications will soon become nothing more than a random walk through the back halls of inadequately functioning institutions. We will have gotten nowhere, our purposes ultimately undefined.

This volume offers some guidelines that will serve both types of change. First, evaluation of change efforts must be built on broadbased conceptions of outcomes—outcomes that reflect changes in academic behaviors of individuals, in the degree of comprehensiveness of services, in school and agency structures and procedures, and in the social contexts within which children grow and develop.

Second, we need to incorporate a variety of research strategies in assessing programs. If the desired outcomes are disparate, not all will be amenable to quantitative measurement. As the Wang, Haertel, and Walberg chapter illustrates, most program evaluations do not offer any information on contextual subtleties or historical contexts that authors of the other chapters have argued to be crucial. This may be somewhat reflective of the inclinations of journal editors to privilege "hard data" evaluations, or of the lack of careful thought by researchers about the diversity of outcomes that are implied by their interventions. The discussions in earlier chapters provide an ample rationale for broadening evaluation frameworks to include other strategies and other kinds of data in evaluations.

Third, we must be willing to grapple with the complexity of balancing the uniqueness of each site with the need to generalize across sites to reach "scientific" conclusions about whether changes have created better or worse conditions for different groups. These chapters have thoroughly documented the power of social context and the specific configuration of participants in creating collaborative services. This power must be acknowledged and accounted for in research designs to evaluate collaborative programs. On the other hand, we must continue to search for understanding that allows us to adopt innovations for new settings and configurations of problems. We can afford neither the time nor the resources to reinvent the entire process each time a new collaboration is attempted.

Finally, these chapters increase the tension between evaluating the marginal contributions of different components of comprehensive programs and evaluating whole programs. We know very little about what results from combining simple elements to build comprehensive programs. To evaluate separate components may cause us to overlook the synergies created by their combinations. To conduct only holistic evaluations may cause us to overlook conflicting effects of components. Future evaluations must combine holistic and component assessments if a broadened perspective is ever to be achieved.

References

Katz, M. B. (1968). *The irony of early education reform: Innovation in mid-19th century Massachusetts*. Boston: Beacon Press.

Tyack, D. (1992). Health and social services in public schools: Historical perspectives. *The Future of Children, 2*(1), 19–31.

Part One

The Policy Debate

Chapter Two

Collaboration to Improve Education and Children's Services

Politics and Policy Making

Michael W. Kirst and Carolyn Kelley

The movement to integrate services for children through collaboration among children's organizations has taken hold as a viable issue of interest to policymakers as well as school and program administrators. The multiple needs of children at risk make the provision of school-linked integrated services necessary to ensure access to a quality education. Students who go to school hungry, abused, or sick are unlikely to engage themselves successfully in the classroom and are likely to experience educational failure, perpetuating the cycles of poverty and delinquency. The collaborative-services movement is an attempt to address the problems of children in a coherent, comprehensive, and intensive manner so that children can focus on obtaining a good education and enjoy a successful adult life.

The 1990s have brought an explosion in local efforts to integrate children's services, spurred on by state and federal policies and private foundation grants that encourage such efforts. This chapter explores the politics and policymaking of the integrated-services movement at the federal, state, and local levels as well as operational considerations that need to be addressed when integrated-services programs are implemented. At the federal level, a philosophy of instrumentalism provides the rationale for improving and rethinking children's services. At the state level, a variety of efforts are under way to galvanize collaboration among fragmented children's services providers, through the creation of children's agencies, broader state legislative committees, technical assistance, and start-up grants.

Foundation and state support for new approaches to service delivery have encouraged and built on an abundance of local efforts to combine services in unique ways and to provide better services to youth at risk of teen pregnancy, dropping out of high school, drug abuse, gang violence, and other delinquent behaviors. Numerous operational considerations that flow from the fragmented and piecemeal structure of children's programs need to be confronted if successful integrated and collaborative programs are to be implemented. Before turning to operational issues, however, this chapter provides an overview of the political rationale, strategy, and potential coalitions that will assist in furthering children's programs.

The Evolution of Federal Policy for Needy Children: Instrumentalism and Incrementalism

An energetic brand of federal leadership led to the creation of special programs targeting poor and disadvantaged children in the 1960s, exemplifying a unique period in the United States in terms of children's programs. Given current economic and social patterns, recapturing that kind of leadership is unlikely. Historically, in the more typical pattern of U.S. policy toward at-risk children, one finds instrumentalism and incrementalism: the former in that interventions are usually justified by their economic or social returns for the larger society rather than the responsibilities of society toward the well-being of the individual, and the latter in that societal interventions in private life have historically required demonstrations of extreme parental dysfunction, with broad preventive action rare and unlikely. Legally, this term has been called parens patriae (see Grubb & Lazerson, 1982).

In part, both instrumentalism and incrementalism are the result of an American political culture that rests moral responsibility for social and personal outcomes on the shoulders of parents, and which has a strong ideological commitment to limited government. Instrumentalism and incrementalism are perpetuated by an organizationally complex intergovernmental system, the notion of parens patriae, and, somewhat ironically, the balkanized nature of the services that have emerged to administer assistance to children in need. The irony is that these services, in large measure established by federal efforts to alleviate poverty in the 1960s, were instituted in a fragmented way that hindered future attempts to create broad and comprehensive approaches toward the disadvantaged. A key thesis of this chapter is that collaboration among agencies for children's services can be justified most effectively based on instrumentalism and incrementalism.

Instrumental rationales often cited include concern over the declining birthrates among the more materially advantaged classes and the rapid growth in numbers of children born in poverty. Business organizations have become alarmed about the future supply of educated labor and more aware that they must rely on children of disadvantage. Indeed, with a shrinking high school population overall, these at-risk children make up a growing proportion of the potential graduate pool.

The present stress on quality education for minorities and the poor stems less from a sense of moral outrage than from the economic self-interest of the business world, adequate social security measures, welfare costs, and the international competitiveness of the nation. Despite widespread pessimism based on the decline of government support during the 1980s, disadvantaged children may, for these instrumental reasons, fare better with government programs in the next decade. The needs of a growing capitalist economy may create the political will to provide disadvantaged children with better health, schooling, and other support. Political efforts will have to contend, however, with the federal budget deficit, a material reality that will limit any potential solutions for disadvantaged children to incremental ones. To set current politics in perspective, it is important to understand the evolution of federal policy for disadvantaged children.

Federal interest and involvement in education (as well as other social arenas) expanded greatly during the 1960s because of a broad concern with racial inequality. Beginning with the New Deal and reaching its apex during the Great Society, elite opinion generally held that the federal government could better represent and satisfy the demands of the poor than could state and local governments, due to a lack of resources at the state and local levels as well as to the often oligarchical and relatively nonrepresentative nature of state and local institutions (Davidson, 1969). The early 1960s was also a time of great optimism about the capacities of government to enact initiatives that could engineer a just society, accompanied by a parallel optimism in the ability of social science to guide the way. In addition, the political landscape included a new and increasingly powerful civil rights movement, a budget surplus, a committed president who built an entire domestic agenda on these issues and had a sympathetic Congress, and a faith in active government that allowed temporary aberrations from the more traditional philosophy of limited government.

In this period the federal government launched the most direct and massive program of assistance to precollegiate schooling in its history, the Elementary and Secondary Education Act (ESEA). One of its strongest components was Title I, which authorized a program of special assistance targeted directly to low-income pupils. In addition, programs for disadvantaged children and youth were created under the Department of Labor and the Office of Economic Opportunity. These included Head Start; Job Corps; Comprehensive Health Services; Medicaid; Women, Infants and Children (WIC); and others.

The period of rapid growth in social programs ended in the late 1960s and early 1970s due to tightening fiscal conditions and a loss in public confidence that social problems could be readily solved through government programs. An emerging body of research found minimal gains for disadvantaged children who participated in Title I, and the apparent gains from Head Start seemed to disappear during elementary school. Although the research providing this evidence has been sharply criticized, the implications of these studies had a deleterious affect on the broad-scale federal intervention that had its heyday in the 1960s.

In the 1980s, the Reagan administration reflected a renewed emphasis on the traditional American philosophy of limited government. The administration sought to restructure the federal government's involvement in social policy as well as to redirect policy interventions back toward their more individualistic bent—in other words, reviving older governmental notions about family responsibility and choice, and turning policy effort away from its former focus on the structural constraints that may inhibit individual authority, such as prejudices that bar equal occupational opportunities. The administration's restructuring efforts were known as the "new federalism," in which many federal tasks were passed down to the state or local governments, private industry, and individuals. In education, twenty-eight categorical grants were consolidated into a single block grant, a shift that had the effect of reducing the funds to large urban districts. The president also attempted (without success) to demote the Department of Education from Cabinet-level status, under the older arguments that had originally opposed a large federal role in schooling.

Moving away from regulatory and other strategies, Secretary of Education Bell and later Secretary Bennett called on federal resources to provide a platform for an agenda that would be carried out and financed elsewhere. Using the secretary's office as a bully pulpit, the administration propounded a discourse on excellence that displaced equity from its position of prominence on the federal education agenda. They emphasized such policies as discipline, merit pay for teachers, higher graduation standards, and prayer in the classroom. The most prominent example of the bully pulpit strategy was the 1983 report of the National Commission on Excellence in Education called *A Nation at Risk,* which highlighted these excellence ideas.

Between fiscal years 1982 and 1988, budget cuts in most other social policy areas, with the notable exceptions of child welfare services and the WIC program, occurred along with some minor program consolidations. The 1994 elections may result in cuts plus consolidation of many categorical programs.

The election of George Bush to the White House brought some moderation to the previous federal stance. While the Bush administration did not radically change the course set by its predecessor, it gave credence to a somewhat greater federal presence in educational affairs and established a discourse less overtly opposed to traditional equity policies. In the latter part of 1989, Bush met with state governors for an education summit to establish a process for setting national educational goals. While reiterating the states' leading role in schooling, the summit also affirmed and outlined a federal role, to promote national education equity, to provide research and development, to disseminate information on successful programs, and to provide technical assistance to states and localities. Bush supported early childhood education and child care through expansion of the Head Start budget by 39 percent in 1990, and through the passage of a comprehensive child care bill.

Inadequacy of Programs

Despite the presence of state and federal programs, over 20 percent of children in the United States live in poverty today, up from 14 percent in 1969. The median income of families in the bottom income quintile has eroded, and the gap between the incomes of the poorest and the wealthiest families has grown (Cohen, 1992). Race and ethnicity, gender, and family structure are strongly associated with the likelihood of poverty. In California, for example, roughly one-third of Asian, Latino, and African-American children were poor in 1989, compared to 10 percent of white children (Kirst,

1989). In 1989, half of single women with children lived in poverty, compared to 12 percent of two-parent families (Cohen, 1992). While many children fare well in households with low incomes, there is a statistical association between poverty and a greater likelihood that a child will die in infancy or early childhood, suffer serious illness, become a pregnant teen if female, drop out of school, or not continue education beyond high school.

In addition to government programs not meeting the needs of a burgeoning population of poor families, the services that are provided are predicated on outdated assumptions about two-parent family structures. Less than a third of all children live in families with two biological parents, where one works in the paid labor market and the other in the domestic economy of the home. Forty-six percent of children live in homes where either both parents or the only parent is working. About one-half of all children and youth will live in a single-parent family for some period of their lives (Cohen, 1992). Institutions and government programs that serve children (and the parents of children) must become more flexible, aware, and supportive of changing needs of families and children.

Building Coalitions for Improving Children's Services

As in previous eras when the United States has faced economic challenge, a conservative rhetoric has emerged that stresses the link between national competitiveness in the international arena and the development of the country's "human capital." Big business groups have stepped up their involvement in educational issues and in fact have provided critical direction and support to much of the excellence reform legislation that swept through states in the 1980s. By 1990, more attention had been focused on out-of-school influences that were obstructing educational attainment.

The Committee for Economic Development (CED), for instance, established an alliance with advocates for at-risk children.

Concrete evidence in the conjuncture of their interests was presented in the report, "Investing in Our Children" (Committee for Economic Development, 1987). The report's underlying argument for cooperation is that despite the many disagreements about the technological nature and skill requirements of the future labor force, there is a general agreement that the growing population of disadvantaged children lacks the "threshold skills" (literacy and problem-solving skills) to be economically productive (Murnane, 1988). The concerns rest as much with the ability of workers on the shop floor as with that of engineers. Employers worry that current and future workers will not be able to understand directions in manuals, ask questions, or assimilate and synthesize information, and will lack the critical thinking skills to solve everyday problems.

The Congressional Office of Technology Assessment projects that the labor force will grow by only 1 percent annually in the 1990s, compared to an annual growth rate of 3 percent in the 1970s. One third of the new entrants into the workforce by the turn of the century will be members of minority groups, among whom rates of poverty and illiteracy are highest (Outzz, 1993). Employers are increasingly cognizant of the problems that will arise for them if the needs of disadvantaged children go unaddressed.

Another important demographic factor affecting the politics of integrated services is the decline of the urban sector and the growing political dominance of the suburbs. The political importance of the suburbs was readily apparent in the presidential campaign rhetoric of 1992, which had a decidedly suburban tone on both the Republican and Democratic sides. Urban centers and the working-class vote, traditional Democratic party strongholds, no longer provide enough votes to win presidential races. As a result, the focus of issues has moved to more conservative suburban concerns (Schneider, 1992). However, the need for integrated services is most apparent in urban centers (King & McGuire, 1991). Therefore, proponents of integrated services will need to rely on instrumental calls for integrated services that appeal to the suburban audience rather than seeking support solely from traditional liberal urban strongholds.

Women's organizations are another potentially strong ally for expanding policies that meet the needs of disadvantaged children. Groups like the Children's Defense Fund and the National Organization for Women have overlapping concerns regarding child care, parental leave, welfare reform for female-headed households, Medicaid extension to poor pregnant women and young children, the WIC program, and fair housing for families with children. Since poverty has become disproportionately an issue for women and children, the lobbies can avoid direct discussions of the redistribution of income—which is political anathema—and argue more generally for the care of women and children. Also, they can shift the child care discussion from the previously unsuccessful tactic of asserting rights and benefits to one that emphasizes its value to economic productivity.

Many observers have stressed the conflict between public dollars for youth and public dollars for older Americans; indeed, starting in 1979, many public programs for children were cut back while those for the elderly expanded (Preston, 1984). However, there is a potential coalition between youth and the elderly that should not be overlooked. Finding common ground on which to act will be necessary because by the late 2020s, according to the Census Bureau, one in five Americans will be sixty-five or older and the Social Security funds for the elderly will rest on the productive capacity of the young. The number of working-age people on hand to support them will drop by almost half, from nearly five in 1990 to about two and one-half in 2030 (Hodgkinson, 1992). The majority of these workers will come from the expanding pool of poor and disadvantaged children. The support of senior groups should be sought for many efforts, but it will require the difficult task of focusing seniors on the conditions of future generations of elderly.

Given the less-than-robust federal budget projections, advocacy groups for the disadvantaged would be wise to envision a federal leadership role that encourages leveraging and coordination to build both a philosophical and organizational basis for broader efforts to address the needs of children at risk.

What are the prospects for broad-based coalitions among children's service providers and advocates, business, women's groups, and senior citizens? Could such a coalition overcome the looming federal budget deficit to give priority to policies for disadvantaged children? Could new or expanded federal programs overcome the problems inherent in the present delivery system to markedly improve the lives of these children?

The answers to these questions are alternatively hopeful and gloomy. No new "War on Poverty" seems likely to catalyze the federal agenda, but efforts will probably find reward and rationale for organizing advocacy coalitions in the more typical set of incremental and instrumental goals of traditional U.S. children's policy. Like the rationales that motivated educational reforms on the state level during the 1980s, business support and a strategy focused on productivity rather than children's rights or social justice will be the likely impetus for action. In the 1960s, new federal policies were crucial in establishing and giving direction to services for poor and disadvantaged populations. In the 1980s and continuing in the 1990s, given budget deficits and the lack of salience of redistributive policies per se, federal leadership has not been as broad but is still important.

A slowing of federal fiscal support for programs, even though those funds are only a fraction of most project dollars, may lead to a general slowing of progress at the state and local levels as well. The discretionary domestic portion of the 1995 federal budget contains no increase over 1993 levels. This budget freeze means that each new domestic spending program of the Clinton administration must be offset by a cut somewhere else. Two points are key. One is that new efforts must attempt to gain middle-class support as well as cross-cut different populations (the elderly, business, and so on) to build the political coalitions necessary for change. The second point is that efforts must operate within the realistic scope of the federal budget deficit and the Republican agenda of balancing the budget in the near future. Given these constraints, attention should continue to be given to encouraging cooperation and collaboration among agencies and levels of government that provide assistance to children at risk. There will not be a huge expansion of new programs, projects, and resources, so the current array of services must be used more efficiently and effectively. But collaboration cannot overcome underfunded and poorly designed services.

The initial proposals of the Clinton administration intensified and expanded the mild interest in collaboration demonstrated by the Bush administration. Clinton proposed to create ten city empowerment zones that would focus on both economic development and coordinated social services for all age groups. In 1993, the Senate did not approve this concept. The Clinton administration is also intensifying coordinated children's services as part of the $14 billion proposed expansion of Head Start, the reauthorization of Chapter 1, a modified welfare reform program based on the 1988 Family Assistance Program, and some Labor Department job retraining efforts.

Nonetheless, the 1994 Congress balked at large Head Start increases and may not approve more than a $250 million increase for future years. The 1994 election implies that even modest incrementalism may be difficult. Clinton's programs are, at most, an incremental buildup from those of the Bush administration, although Clinton won approval for a major increase in the Earned Income Tax Credit. These increases, however, are not paralleled in the overall Clinton education budget for 1995, which is roughly the same as Bush's outgoing proposal in 1992.

State-Level Policies

States play a variety of leadership roles in improving the coordination of children's services. These include creating a vision, setting goals, establishing standards, providing incentives and sanctions, offering technical support, serving as a convener, acting as coordinator, developing a clearinghouse, supporting research and evaluation, and becoming a model for other states (Koppich, 1991). Although the size, scope, and political support for efforts vary, all forty-seven of the states responding to a recent survey reported participating in some type of multiple interagency collaborative activity (Levy & Copple, 1989).

As integration of services has gained political support, numerous states have developed highly visible entities showcasing efforts to improve collaboration among agencies. Usually existing alongside traditional departmental structures, states have developed commissions and legislative committees on children, children's budgets, and children's codes that enable policymakers and administrators to view specific children's policies and programs within a larger context of policies addressing the needs of children and families. In 1989, thirty-three states had a board, commission, council, institute, or office on children. However, legislative activities are typically led by junior female legislators, and executive branch entities created to integrate children's services rarely carry the constitutional authority to control agency activities (Smrekar, 1989). As a result, these entities do not carry the weight that may be necessary to overcome political opposition to radically restructuring state agencies and programs, or to provide integration of children's services from the top down.

Most of the activity of states to integrate children's policies was initiated in the 1980s, following the wave of reports on education that flourished between 1983 and 1986. Typically, state efforts to integrate children's services involve opening channels of communication among the top administrators of children's programs in the state. Smrekar (1989) describes the three primary goals of state children's commissions: "(1) to create a process that establishes communication between departments with responsibility for children's services; (2) to create awareness of children's needs and communicate those needs to policymakers, advocates, and the general public;

and (3) to collect data on the condition of children and the state systems that serve them" (p. 228).

Despite the flurry of activity at the state level to create highly visible organizations or activities that view children's policy as a whole, most states continue to deliver children's services in the traditional fragmented executive agency arrangement. Several states have attempted to improve interagency coordination within this existing structure by providing legislative mandates and incentives for improving interagency cooperation, and by creating task forces and advisory groups to make recommendations on improving children's service delivery (Smrekar, 1989). A few states have taken a more active role in integrating services by designating grant funds to local communities to establish models of collaboration and school-linked services. These activities are usually limited in scope and have been subject to reduction or elimination in recessionary times. For example, an apparently successful effort to coordinate services for at-risk youth in Massachusetts was eliminated by budget cuts in 1990 (Useem, 1991).

Some notable state efforts to provide funds for integrating services include California's Healthy Start Initiative, which provides planning and program grants to local school districts for the establishment of school-linked services in local communities, and New Jersey's Department of Human Services effort to establish school-linked integrated-services programs. The future of these efforts will depend largely on state fiscal conditions and the willingness of individual program personnel to support complementary efforts in other agencies. Under severe fiscal conditions, agencies tend to cling to as much of the fiscal pie as they can, and collaborative efforts are still viewed as reducing potential individual program support.

Local-Level Politics and Policies

A positive political impetus for school-linked integrated services at the local level is the changed attitude of school leaders. In the 1960s after the advent of Title I, schools seemed to feel that they could provide social services and take on the entire task of solving poverty. Compensatory education funds were used for dentistry, health care, and new clothes. School breakfasts proliferated and pupil services expanded. But as federal funds leveled off and children's problems grew, school leaders' attitudes changed. The mood in the mid-1980s emphasized that schools were overwhelmed with negative changes in children's conditions and were not likely to receive funds to construct needed social services under the school's sole authority.

School restructuring provides yet another impetus as school-linked integrated services have become one of the suggested restructuring components. The school-linked services movement, however, is on the fringes of the educational restructuring movement. Most educational restructuring focuses on decentralization from central offices to school sites, teacher participation, and curricular reform. School-linked services, however, need to be viewed as an essential rather than peripheral part of school restructuring if they are to derive substantial political support from large education interest groups like teachers and administrators. Successful school restructuring must address all restructuring components rather than merely pick and choose a few unrelated ones that do not reinforce each other.

It is unlikely that decentralization and school-based management will be sufficient to provide school-linked services *without* leadership from the school board and central administration. The education accountability system must also change to encompass outcomes from school-linked services as well as the traditional student test scores as measures of school success.

This shift will not be easy because educators rarely come in contact with other children's service providers during teacher preparation or staff development. Schools of education deal primarily with classroom concerns and seldom provide prospective teachers with policy contexts of state or central school district offices. Professional meetings of educators rarely include personnel from the broader fields of children's services, so it is difficult to meet health or protective services workers other than through formal referrals. Consequently, building alliances for school restructuring that include school-linked services will take special arrangements and forums bridging the diverse agencies and personnel involved in children's services. School administrators do not know much about health or other children's programs and must become familiar with these before school-linked services can operate at a school. A hopeful note, however, was the National School Boards Association's recent bill (S619) to establish federal linkage for learning demonstration grants that provide coordinated services for at-risk youth at schools. The bill did not pass, but in 1994 Congress allowed up to 5 percent of the $57 billion Title I program to be used for school-linked services.

There is little organized resistance to the concepts of school-linked services, except among groups opposed to contraception assistance at secondary school health clinics and conservatives who may oppose day care. This suggests that the path of least political resistance would be to emphasize prevention in elementary schools. California's Governor Wilson has recommended an elementary school-linked services initiative, but has run into resistance from California education organizations that want full funding for education programs *before* allocating new money for school-linked services.

Positive support for school-linked services is probably sufficient at least to bring about implementation in the near future of large-scale demonstrations of school-linked services. However, school-linked services also must be viewed as an integral part of school restructuring and be related to academic improvements as an important outcome. The goal of integrated services—to make a variety of services available to meet children's individual needs—is a laudable goal that we should seek in order to promote academic and other outcomes for *all* children, not just those in crisis.

Educators also must be willing to participate in linked services that are not school based; in some localities, a family resource center might be a better site for such services than one on or near school grounds. There is no one best location for school-linked services given the diversity of U.S. communities. Some parents feel alienated from schools and would prefer meeting at another facility; in other instances a school may be the best location but lack the necessary excess space to accommodate service delivery.

Operational Strategies and Tactics for Collaboration

If school-linked services are to be successfully implemented, there must be significant change from every level: district leadership, middle management, principals, teachers, and parents (Jehl & Kirst, 1992).

A school district's superintendent or board of education can initiate planning for school-linked services. A county or city health or social services agency can also initiate the process. Regardless of the initiator, however, the executive leaders of the school district must be involved from the beginning and must view themselves as equals with other community agency executives involved in the collaborative process. Individual schools or school principals need the commitment and involvement of district leadership to pave the way for meaningful restructuring and delivery of integrated services.

Before a school district embarks on this process, it should assess its own capacity. The school board and superintendent who place a value on inquiry and consensus will be able to build capacity for successful school-linked services programs; a contentious and divided board has less energy and ability to establish working relationships with other agencies.

The board and superintendent must understand that, in initiating new working relationships with the health and social service agencies in their community, they cannot attempt to dominate these relationships. From the very first contact with other agencies, an atmosphere of mutual respect and collegiality, or shared responsibility and control, must pervade.

In many communities, these school and agency executives will have met only in an official capacity. Furthermore, the budget process in some states and localities will have forced them to compete in the past for available funding. This history must be overcome, and ownership of the collaboration must be shared within the group. If the process of developing school-linked services is seen as an effort to fulfill a particular agency's agenda at the expense of another's, the process will fail.

School district leadership, with executives from other agencies, must undertake two essential planning tasks: conducting a needs assessment and developing a common mission. A needs assessment is essential for the partnership to understand the needs of its community, including its demographics, racial composition, cultural and language diversity, poverty levels, and indicators of risk factors for students. With a needs assessment completed, school district leadership and other agency executives must begin defining their common plan. What will be the scope and purpose of the collaboration? Which children and families will it serve and with what breadth and depth of services? What outcomes are to be expected? What funding will be used? There is no one right answer to these questions; the answers must be tailored to the strengths and needs of the community.

Agency executives must also revamp fiscal strategies to support the tenets of the common mission (Kirst, 1991). For example, if collaboration among agencies is more effective than the current fragmentation, then funding mechanisms should create incentives for collaboration. If service interventions are more effective before problems reach crisis proportions, then financing mechanisms should be redirected to "front-end" priorities. If frontline service providers of the various agencies (teachers, social workers, public health nurses, and the like) need flexibility in determining which services they can provide to families, then financial formulas should provide such flexibility.

Thus, as part of their initial work, agency executives must

review what they currently spend on children's services and identify funds that can be redirected to support the new priorities of the collaboration. When possible, funds should be shifted from narrow categorical programs to more inclusive, school-linked services. For example, specialized funds to combat drugs and smoking might be combined into a broad prevention approach to children's health problems. In general, "back-end" treatment funds should be shifted to increase preventive interventions. Such redirected funds can also leverage more federal dollars by providing the matching funds necessary to make schools eligible for Medicaid or to provide school-based child care under the federal welfare reform program of 1988.

As part of their fiscal review, agency executives must reexamine their categorical funding streams and work for more flexibility in using these funds. Many schools, especially those serving the most disadvantaged students, currently use categorical funds to provide support staff for narrowly defined projects. Schools need to be able to use these funds and staff for the broader purposes of the collaborative project—for example, to take the time spent determining free lunch eligibility and apply it to a larger assessment of initial family eligibility for health and social services.

Finally, financial linkages among agencies can reinforce the common mission of a collaborative, school-linked service project. Sid Gardner (1989) has described these as "hooks," "glue," and joint ventures. Hooks formally link a child's participation in one program with eligibility and participation in another. Glue money allows one agency to subcontract with other agencies to ensure that children can receive services in one place. The lead agency becomes the "broker" for the child. In joint ventures, several agencies create partnerships to raise funds for jointly operated programs.

The Role of Middle Management

Middle managers serve as the link between a change in policy at the executive level and a change in action. At New Beginnings, the San Diego City Schools' Student Information System, school

district middle management provided ongoing staff work and supported the leadership throughout the process of needs assessment
and the formulation of the common mission and financing strategies. These middle-level administrators often had the clearest
understanding of how the schools and other agencies were operating and how funds were being spent.

The role of middle management includes more than providing
information and staff assistance to agency executives. These administrators also act as liaisons with the principals and teachers of the
district, and the line staff of other agencies. This role requires them
not only to become champions of the new collaborative approach
and mission, but also to determine the practical requirements for
implementing the policy change (for example, developing governance agreements among the participating agencies and negotiating changes in personnel policies).

The school principal must assume new roles and utilize new
skills to implement a school-linked service effort. It is likely that
the principal's school leadership training did not emphasize collaborative leadership and shared decision making with other community agencies. Nonetheless, these skills are essential for the
establishment of school-linked services. First, the principal must be
an active participant in developing whatever is to happen on or
near the site, sharing information about the children and the community, connecting the planning group to parents and teachers, and
providing a "reality check" for planners who may not be aware of
the day-to-day workings of school and community. Second, the
principal must serve as an advocate for an expanded school role in
the lives of families and the operation of other agencies, making the
case with his or her peers, community, and school staff. Teachers
especially need encouragement and assistance from the principal to
expand their agenda to work more actively with families while
maintaining their primary focus on academic success. Third, the
principal must reorganize and link key teachers and other staff on
campus with staffs from other community health and social service
agencies. Sometimes the strength of a major collaboration can be

sapped by a lack of interpersonal communication and understanding among these staffs. Fourth, the principal must act as an "enabler," promoting the involvement of staff and community in planning and monitoring a school-linked service effort.

The Role of Teachers and Support Staff

At the school site itself, teaching and support staffs must be actively involved in assessing the need for school-linked services, adapting and adopting the philosophy that undergirds it, and preparing solid working relationships among their own staff as well as those from other agencies. Strengthening the link between teachers and staffs from other agencies is critical and must often be preceded by lengthy discussion in which participants learn from each other. In the past, teachers have typically communicated with outside agencies only in times of crisis, and the teachers were probably frustrated by these agencies' inability to resolve students' problems. Furthermore, separate undergraduate and graduate training; different professional languages and values; and differences in pay scale, working culture, and union representation can deepen the gaps in understanding between teachers and those in other professions.

Thus, teachers need time to think, talk, and plan with the health and social services professionals who are involved in the collaborative effort. The teachers are likely to have many concerns as they begin this process. For example, they may fear that they will be expected to sacrifice their primary focus on teaching in order to become social workers, that they will not be treated as equals by those in other professions, or that school-linked service programs will become another source of "pullout programs" disrupting instructional time for the neediest students. These concerns cannot be easily discounted or disproved, since most educators have never worked closely with professionals in an integrated-services setting. It will take time for teachers to understand that a well-planned program of school-linked services can involve them in a positive, collaborative role with other agencies and provide more effective assistance for children and families. When the collaborative system provides additional information and help for meeting children's needs, the teacher can modify classroom management strategies and instructional and disciplinary approaches as well as work with parents to involve them positively in their children's education.

The Role of Parents

Parents need to be included in collaboration in order to help identify localized needs, but also as a resource. Collaborative efforts must involve assessment and utilization of resources that the community of parents can bring to the school, and individual parents can bring to their own family units.

Greater Emphasis on Outcomes

Another key change for schools launching school-linked services is increased accountability requirements to measure whether outcome goals are met. These outcomes must be broadly defined. Members of school staffs (and policymakers) should resist the temptation to view programs of school-linked services as a quick fix for low test scores or a way to reduce the costs of education and social services. Other academic outcomes are also relevant and may be easier to document, such as increased attendance, a reduced rate of retention in grade, a decrease in the percentage of students designated at risk, and a decrease in the percentage of students designated for special education.

Health outcomes for students might include the number of students who receive immunizations on schedule and the number who have had a health exam within the last year. As programs of school-linked services grow in their ability to support families, outcomes for families might include increased self-sufficiency, improved family functioning, and increased parent involvement with the school.

Such a broad array of outcomes must be monitored consistently and on a long-term basis, involving information feedback with the collaborative agencies to address unmet needs. This often requires schools to adopt new procedures and secure new equipment to collect relevant data. For example, New Beginnings, which provides on-line information about district students in the San Diego City School district, will be linked to a management information system to facilitate the case management process.

Conclusions

Federal, state, and local politics have become favorable toward interagency collaboration for children. The dominant political rationale is instrumentalism and the dominant approach is incrementalism. The existence of federal budget deficits suggests that it will take individual commitment at the local level to advance this movement. Large-scale investments, such as those characteristic of the 1960s, seem unlikely. However, state governments can play a crucial role in stimulating collaborations and providing start-up funds. Collaboration is part of President Clinton's successful legislation for Head Start, Chapter 1, and urban initiatives under leadership from the departments of Health and Human Services, Labor, and Education. Local political trends are reinforcing the movement toward collaboration. The barriers to implementing interagency collaboration, however, are formidable and not easily overcome. The 1994 congressional election makes recent progress at the federal level uncertain. But block grants formed from federal categories that are featured in the Republican contract could make school-linked services easier at the local level. There may be many fewer categories to link together, but there also may be less federal money.

References

Cohen, D. (1992). Despite widespread income growth, study finds increase in child poverty. *Education Week, 11*(40), 24.

Committee for Economic Development. (1987). *The new America: Prospects for population and policy in the 21st century.* Washington, DC: Author.

Davidson, R. H. (1969). The war on poverty: Experiment in federalism. In R. Lambert (Ed.), *Annals of the American academy of political science* (pp. 1–13). Philadelphia: American Academy of Political Science.

Gardner, S. (1989). Failure by fragmentation. *California Tomorrow, 4*(4), 18–25.

Grubb, N., & Lazerson, M. (1982). *Broken promises: How Americans fail their children.* New York: Basic Books.

Hodgkinson, H. (1992). *A demographic look at tomorrow.* Washington, DC: Institute for Educational Leadership.

Jehl, J., & Kirst, M. (1992). Getting ready to provide school-linked services: What schools must do. *The Future of Children, 2*(1), 95–106.

King, R. A., & McGuire, C. K. (1991). Political and financial support for school-based and child-centered reforms. In J. Cilbulka (Ed.), *Politics of Education Association yearbook 1991* (pp. 123–135).

Kirst, M. W. (1989). *Conditions of children in California.* Berkeley, CA: Policy Analysis for California Education.

Kirst, M. W. (1991, April). Improving children's services: Overcoming barriers, creating new opportunities. *Phi Delta Kappan, 72*(8), 615–618.

Koppich, J. (1991). *Lines of authority, levels of responsibility: The perspective of the state in children's policy.* Berkeley, CA: Policy Analysis for California Education.

Levy, J. E., & Copple, C. (1989). *Joining forces: A report from the first year.* Alexandria, VA: National Association of State Boards of Education.

Murnane, R. (1988). Education and productivity of the workforce: Looking ahead. In R. E. Litan, R. Z. Lawrence, & C. Schultz (Eds.), *American living standards: Threats and challenges* (pp. 215–245). Washington, DC: The Brookings Institution.

National Commission on Excellence in Education. (1983). *A nation at risk.* Washington, DC: Author.

Outzz, J. H. (1993). *The demographics of American families.* Washington, DC: Institute of Educational Leadership.

Preston, S. (1984). Children and the elderly. *Demography, 21,* 435–457.

Schneider, W. (1992, July). The suburban century begins. *The Atlantic Monthly,* 33–44.

Smrekar, C. (1989). State policymaking for children. In M. Kirst (Ed.), *Conditions of children in California* (pp. 221–234). Berkeley, CA: Policy Analysis for California Education (PACE), School of Education, University of California, Berkeley.

Useem, E. (1991, April). *What a difference a recession makes: The rise and fall of integrated services for at-risk youth in Massachusetts.* Paper presented at the Annual Meeting of the American Educational Research Association, Chicago, IL.

Chapter Three

Commentary

Renewing Familial and Democratic Commitments

Edmund W. Gordon

Recently, I celebrated my seventy-fourth birthday. I will use my age as an excuse for impatience and irritability on reading the Kirst and Kelley chapter. I have spent the last forty-five years struggling to improve education in general and especially the education available to low-status persons. I have begun to worry that the curtain will be drawn on my life before much progress will have been made toward providing a better education for all our children and especially those whose status does not afford them privilege.

As a person concerned with the problems of American education, and one who has not suffered as much as most low-status persons, I have wondered if we who work in this important field have been too kind to each other. We have thought about the problems, and talked about them, and congratulated each other on the less than optimal work that we have been doing. Sometimes in our circles, we have tried to protect each other's feelings and therefore have not been as candid or open with our criticisms as we should have been. I have thought, particularly in the area of education, that we can no longer afford to protect each other from criticism and excuse our failures. All this is to say that I do not know whether I am really getting old and crotchety or just old and impatient, but I must be critical of Michael Kirst and Carolyn Kelley's conceptualizations of the educational problems that are addressed in their chapter.

I think Kirst and Kelley have missed the boat. Their conceptualizations of the problems of education and services to children in our society are inappropriately narrow. Their analysis begins with a study of the status quo, national and state policies and services that are themselves an aberration of the best the nation has achieved. They have not focused on the nation's education and children's service problems in a comprehensive manner. So, the way in which Kirst and Kelley have framed the issues will not lead to adequate or even productive solutions. The existing frames within which they have discussed integration and collaboration in children's services simply do not permit us to adequately address the problems at hand. I realize that these are harsh claims on my part. I may be overstating my reservations concerning this work by two of our nation's most outstanding public education policy analysts, but time is running out. The problems of education and development for the low-status people of our nation have reached crisis proportions, so much so that the stability of the social order is now threatened. This is not the time for anemic analyses or partial solutions. As it stands, the authors' conceptualization of the problems requires further elaboration.

Kirst and Kelley's conceptual focus is on the needs of low-class children, but this is only one aspect of the nation's much broader education problem. It may be dysfunctional to have our attention restricted to a focus on those children traditionally labeled "at risk." The shifts in the nation's priorities, the banditry and misappropriation of federal funds, and the deliberate redistribution of the nation's wealth to favor an even smaller minority of the most privileged, have placed at risk all children and families. The nation has become less committed to the nurturance of children and the weakest members of the community.

Changes in the nature and structure of families in the United States compound the destructive impact of this shift in national commitment. The patterns of nuclear and extended families are changing. Single parents, homeless families, family mobility, and economic insufficiency in families are all on the increase. Even for affluent families, the national climate and resources available for the education and nurturance of children have been eroded. It is the limited national commitment to the nurturance and welfare of children that is at the core of the problem of school-community connections in support of education. Unless we as educators, national leaders, and citizens shift the focus of deliberations to what is necessary for the nurturance and welfare of all children, and shift the focus of our resource distribution from support for military power and political economic privilege to support for children and their families, we are not going to address adequately the problems of education and development for children at risk, be they rich or poor, or minority or majority group members.

The Changing Political Economy

Kirst and Kelley correctly call our attention to the shifts in national priorities. Unfortunately in some ways, they understate the history of the last twenty years and the importance of the shifts we have seen in national priorities. They do not explicitly highlight the extensive nature of the consequences of these shifts. They neglect to address the fact that our society has not made a commitment to the development of children its first priority. It is certainly true that we have seen a shift from federal leadership to state leadership growing largely out of the distribution of federal funds. However, the real message is that this period has been marked by banditry, exportation of the nation's means of production, embezzlement of the wealth of this nation, and the reappropriation of national resources to favor the privileged and ill-advised military preparedness. As a result, the nation has neglected its most important national resource. When nations fail to invest wealth in human services, they also fail to invest in human development.

Our society has exported capital and jobs over the last twenty years to the extent that autonomous units that acknowledge no allegiance to the country actually control most of the capital that the nation needs. The exportation of the means of production from this country to other countries, and the transfer of the control of our wealth to nontaxable multinational corporations, has displaced our wealth to such an extent that the economy can no longer support the essential needs of the social order. Therefore, even if we had the commitment, we still would have the practical problem of finding the money to meet the human needs of the nation. Thus, the erosion of national resources is a critical part of the problem that Kirst and Kelly leave untreated in their analysis.

A second critical omission is their failure to address sufficiently the question of national will. That is why the manner in which the problem is conceptualized concerns me. To generate the national will, we need to understand the context and nature of the problems with which we are trying to deal. There are real problems related to the way in which local and state governments manage limited resources. There are certainly problems when groups and governmental agencies try to collaborate. Ill-fated efforts at the integration of human services mark the history of social services in this country. We need to do something about all of these. But the fundamental problems of education and facilitation of development in children have to do with the changing nature and status of families, and the changing nature of the political economy of the nation. Policy decisions that do not take these into account will prove inadequate.

The Changing Nature of the Family and of Childhood

Determining public policy and managing collaboration in its integration depend on a recognition of the changing nature of the family. The nature of the family and its functions are influenced by people's access to resources and power. Recent changes in many people's access to resources and power have radically changed the context for and quality of family life and the lives of children that these families intend to nurture and to protect. What we see happening to low-status families, especially, and people's capacities to support families is in many ways a function of changes in the political economy of the nation.

Here, Kirst and Kelley correctly call attention to the urgent needs of the children with the least advantages and status, but they neglect to emphasize the criticality of the need to integrate human services for, and to address more comprehensively, the needs of *all* children. In our postmodern society, the nature of the family and the nature of childhood have been changing. While I may overemphasize the role of economics to the neglect of other factors, these changes are very much related to the ways in which the family structure has evolved. One way in which the nature of childhood has changed has to do with how parents view their children and the choice to have or not have children. It is costly to have children now. Today, those choosing to have children do not make that choice in order to enhance future family or personal security. Certainly, readers familiar with the history of childhood know there was a time when families regarded children as family assets. It is still the case in parts of Africa and other continents that people measure their wealth in part on the basis of the number of children they have. These children are considered potential workers and producers of income. It is the hope that they will enter the labor force and provide some security for their parents as these parents age. In contrast, today, even in the most advanced societies, children are viewed more as a financial liability than an asset for families. Even if in the lower and under classes there continues to be some perceived security advantage to procreation, it is the modal value for the society that drives the nation's priorities. If society at large does not value children, it is even more difficult for low-status families to protect and nurture children.

Another change in the nature of childhood has to do with the change in family structure. The nature of the families that should provide nurturance and protection for children has changed. (I should preface this line of discussion with a disclaimer: I don't want to appear to adhere to the sexist argument that holds that women should be home with children.) It is no secret that most families can no longer support themselves with the income of one member. The gender democratization of the labor force and the changed economic conditions that require most families to have at least two wage earners to support themselves have pulled out of the home the adult who provided the nurturance, the glue for the family. I am not arguing that women should be returned to the home to raise children. I do argue that adults are needed to raise children. Society has to find ways to make adults available to nurture children; it must be reorganized so that it is not nearly impossible for two adults (or even for one adult, as is increasingly common) who choose to have a family to attend to family management and child care.

Incrementalism and Instrumentalism

Kirst and Kelley have introduced the interesting distinction between incrementalism and instrumentalism. Their concern with collaboration rests on these two notions. Incrementalism involves helping only those who are most disadvantaged, whereas instrumentalism argues that promoting society's economic well-being requires most of its people to be educated to the end that doing so produces a more economically competitive society. They assert that collaboration for children's services among agencies can be most effectively justified based on instrumentalism and incrementalism (Kirst and Kelley, Chapter Two, this volume). While such services directed by either rationale certainly may be facilitated by collaborative efforts, a direct relationship of either incrementalism or instrumentalism with collaborative services does not appear to be supported by their argument.

Both of these justifications for collaboration are limited. It is the complexity of human needs and the differential requirements of various services for children that are the energy behind the move toward collaboration. The important issues surrounding incrementalism and instrumentalism are more philosophical, mechanical, and political. They are philosophical in the sense that one's position on the continuum can be value-driven. Followers of the philosopher and social critic John Rawls (1973) could easily argue for the allocation of resources to favor those most in need. Persons driven by political practicality would likely settle for the position on the continuum that could muster the greatest amount of political support. In the current period, that might favor instrumental approaches because most segments of society are hurting financially and are not inclined to favor targeted services. Policymakers who worry about mechanics would probably want to know which approach should theoretically lead to the greatest likelihood of positive social change. Kirst and Kelly are to be commended for calling attention to the dimension of the continuum.

The authors address a number of the efforts at collaboration. They review something of the history of our efforts of bringing services together for children, and they remind us of some of the conditions under which effective collaboration has been possible. Their analysis, however, contributes little to the resolution of the tension between the two positions in the determination of public policy. One could gather from their discussion that the authors favor an instrumental approach with its focus on serving all children. I find myself resonating to their choice, but for different reasons. They seem to endorse the often-stated public justification for human resource development that adheres to the concern for making U.S. nationals more productive economically and more competitive in the global economy. I favor instrumentalism because it is essential to the development of citizens who are able to participate meaningfully in the economic, political, and social intercourse of the society. I see the economic and the social ends as being critical to the roles of citizens as the educators and nurturers of children. Collaboration in the provision of integrated services for all is critical because of our common destiny.

The ideas of incrementalism and instrumentalism may support

a need for collaboration. However, it is not just a question of collaboration. When Kirst and Kelley call our attention to the need for collaboration, they highlight only part of the problem and obfuscate a more fundamental, more crucial issue. While Kirst and Kelley call our attention to the concept of collaboration, it may be that the critical issue is one of commitment and not of collaboration. In my long life, I have sensed that our nation and even groups of its people move rather effectively to collaborate or work independently when they are committed to something. As I look at our children and services to children in our society, I do not think we have had the commitment.

Although it may be appropriate in any system of social justice to favor the people who are most disadvantaged, there must be a more universal understanding and conception of the importance of human development if we are going to move to the commitment and collaboration that are needed in education and human services. In other words, I must understand that such an agenda is important for my children, just as the woman who cleans my house must understand that it is important for her children. We can build the sort of national commitment that we need around that kind of coalition. It is not only children of the poor for whom we want comprehensive and integrated services. It is for *all* children that we struggle. It is a right of childhood that these things be available.

Toward More Humane
Political, Economic, and Public Policy

In general, Kirst and Kelley's work is an inadequate conceptualization of both the problem and the state of the nation as they *are, could be, and must be for children*. A program of services that is informed by this limited conceptualization is destined to be inadequate. Because the society itself is neither committed nor organized to support families as units for the nurturance of children, it is clear that one of the necessary conditions for forward movement is our recognition that *all* of the nation's children are in trouble—children from middle-class or affluent families as well as children from low-income and minority families. Further, it is critical that public policy concerning services for children be informed by the recognition that infancy and childhood for humans require nurturance in stable and economically sufficient social units (families) or institutional surrogates that are sufficient to the comprehensive nurturance of developing persons.

Families or stable units in which adults are available, able, and willing to assume these responsibilities are the only viable models human societies have developed as yet. Assuring the availability of such units to all children is an urgent public policy priority. To implement such a policy will require that the nation make it possible for persons who choose to invest their efforts in the nurturance of children to do so without monumental sacrifice or inconvenience. For persons who bear children and who choose not to make their nurturance a personal priority, the nation must ensure that these children receive the care and nurturance that they need.

When adequate levels of child nurturance cannot be provided in the home, educational and other institutions must be enabled to provide comparable supports for learning. One model for doing so is the integration of child nurturance services. Part of what we are trying to do in comprehensive and integrated services for youngsters is to provide the same quality of nurturance and protection for all children that we want for our own children. There has been an explosion of interest in this model, but I do not think there has been a societal commitment to it. Schooling continues to be viewed as distinct from child welfare.

When I was a beginning student at Teachers College many years ago, my professor of educational administration talked about the responsibilities of school boards and was advancing the notion that school boards really should be child development boards. These boards should be the community authority that protects the interests of children; therefore, they should have almost unlimited control of the resources necessary to support the development of children. That notion never caught on. School boards are usually thought to be responsible for the academic development of children. However, we fight over whether they can have medical services or social services and who will be in control of them. We continue to see these as distinct functions when they ought to be integrated.

There are other good models for alternative or supplementary educational and nurturance services to children, all of which are underfunded, including one of the most popular to emerge in this society, Head Start. Twenty-seven years ago we started Head Start. Almost immediately the president recognized its value, but it still doesn't serve all the children who need it or whose families desire the service. Within the Head Start program, we continue to give more attention to the screening and monitoring of children's needs than to the feeding, treating, and nurturing of children. We continue to hold children and families overly responsible for their failures and inadequacies, and for the nation's failures, rather than assign the responsibility to society through its institutions that should be held responsible.

In the final analysis, it is important that we have adults who can raise children. Stable social units in which to develop children are necessary. Any society has a responsibility to enable its young people to develop the capacity to create and maintain such units. William Julius Wilson (1987) has used the construct *marriageability* to refer to this capacity. He uses the construct when writing about an African-American population. However, the concept he advances is appropriate to any low-status, disenfranchised, poverty-stricken group and perhaps in many ways to the population at large. He uses the marriageability ratio of males in the group as one indicator of the community's health. The ratio is based on the number of males in the group who are viewed as marriageable. I am also working with this construct as a social indicator, but my use does not necessarily have to do with eligibility for marriage. I would prefer to call it *citizenship-ability*, or the capacity to function as an independent person in the discharge of the functions of citizenship.

What does marriageability or citizenship-ability have to do with children? It seems to me that we have worried about how economically productive we make our population and about how vocationally competent our workforce needs to be in order to participate in the global economy. We have not, however, worried about how socially competent we must enable persons to be, in the sense of how competent people are to participate as citizens in this society. A part of that competence relates to participation in the functions of families, including the nurturance of children.

Readers with children must know or will discover that we need to be as concerned about the marriageability or citizenship-ability of our children's peers as we are about our children themselves. When children grow up, many family units will be altered as children choose others with whom to pair off. Because we cannot select partners for them, perhaps the only thing we can do is make sure that the pool is wide and rich enough to give each a reasonable chance of finding a citizenable partner.

So, quite apart from international economic competition, I would argue for the survival of that which we call family and for the survival of the democracy itself. We have got to worry more about the way in which youngsters are nourished and protected as they develop in society. On the citizenship side I often advance the notion that in a democracy we have government with the consent of the persons being governed. But if I am going to give my consent, it must be informed consent. If there are folks who are too physically ill, too mentally ill, too illiterate, and too educationally underdeveloped to give informed consent to government, then they are left out of government. As Conant (1961, 1964) stated more than thirty years ago, we are simply building an increasingly explosive reservoir of discontented, dysfunctional people who will disrupt the society. Therefore, instead of an incrementalist approach, which certainly can contribute to reform, I advocate an instrumentalist approach focused on the enrichment of the pool of human resources, which are the ultimate social capital of the society.

Finally, let it be clear that I am not an economist, but as I look at the issues, it seems to me that any examination of the public policy implications of our efforts at improving the education of children must address the political economy of our nation in the closing years of the twentieth century. The political economy of the region and period in part defines the contexts in which families, schools, and other institutions of child development and nurturance exist. The United States, and the world for that matter, is in a period of severe economic decline and relocation. These changes have influenced the amount of financial resources policymakers feel are available for human services. Even more important, these conditions are influencing the opportunities that people have to find jobs and effectively participate in the economy. In periods of high unemployment and underemployment, without an adequate program of income maintenance, we should expect only personal and family dysfunction and disorganization. A dysfunctional political economy precludes the appropriate discharge of family responsibilities and it impedes the society's will, if not capacity, to support the institutions that might otherwise provide the safety net or supplemental supports for child development and nurturance.

The industrial strength and economic control of much of the nation's wealth today has shifted into the hands of multinational corporations answerable to no nation whatsoever. It has been estimated that since the middle of this century, thirty million jobs have been exported or eliminated by corporations in their search for cheap labor, lower taxes, and freedom from regulation of industrial production and capital development. These political economic developments have critical impacts on the willingness and capacity of our federal government and several states to provide children's services. In such a climate, Kirst and Kelley are correct in recognizing the barriers to collaboration.

It is this climate created by the changing political economy of the nation together with the differences in the ways Kirst and Kelley think of the core problems that lead me to be impatient with their treatment. Were their chapter written twenty or thirty years ago, I would probably have applauded their effort. Their review of federal policy in the past twenty years is accurate, even if it is insufficiently critical of that policy's devastating effects. They make the case for both integration of services to children and collaboration in the delivery of such services. They effectively identify some of the barriers to collaboration. The problem is, if we could implement what they advocate, the children of our nation would still be in trouble; and the children that I worry most about would continue to be at risk, not simply of failure to thrive, but at risk of failure to survive. I wish we still had the luxury of being able to applaud Kirst and Kelley for this effort. But I am growing old. Time is running out. Children are being destroyed in and by the inaction of a nation that can do more to protect them.

References

Conant, J. B. (1961). *Slums and suburbs*. New York: McGraw-Hill.

Conant, J. B. (1964). *Shaping educational policy*. New York: McGraw-Hill.

Rawls, J. (1973). *A theory of social justice*. London: Oxford University Press.

Wilson, W. J. (1987). *The truly disadvantaged: The inner city, the underclass, and public policy*. Chicago: University of Chicago Press.

Chapter Four

Commentary

Local Partnerships as the Source of Innovative Policy

Wayne H. Holtzman

In their thoughtful review of politics and policymaking as these affect integrated services for children, Kirst and Kelley point to certain similarities between the 1990s and the 1960s. The Kennedy-Johnson era was one of great optimism and hope, a period in which the majority of Americans believed that the federal government should be active in nearly all aspects of American life, a departure from the traditional idea of limited government. A budget surplus in the Johnson administration made it feasible to fund hundreds of new programs as we moved from the New Frontier to the Great Society. Harmony between the congressional majority and the White House was essential for rapid change. Many of the federal laws passed in the mid-1960s, such as the Elementary and Secondary Education Act, established new programs and funding streams that still exist today, though at a much diminished level. The 1990s are beginning to look a little like the 1960s with two important exceptions.

First, there is no budget surplus; indeed, there is a monstrous deficit. Second, the level of optimism and hope for the future is considerably subdued. Some political observers have commented that political activism in the United States is cyclic in nature. Every thirty years there appears to have been a rise in federal activism with renewed hope and vigor. In each case, the political party in the White House and Congress has had unified control, making extensive legislation and reform feasible. Within five to ten years, however, such activism runs its course, and a longer period of consolidation and readjustment occurs along more traditional lines.

During the Reagan and Bush administrations of the past twelve years, strenuous efforts were made, often unsuccessfully, to limit the role of the federal government with respect to state and local governments as well as the private sector. Consolidation of categorical grants into block grants for the states, a shift in philosophy from federal to state responsibility and initiatives, and appeals to the private sector, both profit-making and nonprofit, to pick up the difference were repeatedly emphasized throughout the 1980s. Many state governments were greatly strengthened during this period, but in recent years they have all been facing severe budget problems, due to the lack of adequate funds from state tax revenues. Problems at the local level of city and county governments are even more severe and have led to deteriorated urban conditions not unlike those of third world countries in many places. The new federalism has simply not worked as originally anticipated.

When we look realistically at the current state of affairs throughout the country, politically, economically, and socially, it is clear that there is no way we can recreate the favorable conditions of the 1960s during the Johnson era. Fundamental changes have occurred in society that are irreversible, and the growing national debt limits severely what the federal government can do in the next several years. The best that can be expected is a more harmonious working relationship between Congress and the White House, coupled with a growing national resolve to invest in the future rather than squander resources in the present.

The Need for Local Partnerships

For the aforementioned reasons, I believe that the most creative initiatives for the near future will be those that grow out of local partnerships rather than federal mandates. Many such projects are popping up all over the country as communities, both large and small, look to themselves and their immediate surroundings for whatever resources are needed to reach their goals. These partnerships are forming for a number of reasons, some of which have been outlined by Kirst and Kelley. First is the growing concern of employers for skilled, reliable manpower in the future. Business and industry throughout the country have been hearing the steady drumbeat from Washington and elsewhere that America will lose out in the global economic competition if it cannot produce more competent school graduates who are ready and eager to be employed as skilled, responsible workers. Corporations are encouraging their employees to get involved as volunteers in programs for community development, education, and human services.

At a recent Adopt-a-School night in Austin, for example, 1,700 individuals representing hundreds of companies, many of them small, were honored for their volunteer activities within the Austin schools. The Chamber of Commerce has embarked on a new program, supported in part by the Hogg Foundation (referred to in this chapter as the Foundation), called "Employers Support Parenting." This initiative was started by twenty-two companies that are leading the way in developing family-friendly personnel policies that prove to be beneficial to the company as well as to young parents and their children. These range from day care to subsidized parent education, from flextime working arrangements to pregnancy leaves of absence. Strong information networks are being developed as this program spreads among other companies under the leadership of the Chamber of Commerce.

A second reason for the new growth of partnerships in education and human services is the fact that, in many places, the focus is shifting in subtle ways from damage control to prevention in dealing with societal problems. The Texas legislature, a political body not known for its farsighted planning, recently underwent a major shift in its thinking by supporting new prevention initiatives for children and their families. To be sure, large sums of state money are still earmarked for expanding prisons and so forth, but at least a significant start has been made in the other direction. A third reason for partnerships is the growing realization that no single agency or source of support, public or private, state or local, can raise the resources necessary to address the needs of children and families. And finally, the severe disadvantages of categorical funding under state mandates are becoming all too clear in the form of fragmented, disjunctive services that are inefficient, ineffective, and wasteful of limited resources.

Hogg Foundation School-Human Services Initiative

These signs of change in Texas, where the Foundation operates, have been sufficiently encouraging that we embarked in 1990 on a major new program aimed at improving child development, family preservation, and community renewal by integrating health, human services, and education using the schools as the locus for their delivery. This new initiative grew out of statewide commissions appointed by the Foundation in 1987 that spent three years focusing on three major areas—the mental health of young children and their families, the problems of adolescence and becoming an adult, and the issues surrounding community care of the mentally ill. A major consensus throughout the state was achieved that the Foundation should concentrate its efforts on children and their families, supporting demonstration projects with built-in research and evaluation to point the way for the state and local communities.

The Foundation set aside $2 million to fund four major demonstration projects within selected schools and neighborhoods of Austin, Dallas, Houston, and San Antonio. Attention was focused on how traditional education could be integrated with a wide array of health and human services, both treatment and prevention, for which the school would be the locus of delivery. Successful programs elsewhere were used as a basis for developing what soon became known as the School of the Future project. Jim Comer's

School Development Program at Yale (Comer, 1985) and Zigler's School of the 21st Century (Zigler, 1989), which emphasized child care and family support services, were woven into the program design.

Design of the Project

After months of initial planning in each of the four metropolitan areas, neighborhoods defined by one or two elementary schools and a middle school were selected to become sites for the experimental program. Initial grants from the Hogg Foundation of $50,000 per year for five years—a total of $1,000,000—were committed in the spring of 1990, making it possible for each of the communities to appoint a full-time project coordinator. An equal amount of money has been set aside to provide each site with technical assistance and evaluation support. Community agencies and private corporations have joined the Foundation and the school systems as partners in support of the program. Five essential features of the School of the Future characterize each of the four demonstration sites: (1) the integration of a broad spectrum of health and human services in public schools; (2) involvement of parents and teachers in the program activities; (3) involvement of many organizations, both public and private, as partners; (4) a strong commitment to the project by superintendents, principals, and other school administrators; and (5) a willingness to participate in the evaluation of the project (Holtzman, 1992).

Three levels of child development are targeted at each demonstration site: preschool, elementary school (grades K–5), and middle school (grades 6–8). At each level, many approaches are being integrated in a comprehensive program of health and human services, with the particular combination of services dependent on local needs and resources. At the preschool level, examples of services include Head Start, Parents as Teachers, primary health care, and programs for siblings of children already in school. In elementary and middle schools, services will focus on the treatment or prevention of a variety of mental health problems, such as substance abuse, child abuse, school dropouts, teen pregnancy, and suicide as well as on enrichment programs to promote self-esteem, effective interpersonal relations, and sound human development.

Each school develops unique programs and activities to meet the special needs of students and families. Parent involvement, for example, can take many forms. In San Antonio, the Parent Volunteer Corps has been created to help in the classrooms. In Austin, parents are involved in the Community Advisory Committee, which, among many other activities, organized a mental health information fair on the school site. In Houston, parent groups provide valuable information on the needs of community children. In Dallas, the Parents Advisory Committee has been formed to assist in developing programs.

During their first two years of operation, the four projects have developed in ways that are highly appropriate for the social, cultural, and ethnic characteristics of each neighborhood. One of these four programs—the Houston School of the Future project—is described in detail in Harriet Arvey and Alfredo Tijerina's discussion of their first two years of program experience (see Chapter Sixteen this volume).

Local leaders were both greatly stimulated and relieved to learn that the Foundation would support each School of the Future for at least five years. Long-range planning with the involvement of many partners at each site meant stability and reassurance that careful initial planning would pay off dividends in the long run. There is no external monitor insisting on immediate implementation or quick results, which allows each site to proceed deliberately and at its own pace. The parties involved realize that it will take two or three years before all the components visualized as important for the School of the Future are properly in place.

Importance of Research and Evaluation

An essential feature of the School of the Future is the plan to undertake research and evaluation at each of the four sites. The major long-term investment of resources and the opportunity for longitudinal follow-up of thousands of children and their families present a unique opportunity to conduct significant research and evaluation on which future policy decisions can be based. Results of the evaluation will provide individuals and agencies with information on how to start a school-based service program and will offer key decision makers reliable information on which to base future policies. Moreover, the assessment and follow-up of thousands of children and their cohorts in the four sites over many years will yield a unique set of scientifically valuable data on child development, educational practices, school organizations, community attitudes and behavior, and family development. For these reasons, the Foundation and its advisers made special efforts during the project's initial stages to deal with a number of critical questions relating to evaluation design and its implementation.

A full-time behavioral scientist within the Foundation serves as director of evaluation under my direction. An additional full-time psychologist and five doctoral candidates in psychology, sociology, and social work help with data collection and analysis under the director's supervision. A group of evaluation experts including University of Texas faculty members and key advisers in each of the four cities meets regularly to discuss technical issues and offer advice on methods for handling difficult evaluation questions. Special efforts were made in the first year to ensure that adequate baseline data were obtained for as many children as possible at each of the four sites before major installation of new programs and restructuring of the schools. In addition, comparable data have been obtained from other similar schools within each of the four cities to serve as comparison or control cases for the longitudinal study of change in subsequent years.

A finely tuned balance has been achieved between the four local sites and the centralized activities for which Foundation staff and its advisers are assuming responsibility. Every effort has been made to encourage each site to develop its own detailed plans and procedures within the overall guidelines. Representatives of the major stakeholders at each site have their own governance mechanisms that include school personnel, parents, human service agencies, and others.

Toward the Future

While it is too early to say how permanent these four experimental programs will be, it is already clear that each of them has set long-range objectives and intends to continue in an experimental mode for years to come. The publicized, long-term commitment of the Foundation has been particularly valuable in encouraging all participants to be creative, flexible, and farsighted in their vision of what they want the School of the Future to become.

As the School of the Future evolves in the next several years, vigorous efforts and skillful leadership will be necessary to achieve the goals that have been established. Additional partners will have to be drawn into the project, both to provide stronger financial support and to ensure the needed involvement of other community organizations and leaders, as well as the parents and other local citizens within the neighborhoods surrounding the demonstration sites. Several such partners are already joining forces with the original group in each of the communities. In Austin, for example, a major, new partnership has emerged that involves all major elements of the city. Under the leadership of Walt Rostow, former special assistant to President Lyndon Johnson and currently professor emeritus of economics at the University of Texas, a number of political leaders, neighborhood action groups, corporate CEOs, and church organizations have launched what has come to be known as the Austin Project. Several dozen members of the Project's board of directors and others serving on specific task forces have been at work since early 1992 developing a comprehensive investment plan for the young aimed at child and family development, educational reform, urban renewal, and economic productivity. The Austin School of the Future project is a key component of this comprehensive new investment plan.

A great deal is being learned from this experiment on how to involve public agencies, private foundations, business and industry, community activists, school personnel, health and human service providers, neighborhood police, and the children and families themselves in viable partnerships for the common good. While every effort is being made to redeploy existing resources, additional state and federal help will be needed if the successful aspects of such experiments are to be implemented on a large enough scale to achieve the goals that have been set.

As scientists and policymakers, we have learned a great deal about how to strengthen the forces for constructive growth and mental health within children and families. Enough is already known to see more clearly what must be done to help families in trouble if we are to survive as a society. Most families want to be responsible for their own development. Most families also need help to accomplish their goals.

Rekindling the caring spirit in America has already begun. The School of the Future promises to be a key agent for nurturing this spirit while fulfilling a renewed national commitment to high standards of achievement.

References

Comer, J. P. (1985). *The School Development Program: A nine-step guide to school improvement*. New Haven, CT: Yale Child Study Center, Yale University.

Holtzman, W. H. (1992). Community renewal, family preservation, and child development through the School of the Future. In W. H. Holtzman (Ed.), *School of the Future* (pp. 3–18). Austin, TX: American Psychological Association and Hogg Foundation for Mental Health.

Zigler, E. F. (1989). Addressing the nation's childcare crisis: The school of the 21st century. *American Journal of Orthopsychiatry, 59*(4), 484–491.

Part Two

Key Organizational Issues

Chapter 5

Obstacles to Success in Educational Collaborations

Barbara Gray

The Growing Need for Collaboration

Collaborative initiatives are on the rise in virtually every sphere of human endeavor. Examples include strategic alliances among businesses, public-private partnerships to spur economic development, and policy dialogues among diverse stakeholders over environmental issues (Gray, 1989). These initiatives are prompted by intractable problems and increasing interdependence among the parties whom the problems impact. In the educational arena, major initiatives to promote family-community-school cooperation have been launched in the last five years (Kirst & Kelley, 1992; Palanki, Burch, & Davies, 1992). The formation of public/private partnerships and cross-agency partnerships for service delivery has created a new source of energy for tackling the complexities of planning and service delivery (Melaville & Blank, 1993). By marshaling the resources of the public, private, and not-for-profit sectors, these partnerships afford synergistic solutions to problems that are impossible for any single organization or sector to solve through independent action. This synergistic potential, and the possibilities for joint gains that collaborative partnerships afford, have made them not only

This research would not have been possible without funding from the Synergos Institute, New York, NY. Helpful comments and technical support were also provided by the Institute for Developmental Research, Boston, MA, and the Center for Research in Conflict and Negotiation, The Pennsylvania State University, University Park, PA.

attractive but essential new organizational forms. They have also stimulated the consideration of policy issues related to collaboration, since governmental policies at the federal, state, and local levels—as well as agency policies and practices—can enhance or impede collaborative initiatives.

Several factors promoting the need for collaboration around educational problems have been identified (Gray, 1989; Kagan, Rivera, & Parker, 1990; Crowson & Boyd, 1992). Declining productivity growth and increasing competitive pressures have caused the United States to lose its competitive edge internationally. We face a collective challenge as a nation to develop a workforce with technical and "intellective" skills (Zuboff, 1988) that will enable us to regain a competitive advantage in the global marketplace. This challenge falls squarely on the shoulders of the nation's schools (McGrew, 1991).

Despite the demands of these global challenges, however, our school system is decaying in the face of threats from poverty, drugs, homelessness, gang violence, teenage pregnancies, high dropout rates, and astronomical levels of teen unemployment. The interrelationship of these heretofore intractable problems creates an imperative that schools and other social service agencies work together to try to redeem what some are calling a lost generation of youth (Committee for Economic Development, 1989). For hundreds of thousands of at-risk youth, their appalling social environment has a profound negative influence on their ability to function in school. Unless more comprehensive services are provided in parallel with education, schools alone cannot be expected to educate youngsters with severe health and social problems that inhibit their ability to learn. Moreover, the private sector is not immune to this deterioration in educational quality. Businesses, increasingly in need of graduates with basic language and computational skills, can no longer rely on the educational system to provide a pool of competent workers prepared for entry-level positions (Levine & Trachtman, 1985; McGrew, 1991). Growing numbers of young people lack the basic skills they need to be economically productive (Murnane, 1988). Accordingly, collaboration across health, education, and social service agencies, as well as between the public and private sectors, has become a fundamental necessity.

An additional factor stimulating collaboration in education has been the sharp declines in federal revenues for social programs of all kinds, beginning with the Reagan administration (Gray, 1989; Kagan et al., 1990). Collaboration affords an opportunity for cost containment, restructuring, and minimization of interagency rivalries for the scarce resources available (Kagan et al., 1990; Lieberman, 1986; Otterbourg & Timpane, 1986). Such cooperation will necessitate replacing narrow, fragmented, agency-funded projects with state and federal support that facilitates a more holistic response to the problems of children; such integrated-services programs need to be linked with educational restructuring (Kirst & Kelley, 1992).

The Collaborative Process

According to Wood and Gray (1991), collaboration occurs when a group of autonomous stakeholders of a problem domain engage in an interactive process, using shared rules, norms, and structures to act or decide on issues related to that domain. The term *stakeholders* refers to those groups and/or individuals who are affected by the problem under consideration. Organizing for successful collaboration requires new approaches to management, including "efforts to coordinate autonomous organizations without the authority of a formal hierarchy" (Whetten & Bozeman, 1984, p. 21). The outcome of collaboration is a negotiated order among the stakeholders (Gray, 1989; Nathan & Mitroff, 1991) in which the parties have reached some common agreement about the problem domain.

The nature of the collaborative process is critical to the type of outcome that is reached. Three phases in the process have been delineated: problem setting, direction setting, and implementation

(Gray, 1989). The primary objective of problem setting is to give the situation an explicit form or identity that allows stakeholders to communicate about and eventually act on it (McCann, 1983). Direction setting seeks to achieve agreement about the issues affecting the problem domain. Implementation involves carrying out any agreements that require action.

At each phase, a number of issues influence the final resolution. In the problem-setting phase, for example, determining who the stakeholders are is a critical issue, since the participants in the interactive process will influence the nature of the agreements reached as well as the ease of coming to agreement. A critical issue in the direction-setting phase is the way in which information is gathered and exchanged. A joint information search facilitates the achievement of shared solutions because it gives the parties a common basis from which to draw inferences (Gricar & Brown, 1981). During implementation, procedures must be designed and structures created to ensure follow-through on any agreements reached. Inskip (1993) has shown that whereas the three phases are indeed essential, movement through them is often iterative and not necessarily orderly and sequential. If issues are not addressed, however, the probability that the collaboration may be unsuccessful increases.

Obstacles to Collaboration

Capitalizing on the potential afforded by collaboration, however, and transforming it into effective interorganizational relationships that produce tangible program improvement is not an easy task. Collaboration is no panacea. Successful collaborative alliances depend on a host of factors, many of which the partners cannot directly control (Gray, 1989; Sharfman, Gray, & Yan, 1991). The obstacles include (1) institutional disincentives, (2) historical and ideological barriers, (3) power disparities among stakeholders, (4) societal-level dynamics (such as the trend toward individualism in the United States), (5) differing perceptions of the level of acceptable risk, (6) technical complexity, and (7) political and institutional norms. Many of the obstacles are rooted in the philosophy and patterns of activity associated with what Robert Reich (1983) has termed the *management era*, characterized by assumptions about stable environments, standardized mass production, and continued growth. Despite their inappropriateness in a global environment, well-worn practices do not change overnight, and resistance is a predictable response to change (Klein, 1976; Lorsch, 1986). Formidable obstacles to implementing educational partnerships have been enumerated by Crowson and Boyd (1992), including undependable funding, management of logistics, the need for new roles and new leadership, protection of confidentiality, and information management. In addition, change evokes unconscious psycho- and sociodynamics that, as Eric Trist (1989) warns, produce destructive regressions in the process as well as a feeling of hopelessness.

This chapter examines the obstacles to collaboration by analyzing a case study of a collaborative educational partnership that failed to realize its full potential. The subject case involves the Youth Policy Group (YPG), a joint effort among business, civic, government, and educational institutions to deal with youth unemployment in New York City. Despite the formation of a powerful coalition of influential stakeholders, a thorough analysis of the problems, and agreement on a plan of action to redress them, YPG was unable to take or promote action on its plan. This analysis draws heavily on numerous interviews conducted with key YPG members. The background of the case study is presented here, followed by an analysis of the specific obstacles to collaboration that prevented implementation of agreed-on plans. Finally, recommendations are offered for overcoming or minimizing these obstacles to collaboration for future groups.

The Youth Policy Group: Background

In 1980, the percentage of teenagers employed in New York City was considerably lower than the national average for teenage employment (Levine & Trachtman, 1985). In 1982, of the more than 700,000 youth in New York City between the ages of sixteen and twenty-one, 40 percent were unemployed. For African-American and Latino youth, the figure was about 60 percent. Additionally, at least half of youth who were sixteen to twenty-four and who had dropped out of school could not find or were not looking for jobs.

Several explanations were offered for these high numbers. The first blamed the school system for its failure to address the employability needs of students, claiming the schools did not prepare students with conceptions of what it means to work or the necessary skills to enter the workforce as productive employees (Grinker & Walker, 1984). A second explanation focused on the changing requirements of many entry-level jobs which, because of increasing automation, demand both clerical and computational skills. Other accounts blamed students for increasingly unrealistic expectations about what a job should offer and cited the lure of "competing" sources of income available through criminal endeavors. A final explanation acknowledged the social environment of poverty, homelessness, crime, and inadequate health care, which leaves children and youth bereft of the basic developmental needs required for functioning at even a minimum level in school. A study done for the New York City Partnership noted: "It is difficult to overstate the deleterious effect of pervasive unemployment on our young people: For most of them, [it] leads to adult unemployment and a cycle of poverty that often engulfs several generations. Educators and youth unemployment experts are nearly unanimous in agreeing that young people who have jobs as teenagers are much less likely to suffer unemployment as adults. Young people will remain unemployable if they do not receive basic skills upon which job performance depends" (Nochimson, 1985, p. 2).

Almost two decades ago, a few civic and corporate leaders began to realize the implications of youth unemployment for the long-term health of New York City. In June of 1979, a key meeting marked the beginning of a partnership among business, government, and the schools in dealing with youth unemployment issues. Attending the meeting were Mayor Koch, David Rockefeller (chairman of Chase Manhattan Bank), Richard Shinn (chairman of Metropolitan Life Insurance Company), Arthur Barnes (executive director of the New York Urban Coalition), and Ron Gault (commissioner, New York City Department of Employment). They struck an agreement to initiate the first Summer Jobs Program (SJP), a major partnership effort among business, schools, and the city.

The program represented one of the first citywide endeavors among multiple sectors to address the youth unemployment issue. The seeds of collaborative efforts were sown during the SJP and subsequent efforts to create a comprehensive youth employment plan were shaped, in part, by its history. The program continued for several years, with leadership assumed each year by a different major corporation—including Citibank, Phillip Morris, the Daily News, Metropolitan Life, Coopers and Lybrand, IBM, and New York Newsday.

In the year following the inception of the SJP, the New York City Partnership (NYCP) was established by some of the same civic leaders as a more permanent vehicle to stimulate collaborative efforts between business and other organizations for addressing the city's problems. The partnership brought together the New York Chamber of Commerce and Industry and the Economic Development Council. A board of high-level executives of private and nonprofit institutions was formed. The broad mission of the partnership was and still is "to make New York City a better place in which to live, to work and to conduct business" (New York City Partnership, 1984, p. 4). Additionally, NYCP sought to address three critical needs: (1) the preparation of residents for service industry jobs, (2) the retention of back-office (that is, professional support service) jobs, and (3) improvement of the business climate in the city.

By 1982, responsibility for ensuring the continuity of the SJP had fallen under the aegis of the NYCP. Additionally, two committees were formed under NYCP's auspices to address problems of youth in the city: the Education Committee and the Youth Employment Committee. The former was organized by the president of the United Federation of Teachers, and by then-chancellor of the New York City Schools. The chancellor, believing the SJP was too focused on employment, hoped to establish a wider dialogue with business. His priority was to emphasize business participation in education.

The Youth Employment Committee, on the other hand, sought to better understand the complexity of the youth employment problem and to evaluate existing programs. It commissioned two separate reports; these reports underscored the need for additional employability efforts to offset shrinking federal funding and outlined a catalytic role for the New York City Partnership in coordinating new initiatives (Grinker & Walker, 1984; Levine & Trachtman, 1985). The second study specifically emphasized the need for a school-business partnership to address the problems of youth unemployment:

> The problems of New York's public schools are shared by many large urban districts: high dropout rates, low achievement scores, continuing financial constraints, low levels of public support and low teacher morale. The problems are symptoms of a system not meeting the needs of the students or the teachers. A system which can attract, retain, and support the best performance possible from both students and teachers should be the goal of business/education partnerships. The business community and the schools have important contributions to make in moving in this direction [Levine & Trachtman, 1985, p. i–ii.]

Despite these recommendations, no comprehensive effort to address youth employment was underway at the NYCP during the early 1980s. Other than the SJP, the role that the private sector could play in youth employment problems was not well articulated.

Lack of Shared Perceptions Among Stakeholders

A major difficulty in the collaboration was that stakeholders did not share common perceptions of the problems and of each other. Business was perceived primarily as providing funds to support programs initiated by the school system and others. Few corporations embraced a more active role for themselves, and consequently their commitment to youth employment issues was not strong during this period. According to a Citibank executive, many businesses did not recognize the value of hiring young people. However, a handful of companies—including Metropolitan Life, American Express, Time Inc., Citibank, and New York Telephone—had targeted the youth employment issue. An executive at Metropolitan Life characterized as follows their motivation to get involved in the issue: "Emphasis was being placed on the private sector to solve social problems. At Metropolitan we had reviewed the range of community problems and concluded that youth employment was a high priority issue."

An executive at Citibank acknowledged that business has a strong need to work with the Board of Education because the educational system alone cannot tackle all the problems associated with employability of in-school youth. However, he noted, "The school system has to let you get involved." Speaking from the education side, a teachers' union spokesperson observed that "businesses are increasingly recognizing the role they can play as constructive critics of education." However, he cautioned the private sector not to lose patience with the pace of public sector bureaucracy if results were not forthcoming as quickly as expected.

Suspicions among stakeholders about each other's motives and about the feasibility of a partnership were confirmed at the inception of the SJP. According to one participant, "Government was cynical about what business was capable of doing and business was skeptical about the capabilities of government." Clearly, the stakeholders had different agendas. Whereas members of the business community had an overall strategy for economic development in the city, others, such as the New York commissioner of employment and the executive director of the Urban Coalition, sought a more vigorous effort to alleviate the high unemployment in the city. The school system, in turn, expressed concern about the Reagan-era cuts in federal funding for social and educational programs. The mayor, on the other hand, was looking for a project that would produce an immediate impact on the problems of youth in the city. Despite these differences, sufficient agreement was reached to proceed with the SJP.

Formation of the Youth Policy Group

In July 1983, three members of the Youth Employment Committee proposed that the partnership and allied organizations design a youth apprenticeship program modeled after a successful West German program. A staff report indicated that the NYCP was well positioned to develop a pilot apprenticeship program because of its close ties to the city's public school system and the potential for corporate-sector involvement. The report stressed that the NYCP alone could not launch such an undertaking, and that the program "should be broadly collaborative." Among the possible impediments cited were business' skepticism about participating in manpower programs focused on the disadvantaged rather than on the manpower needs of business. As one corporate observer noted: "Business participation needs to have a fixed beginning and ending and be absolutely attainable so that everyone succeeds. The objectives need to be clear, for example, 'We are going to find X number of jobs,' not, 'We're going to solve the youth employment problem.'" Other possible drawbacks were the need to secure public sector funds, to contend with minimum wage regulations, and to attract a critical mass of businesses within a single industry to provide a sufficient pool of jobs.

Despite these concerns, funding was secured from the German Marshall Fund to send business leaders and state and city government officials to Europe to study youth employment programs that might be replicated in New York. A cross-section of stakeholders with a demonstrated interest in youth employment issues was assembled and came to be known as the Youth Policy Group (YPG). The role envisioned for the New York City Partnership was detailed in an August 1984 memo to NYCP's president from one of its vice presidents, who coordinated the YPG: "The Partnership will serve as a broker for the diverse interests represented by the Department of Employment, the New York City Schools, the United Federation of Teachers, the Private Industry Council, community-based training organizations and the private sector. A priority will be to ensure that the work program addresses private sector employment needs" (NYCP, 1984, p. 4). The memo envisioned that, following the European trip, a collaborative effort would produce a pilot program under the auspices of the NYCP.

Twelve stakeholders were selected by an informal group of NYCP staff and corporate and government advisors for the trip; all were high-level professionals in their respective organizations and had a demonstrated commitment to youth employment issues. The participants included officials from a state agency, a city agency, and the New York City public schools; leaders of a labor union and a teachers' union; executives from a life insurance company, a publishing company, a bank, and an investment firm; and officers from the New York City Partnership. Two groups of stakeholders were not included on the committee: community and social service organizations (who deal closely with at-risk youth) and youth themselves. In retrospect, this was a costly oversight. A logical choice to represent community organizations was the president of the New York Urban Coalition, who had participated in both the Education and the Youth Employment Committees and the Summer Jobs Program. According to the Youth Policy Group's report: "The choices were difficult; there are a number of other public sector agencies and officials also concerned with these issues; just as there are other labor unions and other corporations with programs already in place. . . . Leaving those others out of the trip and figuring out ways to bring them back into the planning process later was more problematic" (Dulany, 1985, p.2).

Some argued that the community voice was represented by the City Commission on Employment, but others disagreed. (The Urban Coalition was invited to join the group after it returned from Europe. Youth, however, were never considered.) In preparation for the trip, the travelers met twice to plan an agenda and brief themselves on the European programs that had had the most impact in their respective countries.

The European visit proved invaluable in at least three ways. First, it provided the group a common focus for considering potential program elements for a U.S. program. The value of including multiple stakeholders can be gleaned from the following comment by one of the private sector participants: "I was having a difficult time equating what the three other cultures (German, British, and Swedish) were doing that we could do. I was struggling. I spent most of my time with the Chancellor of Schools who had a much better handle on what could and couldn't work. It was very rewarding."

Second, the trip reinforced the necessity for collaboration in addressing youth employment problems. One of the corporate sector representatives emphasized the strength of the multisector commitments needed: "Solutions to the problems of youth unemployment can only be successfully developed if business, government and labor cooperate. The problem is too great for any one entity or sector to handle alone."

Third, considerable bonding occurred among the group members. In the words of one participant: "We gelled together. This was something that brought us together socially and politically. In was an intense period of time. We became more comfortable and overcame the usual cautions that would prevail across these institutional boundaries." Another noted feelings of trust and friendship that continued long after the trip. Still another observed: "One measure of [the trip's] success was that people became so turned on within a very short time."

Posttrip Activities

The members of the Youth Policy Group met frequently throughout the next year. With the help of a facilitator, the group held several long retreats to digest the European experience and to sort out the questions it provoked about solving youth employment problems in New York. As one member noted, the YPG agenda expanded during these posttrip meetings: "The puzzle became more complicated. Putting together all the pieces became key, [as did] selling it to the Partnership." Some complications arose in reaching agreement about which populations would be served. This argument was characterized as the in-school/out-of-school debate, and centered around whether programs should be targeted for at-risk youth (who had clearly dropped out of school) or only those with the potential to stay in school. The YPG strove to forge a plan that would address the needs of both in- and out-of-school youth with education and employability.

By summer of 1985, the YPG had agreed on broad goals. Collectively the goals represented a comprehensive plan dealing with both in- and out-of-school disadvantaged youth, primarily those sixteen to twenty-one, with some programs extending the age limit to twenty-five. The goals called for an assessment of existing employability, training, and placement programs and consideration of how existing programs could be improved through a collaborative approach. Specific action plans for implementing each goal still needed to be identified. This task was delegated to the NYCP staff to complete and present at a future meeting.

To assist in the development of action plans, the YPG commissioned a consultant to document existing programs and identify unmet needs. The consultant worked closely with partnership staff to flesh out a program, and by September 1985, reformulated goals and objectives were presented to the YPG for consideration. Among the specific proposals the group agreed to was a citywide program to coordinate employment services at each high school. Local businesses would be involved through an advisory board tailored to each school. The purpose was to find jobs to motivate students to stay in school through graduation. Plans called for a pilot program in three schools.

Implementation

Despite the intensive work to gain a consensus and produce a draft program, the Youth Policy Group's recommendations were never implemented. On the surface, the reason for this was the effective collapse of the YPG. Several key members changed jobs at a crucial point in the group's development. The representative from Equitable Life was also chairman of the Private Industry Council and could not maintain substantial involvement after the European trip. The commissioner of the City Department of Employment resigned that post in April 1985. The original Citibank representative was unable to participate in any of the follow-up meetings, although he did send a replacement. Another of the original group, the New York Commissioner of Labor, resigned that post in January of 1986. And a key participant resigned as a vice president of the New York City Partnership in March 1986. According to one member, "We lost momentum because key business people dropped out. We had an opportunity and lost it." The vice president, in particular, was described as "the life force of the group" and "the torch that was carrying this."

Analysis

A comprehensive analysis of why the Youth Policy Group's recommendations were not implemented produced a number of explanations, but five issues stand out. They are (1) inattention to structuring during implementation, (2) failure of group members to understand their different institutional cultures, (3) pervasive historical tensions, (4) institutional disincentives for implementation, and (5) failure to build a constituency. They are also typical obstacles to achieving success in any school-business-community collaborations.

Inattention to Structuring During Implementation

Although care was taken to facilitate the collaborative process during the direction-setting phase, this same attention to structuring was absent during implementation. Structuring refers to creating administrative apparatus to manage the process and to authorize actions to implement the agreement (Gray, 1989). Provisions for implementation were never clearly formulated by the group, and efforts to enlist subordinates in following up on the recommendations were minimal. One observer recalls that there was little follow-through when individual members were charged with seeking input from their subordinates on specific program proposals.

It is not clear, either, that the group conceived of itself as implementers. Among those who went on the European trip, expectations varied about what the group would accomplish. Interviews with YPG members revealed that they did not agree about who would assume responsibility for implementing their recommendations. According to one participant, there was no prior understanding that their work would extend beyond the trip itself or that implementation was a part of their role. Many members saw themselves in an advisory role to the New York City Partnership and looked to it to carry out the recommendations. In contrast, another believed that there was a conscious and deliberate effort among group members to move forward on their return and that trip participants were chosen expressly for their ability to "make something happen." Still, he viewed NYCP as implementer and YPG's task as "selling the Partnership on a plan of action that should be followed." This ambiguity about responsibility for implementation was never clearly resolved. No one was authorized to implement the recommendations and no one took the initiative to do so.

The irony is that implementation required leadership from the very people in the YPG who formulated the recommendations. Without high-level commitment of financial and human resources by the school system, for example, the proposals could not be implemented.

Gaining a commitment of this type is a tricky issue in organizing collaborative efforts. It is unrealistic to expect stakeholders to commit up front to implementing recommendations when they cannot fully anticipate the implications of that action. Yet, as the process unfolds, critical queries regarding the feasibility of the proposed actions need to be built into the deliberations. Specifically, that means clarifying who has the authority to act on agreements that are reached and who will assume responsibility for ensuring that they are carried out. The Youth Policy Group never reached consensus on where that authority resided. Clearly they had the authority—by virtue of their respective offices—to implement many pieces of their proposed plan.

Failure of Group Members to Understand Their Different Institutional Cultures

Differing institutional cultures and work ethics often create one of the most difficult obstacles to successful partnerships (Gray, 1989). Organizations have development cultures that are unique to their organizational mission and history (Schein, 1986; Trice & Beyer, 1993). These cultures reflect the values, assumptions, rituals, and practices that form the basis for conduct of the organizational mission. Professionals, too, have cultures that undergird the practices they employ on a daily basis. When diverse institutional and professional representatives gather to collaborate, they bring cultural assumptions—shaped by their own institutional and professional experience—that often differ substantially. These assumptions create expectations about how other institutions should operate; these expectations frequently do not match the reality of the organizations.

For example, public and private sector expectations about time and authority differ considerably. Unless partners become sensitive to these differences and learn to work within the constraints of the other participating institutions, joint efforts will end in frustration. The private sector need for public visibility and a quick success, for example, must be balanced against the slow-moving, comprehensive approval process of public sector bureaucracies.

Overcoming the obstacles created by cultural assumptions becomes particularly salient in educational collaborations attempting integrated-service delivery. The members of the Youth Policy Group began to appreciate and cope with these institutional differences. Traveling together clearly led to the breaking down of some traditional institutional barriers among the YPG members. The representative from the Teacher's Union commented, "We had to go beyond just the union and the school system." A Citibank representative offered similar observations about the relationship among education, the private sector, and the union: "The insulation between education and business is beginning to erode. The union is becoming more willing to let business come in and teach, whereas before the systems didn't even talk to one another. There is more open communication now. Things have changed." One member recalled a specific instance in which the consultant "got them [the Private Industry Council, the Department of Education, and the Chancellor of Schools] to get off turf issues and to reveal to each other the specifics of the youth programs they had in place." Despite these early successes, historical institutional differences became personified in individual conflicts (such as the in-school, out-of-school debate) that inhibited implementation.

Pervasive Historical Tensions

Any collaborative effort can expect to encounter tensions, but those that affected the Youth Policy Group were particularly pervasive.

Tensions Within the New York City Partnership. A lack of internal support from the partnership's president for the formation of the Youth Policy Group and for its recommendations appears to have contributed directly to the implementation failure, according to some YPG members. The president, who was also the former chancellor of schools, was in a position to use his influence both within and outside the New York City Partnership to generate support for the Youth Policy Group's recommendations. Theoretically, he might have used his influence to cultivate support from the mayor or from a wider set of private sector participants including those represented by the Chamber of Commerce and Industry, but did not. Presumably, the president's previous association with the schools led him to bring to the NYCP a preference for addressing the needs of in-school youth. Although he agreed that the schools needed to teach a work ethic, he viewed programs for dropouts as a safety net. He believed, "By acknowledging dropping out, you ratify it." In contrast, the NYCP president described the vice president's agenda as "more global than mine. She was interested in transforming schools; I saw transformation as much more gradual. The culture I was trying to create was that adults would be comfortable in the presence of kids."

From the vice president's perspective, the Youth Policy Group's efforts were not supported by the partnership's president. It is perhaps not surprising that the president raised objections to the German Marshall Fund project during its conception and did not actively promote action on the Youth Policy Group's recommendations. Instead he focused on the administrative and financial concerns of the NYCP, which required considerable attention since the president's post had been vacant for several months. Other observers, however, saw him as still closely tied to a school agenda at the NYCP, and, as a result, "the Partnership never came clean on its schools agenda." One member of the YPG commented on the role the president might have played: "[He] was a close ally of the mayor and in close alliance with government officials. He could have put together political and financial support to implement our proposals. He was the logical spokesperson, as opposed to any of us."

Tensions Between the New York City Partnership and the Chancellor of Schools. A related consideration was the tension between the president and his replacement as chancellor of schools. It seems likely that the strained relationship between the New York City Partnership and the schools directly inhibited implementation. The president's move from chancellor of the New York City Schools to president of the partnership created a substantial rift between the two institutions that persisted during the tenure of the next two chancellors. He became a kind of "chancellor in exile" whose presence and posture at the partnership inhibited the development of a constructive working relationship between the schools and the NYCP. The president said he elected to "mind my own business" to give the new chancellor of schools room to maneuver. The animosities were so strong, however, that the new chancellor initially refused to work on NYCP projects, and his successor only agreed to participate in the YPG after considerable hesitation. This underlying historical tension may help explain why New York City Partnership staff found little leadership from the school system for implementing the recommendations.

Tensions Between Business and the Schools. Implementation was further thwarted by the frustration of the business community with the school system bureaucracy. Tensions between several key corporations and the school system became increasingly strained when plans for a High School of Communication Arts (a proposed joint venture between Time, Inc. and the schools) were never implemented.

Institutional Disincentives for Implementation

Overall, the New York City Partnership's role can best be described as that of convener and catalyst. It played the convening role by identifying the European travelers and by handling arrangements for the trip. The partnership played a catalytic role by mustering resources and energizing the group. Unfortunately, the link between the Youth Policy Group and other partnership committees was never clearly forged. NYCP's vice president was the primary organizing force, playing the role of group leader within the Youth Policy Group, and staffing both the Education and Youth Employment committees of the New York City Partnership. She, then, was the primary conduit from the group to the rest of the NYCP's organization.

The committees, however, had little ownership of the Youth Policy Group's work. Only one YPG member sat on the Youth Employment Committee. Four other YPG members played key roles in the working groups of both committees, but had no decision-making role within the partnership. Nor did the Youth Policy Group have a mandate from or the sponsorship of either committee. In short, the link between YPG's work and the NYCP committees was tenuous at best. Without the support and leadership of the CEOs who sat on these committees, there was no one to spearhead implementation of the YPG's recommendations.

In order to move from the comprehensive agreements reached by the Youth Policy Group to a major programmatic multiagency initiative, someone had to champion the cause and enlist the commitment of the respective organizations in adopting and carrying out a program. The New York City Partnership's committee structure posed some natural obstacles to collaboration on the youth employment problem. The YPG's deliberations touched on both education and employment, yet neither committee provided leadership to or sponsorship of the Youth Policy Group. The chair of the Youth Employment Committee retired at a critical time, when private sector leadership was needed to broaden the base of support for the recommendations, and the Education Committee did not pick up the gauntlet for youth unemployment. According to one corporate member of the Youth Policy Group: "This was some good work. But it wasn't going to be driven by business. It was the worst time for business. They didn't want to hear about the underclass and weren't trained or set up to help train and manage apprenticeship programs."

The typical model of implementation within the New York City Partnership was the lead company approach, in which one corporate CEO spearheaded a project using his or her own staff resources to coordinate it. Since the Youth Policy Group plan did not operate with a lead company model, corporate support did not materialize. As one YPG member explained, "No one could administer the joint agreement. The Partnership did not have the will or the authority to do so." Ownership of the YPG's efforts could have been more widely distributed had either or both committees ratified the group's mission and formally charged it to return with recommendations. Clarification about who was responsible for implementation would more likely have occurred if there had been accountability to one of these committees. Thus, the inability of the New York City Partnership to muster and sustain high-level corporate support for the YPG recommendations was a major reason for the lack of implementation.

The consultant's report stated that structurally there were no provisions in place at the partnership for carrying forward the Youth Policy Group's product. The report identified several problems with implementing the Youth Policy Group's recommendations: "The above recommendations require joint planning and collaborative programming among and between disparate public agencies and the private sector. There is currently no body in New York capable of framing, promoting and implementing a coordinated, comprehensive effort for investing in the human capital of young people" (DeLone, 1985, p. 5). The report called for a streamlining of existing NYCP committees and leadership from a group of high-level public and private sector executives to develop and implement the recommendations.

Limited Stakeholder Set and the
Failure to Build a Constituency

A final factor that thwarted implementation was the exclusion of some stakeholders from the Youth Policy Group. The YPG emerged out of the European trip and its members were largely those who had taken the trip. The stakeholder group that traveled together represented several organizations who had a real interest in the youth employment issue and historically were committed to improving the situation. However, other groups in New York who also had a stake in the youth employment issue were not included. Groups who were not involved included the mayor's office, and youth and local groups in communities with high levels of unemployed youth. Their exclusion had the net effect of limiting enthusiasm for the project. These groups were in a position to create an interested audience and political support for the recommendations, but this never materialized.

Finally, since there was little involvement of grassroots community groups in the Youth Policy Group, there was no constituency to apply continued pressure to the New York City Partnership to follow through with its plans. If the community groups had had a stronger voice in the planning, and a role in ensuring implementation, their influence might have kept the recommendations alive. As the Urban Coalition representative noted, this may have hurt the partnership in the long run: "Community groups can't be represented by a government agency. What I represent is a different politic. There was a struggle to get other community organizations involved. They were stakeholders, but they represented a different racial mix than the Partnership could handle. By not including them and the mechanisms to legitimate these individuals, the Partnership undermined its own power. No one was waiting for what the Partnership was going to say. Not including them limited the quality and the political force of the recommendations and drained power from the organization."

Epilogue

In the spring of 1988, a program very similar to that proposed by the Youth Policy Group was initiated by the New York School and Business Alliance (SABA). The principals in launching this effort were the former chairman of NYCP's Education Committee and the president of the New York City Board of Education. It is interesting to note that the SABA initiative, in contrast to the YPG plan, had a corporate champion and that many of the recommendations made by the Youth Policy Group were implemented by this alliance. One former YPG member observed: "The process was never finalized, but it left us with good ideas about what the future should look like. I identified in New York Working the same concepts that we had started in the YPG plan."

Specifically, New York Working's program (drafted with the assistance of the same consultant who had worked with the Youth Policy Group) called for a Career Development and Employment Office in each high school. The office would coordinate counseling and training efforts already in place within the schools, and identify local job opportunities for graduates. In addition, a central staff would solicit job pledges from businesses and financial support for the program. Although New York Working was initially developed under the auspices of a separate school-business partnership, in late 1988 SABA and the New York City Partnership began working collaboratively to implement it. NYCP housed the program, and implementation responsibility fell under the NYCP president. The program was slated to begin in six schools in fall of 1988. Many of the former YPG members were guardedly optimistic about New York Working. With respect to the impact, one YPG member noted, "The jury is still out."

Over the next several years, the New York Working Program was instituted in nine high schools in the most needy communities in New York City. Each school has an employment and career development center staffed jointly by education and community representatives. Businesses provide mentors, internships, and technical assistance. The program is funded through the governor's office and was administered by the New York City Partnership until 1994 when responsibility for it shifted to the United Way.

Conclusions and Recommendations

The Youth Policy Group experience highlights several obstacles that can interfere with successful collaboration. An important question, in hindsight, is whether their deleterious effects could have been prevented or ameliorated, and how similar groups might avoid these difficulties in the future. Evidence from other collaborative ventures suggests that a different outcome might have been achieved had there been careful attention to process issues throughout the effort. Critically important was forging a strong tie between the planners and implementers from the outset, requiring a multiplicative process in which the education and youth employment committees were involved from the early stages and their input incorporated throughout the planning. A related process issue concerns the involvement of multiple representatives from each stakeholder institution during the early phases, so that losses due to attrition have minimal effects.

While institutional barriers were temporarily overcome by the joint data gathering afforded by the European trip, the issue of barriers requires continual revisiting throughout the collaborative effort. In the case of the Youth Policy Group, since little attention was paid to issues of implementation early on, institutional differences concerning implementation were never explored constructively nor were alternatives considered.

With respect to stakeholder participation, a model similar to that used in the Newark Collaboration would have proven beneficial. In Newark, organizers initially cast a broad net for stakeholders and absorbed newly identified stakeholders into the process as it evolved. Additionally, they encouraged intraorganizational planning parallel to the cross-stakeholder discussions (Strauss, 1988) so that constituent organizations were continually "in the loop."

Historical tensions are, perhaps, the most difficult obstacles to overcome. A collaborative process that permitted more balanced participation by several corporations, rather than a lead company approach, might have overcome the lack of support of the New York City Partnership's president. On the other hand, there is evidence that some collaborative initiatives succeed only through the efforts of a champion who inspires others to participate (Westley & Vredenberg, 1992). With a detractor rather than a champion, the Youth Policy Group's efforts may have been doomed from the start. A final issue concerns timing and the readiness of the wider environment for the collaborative initiative (Sharfman et al., 1991). Achieving successful collaboration requires aligning the collaborative efforts with a receptive environment.

The last issue to be considered here, and one that has enormous effect on collaborative efforts, concerns policy. In the last several years the climate for cross-agency and cross-sectoral collaboration has shifted considerably (Potapchuk & Polk, 1993). Countless initiatives have sprung up, particularly in the area of integrated services. Among the more successful ones are the Walbridge Caring Communities Project, New Jersey's School-Based Youth Services Program, Minnesota's Childhood Family Education Program, and the Annie E. Casey Foundation's "New Futures" programs in four U.S. cities. Despite some successes among these model programs, and the instrumental incentives promoting collaboration in education, obstacles at the policy level must also be overcome if the potential of collaborative opportunities is to be realized and the lives of children are to be improved.

Among the most critical obstacles at the policy level are (1) an unrealistic appraisal of the time and resources required to successfully convene a collaborative process, (2) fragmentation of agency grants that discourages cross-agency efforts to solve complex problems, (3) limited resources, and (4) barriers to intergovernmental coordination that exacerbate problems of fragmentation. At a recent conference entitled "Building the Collaborative Community," participants identified several steps that could improve the climate for collaborative initiatives. First, grantors should amend the request for proposal (RFP) process to ensure sufficient lead time for communities to undertake the preliminary steps of convening a collaborative group. Identifying stakeholders and garnering their commitment to collaborate are essential first steps in launching a successful alliance (Gray, 1989). However, these require sufficient time frames and networking to identify the right participants.

Second, in many communities, a core set of stakeholders may be involved in multiple collaborative efforts, each initiated by a different federal or state agency or by multiple programs within agencies. Government agencies that mandate collaborative processes as a requirement for the disbursement of their funds should allow (and encourage) existing collaboratives to apply for new resources without having to begin anew each time. Third, agencies should review the negative incentives to collaboration embedded in categorical grants (Potapchuk & Polk, 1993). Fourth, in areas such as services to children and youth, multiple agencies provide funding and generate a myriad of programs and policies, but these often inhibit local implementers from working across agencies precisely when collaborative efforts are needed. Intergovernmental review of the obstacles created by federal agency barriers is of highest priority if the limited funds for at-risk children are to be used most effectively. Finally, conveners and sponsors need to garner the necessary authority to address obstacles to implementation throughout the process. Often political clout and leadership are needed to muster the appropriate representation of stakeholders and the necessary follow-through from those authorized to implement collaborative agreements.

References

Committee for Economic Development. (1989). *The new America: Prospects for population and policy in the 21st century.* Washington, DC: Author.

Crowson, R. I.., & Boyd, W. L. (1992). Coordinated services for children: Problems of organization and implementation. *The CEIC Review, 1*(2), 3–5, 8.

DeLone, R.H., and Associates. (1985, Summer). *Tomorrow's work force: Issues and opportunities for human capital investment in New York City.* Executive summary of report prepared for the New York City Partnership, Youth Policy Group.

Dulany, P. (1985, Fall). *German Marshall Fund Report.* Unpublished, internal report of the New York City Partnership.

Gray, B. (1989). *Collaborating: Finding common ground for multiparty problems.* San Francisco: Jossey-Bass.

Gricar, B., & Brown, L. (1981). Conflict, power, and organization in a changing community. *Human Relations, 34*(10), 877–893.

Grinker, W. J., & Walker, G. C.. (1984). *Report on a youth employment program strategy prepared for the New York City Partnership's Committee on Youth Employment.* New York: New York City Partnership.

Inskip, R. A. (1993, July). *A study of facilitating interorganizational collaboration.* Paper presented at the CAIS/ASCI Conference, Antigonish, Nova Scotia.

Kagan, S. L., Rivera, A. M., & Parker, F. L. (1990). *Collaboration in practice: Reshaping services for young children and their families.* New Haven, CT: Yale University, Bush Center for Child Development and Social Policy.

Kirst, M. W., & Kelley, C. (1992, October). *Collaboration to improve education and children's services: Politics and policymaking.* Paper presented at School-Community Connections: Exploring Issues for Research and Practice (an invitational conference sponsored by the National Center on Education in the Inner Cities), Leesburg, VA.

Klein, D. (1976). Some notes on the dynamics of resistance to change: The defender role. In W. Bennis, K. D. Benne, R. Chin, & K. E. Cory (Eds.), *The planning of change* (pp. 117–124). Troy, MO: Holt, Rinehart & Winston.

Levine, M., & Trachtman, R. (1985, October). *School/business partnerships: A share in New York's future.* Report prepared for the New York City Partnership. New York: New York City Partnership.

Lieberman, J. K. (1983). *Litigious society.* New York: Basic Books.

Lorsch, J. (1986). Managing culture: The invisible barrier to strategic change. *California Management Review, 2*(2), 95–109.

McCann, J. E. (1983). Design guidelines for social problem-solving interventions. *Journal of Applied Behavioral Science, 19,* 177–189.

McGrew, J. (1991). Developing a shared vision: Business, government and education. *National Civic Review, 80*(1), 31–35.

Melaville, A. L., & Blank, M. J. (1993). *Together we can: A guide for crafting a profamily system of education and human services.* Washington, DC: U.S. Department of Education and U.S. Department of Health and Human Services.

Murnane, R. (1988). Education and productivity of the workforce: Looking ahead. In R. E. Litan, R. Z. Lawrence, & C. Schultz (Eds.), *American living standards: Threats and challenges* (pp. 215–245). Washington, DC: The Brookings Institution.

Nathan, M., & Mitroff, I. (1991). The use of Negotiated Order Theory as a tool for the analysis and development of an interorganizational field. *Journal of Applied Behavioral Science, 27*(2), 163–180.

New York City Partnership. (1984, March). *The partnership blueprint: Strengthening New York as a world city.* New York: Author.

New York City Partnership. (1984, August). Internal memo.

Nochimson, K. (1985, September). *Report prepared for the New York City Partnership's Youth Policy Group.* New York: New York City Partnership.

Otterbourg, S.D., & Timpane, M. (1986). Partnerships and schools. In P. Davis (Ed.),*Public-private partnerships: Improving urban life* (pp. 60–73). New York: Academy of Political Science.

Palanki, A., Burch, P., & Davies, D. (1992, March). *Mapping the policy landscape: What federal and state governments are doing to promote family-school-community partnerships* (Report no. 7). Baltimore, MD: Johns Hopkins University, Center on Families, Communities, Schools, and Children's Learning.

Potapchuk, W. R., & Polk, C. (1993, July). *Building the collaborative community.* Paper presented at Building the Collaborative Community, a conference sponsored by the National Institute for Dispute Resolution, the National Civil League, and the Program for Community Problem Solving, Washington, DC.

Reich, R. B. (1983). *The next American frontier.* New York: Times Books.

Schein, E. H. (1986). *Organizational culture and leadership.* San Francisco: Jossey-Bass.

Sharfman, M., Gray, B., & Yan, A. (1991). The context of interorganizational collaboration in the garment industry: An institutional perspective. *Journal of Applied Behavioral Science, 27*(2), 181–208.

Strauss, D. (1988, March). *Process management: Planning the plan to do.* Presentation given at the Conference on Collaboration and Conflict Resolution in Community Problem Solving: Emerging Trends and Methods, Washington, DC.

Trice, H. M., & Beyer, J. M. (1993). *The cultures of work organizations*. Englewood Cliffs, NJ: Prentice Hall.

Trist, E. L. (1989). Foreword (pp. xiii–xvi). In B. Gray (Ed.), *Collaborating: Finding common ground for multiparty problems*. San Francisco: Jossey-Bass.

Westley, F., & Vredenberg, H. (1992, August). *Managing the ark: Interorganizational collaboration and the preservation of biodiversity*. Paper presented at the Academy of Management Meeting, Las Vegas, NV.

Whetten, D. A., & Bozeman, B. (1984, May). *Policy coordination and interorganizational relations: Some guidelines for sharing power*. Paper presented at the Conference on Shared Power, Hubert H. Humphrey Institute and School of Management, University of Minnesota.

Wood, D. J., & Gray, B. (1991). Toward a comprehensive theory of collaboration. *Journal of Applied Behavioral Science, 27*(2), 139–162.

Zuboff, S. (1988). *The age of the smart machine*. New York: Basic Books.

Chapter Six

A Communication Perspective on Interorganizational Cooperation and Inner-City Education

Eric M. Eisenberg

As a society and as a species, we have entered an age of limits. Whereas past generations were afforded the slack to make bad decisions and still survive—even thrive—we no longer have this luxury. Shrinking resources have led managers and administrators to seek ways (and the rhetoric is by now painfully familiar) to "do more with less" and to "work smarter, not harder." Of course, for some people scarce resources have always been a way of life. What is different now is the near-universal scarcity of resources across every type of organization and industry, from hospitals and schools to private businesses and government agencies (Eisenberg & Goodall, 1993).

When times are tough, one natural tendency is to pull together to support one another. The 1990s have thus far been marked by an explosion in joint ventures, partnerships, and strategic alliances that shows no sign of abating. A fair conclusion would be that in good times, plentiful resources permit agencies and organizations to conduct their business independently with little concern for one another. Given scarce resources, however, interorganizational cooperation becomes essential as a means of managing a turbulent organizational environment.

While noble in concept, interorganizational cooperation is risky business in practice. The success rate of such partnerships, whether private-private, public-private, or public-public, is in fact quite low.

Interorganizational arrangements share a common characteristic: they require participating organizations to give up some degree of autonomy in exchange for the potential synergies and rewards that may come from the partnership. Once this reality of collaboration becomes clear to all parties, there is often a steady withdrawal from cooperation and communication. Consequently, the number of organizations that consider various forms of interorganizational arrangements far exceeds the number that actually go through with them. Over time, the actual realized benefits from cooperation fail as a rule to outweigh the considerable costs. For these reasons, I am tempted to begin with the assertion that interorganizational cooperation *does not* work, and to consider instead some fundamentally different alternatives.

This view seems overly pessimistic, however, particularly in light of Carol Truesdell's comments later in this volume. In regard to her work with the Minneapolis Youth Trust, she feels a "real readiness for doing something radically different," and that frustration is reaching such a level that the "need to cooperate is greater than any sacrifices that may be required" (see Chapter Nine, this volume). A similar sort of hopefulness is associated with the New Beginnings program in San Diego, where preliminary data collection on interagency collaboration revealed that change was necessary since service delivery agencies could hardly do any worse than current arrangements. While I share this perception of the growing motivation for change, I realize that there are not as yet reliable models for successful interorganizational cooperation. More to the point, I will argue in this chapter that interorganizational cooperation may indeed be possible, but only if we come to think differently about how and why it might work. Specifically, *current approaches to interorganizational cooperation are based on fundamentally flawed ways of thinking about the nature of effective communication, and of the relationship between communication and coordinated action.* An alternate view of these processes will allow us to foster interorganizational arrangements that have a greater chance of success.

Historically, the dominant approach to interorganizational cooperation has been a rational one, based on an ideologically motivated, modernist view of communication that values agreement, openness, and prospective planning as the preferred route to coordinated action (Eisenberg, 1984, 1990). The payoff from this approach has been minimal. As an alternative, I offer a *counterrational* approach to cooperation, one that values dialogue, diversity of experience, and coordinated action over agreement and open communication. Specific implications for school-community connections are offered throughout.

Rational Approaches to Interorganizational Cooperation

Traditionally, interorganizational cooperation is viewed as an attempt by one or more organizations to address perceived uncertainty in the environment. Two models have been applied to understanding the process of interorganizational cooperation: *resource flow* and *information flow*. The resource flow model "treats environments as consisting of resources for which organizations compete . . . the process through which information about environments is apprehended by decision-makers is not given much attention" (Aldrich, 1979, p. 110). By contrast, the information flow model "relies heavily on theories of perception, cognition, and decision making, focusing on environment as seen through the eyes of organizational members" (Aldrich, 1979, p. 110).

Many types of information and resource flows can be established between organizations. In manufacturing organizations, a common strategy is to promote vertical linkages between assembly houses and suppliers to ensure a reliable flow of high-quality parts and sub-assemblies. Among service organizations, horizontal linkages are more common. Agencies involved in treating cancer patients, for example, may cooperate to make it easier for an individual to navigate the journey from the screening clinic to a physician, then to a hospital, and finally to a hospice or support group for cancer survivors. Schools may cooperate with community-based social service agencies to increase the likelihood that disadvantaged students come to classes physically and emotionally prepared to learn.

It is misleading, of course, to consider interorganizational linkages as if they were all the same. In an earlier study (Eisenberg et al., 1985), my colleagues and I devised a classification scheme identifying three levels of interorganizational cooperation. First, an *institutional* linkage occurs when information or resources are exchanged between organizations without the immediate involvement of specific organizational roles or personalities (for example, data exchange between bank computers). These types of exchanges are becoming much more frequent. Second, a *representative* linkage occurs when a person who officially represents one organization has contact with the official representative of another organization (for example, a labor union leader meets with a school principal to work out a job training program). These contacts are common, and the emphasis is on the official nature of the individual's purpose and roles. Third, a *personal* linkage occurs when an individual from one organization exchanges information or resources with someone in another organization but in a nonrepresentative and unofficial capacity (for example, friendship, kinship, old-school ties). Personal linkages, while risky and difficult to control, are at times the most likely source of successful cooperation.

The level at which the linkage between organizations takes place is only one way of characterizing differences among types of collaboration. Later in this volume, Michael Grady (Chapter Eight) makes the excellent suggestion that, at least in the realm of school-community connections, there are many different "flavors" of interorganizational relationships. Specifically, Grady argues that such ventures can be classified along a continuum, reflecting the extent to which each participating organization is required to change its "deep structure" in order to cooperate. For example, one kind of school/industry partnership might simply provide information and role models for students through a guest speakers program, necessitating no significant changes on the part of either the school or the business. Alternatively, a business might offer an extensive scholarship and apprenticeship program for students, but only on the condition that the school revamp its curriculum (as well as its methods of evaluation) to better prepare students for the business world. This latter arrangement would require much more substantial change on each partner's behalf. Collaborative ventures requiring deep structure changes are more likely to fail, but are also most likely to bring about breakthroughs in large-scale systems change.

Whatever the degree of change required, underlying the traditional approach to interorganizational cooperation is the belief that interorganizational arrangements are undertaken for mainly rational reasons, with each agency attempting to maximize its own goals while at the same time giving up as little autonomy as possible. In some cases, entire communities (Ackoff, 1981) and industries (Emery & Trist, 1965) have come together to develop superordinate goals and plan methods of cooperation. Such efforts are rational and prospective, and involve, in general, the identification of key stakeholders, joint definition of the problem, and a commitment to reach agreement on a chosen course of action. The practical value of each of these activities is critiqued in the next section.

Critique of the Rational Approach

With rare exception, the rational approach to interorganizational cooperation is problematic. The difficulties are by now quite familiar to those who have tried it:

- Differences in professional training and background result in widely divergent values and priorities, expressed as incommensurable vocabularies (that is, the stakeholders don't "speak the same language").

- Fear of loss of autonomy leads to stalling and unwillingness to carry through on planned actions, especially when deep structure changes are called for.

- In general, there is an "inefficiency" of cross-professional dialogue that results from misguided attempts to reach agreement on values, beliefs, and terminology.

This is the problem in a nutshell: efforts to lead diverse groups toward agreement on core values or assumptions naturally result in a focus on differences, which are often divisive (Weick, 1979); in watered-down plans that can amount to bad compromises satisfying no one; and in a lack of follow-through on actions, since once the planning is over, it is very hard to apply these agreements back in each organization's specific culture.

I have seen the rational approach to interorganizational cooperation fail dramatically in a number of different settings; two examples are especially memorable. In the early 1980s, the National Cancer Institute funded the Metropolitan Detroit Cancer Control Project (MDCCP) to improve coordination across diverse professions dealing with cancer in Detroit. The grant was made for a five-year period. Initial obstacles to communication were significant—physicians and hospital administrators felt little motivation to speak with members of social service organizations with vastly different training, status, and goals. Nevertheless, new linkages were forged among these individuals, discussions were held, cooperative plans were made, and a sense of hopefulness pervaded the community—until the money ran out. The fourth and fifth years of the grant were marked by a rapid retreat from cooperation to renewed isolation. By the time the five years was up, although a few improvements were made, one was hard-pressed to find evidence that the project had ever happened.

A second experience with the limitations of the rational approach to cooperation involved a federally funded seminar to promote school-industry collaboration on student career readiness. I remember this workshop especially well because I was co-facilitator. Rather than identify and discuss the differences in values and opinions between labor leaders and sixth-grade teachers, I struggled to keep the focus on joint actions that could be implemented immediately. We had two excellent days of work, until the senior project manager showed up. He opened the final session by asking people to "communicate openly" and to share their strongest feelings about how well things were working in the field and about what needed to change. Things degenerated quickly into a shouting match, with each "side" blaming the other, mouthing well-worn positions. I was appalled to see the fragile connections that had been built for two days broken apart; but the project manager thought the outcome was somehow healthy in that at least now they had "cleared the air."

I fear these examples are typical. The reason the rational approach is so difficult to implement is because it is grounded in faulty models of human communication that also pervade American culture. Specifically, it is based on the following three assumptions, which I discuss in turn: (1) the goal of "effective" communication is to reach agreement; (2) effective communication is open and honest; and (3) it is best to plan before you act.

Effective communication seeks to reach agreement. The idea that organizations should communicate to create shared assumptions, values, and beliefs gained popularity in the 1980s, with the publication of Peters and Waterman's (1982) *In Search of Excellence* and Deal and Kennedy's (1982) *Corporate Cultures.* Overnight, businesspeople were talking about the benefits of "strong cultures," homogenous monoliths characterized by a high degree of value consensus. It did not take long, however, to see the problems and abuses that accompany such a commitment to agreement, such as the loss of diversity and the potential for groupthink. Many of Peters and Waterman's excellent companies have failed, or have been tagged as unpleasant places to work. What is more, the desire to resolve differences and to strive for agreement (rather than learning to live with differences) has been recognized as peculiarly American and far from the standard worldwide (Moore, 1983). Most important, the idea of a "strong" culture was dismissed as a folk notion borrowed from anthropology with little supporting evidence for either its actual prevalence or effectiveness. In contrast, some extraordinary examples of coordinated action can occur under conditions of limited agreement and shared understanding (Eisenberg, 1990). People can understand, appreciate, and respect one another's experiences and world-views *without* seeking agreement.

Effective communication is open and honest. Closely allied with the drive for agreement is an ideology of openness that pervades American social life (Eisenberg & Witten, 1987). The ideology of openness says that (despite considerable research and lived experience to the contrary—see Bochner, 1982) effective communication is open, clear, and honest. In real organizations, however, closed communication is as a rule rewarded over open communication (Conrad, 1983). Nevertheless, people maintain the ideal of openness as the best way to approach organizational communication. But there is neither the time nor often a good reason to be open in organizational communication (Parks, 1982). Openness reveals differences that are not easily resolvable and may consequently lead to paralysis. In opening up fully to one another, we may lose the ability to act together.

Planning is key to the rational interorganizational project. The complete argument goes something like this: effective cooperation depends on getting the right people together to communicate openly and build a shared understanding that will serve as a basis for action. While there is considerable anecdotal evidence to suggest that planning actually works, research has in many cases supported just the opposite—that people act first, then make sense of their actions later. Karl Weick (1979) calls this "retrospective sensemaking" and argues that, in many cases, people figure out what they think only *after* seeing what they do and say. In other words, plans are myths, or "useful fictions." Things rarely work out as planned.

It has been my experience that, counter to rational arguments, an emphasis on open communication, a drive toward agreement, and a desire to plan before acting can create more roadblocks to effective interorganizational cooperation than they remove. The rational approach might be classified as modernist in that it puts faith in rational thought and discourse to solve the problems at hand. By contrast, I wish to offer a counter-rational, postmodern view of interorganizational cooperation, one that focuses less on planning, agreement, and open communication and more on coordinated action.

A Counter-Rational Alternative

In my experience, effective interorganizational cooperation does not require shared purposes, common goals, common language, an agreed-on plan, or even open communication. Instead, it requires a commitment to coordinated action. Although this commitment *can* be reached through fostering agreement on goals, plans, and beliefs, this may in fact be the most difficult approach— sort of like climbing the sheer face of a mountain when there is a well-maintained road that runs up the other side. Attempts at fostering agreement may be motivated more by ideology than pragmatics, the result of an unquestioned set of beliefs about communication. But aren't there alternative routes to coordinated action?

I am sure you will have noticed by now that I have avoided using the word *consensus* thus far in this chapter, since the concept is often misunderstood in important ways. The technical definition of consensus is "agreement to implement," which is not the same as agreement on a set of values, beliefs, or assumptions. While this definition of consensus allows for coordinated action despite diverse ideas and opinions, the term is usually applied incorrectly to mean a process for reaching unanimous agreement. I have no problem with consensus building that seeks as its primary goal the cultivation of *sufficient* understanding to permit coordinated action. I do object when consensus is used as a synonym for unanimity.

Following are guidelines that I have used effectively to promote collaboration that does not depend on agreement, openness, or a common plan.

Begin with the Client's Voice. The goal of many interorganizational efforts is to have a positive impact on the perceptions and experience of the end user or client. One good way to build this goal into cooperative efforts is to begin by introducing to the stakeholder group the *voice* of these clients' experience. This tactic also minimizes irrelevant tangents and professional crosstalk. If inner-city families are the concern, begin the meeting with *their* talk, through interviews, ethnography, films, tapes, or even better, *their participation in person*. For example, conferences on education could as a matter of course begin with the testimony of students. Conferences on the reproductive choices of unwed Latino women could include such women at various stages of their development. Make the language and priorities of the end user the common denominator for the group.

The effects of such a shift in perspective are significant, with two implications being especially notable. First, when this approach is adopted, the burden of "translation"—from technical to nontechnical language—is where it should be: with the service provider. Technical language either gets demystified through such an encounter or is revealed to be superfluous. Second, including the client in the conversation influences how and where such conversations take place. This process alone is instructive, as the coordinating groups are forced to address some of the obstacles facing their target population (for example, transportation, child care) in an immediate way.

Postpone Master Plans. Explicitly and purposefully avoid drafting any master plan for interorganizational cooperation. Table, defer, and filibuster all attempts to do so. Focus instead on small, definable, achievable joint actions—"small wins"—that over time will build on each other (Weick, 1979). Reorient your definition of success to mean incremental action sustained over a long period of time. Commit yourself to celebrating these successes, and to identifying them publicly as "wins," as examples of how cooperation can work.

Once significant progress has been made, then and only then should a plan be constructed, when it is no longer a threat to action and will at the same time inform others (and yourself) about what you have been doing all along. In this sense, planning in interorganizational efforts is a kind of "retrospective sense-making" (Weick, 1979) wherein the stakeholders create a story about how well they worked together (and how they didn't). The actual nature of cooperation is, of course, quite unlike this "plan." Instead, it is lumpy, serendipitous, messy, and unpredictable. This should not be seen as a problem since the formulation of better up-front plans does not make the coordination process more rational or manageable in any case.

Cultivate Weak Ties. One of the first steps people take in orchestrating an interagency effort is to make a list of the key stakeholders who must be involved in the planning process. As is the case in the private sector, within any reasonably defined community or region of the country, the same people keep showing up on such lists. These are the "movers and shakers" in industry, government, and education who have the expertise to make such a program work, and/or the power and influence to promote it (or potentially stop it).

A problem exists, however, if coordination efforts are limited to these "key players." Mark Granovetter (1973) found that for many organizational decisions, the people you think of first—those who are most familiar with the issue at hand—are also least useful in providing critical, novel information needed to make good decisions. This is because these "strong ties" already share the same knowledge base, and most likely have access to information that is already familiar to you.

Consequently, in contemplating any interorganizational effort, first make a list of the twenty or so "key players" who are most identified with the issue. Then set this list aside. Next, make a list of twenty other intelligent, powerful people in (and outside) the community who are at most tangentially related to the problem at hand. Spend your time cultivating them.

Create Joint Plots. Walter Fisher (1987) argues that humans operate using "narrative rationality" more than formal logic. In other words, what is of primary importance in human decision making is whether the "story" being told rings true. View the task of interorganizational cooperation not as one of fostering agreement among people speaking diverse vocabularies, but rather as an effort to craft a joint plot or story that all agencies and organizations will find resonant. Stress experience over ideas—both the experience of the end clients or users and the experiences of the various professionals. Write in prose what the "story of their cooperation" might look like, and avoid attempts to move the conversation to abstract ideas, values, or commitments. Be tolerant of subplots that run in different directions; the story should work like a web that weaves together experience without declaring any one individual or group's account superior (there is more on this point in the final section on dialogue).

This idea also works well with pictures. I once saw a cartoonist document the past, present, and potential future of an organization on a long sheet of paper hung across a huge wall. All the critical events that contributed to the development of the organization were there, along with the likenesses of key people. The result was that people focused more on the fact that there was a coherent story that they could all refer to and laugh about than they did on their specific interpretations of key individuals or events.

Act Globally, Reap Locally. An overly narrow focus on the defined problem and the most immediately affected population may blind us to broader social patterns that hinder cooperation. Always keep your project out in front of you, bigger than whatever problem you are working on at the moment. Rather than focus on the constituency of interest (for example, stressed families from the inner city), try addressing a broader client population than you are directly interested in serving (for example, the Korean-American community). Working at higher levels of generality can help build political support for change. Some believe, for example, that the social programs of the 1960s had limited success because they focused too narrowly on the poor to gain a significant political constituency. In addition, envisioning a different client population from the one you think you are targeting works similarly to cultivating weak ties—it opens you up to a far greater number of ideas and possibilities than you might uncover otherwise.

Cultivate Boundary Spanners. One important legacy of open systems theory is the conception of organizations as existing in continuous interaction with environments across permeable boundaries (see Adams, 1980). Some jobs are especially focused on communication across boundaries. For example, a social worker or parole officer who has most of his or her contacts with individuals outside the organization is clearly a boundary spanner. In for-profit organizations, receptionists, salespeople, customer service representatives, and market researchers are all examples of boundary spanners.

It is important to remember that boundary spanners have significant power because they provide a communication linkage between disparate groups. Unfortunately, their training and development is often neglected by their employers. This is why the reputation of a multimillion dollar bank, for example, can be adversely affected by the poor communication skills of a single teller or telephone receptionist who is earning minimum wage.

Similarly, in interorganizational efforts, new interfaces among organizations are often worked out at the higher levels, but rarely taken into account are the boundary spanners who will actually facilitate the day-to-day connections. For example, a high school may have an arrangement with a job training program to refer their non-college-bound students for job-specific training. The specific people who will make the arrangement work—teachers, guidance counselors, secretaries, administrators and their assistants—must all be involved and informed (especially about the ways in which their jobs will change) to ensure the greatest likelihood of success. Boundary spanners may be identified through communication network analysis (see Monge & Eisenberg, 1987) and explicitly involved in planning and implementing the details of the collaboration.

Think the Unthinkable. Whether or not you are willing to buy into this idea, I would nevertheless urge you to spend at least some time considering seriously the statement I made earlier—that interorganizational cooperation and cross-professional dialogue is impossible. If this were a true statement, what would you do then? This way of thinking refocuses your energies on the goals of cooperation, when all too often we get caught up in the politics of the process, which are not at all the concern of the clients or end users. For reasons I have already suggested, the likelihood of successful interorganizational cooperation is sufficiently low that if viable alternatives exist, they should be carefully considered.

Foster Dialogue. Adopting a counter-rational approach to interorganizational communication does not mean avoiding communication or regarding interaction as futile—quite the contrary. This is the key difference: instead of seeing communication as a tool for building shared attitudes, values, or beliefs, one can see communication as *dialogue*. But what are the defining characteristics of interorganizational dialogue? The three dimensions of dialogue that I consider to be most important have to do with equalization of voice, empathy for another's perspective, and respect for another's experiences (Eisenberg & Goodall, 1993). I discuss each of these in turn.

First, at the outset of any interorganizational effort, it is a given that some people's voices will "count" more than others. In fact, the systematic exclusion of the client population from such sessions is an extreme case of this phenomenon. But even among invited participants, preexisting power relations often lead to uneven participation. The first step in establishing dialogue is to promote and allow for equalization of participant voices through the strategic use of facilitation techniques and the agenda. A necessary but not sufficient condition for interorganizational dialogue is that all parties have a comparable opportunity to speak.

Second, interorganizational dialogue requires participants to empathize with others' positions and perspectives. The most common obstacle to cooperation is the individual's entrenched belief that his or her worldview is the only correct one. In practice, a change in this area requires participants to be trained in active listening skills so they may get beyond the initial resistance that naturally comes from being exposed to a different position from their own. Empathy is another necessary but not sufficient condition for dialogue, although it is harder to achieve than comparable opportunities for voice, since it exists in the realm of emotions and egos.

The third step in cultivating interorganizational dialogue regards the treatment of personal experience in conversation. The key notion here is that fostering dialogue is not so much about sharing ideas as it is a way of cultivating experience. Much too often, participants treat conversations with each other as a kind of free market of ideas in which different perceptions are in competition with one another and the goal is to advance one's own perspective at the expense of all others. In the process, people rarely speak directly from experience.

Alternatively, in dialogue people speak from their experience and listen for the experiences of others. In this way, dialogue is additive; each new experience that is recounted is a contribution to the whole, and no individual's remarks invalidate what has come previously. The result is a varied collection of multiple "voices" that form a richly textured account of "how things really are" without forcing adherence to any one viewpoint or perspective (Eisenberg & Goodall, 1993). What is more, there is no goal of integration of experience, and such attempts at synthesis are resisted. In dialogue, what is fostered is not agreement but mutual understanding; interestingly, it is this mutual understanding and respect that is most likely to lead to coordinated action. In dialogue, participants feel they have had their say, feel their voices have been heard, feel they have truly heard others, and despite apparent differences, are ready to work together.

Interorganizational dialogue is possible—I have seen it work. What is needed to make it work is an advocate or group of advocates who encourage the expression of experience by all participants, including clients, and discourage attempts to reach agreement that are based on the devaluation of some individuals' experience. This is another way of saying that the mechanics of valuing "diversity" occur in communication, and with repetition become normative within a group. What is most needed (and most difficult, it must be said) is a shift away from arguments over ideas and values toward the expression of experience, away from plans for action and toward acting in the absence of plans.

Needless to say, dialogue "feels" very different from the typical arguments and debates among stakeholders, and if judged by modernist standards, seems unfocused and unresolved. What is most persuasive from my perspective, however, is that successful and sustained joint action follows more surely from dialogue rooted in diversity and mutual understanding than it does from traditional attempts at fostering agreement.

Implications for School-Community Connections

The document outlining the purpose of the conference for which these chapters were originally written underscores the need to

"mobilize school and community resources in the service of children and youth" (Rigsby, 1992, p. 3). The importance of such an
effort is unquestionable. What *can* be questioned further is useful
routes to such mobilization. The document reflects further on "the
complexities of communication" but concludes that the goal should
be "*coherent* [italics added] multiagency support and assistance . . .
to the children and their families" (pp. 2–3). Whereas the need for
such support is undeniable, I am always skeptical of calls for coherence. The history of many academic disciplines, for example, is an
unending struggle for coherence that is in the end unattainable in
any specific way due to multiple incommensurable language communities. Preferable to coherence in promoting coordinated action
is *cohesiveness*, the willingness to work together in the absence of
shared understanding (Bochner & Eisenberg, 1984). In business,
and in politics, for me one key to effective coordination is a strategically ambiguous vision or mission, which simultaneously motivates action and permits individuals to retain their idiosyncratic
meanings and beliefs (Eisenberg, 1984).

The idea of an improved "cross-professional dialogue" is also
mentioned repeatedly in the purpose statement for the conference.
This is clearly needed, not just in relationship to this set of issues,
but globally in regard to many isolated interest groups. Two things
are worth noting about how such a dialogue is operationalized.
First, professionalization itself may prove an obstacle to dialogue,
both among members of organizations and between such individuals and the stressed population of concern. As mentioned earlier,
the common denominator should be the experience and vocabulary of the client. Professionalization as a concept isolates individuals physically, attitudinally, and linguistically from many kinds of
dialogue by erecting disciplinary language barriers. Second, we
should consider carefully the precise definition of dialogue that we
wish to advocate. As I have described above, dialogue for me has
a very specific meaning—it is a conversation that is not oriented
toward agreement, but instead toward cultivating the diversity of
experience.

And it is precisely this diversity of experience—the fact that people representing businesses, families, churches, schools, and government agencies have partial and different readings of the current situation—that should be the starting point for a productive interorganizational dialogue. A well-meaning sense of urgency may lead us to attempt to orchestrate this dialogue in ways that produce greater openness, agreement, and plans. We should resist these temptations, inasmuch as experience teaches us that such efforts as a rule backfire. Instead, we should concentrate on transforming attempts at interorganizational communication into dialogue, and on promoting coordinated action in the explicit absence of agreement.

References

Ackoff, R. (1981). *Creating the corporate future*. New York: Wiley.

Adams, J. S. (1980). Interorganizational processes and organization boundary activities. *Research in Organizational Behavior, 2,* 321–355.

Aldrich, H. (1979). *Organizations and environments*. Englewood Cliffs, NJ: Prentice Hall.

Bochner, A. (1982). The functions of human communication in interpersonal bonding. In C. Arnold & J. Bowers (Eds.), *Handbook of rhetoric and communication theory* (pp. 544–621). Newton, MA: Allyn & Bacon.

Bochner, A., & Eisenberg, E. (1984). Legitimizing speech communication: An examination of coherence and cohesion in the development of the discipline. In. T. Benson (Ed.), *Speech communication in the 20th century* (pp. 299–321). Carbondale: Southern Illinois University Press.

Conrad, C. (1983). Organizational power: Faces and symbolic forms. In L. Putnam & M. Pacanowsky (Eds.), *Communication and organizations: An interpretive approach* (pp. 173–194). Newbury Park, CA: Sage.

Deal, T., & Kennedy, A. (1982). *Corporate cultures*. Reading, MA: Addison-Wesley.

Eisenberg, E. (1984). Ambiguity as strategy in organizational communication. *Communication Monographs, 51*(3), 227–242.

Eisenberg, E. (1990). Jamming: Transcendence through organizing. *Communication Research, 17*(2), 139–164.

Eisenberg, E., Farace, R. V., Monge, P., Bettinghaus, E., Kurchner-Hawkins, R., Miller, K., & Rothman, L. (1985). Communication linkages in interorganizational systems: Review and synthesis. In M. Voight & B. Dervin (Eds.), *Progress in communication science* (Vol. 6, pp. 231–261). Norwood, NJ: Ablex.

Eisenberg, E., & Goodall, H. L. (1993). *Organizational communication: Balancing creativity and constraint*. New York: St. Martin's Press.

Eisenberg, E., & Witten, M. (1987). Reconsidering openness in organizational communication. *Academy of Management Review, 12*(3), 418–426.

Emery, F., & Trist, E. (1965). The causal texture of organizational environments. *Human Relations, 18*(1), 21–32.

Fisher, W. (1987). *Human communication as narration: Toward a philosophy of reason, value, and action*. Columbia, SC: University of South Carolina Press.

Granovetter, M. (1973). The strength of weak ties. *American Journal of Sociology, 78*(6), 1360–1380.

Monge, P., & Eisenberg, E. (1987). Emergent communication networks. In F. Jablin, L. Putnam, K. Roberts, & L. Porter (Eds.), *Handbook of organizational communication* (pp. 304–342). Newbury Park, CA: Sage.

Moore, M. (1983). Culture as culture. In P. Frost, L. Moore, M. Lewis, C. Lundenberg, & J. Martin (Eds.), *Organizational culture* (pp. 373–378). Newbury Park, CA: Sage.

Parks, M. (1982). Ideology in interpersonal communication: Off the couch and into the world. In M. Burgoon (Ed.), *Communication Yearbook* (Vol. 5, pp. 79–108). New Brunswick, NJ: Transaction Books.

Peters, T., & Waterman, R. (1982). *In search of excellence*. New York: HarperCollins.

Rigsby, L. (1992). *School-community connections: Exploring issues for research and practice*. Prospectus for a conference on school-community connections. Philadelphia: National Center on Education in the Inner Cities.

Weick, K. (1979). *The social psychology of organizing* (2nd ed.). Reading, MA: Addison-Wesley.

Chapter Seven

Integration of Services for Children

A Political Economy of Institutions Perspective

Robert L. Crowson and William L. Boyd

"Stripped to its essence, the goal of the current educational reform is to change the behavior of individuals and institutions" (Timar & Kirp, 1987, p. 311). This philosophy is reflected in terms like *teacher empowerment* and *school restructuring*. School choice advocates suggest that greater competition among schools will lead to improved internal operations in "surviving" schools. The Chicago-style decentralization of schooling seeks to change the city's top-heavy bureaucracy by increasing community control (Hess, 1991). In a similar vein, advocates of children's service integration describe their proposals as "the beginning of a significant effort to restructure the way health and social services are delivered to school-age children and their families" (Larson, Gomby, Shiono, Lewit, & Behrman, 1992, p. 7). The rationale for integration is that children have multiple and interconnected needs, yet the current service delivery system tends to be specialized and disjointed, with various service providers often functioning nearly at cross-purposes. Service integration, it is argued, can be "a strategy to reduce these systemic problems" (Larson et al., 1992, p. 8).

Thus, reform proposals ranging from consumer choice to site-based management to service integration all seek indirectly to counter systemic problems and alter the very nature of public service institutions. A well-implemented reform can feed back into significant changes in organizational behavior; Odden and Marsh (1989) document the effectiveness of this model of indirect institutional change. However, contrary evidence suggests that the model is often ineffective because reform efforts are defeated by the many "intractabilities" of public sector institutions (Sarason, 1971, 1990).

Evidence describing intractable institutions has recently spurred renewed interest in moving toward a model of more direct institutional change. This movement can be described as a "new institutionalism" in the theoretical and research literature on public sector behavior (Moe, 1984; Wilson, 1989). Described by March and Olsen (1984) as a "resurgence of concern with institutions" (p. 740), this perspective is the first to emphasize the institutional contexts that embed individual behaviors and the complexity and relative autonomy of institutions amid their social and political environments (Searing, 1991). Two questions are central within this perspective: Why do institutions respond poorly to reform? What can be done to improve the track record of institutional change?

As efforts to link institutions in shared endeavors, today's service integration experiments offer rich opportunities for learning more about the two institutional change models and for investigating how key constructs of new institutionalism apply to the children's services arena. This chapter builds on a review of the growing literature on children's service integration and some early fieldwork at selected cross-agency collaboration sites. We offer tentative management-related observations on service integration, using a new institutional perspective that highlights organizational rewards, rules, and roles.

The Political Economy of Rewards

Most reform-minded solutions to the "systemic problems" of institutions assume that altered reward systems will change individual behavior. Thus, teacher empowerment looks to shared decision making to build professional collegiality and cooperation. School choice advocates assume that the budgetary requirements of maintaining enrollments will lead to improved school quality. Chicago-style reform envisions improved schooling and increased community responsiveness through reduced bureaucracy. Children's service integration advocates seek to increase professional cooperation; overcome fragmentation; and improve the health, well-being, and education of young people (Morrill, 1992).

While researchers and reformers pursue the rewards of integration, they acknowledge that the reward systems of institutions— and the interplay of reward systems in cooperating institutions—are poorly understood (Baron & Cook, 1992). Institutions are complex political systems with idiosyncratic tendencies; they position rewards at cross-purposes, reward behaviors that fail to fit organizational objectives, and hide powerful disincentives in the very structures that are intended to reward (Pfeffer, 1982; Wilson, 1989). Public schools, as institutions, contain perverse incentive patterns in which school improvement is not encouraged, seniority is rewarded above performance, stability above change, client management above client satisfaction, and conflict avoidance above risk taking (Boyd & Crowson, 1981; Boyd & Hartman, 1988; Boyd, 1991).

The Extant Literature

The literature on children's service integration recognizes important issues of reward structure in interagency collaborations. Kirst (1991), for example, acknowledges the importance of "glue money" as a means for attracting agencies into service partnerships. Kahne and Kelley (1991) note that the separate accountability systems of agencies reward individuals for compliance with their own rules and regulations rather than those of shared programming. They claim that such a system "fosters fragmentation by focusing on narrowly defined programmatic and procedural criteria, and fails to provide an assessment of the general well-being of clients" (p. 20). Likewise,

Gray and Hay (1986) observe that unless "other compelling incentives exist, powerful stakeholders will resist collaborative interventions so that they can preserve their individual control over the domain" (p. 99).

Evaluation and research of on-site experiments highlight similar barriers to service integration. For example, there are no incentives for agencies to share power and authority, and the rewards are insufficient to make individual professionals change course (see Policy Memorandum SYR 71–5, 1971; Stake, 1986; Wehlage, Smith, & Lyman, 1991). Changing course may be particularly difficult if individual children's service agencies offer conflicting rewards for similar actions. Both Zellman (1990) and Finkelhor (1984), for example, found that child-protection agencies tried to reduce their caseloads by narrowing their definitions of abuse and screening out all but the most serious cases. Conversely, school professionals were encouraged to report all suspected cases of abuse and to expand their perceptions of what might indicate abuse.

Early fieldwork examining a collaborative service project in Chicago (Crowson, Smylie, & Hare, 1992) indicates that building principals of cooperating schools—long rewarded for maintaining control—tend toward overmanaging. Although a recently added array of discretionary professional activities in these newly service-rich schools considerably broadened each site administrator's sense of risk and responsibility, the reward system—long attuned to evidence of managerial control—was threatened when increased professional autonomy confronted principals' direct control. Such tendencies toward control or domination are a major reason that scholars argue for a community-based rather than school-linked approach to service integration. Specifically, Chaskin and Richman (1992) claim that embedding services within established institutions such as schools "runs the risk of bureaucratic rigidity and the diminution of pluralist, citizen-based planning" (p. 108).

Citizen-based planning and community involvement in service coordination often constitute key elements in the reward system of proposed integrated services. Community and parent involvement are assumed to have important advantages. Furthermore, Gardner (1992) maintains that, "Without [parents'] support at home, the interventions at school and in the agencies will lack indispensable reinforcement" (p. 88). Integrated-services proposals assume that parental involvement and knowledge of access to services will translate into (1) use of the services and (2) a parent/provider partnership that supports effective services (Melaville & Blank, 1991).

Fieldwork with inner-city families suggests, however, that families living in poverty seldom believe professionals are willing to work as partners (Brinker, Frazier, & Baxter, 1991). "For the disenfranchised, school may be the last place they would turn for help" (Chaskin & Richman, 1992, p. 111). Brinker, Frazier, and Baxter (1991) suggest that encouraging impoverished families to turn to coordinated children's services for assistance may necessitate a program of incentives (for example, food, clothing, shelter). Furthermore, these incentives must be provided with an awareness of the larger ecology of inner-city life. For instance, families may be afraid to move about in gang-dominated neighborhoods, have bad memories of previous encounters with caseworkers from welfare and child and family services agencies, be fighting drug or alcohol dependency, and be struggling daily to obtain food, milk, diapers, or clothing.

Rewarding Service Integration

In summary, public service institutions simultaneously exhibit incentives for and disincentives against compliance with their goals. Integrated-services advocates acknowledge that if compelling start-up incentives are not offered, incentives for noncooperation may prevail. Evaluations of existing experiments also acknowledge that cooperation incentives must counter deep structural problems such as disjointed professional practices, managerial controls, and the competing needs of partners and clients. However, while advocates recognize both the structural barriers to success and the importance of careful planning toward collaboration, they rarely discuss ways to design effective reward systems. We offer two observations derived from a model of more direct institutional change.

Rewarding Institutional Participants

First, a review of the relevant literature indicates the need for a carefully framed model of rewards to institutional participants. Gray (1989) suggests that institutional needs for effective responses to increasingly turbulent environments can serve as a powerful incentive for collaboration. Although she primarily discusses private-sector collaboration, some elements of business-sector environmental turbulence also provide the rationale for children's service integration, including urban crisis, shrinking revenues, a fragmented and overlapping menu of children's services, and the subsequent need for increased efficiency in service delivery.

Gray (1989) also suggests a negotiated or "stakeholder" approach to collaboration, in which each party's interests are at least partly addressed through negotiation. Crowson and Boyd (1992) note the difficulty of identifying the stakeholders and stakes in children's service integration. For example, as mentioned above, program planners often assume, sometimes incorrectly, that parents have a stake in participating in decisions or in accessing enriched services. Similarly, although classroom teachers can be vital players because of their close daily contact with children, their stakes may often be best defined by their perceptions of threats to teacher autonomy, their limited time, and an already heavy burden of noninstructional duties.

Many service integration experiments have been specially funded, usually with foundation-related assistance. When institutions offer special funds, they also typically introduce additional stakeholder interests and expect experimenters to produce short-term payoffs. Farrow and Joe (1992) address longer-term funding of integrated services, recognizing that current categorical funding and the rules that often accompany it (for example, services offered only after families reach crises) are unlikely to build institutional collaboration. Instead, they suggest a fiscal strategy that directly supports core social service staff by redirecting existing funds through strategies such as staff reassignment, budget reallocation, and decategorization.

Such suggestions are vital to institutional collaboration because resource dependency is the strongest impetus for interorganizational coordination (Van de Ven & Walker, 1984). Nevertheless, many additional incentives at the institutional level must also be a part of the planning process. Van de Ven and Walker (1984) found that resource dependencies may lead to increased communication between institutions, through which "inconsistencies in the assumptions brought to the relationship begin to emerge"; paradoxically, this "latent conflict" may lead to a drive for greater autonomy and reduced resource dependency (p. 619).

At the institutional level of children's service integration, incentive plans must consider rewards that encourage shared notions of goal attainment, new patterns of upward employee mobility, regenerated client and service-provider commitment, a redistribution of collegial power and control, and an integration of both children and client/community needs. Moreover, as Moe (1984) suggests, an effective incentive structure must find a way to help participants not only pursue institutional objectives beyond their own interests but also participate in developing an effective monitoring system. Interestingly, although there is increasing recognition of the importance of overall evaluation in service integration (see Gomby & Larson, 1992), little attention has been paid to program and performance monitoring, a function that, with current trends toward decentralized decision making, seems to carry overtones of administrative control.

Rewarding Individual Participants

The implications of rewarding individual participants in children's service integration need careful reexamination. Some organizational scholars prefer to apply the concept of organizational culture to an institutional whole (Deal & Kennedy, 1982; Peters & Waterman, 1982). Others see organizations as amalgamations of multiple, interacting subcultures with frequent opportunities for both cooperation and conflict (Jelinek, Smircich, & Hirsch, 1983; Morgan, 1986). Alongside institutional reward structures are multiple, subcultural incentive systems that collectively supply a rich menu of reward options to the individuals within an organization (Wilson, 1989). Hannaway (1988) and Crowson and Morris (1991) document the tendency of public school administrators to seek safe ground in managerial control and to manage risk in volatile institutional environments.

Remarkably little is known about the intraorganizational distribution of rewards in either public or private sector institutions (Baron & Cook, 1992). Even less is known about how the distribution of rewards to individuals within cooperating institutions may affect the success of service integration efforts. Zellman's (1990) findings "raise real concerns about the ability of the child protective agencies and the schools to interact effectively to protect children" (p. 52). Similarly, Rosenheck's (1985) study of collaboration between psychiatrists and community police officers found the two groups operating with very different incentives with regard to key questions of client control, surveillance, tolerance of misbehavior, enforcement of regulations, and use of force.

Whether a project is school linked or school based, the assumption of service integration is that the separate contributions of educators, health professionals, social services experts, and others can be shaped to complement the needs of a common clientele. Advocates of service integration acknowledge constraints in the separate professional training of service providers, the misunderstanding and distrust among professions, the independence of governance and communication/information systems, and the territoriality of professionals (Levy & Shepardson, 1992). In terms of the latter, although public schools have long been the settings for children's services other than education (Tyack, 1992), the tradition has been only minimally integrative—school guidance counselors, social workers, nurses, teachers, and others all work on their own "turf," with little sense of a shared contribution to each child's "whole."

The model of indirect change recommends oversight committees, liaison groups, specific written agreements, renegotiated personnel policies, and joint planning arrangements as ways to resolve barriers (Skaff, 1988; Levy & Shepardson, 1992; Gardner, 1992). However, to date, little attention has been paid to "deep structure" changes in role-specialized incentive systems.

The Political Economy of Rules and Roles

Institutions become humanized by pursuing equally their own and their members' purposes (Trist, 1977; Ackoff, 1974). Although the interplay between the institution and the individual is key, institutions must also, by relating themselves to the purposes of society, become "environmentalized" (Trist, 1977).

Institutions that act independently but share a common field (for example, providing similar or overlapping services, sharing a clientele, or drawing on the same resource base) may add considerably to the turbulence of one another's environments (Gray, 1989). Turbulence can lead not only to an added recognition of institutional interdependence but also to higher levels of individual and shared uncertainty (Trist, 1977). For example, as public schools join forces with other social service providers in the community, the cooperating institutions engage in a renewed environmentalization of their structures. Consequently, they may raise considerably their levels of institutional turbulence and uncertainty.

A public school that confines itself to the traditional curriculum and remains closed to parent/community involvement inhabits its own environment; a public school that shares space with the parks department and operates an on-site community health clinic operates in a more complex environment. Its professional life space becomes defined not only by school rules and regulations but also by health, recreation, social work, and library rules. School politics characterize its activities, but professional and neighborhood politics become defining characteristics of its institutional persona.

The issue of confidentiality is perhaps the best example of turbulence in children's service integration. Client information constitutes the most significant property right held by each profession, in that property rights protect the basic value of a service or commodity that is available for exchange (Demsetz, 1967). Important issues must be considered when service providers pool information about children and families; confidentiality restrictions are rooted in constitutional guarantees of personal privacy, statutory provisions, and the ethical standards of various professions. Thus, confidentiality must be protected, although shared information may help maintain continuity in children's service delivery and improve efficiency and effectiveness in the use of child-assistance resources (Behrman, 1992; Joining Forces, 1992; Kahne & Kelley, 1991).

Several methods have been proposed to resolve confidentiality issues, including family consent agreements, release forms, and careful guidelines for securing access and limiting data for automated information systems. There are, however, more critical deep-structure problems for cooperating institutions, including feared loss of turf control, distrust of other professionals' use of confidential information, and ethical and legal concerns (including fear of lawsuits) when information leaves traditionally closed systems.

Thus, partner institutions in children's service integration experience increased environmental turbulence, manifesting in conflicts over legal controls (beyond those involved in information sharing), fund commingling, professional training and retraining issues, issues of administrative authority, workplace and facilities usage, and client-referral issues. All these have surfaced in evaluations of service integration experiments since the 1960s (Crowson & Boyd, 1992) and are therefore concerns for people attempting to create guidelines for experimenters (*At-Risk Youth in Crisis*, 1991; Bruner, 1991; Melaville & Blank, 1991).

Although professional service integration experiments are relatively new, and the instructive literature therefore nonspecific, there are several existing proposals for effective collaboration. Employing the model of indirect institutional change through careful reform implementation, Van de Ven, Walker, and Liston (1979) suggest a personal-level strategy of awareness and consensus building using an interagency network. Another proposal calls for creating the special roles of case management specialist, facilitator, or liaison director (Gray, 1989; Melaville & Blank, 1991). Hall, Clark, Giordano, Johnson, and Van Roekel (1977) and Shedd and Bacharach (1991) argue for more direct procedures such as preimplementation contract negotiations, formal participation structure agreements, or legal mandates.

Both direct and indirect integration proposals renew interest in questions of rule establishment and role definition, which had declined in the past few decades. Coincidentally, formal rules and regulations have lost academic popularity and, as well, have been identified as key aspects of bureaucratic overcentralization (Searing, 1991).

Rules and Roles in Children's Services

Paradoxically, observing rules is vital to understanding processes of organizational change. Even though rules are often regarded as the static fixtures of institutions, their relative stability provides a window of opportunity into organizational adaptability and the ecology of institutions in interaction with their environments (March, 1981).

To date, the promotional, analytical, evaluative, and instructive literatures have not focused on the direct model panoply of potential revised rules and regulations for effective service integration. Many constraining rules and regulations are widely recognized in the literature, particularly those on information sharing, resource integration, and the various governmental controls affecting public service professionals (Kirst, 1991).

The literature provides many examples of constraining rules. In their investigation of the Chicago experiment, for example, Crowson, Smylie, and Hare (1992) examine a civil service system that threatens the project because it lacks flexibility and categorizes important new family services roles at only the lowest civil service rates. Some literature also recognizes the subtle, less formal rules constraints on service integration, particularly the separate professional cultures that attain quasi-rule status and are not easily merged (Johnson, Ransom, Packwood, Bowden, & Koean, 1980; Kahne & Kelley, 1991).

In an attempt to move toward new structures of rules and regulations, efforts have increased at the state and federal level to facilitate children's services integration (Gerry & Certo, 1992). At the local instructive level, however, the best advice to date highlights the technical difficulties encountered in differences of rules and regulations in that they make up an institution's unique identity. Melaville and Blank (1991) suggest that partners committed to sharing and reform through process can nevertheless negotiate effectively to "overcome the barriers that policy differences create" (pp. 29–30). This willingness to negotiate, however, may not overcome most rule and role constraints. Such constraints are not only a part of separate institutional identities among public service professionals, but are well embedded in the deep structures (Tye, 1987) and the production technologies (Thompson, 1967) of organizations. They are certainly a part of the intractability of institutions (Sarason, 1971, 1990).

It may be helpful, therefore, to reconsider existing conceptions of rule and role constraints. To date, the literature suggests that differences in rules and roles can change through intra-institutional planning and liaison committees, statutory changes (if needed), and "whatever-it-takes" negotiations. Further, procedural innovations such as case management strategies, improved clientele feedback and input, and professionally shared or integrated decision making can help build a changed system of services to individuals and families (Gerry & Certo, 1992).

Alternatively, we suggest that the drive toward service integration should start with the separate institutional structures of cooperating institutions and thoroughly examine how these structures now serve their institutions by "imposing elements of order on a potentially inchoate world" (March & Olsen, 1984, p. 743). One such structure, the temporal order of institutions, includes event cycles, time allocations, and queues. Indeed, a powerful argument in support of integrated services is that the timing of services to families is currently far from optimal; that is, earlier interventions could prevent later consequences. More important, the current system of queuing in many service arenas tends to lose the value of prevention by waiting for crises to develop before providing special services (Larson et al., 1992; Melaville & Blank, 1991).

Although there is recognition that constraints such as differing organizational life cycles are problems for children's service integration (Gardner, 1992), little attention has been paid to deep-structure alterations in the temporal orders of cooperating institutions. Schools in inner-city environments have increasingly lengthened the school day, year, and often week, and the age of school entrance has lowered to the "child care" years. These changes reflect a new focus on the child development role of the school.

Nevertheless, the timing of needed services for children and families generally conforms poorly to education schedules. Late nights, weekends, and summers are often the times of greatest need. Although services provided at these times often have a crisis origin, out of such crises may arise a receptivity to prevention. The timing of a child development and prevention orientation is far different from that of a services orientation that requires being there as events unfold, responding quickly and comprehensively to need, and being reactive as well as proactive. Not yet addressed in children's service integration are procedures (rules and roles) that somehow blend institutional life cycles and queues.

A second institutional structure (the source of rules and roles) is symbolic order (March & Olsen, 1984). Although there is recognition of the constraints to collaboration that reside in differing institutional cultures (Gray, 1989), there has been little analysis of the integrating power of symbols, rituals, ceremonies, stories, and drama. Public schools are bastions of ritual and ceremony—ranging from formal collegiality (for example, addressing teachers by last name only) to recognition ceremonies (for example, commencement, honors awards) to a comforting sameness in numerous details, from the annual calendar to the weekly lunchroom offerings.

Compare, for instance, some of the conventions of hospitals with those of public schools. Increasingly, visitors in hospitals are recognized as a valuable element in the healing process. Although there are usually sign-in procedures and visiting hours, these rules are often only loosely observed. Close family visitors are increasingly permitted to stay overnight and are able to assume quasi-nursing roles. By contrast, public school visitors, while more welcome than in years past, are not typically regarded as integral to the learning process. Other key differences in convention include these:

- The hospital summons its best, organizes itself around, and coalesces its resources for crises. The public school typically seeks to avoid any hint or charge of a "crisis orientation." Crisis is best avoided in the greater interest of long-term development.

- The hospital uses pull-out specialist services as an integral part of a holistic diagnosis and recovery for each patient. Despite the individual education plan (IEP) tradition from special education, the public school tends to fragment its professional services, and regular classroom teachers often resent time taken from what they regard as the real work of the institution.

- In health care, the most important people are not necessarily those who "live" occupationally in the human service institution. Many people, especially physicians, use the institution as a base but have a practice (and spend much of their day) elsewhere. In public schools, the most important people "live" in the institution and are closely tied (career-wise, psychologically, and so forth) to the day-to-day affairs of the organization. In the former, primary loyalties to the organization may be less important to effective service provision than in the latter.

- In health care, there is frequently much more procedure, ritual, rule following, and care taken at the intake end than at the release end. In public education, clients are not released; rather, their completion of the program is celebrated, often with close friends and relatives joining in a large-scale celebration. In the first case, a matching of service with client diagnosis and need is primary; in the second the emphasis is on evidence that the client has met the institution's standards for performance.

Key differences such as these in the workaday drama of public service institutions are also to be found among public schools and institutions for criminal justice, public housing, parks and recreation, child protection, and family assistance (see Lipsky, 1980). The differences are a central part of the separate order of each institution; they provide the symbolic, normative, and demographic structures (rules and roles) that surround and define their work. Integration of professional services must seek to understand and find commonality among these sometimes fundamental differences in institutional order. Further, deep institutional differences such as these are unlikely to respond easily or well to a model of institutional reform that seeks, through the simple impact of the reform itself, to change institutional incentives, rules, and roles.

Summary

Much of the current effort to reform education finds its rationale in institutional failure. Top-down, centralized control must be replaced by a bottom-up, decentralized restructuring of schools. The institutional survival mechanisms sparked by consumer choice will likely improve school quality. Linking services for children will hopefully turn a now-fragmented institutional and professional framework of public service into a more productive whole.

The difficulties and constraints surrounding any of these objectives are well recognized. Nevertheless, with typically American pragmatism and optimism, many locales have entered into experiments in school restructuring, choice, and coordinated services. The results, predictably, are never uniform and often puzzling. Reform seems to work in some places, but not others; some projects flounder, some barely survive, while others quickly become part of the "we-tried-this-before" history of the institution. Some projects move in unforeseen (but not always bad) directions, some are blamed for doing more damage than good, and some provide valuable "lighthouse" lessons for future reformers and reform projects.

This may well be the best change-the-institution model. Experiment, evaluate the results, hopefully learn a lesson or two, develop a literature on how to do it better, and then experiment some more. As problems surface, solve them, then determine whether the solutions are working. Such a model is powerful and exciting, for it gives projects and participants a sense of pioneering—a chance to enter anew the unknown jungles of institutional behavior, seeing what might be done to tame them.

However, critics (not all of whom are die-hard pessimists) claim that most of the reform-minded experiments fail to cut paths through the jungles. Institutions are stubbornly intractable. Their structures and procedures, reward systems, and cultures are heartily resistant to change. Tye (1992) argues that seldom in the reform/ restructuring movement "is adequate attention given to *institutionalizing* the new behaviors that employees have to exhibit—consistently and permanently—if the desired organizational changes are to occur" (p. 10).

Currently surfacing from a renewed interest in the study of institutions is the notion that a clearer understanding of institutional features is a central element of the very model of reform-minded change (Shepsle, 1989). The new institutionalism may be especially appropriate as a window into the integrated-services movement. Because efforts to integrate children's services involve combinations of institutions, structural issues in changing organizational behaviors are several times magnified. Furthermore, there are increased research opportunities to learn about the behaviors of public sector institutions when they attempt to integrate some of their child and family services.

Although this chapter lacks the depth or scope of treatment that the subject ultimately deserves, we have tried to suggest that researchers need to be more attentive to some key issues of institutionalism in thinking about children's service coordination. It is well recognized that institutional reward systems are at stake in service integration, and that a powerful bit of "glue" is vital. The literature is already well supplied with evidence of incentive constraints in convincing individuals and institutions to change course. In addition, there is some evidence that rewards in service coordination are not always effectively consistent with client needs, administrative control systems, or individual employee preferences/interests.

Similarly, it is well recognized that prevailing rules and roles can be powerful stumbling blocks in the evolution of such necessities as a shared information system, common eligibility or participation requirements, combined budgets, and a shared professionalism in place of territoriality. Nevertheless, very little is known about how such deep structure elements as the differing temporal orders and the differing conventions of institutions can be brought toward common purposes. Institutions are complex, hardy, and resilient creatures.

References

Ackoff, R. I. (1974). *Redesigning the future*. New York: Wiley.

At-risk youth in crisis: A handbook for collaboration between schools and social services. Vol. 1: Introduction and resources. (1991, June). Eugene, OR: ERIC Clearinghouse on Educational Management.

Baron, J. N., & Cook, K. S. (1992, June). Process and outcome: Perspectives on the distribution of rewards in organizations. *Administrative Science Quarterly, 37*(2), 191–197.

Behrman, R. E. (Ed.). (1992). School-linked services. *The Future of Children, 2*(1).

Boyd, W. L. (1991). What makes ghetto schools succeed or fail? *Teachers College Record, 92*(3), 331–362.

Boyd, W. L., & Crowson, R. L. (1981). The changing conception and practice of public school administration. In D. C. Berliner (Ed.), *Review of research in education* (Vol. 9, pp. 311–373). Washington, DC: American Educational Research Association.

Boyd, W. L., & Hartman, W. T. (1988). The politics of educational productivity. In D. H. Monk & J. Underwood (Eds.), *Distributing education resources within nations, states, school districts, and schools* (pp. 271–308). Cambridge, MA: Ballinger.

Brinker, R. P., Frazier, W., & Baxter, A. (1991). *Maintaining involvement of inner-city families in early intervention through a program of incentives: Looking beyond family systems to societal systems.* A draft report to the U.S. Department of Education, Office of Special Education and Rehabilitation Services. Chicago: University of Illinois at Chicago.

Bruner, C. (1991, April). *Thinking collaboratively: Ten questions and answers to help policymakers improve children's services.* Washington, DC: Education and Human Services Consortium.

Chaskin, R. J., & Richman, H. A. (1992). Concerns about school-linked services: Institution-based versus community-based models. *The Future of Children, 2*(1), 107–117.

Crowson, R. L., & Boyd, W. L. (1992, February). *Coordinated services for children:*

Designing arks for storms and seas unknown. Philadelphia: National Center on Education in the Inner Cities.

Crowson, R. L., & Morris, V. C. (1991). The superintendency and school leadership. In P. W. Thurston & P. P. Zodhiates (Eds.), *Advances in educational administration. Vol. 2: School leadership* (pp. 191–215). Greenwich, CT: JAI Press.

Crowson, R. L., Smylie, M. A., & Hare, V. C. (1992, April). *Administrative issues in coordinated children's services: A Chicago case study*. Paper presented at the annual meeting of the American Educational Research Association, San Francisco.

Deal, T. E., & Kennedy, A. A. (1982). *Corporate cultures: The rites and rituals of corporate life*. Reading, MA: Addison-Wesley.

Demsetz, H. (1967). Towards a theory of property rights. *American Economic Review, 57*, 347–359.

Farrow, F., & Joe, T. (1992). Financing school-linked integrated services. *The Future of Children, 2*(1), 56–67.

Finkelhor, D. (1984). *Child sexual abuse: New theory and research*. New York: The Free Press.

Gardner, S. L. (1992). Key issues in developing school-linked integrated services. *The Future of Children, 2*(1), 85–94.

Gerry, M. H., & Certo, N. J. (1992). Current activity at the federal level and the need for service integration. *The Future of Children, 2*(1), 118–126.

Gomby, D. S., & Larson, C. S. (1992). Evaluation of school-linked services. *The Future of Children, 2*(1), 68–84.

Gray, B. (1989). *Collaborating: Finding common ground for multiparty problems*. San Francisco: Jossey-Bass.

Gray, B., & Hay, T. M. (1986). Political limits to interorganizational consensus and change. *The Journal of Applied Behavioral Science, 22*(2), 95–112.

Hall, R. H., Clark, J. P., Giordano, C., Johnson, P. V., & Van Roekel, M. (1977). Patterns of interorganizational relationships. *Administrative Science Quarterly, 22*, 457–474.

Hannaway, J. (1988). *Managers managing: The workings of an administrative system*. London: Oxford University Press.

Hess, G. A., Jr. (1991). *School restructuring, Chicago style*. Newbury Park, CA: Corwin Press.

Jelinek, M., Smircich, L., & Hirsch, P. (1983). Introduction: A coat of many colors. *Administrative Science Quarterly, 28*, 331–338.

Johnson, D., Ransom, E., Packwood, T., Bowden, K., & Koean, M. (1980). *Secondary schools and the welfare network*. London: George Allen & Unwin.

Joining Forces. (1992, January). *Confidentiality and collaboration: Information sharing in interagency efforts*. Denver, CO: Education Commission of the States.

Kahne, J., & Kelley, C. (1991, October). *Assessing the coordination of children's services: An organizational approach.* Unpublished paper. Stanford, CA: Stanford University School of Education.

Kirst, M. W. (1991). Improving children's services: Overcoming barriers, creating new opportunities. *Phi Delta Kappan, 72*(8), 615–618.

Larson, D. S., Gomby, D. S., Shiono, P. H., Lewit, E. M., & Behrman, R. E. (1992, Spring). Analysis. *The Future of Children, 2*(1), 6–18.

Levy, J. E., & Shepardson, W. (1992, Spring). A look at current school-linked service efforts. *The Future of Children, 2*(1), 44–55.

Lipsky, M. (1980). *Street-level bureaucracy: Dilemmas of the individual in public services.* New York: Russell Sage Foundation.

March, J. G. (1981). Footnotes to organizational change. *Administrative Science Quarterly, 26,* 563–577.

March, J. G., & Olsen, J. P. (1984, September). The new institutionalism: Organization factors in political life. *American Political Science Review, 78*(3), 734–749.

March, J. G., & Olsen, J. P. (1989). *Rediscovering institutions: The organizational basis of politics.* New York: The Free Press.

Melaville, A. L., & Blank, M. J. (1991, January). *What it takes: Structuring interagency partnerships to connect children and families with comprehensive services.* Washington, DC: Education and Human Services Consortium.

Moe, T. M. (1984). The new economics of organization. *American Journal of Political Science, 28*(4), 739–777.

Morgan, G. (1986). *Images of organization.* Newbury Park, CA: Sage.

Morrill, W. A. (1992) Overview of service delivery to children. *The Future of Children, 2*(1), 32–43.

Odden, A., & Marsh, D. (1989). State education reform implementation: A framework for analysis. In J. Hannaway & R. Crowson (Eds.), *The politics of reforming school administration* (pp. 41–59). New York: Falmer Press.

Peters, T. J., & Waterman, R. H., Jr. (1982). *In search of excellence: Lessons from America's best run companies.* New York: HarperCollins.

Pfeffer, J. (1982). *Organizations and organization theory.* Boston, MA: Pitman Publishing, Inc.

Policy Memorandum SYR 71–5. (1971, December 31). *The potential role of the school as a site for integrating social services.* Syracuse, NY: Educational Policy Research Center, Syracuse University Research Corp.

Rosenheck, R. (1985). From conflict to collaboration: Psychiatry and the hospital police. *Psychiatry, 48,* 254–263.

Sarason, S. B. (1971). *The culture of the school and the problem of change.* Boston, MA: Allyn & Bacon.

Sarason, S. B. (1990). *The predictable failure of educational reform.* San Francisco: Jossey-Bass.

Searing, D. D. (1991). Roles, rules, and rationality in the new institutionalism. *American Political Science Review, 85*(4), 1239–1260.

Shedd, J. B., & Bacharach, S. B. (1991). *Tangled hierarchies: Teachers as professionals and the management of schools.* San Francisco: Jossey-Bass.

Shepsle, K. A. (1989). Studying institutions: Some lessons learned from the rational choice approach. *Journal of Theoretical Politics, 1*(2), 131–147.

Skaff, L. F. (1988). Child maltreatment coordinating committees for effective service delivery. *Child Welfare, 67*(3), 217–230.

Stake, R. E. (1986). *Quieting reform: Social science and social action in an urban youth program.* Urbana: University of Illinois Press.

Thompson, J. D. (1967). *Organizations in action.* New York: McGraw-Hill.

Timar, T. B., & Kirp, D. L. (1987). Educational reform and institutional competence. *Harvard Educational Review, 57*(3), 308–330.

Trist, E. (1977). Collaboration in work settings: A personal perspective. *Journal of Applied Behavioral Science, 13*(3), 268–278.

Tyack, D. (1992). Health and social services in public schools: Historical perspectives. *The Future of Children, 2*(1), 19–31.

Tye, B. B. (1987). The deep structure of schooling. *Phi Delta Kappan, 69*(4), 281–284.

Tye, K. A. (1992). Restructuring our schools: Beyond the rhetoric. *Phi Delta Kappan, 74*(1), 8–14.

Van de Ven, A. H., & Walker, G. (1984). The dynamics of interorganizational coordination. *Administrative Science Quarterly, 29*, 598–621.

Van de Ven, A. H., Walker, G., & Liston, J. (1979). Coordination patterns within an interorganizational network. *Human Relations, 32*(1), 19–36.

Wehlage, G., Smith, G., & Lyman, P. (1991, May). *Restructuring urban schools: The new futures experience.* Madison: Center on Organization and Restructuring of Schools, School of Education, University of Wisconsin-Madison.

Wilson, J. Q. (1989). *Bureaucracy: What government agencies do and why they do it.* New York: Basic Books.

Zellman, G. L. (1990). Linking schools and social services: The case of child abuse reporting. *Educational Evaluation and Policy Analysis, 12*(1), 41–55.

Chapter Eight

Commentary

The Case for Assessing Intermediate Outcomes

Michael K. Grady

It is my feeling that the Gray, Eisenberg, and Crowson and Boyd chapters handled the topic of school-community collaboration quite a bit more successfully than earlier writings on the subject, particularly in defining the essential obstacles to collaboration and describing them in practical terms. Readers who will be engaged, or are currently engaged, in the collaboration enterprise will find these descriptions very helpful. There is also a sober tone to these three chapters; they all recognize that real collaboration is enormously difficult to do, and quite frankly, usually fails.

Common Points of View

The chapters are all strong in identifying the perils of collaboration from the three distinct academic perspectives of the authors: a professor of business administration who specializes in collaboration (Gray), two educational policy experts (Crowson and Boyd), and a communications professor (Eisenberg). Despite the significant differences in perspective and academic training of the authors, the three chapters converge on a number of important points. The first is that institutional collaboration is a worthy goal, which is not something that relevant professionals would necessarily have agreed on five or six years ago. Properly implemented, collaboration can effect positive outcomes for youngsters. Recognition of the growing complexity of social problems is clearly articulated in these chapters, as is the need for an institutional response that under-stands that the very nature of these problems crosses agency bound-aries and, therefore, requires agencies to do the same to respond in a coordinated, coherent fashion. This idea is contrary to the cur-rent emphasis on categorical funding structures, which discourages integration of services provision, budget, and, in some cases, orga-nizational philosophy.

The authors also make it clear that interagency initiatives are easier to start than to sustain, and that they often fail to accomplish what they set out to do. For example, according to Crowson and Boyd, good wishes and a willingness to negotiate are a good start-ing point. However, my experience tells me that the willingness to negotiate in some cases is less a starting point and more an inter-mediate outcome after which the real work begins.

Several critical issues are related to what I would classify as human resource concerns. The first is leadership stability, which includes not just the high mobility rate of professionals in public service agencies but also the impact of new dynamic leadership that may or may not mesh with the philosophy and mission of the col-laboration. In terms of school superintendents (who have a high turnover rate, particularly in urban areas), it is very common for a new superintendent to bring a new plan and vision of restructuring reform. There needs to be some clear thought given to how the col-laboration is going to cope with the addition of this viewpoint, especially if it may represent a challenge to the existing regime.

A second human resource concern is evident in the point Eisenberg makes about the search for cohesiveness among collabo-rating organizations, recognizing that there is a certain amount of getting-to-know-you that must occur. In personal terms, cohesive-ness means a willingness (which I believe is vital to the success of a collaborative effort) to work together toward common goals, per-haps even in the absence of a shared consensus or shared under-standing. Crowson and Boyd discuss cohesiveness in terms of a "new institutionalism" or cross-perspective understanding—that is, they examine deep-structure elements that relate to essential questions: How do these collaborating organizations work? How do they think? What do they think of each other?

Another significant theme common to these chapters is an appreciation for the importance of a sense of shared purpose in integrated children's service efforts that revolves around the question: What is best for children? This point was underscored by Eisenberg midway through his chapter when he stated that if a collaboration does not focus from the outset on an intended benefit for youngsters, it is certainly not worth starting in the first place.

Variations on a Theme

I found important differences, however, in the authors' treatment of the purposes and effects of collaboration. The first centers on when and why collaboration breaks down. Barbara Gray focuses on the process side of collaboration and examines key decision points and necessary transitions. She points out that a collaboration's structure must be sound in order to provide follow-through. Failing to accomplish this will result in a fate similar to that of the New York City Partnership/Youth Policy Group. Collaborations must invest heavily in the up-front process of defining roles and responsibilities: Who are the planners? Who are the implementers? Who is going to carry the collaboration through when the cameras go away?

Gray also touches on the probable clashing of perspectives of the various players in the collaboration, particularly in the area of public-private partnerships. For example, the orientation that public servants will bring to the table—what they think about business and business people—may be a source of friction. In some cases, there is a suspicion of motivations and a questioning of the ability of business expertise to contribute to the solution of what is basically a social service problem. On the other hand, business's orientation toward the public sector may conform to the traditional lay image of rigid, lumbering, inefficient, ineffective bureaucracies. These are the kinds of perspectives that may or may not need to be dealt with from the outset of collaboration to avoid problems later. Crowson and Boyd focus more on misalignment between the ultimate goals of the initiative and reward structures, the needs of clients, and rules and policies, particularly those that govern the funding of collaborative ventures. Finally, Eisenberg admits to having a cynical attitude about a need to invest great energies in reaching consensus in shared understanding. Rather, he seeks a cohesiveness, a willingness to work together.

Collaborative efforts of the type discussed in this book can assume a variety of configurations, or what some of the authors refer to as interorganizational relationships. Gray presents an analysis of the New York City Partnership/Youth Policy Group, a public-private undertaking to reduce youth unemployment in New York City; Eisenberg's reference point, however, is interorganizational cooperation, while Crowson and Boyd's chapter focuses on integrated services, which is probably closer to what I have come to recognize, through my experiences with the Annie E. Casey Foundation (referred to throughout this chapter as the Foundation), as full-scale collaboration. Clarifying these different conceptualizations of collaboration is facilitated by using a continuum that arrays collaboration efforts by the degrees to which participating organizations are asked to change their "deep structures" rather than simply add to or enhance current operations.

We might be able to plot these different initiatives by measuring the extent to which change must occur within organizations if collaboration is to be successful. In the case of the Foundation investments, for example, deep-structure changes in children's mental health, community-based family foster care, and juvenile detention alternatives constitute commitments by participating organizations not simply to add to or subtract from their current service array, but to transform how they finance and where they provide services, modify policies regarding information sharing and the development of management information systems, and reform professional training programs.

Policies and Programs

Learning the significance of determining the proper mix of policy and program in the work of a collaborative initiative has also been a valuable aspect of my experiences with New Futures, a Foundation collaborative initiative designed to reform youth-serving systems in five cities. These two features should not be separated; a successful collaboration utilizes a fair amount of activity at the policy level coupled with concurrent activity in program innovation, specifically in schools and communities. Without sound policy, collaborative initiatives too often become laden with add-on programs, and without programs, policy in a vacuum. In short, there needs to be attention to both as part of the work of the collaborative body.

The importance of early and continuous evaluation, my primary responsibility at the Foundation, cannot be overstated. The evaluation of the implementation and impact of the collaborative effort needs to be seated directly at the center of the development process. If evaluation is conducted properly, it will reveal much about the effect the collaboration is having at the program sites, and what might need to change about both the original project design and current implementation strategies.

When assessing impact, decision makers need to think in terms of both intermediate and long-term outcomes. Simply attempting to measure what appear to be distal effects (which, incidentally, might not be visible for five or six years in many cases) can be disillusioning for those individuals responsible for program implementation. My experience has shown the wisdom of taking small steps in stating expectations and hopes for impact in the near term. This approach will affect positively the morale of the collaborating partners and provide for the development of realistic long-term goals.

A final recommendation is that there be stable support for development of the evaluation and research technology needed to study the impact of social service collaborations. This is an area that has not been sufficiently researched. Case study methodology has improved over the last five or six years, but we have not come very far in mounting comparative tests of the effects of collaboration on communities, organizations, families, or children. This type of research is both very difficult and very expensive, but it must be supported if we hope to learn about the process and product of these initiatives with useful and compelling evidence for policy audiences.

Chapter Nine

Commentary

On Building Trusting and Mutually Beneficial Partnerships

Carol B. Truesdell

The context for my comments is my experience with the Minneapolis Youth Trust, a nonprofit organization dedicated to developing partnerships and collaborations focused on mentoring and workforce development for Minneapolis youth. The mission of the Youth Trust, of which I am currently executive director, is to be a bridging organization; its business is promoting, initiating, and developing partnerships to help children and youth from kindergarten through twelfth grade become ready for life and work.

The scope of our outreach includes more than 150 employer organizations in the Minneapolis area (most of which are for-profit), 70 youth-serving agencies, and the Minneapolis Public Schools, which serve 45,000 children in 75 schools. In general, Youth Trust partnerships are focused on the development of life and work skills, with specific attention to mentoring, education, and work readiness. Each focus area is managed by a division that is governed by the partners involved in that field.

The Youth Trust does not provide direct services to youth; it provides direct services to organizations that serve youth, specifically, employers, schools, and agencies. We add value to current programs, improve the quality of current services, stimulate innovation and reform, and eliminate duplication of effort and cost.

My comments are based on lessons learned from the Youth Trust's experiences convening agencies with strong mentoring and employment programs; developing school partnerships that involve businesses, social service agencies, and community organizations; and launching multisector collaborations, including the North High Career Center, and a more recent initiative, New Workforce. Through New Workforce, the Youth Trust is facilitating the development of a communitywide vision and strategy to prepare young people for a future after high school; aimed specifically at career-oriented employment, New Workforce includes youth apprenticeships and/or postsecondary education and training. This is not another "pull-out program" for at-risk youth; it represents an effort to change systems that are not working for kids. To achieve this goal, the Youth Trust is inviting major institutions to "come to the table" to help young people succeed. Local stakeholders include Minneapolis Public Schools; employers, including the Minnesota Business Partnership and the Greater Minneapolis Chamber of Commerce; Minneapolis's existing youth employment programs; a variety of postsecondary institutions, including technical schools, community colleges, and a representation of four-year colleges, both private and public; and social service agencies and community-based organizations.

Since the Youth Trust does its work through others, board, staff, and partner organizations are learning a lot about what makes partnerships and collaborations work—and not work. There is no road map; we are learning as we go. We are committed to solving complex problems by bringing people together to craft solutions that they develop and deliver. No one sector or organization, however skilled and caring, can do it alone. Our basic belief is that it is the community's responsibility to prepare youth for life and work. In the words of an often-cited African proverb, "It takes a whole village to raise a child."

Response to Barbara Gray

I would like to react to the chapters individually from the perspective of these Youth Trust experiences. One thing I have sensed (as did Barbara Gray in Chapter Five) is that there is a real readiness for doing something radically different. This means pulling people together and asking them to move beyond their own self-interests to accomplish something bigger that benefits the broader community. The challenge is to position the collaboration so that the need to cooperate is greater than any sacrifices that may be required.

The Youth Trust's experiences, particularly those arising from the New Workforce initiative, are parallel to Barbara Gray's findings. Some brief observations based on those similarities follow. First, I believe that the elimination of social service agencies, particularly youth-serving agencies, from the collaborative mix represented by the Youth Policy Group was a critical mistake. On the other hand, I can see why it happened. In our experience, agencies are clearly the most difficult and challenging sector with which to work, owing to their distinct differences in mission, their ongoing competition for limited cash and human resources, and their feelings of powerlessness. Often agencies are the most turf-oriented of all stakeholders, believing that they have the most to lose from collaboration.

Second, it is critical to recruit chief executive officers (CEOs) and their frontline designees at the same time. My strategy is to ask each CEO to sign on to the vision and conceptual framework and then to ask him or her to designate a person with the skill, decision-making authority, and collaborative spirit to participate in the multisector planning process. Unless a hands-on, operating person is present at the table, it is easy to miss the barriers or issues that may block progress. In addition, if the goal of the initiative is to gain an organization's commitment to contribute resources to the collaboration, it is critical that its staff have ownership in the success of the undertaking; this can be achieved only if the people who are responsible for making it work are involved in its development.

Third, another problem with the New York example was the inappropriate and limited role of business. I worked for the Pillsbury Company for five years in the area of community relations, and this experience has given me a broader perspective on the assets of the business community. Since the capacities of corporations are often misunderstood, requests for contributions are frequently limited to dollars alone. Employee volunteers as tutors and mentors, product donations, and many different kinds of technical expertise and assistance are usually overlooked. In addition, businesses can release employees to be career role models and provide opportunities for job shadowing; they can offer summer internships, year-round part-time jobs and youth apprenticeships, and last-dollar scholarship support, as well as internships for teachers, opportunities for staff development, and business participation in curriculum development.

Fourth, the lack of attention to process that Gray referenced is a significant problem. In collaborative efforts, we have found that process is an important product, critical to building respect and trust across sectors. Differences in the values, motivations, cultures, and work environments of different organizational partners cannot be overestimated. If time and energy are not invested in bridging these differences, the partnership or collaboration will fail, sooner or later.

Fifth, I respond positively to Gray's recognition that the role of a convener is critical to the success of multisector collaborations. This is the role played by the Youth Trust. From our experience, we can document the value of a neutral organization as a facilitator, one that has no particular agenda to advance, one that values the unique contribution of each sector or organization, and one that can find common ground, build consensus, and ask for short- and long-term commitments.

Response to Eric Eisenberg

With regard to Eisenberg's chapter (Chapter Six), I certainly agree that we are in an age of limits to a greater degree than ever before, yet I believe that this trend works against organizational collaboration rather than for it. I base this belief, in part, on the reality that private, nonprofit organizations are hardest hit by the reduction in charitable resources. The scramble for ongoing operating funds is resulting in intense competition among organizations that should be working together rather than against each other. Outcomes include greater isolation, increased "turfism," and hesitancy to collaborate for fear of losing the few resources they have. In general, I've seen very little movement toward interorganizational cooperation on a systemic basis among the private, nonprofit community. There is cooperation, however, around more limited objectives and a narrower range of outcomes. To date, multisector collaborations and organizational mergers have not been successful for a variety of reasons.

As a footnote to the previous comments, funders and businesses are frustrated by the plethora of nonprofit organizations in the Twin Cities area, many of which seem to duplicate each other. Fueling this multiplicity is the trend of nonprofits to become narrower and narrower in their scope in order to better serve increasingly needy, highly targeted populations.

With regard to Eisenberg's irrational approach, although directionally correct, the argument is flawed. Perhaps it is a rhetorical difference, but I disagree with his assumptions. In developing a mutually beneficial partnership, there has to be shared understanding, agreement, and consensus around issues of task—consensus on the vision or purpose, the matching of needs and resources, identification of priorities, and decisions regarding structure and staffing, as well as agreement on a communications strategy.

Communications, obviously, must be open in the sense of acknowledging differences in values, work style, language, and motivations. If those differences are accepted verbally, without efforts to reach consensus on any one approach, it is a way to move forward. However, ignoring the existence of differences can become a significant barrier in and of itself.

I also believe in planning to a modest degree. In our experience, partnerships that jump too quickly into activity often must return later to planning in order to reach consensus on purpose, priorities, and structure. I agree, too, that it is best to begin collaborations by developing areas of consensus at the conceptual or policy level to build support for change, rather than starting with the "how to's" of the project. This is the Youth Trust's approach in its New Workforce initiative. The first tasks of the planning team have included agreement on vision, mission, principles, strategies, and outcomes. Before long, however, we must move beyond generalities to identify, specifically, what needs to be changed between grades six and twelve to prepare young people adequately for a future after high school. Soon after that, we must demonstrate that institutions are doing things differently and that current practices are changing, or we will lose credibility with our partner organizations.

I agree strongly with Eisenberg on the concept of recruiting "boundary spanners" as stakeholders. I would define them as people who are personally centered, comfortable with the big picture, open to change, flexible in their thinking, creative in their use of resources, and empowering of others. Therefore, I would select people not only on the basis of their position but also on their style. I also agree with Eisenberg's concept of dialogue as a tool for building consensus: that each experience is valid, that it is not to be challenged, that there is no need to force adherence to one person's view, and that the goal is mutual understanding and respect. In summary, I am in agreement with Eisenberg's observation: "The key to effective coordination is a strategically ambiguous vision or mission, which simultaneously motivates action and permits individuals to retain their idiosyncratic meanings and beliefs" (see Chapter Six).

Response to Robert Crowson and William Boyd

Finally, with regard to Crowson and Boyd's chapter (Chapter Seven), I appreciate the way they articulated the underlying issue. I have worked either in or with the Minneapolis Public Schools for more than two years, and I continue to be overwhelmed by the variety of initiatives and reforms that are operating there, each one with the promise of "fixing" the system. The ones with which I am familiar include school choice, site-based management, school reorganization, agency co-location, tech prep, outcome-based education, authentic assessment, and new approaches to parent involvement. All are on parallel tracks, each one assuming it will be "the" answer. With leadership, with planning and coordination, with leveraging of resources, and with a sustained effort, the logjam could be broken. When the pain of maintaining the status quo is less than the pain of changing the way things are done, the system will change.

Crowson and Boyd's observation about the need for "compelling glue" to bring health and social agencies into schools is a very powerful concept, since I don't believe it currently exists. Unfortunately, a turbulent environment will not bring people together in and of itself. The disincentives for collaboration between agencies and schools are just too great, including lack of time, staff, and resources, as well as distrust and fear of the unknown. The only exception to this analysis is the existence of very short-term, highly focused initiatives spawned by community crises, leading to the collaboration of disparate organizations for a brief period of time around a limited agenda.

My experience with co-location, or bringing agencies into service delivery with schools, has been in situations where new money has been available for additional staff and new program development. Since private funding for initiatives like these will not be available in the future, incentives for co-location must come from the redirection of existing public funding streams and/or from community pressure to change agency service delivery systems. More than funding will be necessary to make co-location successful. Because school and agency cultures are dramatically different, it will take time and effort to build trusting, mutually beneficial work relationships. At best, accomplishing this is a challenge.

I think Crowson and Boyd are right when they observe that we are in a period of experimentation with institutional change, in which one experiments, evaluates, learns, tries again, and experiments some more. That has been my reality as the executive director of the Minneapolis Youth Trust, as I suspect it will be for the members of any collaborative initiative attempting to build partnerships to ready youth for life after school.

Part Three

The Social Context

Chapter Ten

The Macroecology of Educational Outcomes

David W. Bartelt

After three decades of debate about the causes of educational deficits in our urban schools, beginning with Conant's seminal work (1961), both Katznelson and Weir (1985) and Kantor and Brenzel (1993) have forced us to confront the possibility that the changing makeup of our cities, not necessarily the schools themselves, accounts for much of the failure of our educational system. In arguments that correspond with the debates over the origins, characteristics, and perpetuating mechanisms of the underclass, these works focus on the rapid changes in urban communities that form the local context of schools. The movement of resources, jobs, and people from central city to suburb has created a much more hostile environment for communities and their institutions within the inner city. This is particularly striking when we examine the impact of these forces on the educational success of children and young adults in these areas.

As researchers and as prescriptors of public policy, our task is to examine the ways that change in urban economic, residential, and fiscal conditions creates constraints on the effective operation of schools. This task has several dimensions, the first of which is to establish that there is an empirical relationship between these

This chapter would not have been possible without the able assistance of Sue Baker, who has been largely responsible for the development of the database used in the analysis. I would also like to express my appreciation to Leo Rigsby for careful editorial work and several helpful suggestions.

macrosocial forces (specifically, those affecting the ways in which cities grow and decline relative to one another) and educational accomplishment. A further implication of this approach is that the educational system—including its students—is part of a larger urban ecology than is usually considered, namely an interurban relationship among metropolitan areas. This "macroecology" of urban relationships treats the educational system as a part of the institutional infrastructure of urban areas that helps some and hinders others in the pursuit of a comparative advantage in the competition among urban areas for economic resources, population, and a tax base.[1]

This chapter contains both a conceptual and an empirical discussion of the macroecology of inner-city schools, particularly the ways in which schools are constrained in terms of resources by their urban context, and how they must contend with a set of forces impinging on the educational process. Educational policy is often ill-equipped to deal with these constraints.

Toward an Ecology of Education

At the heart of analyses that focus on city change rather than on educational failure is a paradigmatic shift in focus, from schools to urban processes. Schools do not disappear from the analytical frame; rather, the network of institutions and processes that affect the schools becomes the focus of concern. This analysis seeks to weave a set of connecting threads between research on inner-city schools and research on the dramatic shifts in the nature of urban life at a national and metropolitan level.

The main organizational feature of American education is that it is simultaneously embedded in national and multinational institutions and very localized in its point of delivery. American education is rooted in the concept of the community school; American educational policy is rooted in the problem of adapting to economic, political, and social agendas that transcend local schools; and American schools must contend with rapidly changing communities in which their student composition, educational mission, and resource base are largely determined by factors external to any individual school or school system.

Educational critics and policymakers have long recognized this essential dilemma, particularly with respect to urban schools (Havighurst, 1966; Schrag, 1967; Hummel & Nagle, 1973). The response has essentially been a prescriptive one, in which various alternative strategies are suggested, such as magnet schools, busing, and voucher programs (Ravitch, 1983). What is missing is an analytical attempt to systematize the nature of the various contexts within which educational policy and practice are carried out.

Schools are embedded in a network of social processes. They do not start with the same set of resources, with equivalently motivated students, with randomly assigned students, or with reputations for either quality or failure, any more than any other social institution in American society. The ecological model suggests that it is possible to distinguish the salient characteristics of the social arrangements within which schools are embedded as a means of better understanding the outcomes of the educational process. By extension, it also suggests that we can identify the support services that may need to be integrated into and coordinated with the educational process in order to improve educational outcomes, particularly in inner-city schools.

The central concept of this chapter is that of "nested" ecologies of education. As we examine macroecologies, we uncover a second or third ecological system at work, much like the nested Russian dolls children play with. A classroom exists within a school and its ecology of teachers, classrooms, physical structures, and the like. Schools exist within a network of competing, complementary, and other relationships—and in cities, within a system of distribution of resources and constraints. Schools are only one part of the institutional ecology of cities and are affected by the neighborhood ecology of the city. Finally, cities are linked to each other in a complex ecology in which population, opportunities, and fiscal capacities are distributed differentially within the network. In other words, any educational reform effort occurs within the limits of the ecological niche that a school district and its students occupy in the national urban network.

Cities, which form the largest embedding context, are forms of social organization that include both a network of communities and an institutional matrix of private and public organizations addressing various political, economic, and social activities. This chapter examines the extent to which the interactions of a group of cities affect their opportunity structure (for example, the presence or absence of jobs, their population and job development "trajectories") and educational outcomes.

Inner cities and *inner-city schools* denote a geographic referent that includes processes of racial and class stratification but that also taps into the effects of concentration and isolation by race and class (Wilson, 1987; Kasarda, 1989). Much of the literature on the educational deficits of urban schooling implicitly or explicitly ties educational outcomes to one of two major variables that can (in principle) be linked to these stratifying forces. Distributional problems/inequities in direct educational financing or other finance-related resources (for example, computers, books, audiovisuals, support staff, and so forth) shape one literature (Hummel & Nagle, 1973; Verstegen & Ward, 1991). "Family" variables such as income level and "penalties" associated with poverty shape the second (Kennedy, Jung, & Orland, 1986; Crane, 1991; Mayer, 1991). In both instances, particularly the latter, recent analyses of the "underclass" have suggested that racial isolation and the concentrated effects of poverty combine to affect negatively the likelihood of students' educational success and their ability to use education as a means of social or geographic mobility.

This chapter systematically examines the consequences of economic transition, national migration, and urban decentralization on a major indicator of educational success—the proportion of students aged 16–19 (the typical age bracket for achieving a diploma) who are either not in school or have not achieved a degree. This examination should reveal the degree to which schools in urban areas experiencing the most significant negative changes are coping with a population that, due to these large-scale economic and demographic forces, is likely to experience not only educational torpor but a cluster of social problems. These problems interfere both with students' educational prospects and with the fiscal capacity of local governments to meet the demands exerted on it by these problems and the educational endeavor.

Using a data set from fifty-three cities, I suggest the following findings, relevant to the discussion of educational outcomes: (1) there is a suggestive relationship between city development trajectories and patterns of educational funding; (2) there is a distinct pattern to the levels of racial segregation found in cities, strongly linked to the economic history of those cities; and (3) strong ecological relationships exist among the economic development of cities, opportunity structures, funding levels, and the degree to which cities have a dropout problem. Finally, if we accept the findings of this model, the correlates of the position of cities in the system of cities suggest that educational outcomes are highly correlated with other products of the system, such as economic opportunities and the relative presence of single-parent households. Taken together, these findings suggest that the macroecological framework yields significant insights into the "externalities" affecting educational activities in the urban environment and provide a sound basis for the development of an alternative modality for the discussion of educational policy, based on concepts such as "resistance" or "degree of difficulty."

As Raffel, Boyd, Briggs, Eubanks, and Fernandez (1992) have stated, any approach to educational policy in our cities must be comprehensive in nature, addressing the public health, nutrition, and other supportive service needs of the community. What we expect to demonstrate is the essential basis for the current educational dilemma facing inner-city schools—that cities rooted most deeply in older economic bases face the most serious educational deficiencies, have a significant set of related problems that intersect those being addressed by the schools, and have a counteracting set of negative fiscal factors.

This argument asserts the interdependence of inner-city educational systems with their urban contexts, particularly the ways in which macro-urban changes affect both the context and the outcomes of schools. The analysis will move from changes in the national system of cities to the ways in which these changes affect the educational process. We then consider the implications of this argument for the social context of inner-city education—namely, that the same forces that give rise to educational difficulties yield a series of related community characteristics that affect the educational process. The chapter concludes with a discussion of policy alternatives aimed at the complex of issues surrounding educational achievement and the place of the school within the new urban setting. We aim to demonstrate the further embeddedness of urban systems in a wider, national system of urban processes—cities as systems in systems of cities, to use Berry's (1972) approach.

If this larger context proves useful, it will suggest that at least some of the educational policies that we aim to alter must be addressed at the nonlocal level if true educational progress is to be made. This realization will require our stepping away from the traditional political perspectives of left and right and considering the issues confronting inner-city schools from a more systemic perspective. As Kantor and Brenzel (1993) have argued, "Neither liberal nor conservative analyses of the contemporary crisis in urban education explain adequately why the educational initiatives begun in the 1960s have failed so frequently to live up to the expectations of their proponents or why conditions in urban schools have not substantially improved over the past two decades" (p. 368).

The Macroecology of Postwar American Cities

This argument rests on three intersecting macrosocial forces that have dominated American urban life since World War II. The explosive growth of suburbs, combined with the persistent flight of manufacturing from relatively high-waged regions of the country to more hospitable environs, has created a new, decentralized form of urban life. This shift spatially segregates, by poverty and race, a smaller, less economically viable, and more African-American city from its more prosperous suburbs (Wilson, 1987). In addition, the significant growth of a "postindustrial" economy, dominated by the service sector, has impacted the economic externalities of education, affecting both employment possibilities (Bluestone & Harrison, 1982; Harrison & Bluestone, 1988; Kasarda, 1989) and the fiscal health of cities (O'Connor, 1973; Noyelle & Stanback, 1983; Rusk, 1993).

Thus, inner-city schools are increasingly the schools of remnant populations and communities trapped by their economic irrelevance or their links to diminished labor markets. Further, they are increasingly dependent on an overloaded and endangered fiscal base. But another characteristic of this period is the unevenness of these changes. Not all cities experience them equally, and not all began with the same resources and constraints after World War II—demographically, economically, or fiscally. Just as schools differ in their community context and student composition (Yancey & Saporito, Chapter Eleven this volume), they vary by city.

Two major processes have occurred with tremendous impact on the opportunity structure of the American city. First, and most noticeably, the city of the late twentieth century is decentralized. Whether one calls it sprawl, "edge city," megalopolis, or "the malling of America," the Dickensian world of the nineteenth century, with its overcrowding, narrow streets, and noisy city tenements, is largely a thing of the past.

Second, the nature of the economic activity that undergirds urban life has changed dramatically. The urban explosion of the late nineteenth and early twentieth century was fueled by factories and railroads, and by immigrants looking for work. Mass education in that era taught work discipline, common language, and rudimentary mathematical skills (Katz, 1971). In the late twentieth century, the American economy has changed to a service sector economy (Noyelle & Stanback, 1983) and expectations have grown regarding the nature of job skills within at least the upper-level service occupations (such as those related to medicine, law, and management).[2]

In terms of inner-city education, the implication of these events is that a city's capacity to address changing educational needs and the kinds of extraeducational influences on schools are contingent on the city's success in dealing with these changes in urban social structure. A major focus of our analysis is thus the insistence that we identify different forms of urban development and locate the educational system within them. Schools are therefore likely to be different from one city to another along distinct trajectories responsive to the forces of decentralization and economic change. For instance, contrasts between Sun Belt and Rust Belt cities have been offered as prima facie evidence that a new urban perspective was required, oriented to both analysis and policy (Perry & Watkins, 1978). When benign neglect emerged as the actual policy during the 1980s, this was in many ways a de facto acknowledgment of the declining importance of "urban" areas in public policy discourse— particularly at the national level.

This decline was unfortunate, particularly for discussions of inner-city schools, because it masked real losses in jobs while allowing the traditional conception of the school as the major intervening force in people's lives—and hence a major mechanism for escaping poverty and the effects of racial discrimination—to remain unquestioned (but see Jencks, 1972; Mosteller & Moynihan, 1972).[3] As urban problems worsened during the 1970s and 1980s, benign neglect combined with persistent urban fiscal problems (and the increased devolution of social policies from federal to local and individual responsibility) to remove direct national intervention into urban affairs as a viable policy option. At the same time, the traditional conception of the school as a lever for community and personal improvement focused significant pressure on the urban educational system as one of the few remaining social and bureaucratic structures available to address the increasing panoply of urban ills.

Indeed, as cities began to experience the pangs of economic dislocations, particularly in jobs, a frequently heard critique of traditional inner-city locations for businesses and jobs was the inadequate preparation being offered by the schools. This may have been partly true, but flight from unionization, tax incentives in other locations, and the inadequacy of inner-city economic infrastructures and venture capital were equally important factors (Bluestone & Harrison, 1982; Noyelle & Stanback, 1983). The attention paid to educational deficits and to the graduation of ill-prepared students masked a more invidious relationship—namely, the decline in jobs available even to the graduates of the educational system. Particularly in the case of the public school system, the inducement for remaining in the system, for pursuing college-bound tracks as well as vocational training, and for obtaining a diploma, traditionally has been an explicitly economic payoff such as a job or a form of economic mobility.

The dual change in the macro-urban ecology—the shifts in capital, people, jobs, and development from Frost Belt to Sun Belt, and from central city to suburbs—has thus disrupted the entire context within which the American public school emerged. As Massey and Denton (1993) argue, this change not only undercut urban communities but also increased the effects of racial and income segregation across many facets of urban life, including education.

Further, the forces that were impacting cities and changing their internal community dynamics—their ecologies—were beyond the control of either school systems or most local institutions, including municipal governments. Policy debates, both urban and educational, lacked the analytical framework to handle changes in both the internal dynamics of cities and the distribution of resources and people across metropolitan areas.

The standard works on metropolitan development in the United States have typically posited a persistent, largely stable hierarchy of economic and political importance among cities (Duncan, Scott, Lieberson, Duncan, & Winsborough, 1960; Duncan & Lieberson, 1970; Berry, 1972). Few posited rapid changes within the interurban hierarchy that emerged from these dramatic economic and demographic shifts, nor could they have predicted the dramatic new waves of immigration that have fueled the cheap labor markets of the new industrial development of the South and West. And none effectively predicted the transformation in urban thought and urban reality that yielded an increasingly abandoned inner city replacing the vital core of the larger metropolis (Sternlieb & Hughes, 1981).

The urban context for education has changed dramatically, then, as cities lose population and jobs, some to the suburbs, but most to other regions or countries. This shift in both the nature and location of work has created a significant set of educational problems and constraints in its wake—ones that are best seen in an ecological context. Wilson (1987) has identified this trend in its most extreme form as the development of the underclass (also see Kasarda, 1989).

The System of Cities and Its Educational Indicators

The argument advanced thus far can be condensed as follows: (1) schools are organizations that are particularly sensitive to their urban context; (2) students reflect the economic and social dynamics and conflicts of their neighborhood and their city; (3) the schools themselves are driven by both the educational process and the fiscal climate within which they must operate; and (4) effective schools and effective schooling depend on a series of mutually supporting community, family, and economic institutions. To the extent that cities are decentralizing, their economic base declining, their fiscal climate becoming more distressed, and their population exiting, schools face an increasingly difficult task.

This model must demonstrate that real differences exist across cities, and that the same factors that categorize cities point to differences in educational practices and outcomes. In other words, educational outcomes are embedded in a set of institutional and community relationships, such that the forces impacting cities and communities are reflected in the relative success or failure of their schools.

If we are to examine empirically the ways the systemic, macroecological character of the inner city manifests itself, we must set the educational variables in the context of the factors driving the national system of cities. Such an examination should include a recognition of changes in both the types and location of jobs in metropolitan areas as well as corresponding shifts in population, including size, racial concentration, and immigration. Both the financial support of public schools and the ability of schools to retain students at least until they earn their high school diplomas are characteristics of cities hypothesized to be sensitive to students' developmental path.

The data set developed to examine this hypothesis is a synthesis of several economic, population, and government census data sets, aggregated to the level of central cities and their metropolitan areas.[4] The database is historical in nature, covering economic census materials from 1929 through 1987 and population data from 1930 through 1990. Materials specific to the operations of school districts in 1986–87 were obtained from the 1987 Census of Governments. Table 10.1 briefly summarizes the major variables used in this analysis.

Table 10.1. Major Variables in the
Macroecology of Educational Outcomes.

Variables	Source
Manufacturing Ratios, 1930, 1990 (Manufacturing jobs/Total jobs)	Economic Census of 1929, 1987
Population 1930, 1990 (Total; African American)	Decennial Census, 1930, 1990
School Revenues, Expenditures, 1990	Census of Government, 1987
School Enrollment, 1990	Census of Government, 1987
Linguistic Isolation	Decennial Census, 1990

The data set was collected for a sample of fifty-nine metropolitan areas, based on the sample first developed by the American Housing Survey. This is a purposive sample, stratified by size to ensure that all sizes of central cities are contained within its metropolitan statistical area (MSA) sample frame (Abt Associates, 1984). Honolulu has been eliminated from the study, largely because of inconsistent data from the earlier time periods, leaving a fifty-eight-city data set.

In earlier work (Bartelt, 1985, 1990), the basic variable, which is very effective in characterizing cities and their developmental paths since 1929, is the manufacturing ratio—the proportion of jobs held within the manufacturing sector compared to those of the wholesale, retail, service, and manufacturing sectors combined. This simple index, when examined over time, indicates the degree to which a city is a major manufacturing center, as well as the shifts it makes toward a more service-oriented economy. In general, the literature on urban change suggests that urban fiscal problems are associated with persistent attachment to a manufacturing base, as are problems associated with the thinning out of cities—abandoned housing, pockets of isolated poverty (for example, underclass communities), and persistent high levels, sometimes increasing, of racial segregation.

The City System and Postindustrial Society

Table 10.2 lists the fifty-eight central cities, cross-classified by the different levels of their manufacturing ratios (MRs) in 1930 and in 1990.[5] Dividing the levels into three categories (low, medium, and high) allows at least a simple understanding of the shifts that various cities have experienced. Even examining the marginal distributions suggests that the basic shift from a manufacturing to a nonmanufacturing economy has been substantial. Manufacturing ratios in 1990 are much lower across the categories, with the point of division between high and moderate levels in 1990 falling below the corresponding point for the lowest category in 1930. Put differently, a city in 1990 can be regarded as heavily manufacturing if more than 290 of every 1,000 jobs is in that sector, whereas in 1930, the corresponding level would be 559 of every 1,000.

As we examine the categories along the diagonal from upper left (low manufacturing ratios at both times) to lower right (high manufacturing ratios at both times) in this classification, it is important to note that in a relative sense, there is a significant amount of persistence in the level of manufacturing between 1930 and 1990. Cities that traditionally had either mixed local economies (for example, Denver and San Francisco) or highly specialized nonmanufacturing economies (for example, Las Vegas, Miami, Orlando, Washington, D.C.) had low manufacturing ratios in 1930, and they maintained that position in 1990. Major manufacturing cities in 1930, such as Allentown, Buffalo, Cleveland, Newark, and Paterson, remain to this day more heavily manufacturing than their sister cities. Although there are no examples of cities that had a high manufacturing ratio in 1930 and developed a low one in 1990, cities contained in the lower left cells show a stronger movement away from manufacturing jobs over time, while those contained in the cells to the right and above the diagonal are cities that have become relatively more important as manufacturing centers even though their actual level of these jobs may have been fairly modest by 1930 standards.

Table 10.2. Comparison of City Manufacturing Ratios (MR), 1930 and 1990 (58 Cities).

	1990 Low MR <.215	1990 Medium MR ≥.215-≤.290	1990 High MR >.290
1930 Low MR <.365	Denver, Las Vegas*, Miami*, Orlando*, Raleigh*, San Antonio, San Francisco, Spokane, Washington, D.C.	Colorado Springs, Dallas, Kansas City, Oklahoma City, Phoenix, Salt Lake City, San Diego	Anaheim, Fort Worth, Wichita
1930 Medium MR ≥.365-≤.559	Albany, Atlanta, Boston, Hartford, Houston, Madison, New Orleans, Omaha, San Bernardino, Seattle	Birmingham, Columbus, Memphis, Minneapolis, New York, Pittsburgh, Portland, Sacramento	Los Angeles, St. Louis
1930 High MR >.559	Baltimore, Philadelphia, Springfield, Tacoma	Louisville*, Milwaukee, Newark, Newport News, Paterson, Providence, Rochester	Allentown, Buffalo, Chicago, Cincinnati, Cleveland, Detroit, Grand Rapids, Indianapolis

*Excluded from further analysis

Note: Manufacturing ratio is manufacturing jobs as a percentage of all jobs.

By itself, this cross-classification offers little but basic information about which cities have changed most in dealing with the fundamental deindustrialization process. Table 10.3 contains a summary of some of the basic variables discussed earlier as they reflect changes in both the manufacturing ratio and associated indicators of economic opportunity, decentralization, and the uneven migration of African Americans across the city system. The manufacturing ratio increased on average (median) in only one category of city, those cities low in manufacturing in 1930 but high in 1990. Both Fort Worth and Wichita emerged as major urban areas after serving largely as agricultural railheads prior to 1930, while Anaheim's manufacturing increase can be traced to the very specific intervention of the aerospace industry, beginning during World War II. It is also interesting to note that cities in this set were the only ones to experience growth in the proportion of residents in the metropolitan area living within the central city.

In all other cases, the basic pattern of decentralization and migration is evident. Older manufacturing centers have lower population increases and, in the most heavily industrial cities, clear losses. This is also generally reflected in the city-to-suburb ratio of population, where higher manufacturing ratios in 1930 are reflected in a higher level of suburbanization (higher negative values). The only exception to this rule is cities that have persistently been in the low range of the manufacturing ratio. The older and more developed cities, such as Washington and San Francisco, which have experienced significant regional growth, provide some clue to a countervailing process to simple manufacturing decline. In other words, there are reasons for growth apart from simply a shifting economic base, such as the development of southern and western metropolitan areas as a reflection of the Sun Belt shift, apparent in most of the cities in this cell. Washington, on the other hand, provides evidence of a singular form of metropolitan development, tied to the government, regulatory, and supportive office structures.[6]

Of particular interest in this table are the striking data on racial change in cities. If we were to examine only the data on the changing

Table 10.3. Change in Median Levels of Economic and Demographic Indicators, 1930 to 1990.

1930 MR Level	Variables	1990 Low MR (<.215)		1990 Medium MR (≥.215–≤.290)		1990 High MR (>.290)	
		Actual Change	%Change	Actual Change	%Change	Actual Change	%Change
1930 Low MR <.365	Manufacturing ratio	−0.146	−47.5	−0.0007	−2.6	0.142	46.8
	Jobs per capita	0.227	215.8	0.170	168.2	0.285	214.5
	Population ('000s)	171.0	223.0	259.7	241.3	255.4	174.6
	African American ('000s)	52.8	483.7	56.4	666.6	14.4	343.2
	Percent African American	8.6		7.5		2.3	
	City/suburb ratio	−0.715	−71.0	−0.632	−45.4	0.042	11.2
1930 Medium MR ≥.365–≤.559	Manufacturing ratio	−0.217	−52.3	−0.237	−49.0	−0.095	−20.5
	Jobs per capita	0.166	111.7	0.145	86.2	0.173	87.5
	Population ('000s)	122.9	43.5	205.3	25.2	910.5	64.9
	African American ('000s)	48.2	678.9	62.3	438.6	217.8	627.6
	Percent African American	16.7		15.4		23.5	
	City/suburb ratio	−0.617	−61.8	−0.499	−52.6	−0.803	−61.9
1930 High MR >.559	Manufacturing ratio			−0.322	−53.0	−0.240	−36.2
	Jobs per capita			0.066	34.7	0.106	47.1
	Population ('000s)			−31.0	−2.0	−87.0	−17.1
	African American ('000s)			160.3	531.9	87.0	365.0
	Percent African American			22.8		28.3	
	City/suburb ratio			−1.294	−73.2	−0.928	−70.3

Note: MR=manufacturing ratio; that is, manufacturing jobs as a percentage of all jobs.

numbers of African Americans in cities, by far the largest proportional increases occur in cities having lower manufacturing ratios in 1930. On closer examination, however, we see this as clearly an increase that depends on the relatively low numbers of African Americans present in 1930; the largest growth in percentage of African Americans occurs in the cities with the highest manufacturing ratios in 1930, and those that became more highly manufacturing in 1990 than in 1930 (Los Angeles and St. Louis).

These findings are consistent with recent research on the sources of twentieth-century African-American migration to urban industrial centers, and the relative immobility of both low-income and African-American households in recent decades. Frey (1978) points to the highly selective nature of African-American migration throughout the twentieth century, while Long (1988) notes that recent migration streams indicate a persistent direct relationship between educational levels and migration rates. Thus, migration is no longer the option for the unskilled laborer in search of a job but is increasingly a pattern associated with increased educational attainment. Further, Farley and Allen (1987) state that geographic mobility is increasingly associated with intact families and a significant household resource base.

Put directly, African Americans migrated to older centers of manufacturing industry at virtually the same time that whites were beginning to move to the emerging economic centers of the Sun Belt (Long, 1988). As the character of migration changed, lower-income and less-educated households—particularly, but not exclusively, African-American households—remained behind. In a larger context, as population and capital relocated after World War II, it tended to leave cities where African Americans had resettled during the prewar and immediate postwar periods.

The summary data presented here suggest that the shift from a manufacturing to a service sector economy, which underlay much of the geographic shift in urban resources, occurred differentially across the system of cities. While there is some degree of continuity in the relative dependence of cities on the manufacturing sector,

there is also convincing evidence that this shift to a nonmanufacturing economy has been facilitated in some cities and retarded in
others. In addition, patterns of racial concentration and suburbanization may well be linked to this process, although not in a simple
monotonic relationship. Indeed, the data on jobs per capita, a crude
indicator of the changing opportunity structure, suggest that older
manufacturing centers have changed less in this respect than other
cities. Broadly speaking, the lower the dependence on manufacturing in 1930, the better the employment picture for cities today.
Given a relative decline in job opportunities, outmigration and suburbanization are viable options for those able to make the move.

Implications for Education

While the economic base of cities has certainly changed, the
accompanying decentralization of cities appears to have had
the strongest direct relationship with inner-city educational issues
(Katznelson & Weir, 1985; Kantor & Brenzel, 1993). In particular,
the spatial deconcentration of population in urban areas inter-
acts with economic dislocation to decrease the access of inner
city households to jobs and wages (Noyelle, 1987; Kasarda, 1989;
Adams et al., 1991). Suburbanization of people in cities is as much
an economic as a social response to a changed urban economic
order.

This suburbanization process can be examined across our sample of cities. If we use a simple measure of decentralization, the proportion of a metropolitan area's residents living within the central
city, we can directly examine some of the relationships between
decentralization and education.

Table 10.4 contains a three-by-three breakdown of cities by their
level of central-city metropolitan population. The lower the central city's proportion of metropolitan population, the greater is its
degree of suburbanization. Again, the marginal values indicate that
the degree of central-city dominance expressed in this measure was
uniformly higher in 1930 than in the contemporary metropolis. The

Table 10.4. City Population as a Proportion of Metropolitan Population, 1930 and 1990.

	1990 Low <.239	1990 Medium ≥.239–≤.386	1990 High >.386
1930 Low <.500	Albany Allentown Anaheim Atlanta Boston Minneapolis Newark Pittsburgh Providence San Bernardino San Francisco	Birmingham Paterson Sacramento Springfield	Phoenix
1930 Medium ≥.500–≤.648	Cincinnati Hartford Rochester St. Louis Salt Lake City	Buffalo Fort Worth Grand Rapids Kansas City Philadelphia	Colorado Springs Columbus Dallas Indianapolis Los Angeles Madison Memphis Oklahoma City Wichita
1930 High >.648	Denver Washington, D.C.	Baltimore Chicago Cleveland Detroit	Portland Seattle Tacoma Omaha San Antonio San Diego Spokane

cutoff point for cities having a relatively high degree of suburbanization in 1930 is more than 30 percent higher, on average, than
for the same proportion of cities (one third) today.

In Table 10.5, we use the same breakdown to isolate data on
school expenditures (revenue per capita and educational expenses
per student), the relative size of the school population, and the proportion of school-age children (16–19) who are not enrolled in
school and do not have a high school diploma. The data show, as
might be expected from the arguments of Kantor and Brenzel
(1993), that there is a distinct relationship between decentralization and the fiscal climate of schools. If we look at the revenue base
for schools—the revenue load in cities that are highly decentralized in 1990—the average amount of revenue generated across a
city's population is higher than in less decentralized cities. In the
most decentralized cities in 1990, between $681 and $739 per person (averaging $697 per person) is generated for schools, whereas
in the more centralized urban areas the load ranges between $407
and $579 (averaging $568 per person).[7] To some extent, this is
linked to the early presence of some highly decentralized cities, and
their persistence over time. This is best seen in an inspection of the
diagonal cells from those persistently decentralized (the upper left
cell) to those in which the city maintains a strong proportion of the
metropolitan population.

In the case of instructional expenditures for students, a similar
pattern exists. City schools spend between $2,743 and $2,828 per
student (overall average of $2,775 per student) in the categories
indicating highly decentralized areas, whereas they spend less per
student, from $1,953 to $2,269 (averaging $2,200 per student), in
metropolitan areas that are heavily decentralized in 1990. Again,
while there is some effect that might be tied to the persistence of
decentralization, this trend is most strikingly evident in cities that
are highly decentralized in both time periods.

The pupil-to-population ratio was essentially included as a control variable. It would have been interesting if either the revenue

Table 10.5. Educational Indicators by
City/Suburban Population Ratio, 1930 and 1990.

	1990 Low <.239		1990 Medium >.239–<.386		1990 High >.386	
1930 Low	Mean	Median	Mean	Median	Mean	Median
Revenue/Population	.681	.579	.592	.605	.407	.407
Expenses/Pupil	2.743	2.455	2.283	2.334	1.953	1.953
Pupil/Population	.130	.119	.150	.152	.110	.110
Dropout Estimate	.134	.120	.153	.145	.185	.185
1930 Medium						
Revenue/Population	.739	.653	.614	.617	.579	.529
Expenses/Pupil	2.828	2.682	2.178	2.232	2.269	2.062
Pupil/Population	.146	.143	.144	.135	.144	.142
Dropout Estimate	.166	.160	.147	.149	.140	.138
1930 High						
Revenue/Population	.683	.683	.671	.641	.577	.549
Expenses/Pupil	2.817	2.817	2.285	2.463	2.153	1.936
Pupil/Population	.135	.135	.145	.151	.148	.134
Dropout Estimate	.150	.150	.161	.171	.127	.132

or the expenditure amounts consistently varied by the relative level of students in these cities. That is, if cities that were highly decentralized also had a consistently lower number of students relative to the general population, we might expect that some political factor might be at work, in which scarce resources were allocated to noneducational uses. There is, however, no such trend present in the student/population ratio. Instead, there is a counterintuitive finding that suggests a plausible explanation for much of the political conflict over educational policy. The data we have examined demonstrate that the more decentralized a city is, the higher the level of instructional expenditure, and the heavier the economic burden on the taxpayer.

The literature on fiscal health of cities suggests that decentralization is a significant correlate, and possibly causally linked, with fiscal distress (Rusk, 1993). Essentially, these data suggest that schooling in decentralized cities is more expensive and brings a correspondingly heavier burden on the taxpayer. This strongly suggests that cities experiencing the greatest population losses and, by extension, a more diluted tax base, are simultaneously being asked to carry an increasingly costly educational system.

It is beyond the scope of this analysis to examine the components of educational expenditures (for example, wages, special and compensatory educational costs, materials, and so forth). By focusing our attention on instructional expenditures, we essentially controlled for variations in bureaucratic overhead as much as possible. Further research should address this issue in some detail before reforms of educational expenditures are suggested. Clearly, calls for reduced educational funding—or at least the demonstration of positive educational effects as a condition of increased expenditures— will fall on attentive ears in cities with highly decentralized metropolitan areas. Rusk (1993) has pointed to these cities as exactly the ones with higher neighborhood and educational segregation levels, and suggests that these factors interfere with educational effectiveness as well.

This chapter focuses primarily on the last variable in the table, the estimate of a city's dropout rate. The ratio is expressed in a decimal format, which can be reinterpreted in one of two ways. In cities that were highly decentralized in both 1930 and 1990, 134 of every 1,000 young adults (sixteen to nineteen years old) neither were in school nor had a high school diploma. Alternatively, 13.4 percent of the young adult population could be considered to have dropped out.[8] In cities with the lowest proportion of central city population, the average ratio varies between .134 and .166. Strikingly, there is no evidence of a simple linear relationship between decentralization of cities and the number of dropouts in 1990.

Two possible explanations come to mind. First, evidence of simple relationships is usually hard to find in social science research. Dropout rates may be better explained by a more complex model than decentralizing metropolitan dynamics. (In fact, the analysis turns to just such an approach in the following section.) But it may also be fruitful to think somewhat further about the nature of the dropout process.

Discussion of school dropout is usually considered within the framework of schools failing students (Natriello, 1987). However, Fine and Zane (1989), in their study of young women dropouts, find that students are reacting both against school and against pressures from their communities to become early adults. Pallas (1980) found in his national study of dropout rates that students in many communities were both turned off by school and opting toward another set of choices, typically linked to economic opportunities. This fits with anecdotal evidence collected in field studies in Philadelphia's Latino community, in which education past ninth grade is often regarded as a luxury because of the need to have another bread-winner in the family.

The practical consequence of this discussion is that dropout rates may be high in cities experiencing economic and educational deprivation, but are also high where economic opportunities are sufficiently present to lure students from schools into the labor force.

In any case, the next step in the analysis allows us to sort out some of these relationships empirically. Using the dropout rate as a dependent variable, we tried to discern the set of predictive factors that would help explain the variation of these rates across the fifty-three cities. In trying to capture the possibility of increased opportunities affecting dropouts, we composed a variable that indicated the metropolitan area's growth rate from 1930 through 1990—that is, the proportional growth of metropolitan areas since 1930. We also added a variable, new to the 1990 census, called linguistic isolation, which indicates the proportion of households in which English is not the primary language and represents a proxy for the effects of immigration on the educational process.

In early attempts to predict dropout rates, decentralization had a negligible and nonsignificant relationship to the number of dropouts, and thus does not appear in the final equation analysis reported in Table 10.6. This finding is not unexpected, given our earlier discussion. What is striking is the way city system factors interact with fiscal forces to predict school dropout rates. The R^2 of .54 represents a significant level of explained variance. Further, the beta weights indicate a strong pattern of support for a systemic, or macroecological, interpretation of dropout rates.

Table 10.6. Regression Analysis of Dropout Rates.

Variables	Beta
Manufacturing Ratio	.279*
Percent African American	.341*
Revenue/Population	.297*
Per-Pupil Expense	−.368*
Linguistic Isolation	.292*
Metropolitan Growth Rate	.274*
R^2	.54

*Significant at .01.

As the analysis indicates, city dropout rates appear to be a function of both opportunities and constraints. Dropout rates tend to be higher in cities that remain highly manufacturing in their makeup, and in which the percentage of African-American population is high, holding the other factors constant. These are cities in which the revenue load is high but the instructional expense is somewhat lower, and where the instructional needs of students tend to be higher due to linguistic isolation. Interestingly, the dropout rate is also affected by the growth rate, indicating that there are conditions in which potential increased opportunities are associated with dropping out.[9]

Discussion and Implications

The vast bulk of the educational literature suggests that differences in race, class, segregation, and family resources (both social and economic) are reflected in differential educational attainment, and that they codetermine, with educational credentials, the economic attainment of students. Education, apart from its internal agenda of transmitting knowledge and skills, is recognized as the credentialing arm of the labor market (Katz, 1971; Burtless, 1990; Collins, 1979).

From a macroecological perspective, education systems link households and the labor market. This analysis argues that the performance of a city's schools reflects the operations of its political economy and specifically the relative strength of its opportunity structures. In this model, based on a dynamic system of cities, the evidence on school retention suggests that schools succeed differentially, depending on the city in question. It is less clear whether the schools control the extent to which they can succeed. Put bluntly, the argument in policy circles and in the general public is increasingly that inner-city schools are "failing." However, schools should be assessed within the context of the resource base and the opportunity structures that provide the context for their operation.

The relative success or failure of schools can never escape the social processes in which they are deeply enmeshed in day-to-day operations. These social processes create an educational task that schools are often not well equipped to handle, particularly in the instance of communities and people coping with rapidly emptying cities and declining economic and political opportunities.

Thus, the implications of this approach are far-reaching, as they indicate that educational policy cannot proceed in an institutional and relational vacuum if it is to be effective. Instead, policymakers need to be aware of the intersection of the same macroeconomic forces that have created remnant communities, isolated from economic and social opportunities and increasingly the source of a despair that challenges even the most effective of schools (Kozol, 1991).

Striking evidence of this phenomenon can be generated from the 1990 Census of Population and Housing. Using dropout rates and manufacturing ratios as indicators of the educational and city system factors, we generated a correlation matrix from a set of indicators of poverty or competing fiscal demands. These variables were deliberately selected on the following basis: they reflect changes in urban income levels, unemployment, and labor force participation as direct measures of additional economic effects of deindustrialization and decentralization. They also include other claims on local fiscal climates, such as in the welfare, housing, mental health, crime, and homelessness levels. Taken collectively, they represent the potential correlates of economic dislocation. The results, presented in Table 10.7, are very striking.

One very clear force that intersects economically changing cities and the family background of students is the substantial correlation between female-headed households with children and both dropout levels and levels of manufacturing in 1930. Further, the correlation of percentage of African Americans with female-headed households in this sample is .752. A simple extension of the argument offered in the regression analysis suggests that the entrapment of poor, predominantly African-American households occurred contemporaneously with the growth of single-parent households. In a city with limited economic opportunities, and where the evidence suggests that dual-income households are often a necessity to avoid poverty-level incomes (Adams et al., 1991; Burtless, 1990), the presence of single-parent households is economically problematic for the families involved—particularly when fiscal constraints reduce welfare payments. Modest but significant correlations are found between dropout rates and female-headed households, unemployment rates, percentages of people on welfare and in poverty, lower income levels, and the proportion of the population living in prisons, mental hospitals, and other nonmilitary, noneducational institutions, or in the homeless system (the percentage institutionalized).

This evidence suggests that when cities experience the economic deprivation accompanying economic change and dislocation, the impact transcends any given institution and involves a series of interrelated public problems. The picture drawn here is one in which unemployment and lowered workforce participation are

Table 10.7. Correlation Matrix: Economic Base, Dropouts, and Poverty-Related Variables.

	Female Head of Household	Not in Labor Force	Unemployed	On Welfare	% in Poverty	Median Income	% Boarded Up	% Institutionalized	Dropout	Manufacturing Ratio, 1930	Manufacturing Ratio, 1990
Female Head of Household											
Not in Labor Force	.628										
Unemployed	.816	.585									
On Welfare	.863	.744	.815								
% in Poverty	.888	.704	.842	.837							
Median Income	-.779	-.745	-.706	-.672	-.876						
% Boarded Up	.484	.511	.551	.436	.596	-.583					
% Institutionalized	.337	.212	.174	.282	.288	-.188	.148				
Dropout	.422	.069	.544	.355	.404	-.332	.382	.193			
Manufacturing Ratio, 1929	.591	.467	.442	.614	.448	-.471	.246	.020	.203		
Manufacturing Ratio, 1987	.298	.061	.317	.237	.156	-.212	.076	-.228	.357	.607	

both significantly associated with the degree of manufacturing dependence in cities. So are welfare rates, poverty rates, and lowered income levels.

In this context, it is impossible for us to limit the discussion of educational effectiveness to a within-classroom or within-school process. The limits placed on schools as organizations, the challenges facing them by students who bring the correlates of economic desolation with them to the school, and the bleak futures facing these children as they contemplate restricted labor markets make a limited educational intervention foolish at best.

What form should interventions that adopt an ecological approach take? In the first instance, a major part of the problem facing us as educators is that our paradigms do not fit the dimensions of the problems. A useful first step is recognizing the ways in which our educational problems are inextricably tied to the collective set of problems facing inner cities in an era of decentralization and deindustrialization.

A new framework for grappling with the issues is not, by itself, enough. Consider the school as the focal point in a network of family, community, and economic relationships. A significant thread of redistribution emerges from some of the earlier results; that is, the increased costs associated with keeping students in schools through raising instructional expenditures only adds to the comparatively heavy burden felt by the taxpayers of these cities.

In addition, the concentration of African-American households in many of the most severely affected cities suggests that they will be asked to provide more in the way of resources and to gain less in the way of educational benefits. Discussions must continue around issues of fiscal equity in schools, no matter how difficult recent court decisions and political struggles have made it.

If we limit our discussion to the simple matter of retention (a prerequisite for students gaining further content and other educational benefits), our earlier results, combined with the correlations just discussed, indicate a series of broad strategies needed to accompany educationally specific interventions. In particular, business and job development programs need to be directly linked to educational programs. Similarly, greater educational opportunities, even to the level of guaranteed admissions to postsecondary institutions, need to intersect.

At some point, we also need to recognize the intractability of the nexus between family structure and educational participation. While the relationships we explored here are largely ecological in nature, the essential logic of our arguments suggests that increased economic opportunities reduce the level of single-parent households, and, by extension, increase the likelihood that a more viable set of urban communities is generated.

The implications of such an approach are straightforward: educational and economic development efforts must be made to run in tandem. And until these efforts generate a turnaround in inner-city neighborhoods, educators should be prepared to discuss the ways in which social welfare, child care, increased instructional costs, housing, and supplementary educational programming need to reinforce each others' efforts both within the classroom and within the arenas of fiscal debate.

Notes

1. The cities are discussed here solely within their U.S. context, whereas the forces that have affected them are discernible on a global level as well. Thus, U.S. cities no longer simply compete with each other, but with other trade, production, and financial services hubs across the world.

2. It leaves aside, of course, the issue of lower-level service jobs. We do not yet have a clear signal of what is expected of orderlies, janitors, or street cleaners.

3. The debate over "inequality," emotional as it was, masked an important shared assumption between Jencks (1972) and many of his critics: namely, that there were factors more

important than school structure, pedagogy, or other internal school forces that impacted student success within and beyond school years. In effect, Jencks and many of his supporters were pointing out that the sorting function of schools may well have been made redundant by the effects of spatial segregation and economic change.

4. Metropolitan areas are determined by the Census Bureau as aggregations of counties, generally surrounding a large (50,000+) central city. In addition, most economic census data are reported on a county basis, especially in reports prior to 1960. The metropolitan areas used here are those defined by the Census Bureau effective in 1972.

5. 1930 (representing the 1929 economic census) and 1990 (actually the 1987 economic census) are used for these tables, to allow easy comparison to the population census dates. Also, five cities, indicated by asterisks, contain uniquely structured school districts, making it impossible to distinguish central-city school data from suburban data. They were withdrawn from later analyses of educational expenditures, dropout measures, and the like.

6. Borchert (1982) has referred to this form of development as "command and control" center development. It is beyond the scope of this analysis to develop the full implications of this analysis.

7. Not all funding necessarily comes from the city itself; in a few of the cities represented here, a statewide equalization formula is used.

8. This may seem a low estimate to many persons whose focus is on schools and districts in which the dropout rates are much higher. But these are compiled by the educational system, using different criteria across systems to identify dropouts. Actually, three factors may account for differences in Census Bureau and local district estimates. First, the census is essentially a self-reported survey, in which some degree of misrep-

resentation is possible. Second, public school systems report on only a limited set of all students in the 16- to 19-year-old category, so the census indicator may reflect significant differentials in private school dropout rates. Third, some students move out of the school system and achieve a general education development (GED) certificate after leaving school.

9. A preliminary path analysis of this equation suggests that the effects of historical city system variables are mediated through several key factors, such as the degree of annexation, shifts in job locations, and average wage levels, the effects of which are mediated through the revenue stream, the concentration of African Americans in certain urban areas, and the degree of linguistic isolation present in a city.

References

Abt Associates. (1984). *The American housing survey codebook*. Cambridge, MA: Author.

Adams, C., Bartelt, D., Elesh, D., Goldstein, I., Kleniewski, N., & Yancey, W. (1991). *Philadelphia: Neighborhood division and conflict in a postindustrial city*. Philadelphia: Temple University.

Bartelt, D. (1985). *Economic change, the system of cities and the "life cycle" of housing*. Final Report, AHS Research Grant. Washington, DC: U.S. Department of Housing and Urban Development.

Bartelt, D. (1990). *Cities divided: Race, redlining and restructuring*. Paris: Fourth International Research Conference on Housing.

Berry, B.J.L. (Ed.). (1972). Latent structure of the American urban system, with international comparisons. In B. Berry (Ed.), *The city classification handbook* (pp. 11–60). New York: Wiley.

Bluestone, B., & Harrison, B. (1982). *The deindustrialization of America*. New York: Basic Books.

Borchert, J. (1982). Command and control centers in American cities. *Annals of the Association of American Geographers*, pp. 352–373.

Burtless, G. (Ed.). (1990). *A future of lousy jobs: The changing structure of U.S. wages*. Washington, DC: The Brookings Institution.

Collins, R. (1979). *The credential society: An historical sociology of education*. New York: Academic Press.

Conant, J. (1961). *Slums and suburbs*. New York: McGraw-Hill.

Crane, J. (1991). Effects of neighborhoods on dropping out of school and teenage childbearing. In C. Jencks & P. Peterson (Eds.), *The urban underclass* (pp. 299–320). Washington, DC: The Brookings Institution.

Duncan, B., & Lieberson, S. (1970). *Metropolis and region in transition*. Baltimore: Johns Hopkins University Press.

Duncan, O. D., Scott, W. R., Lieberson, S., Duncan, B., & Winsborough, H. (1960). *Metropolis and region*. Baltimore: Johns Hopkins University Press.

Farley, R., & Allen, W. (1987). *The color line and the quality of life in America*. New York: Russell Sage Foundation.

Fine, M., & Zane, N. (1989). Bein' wrapped too tight: When low-income women drop out of high school. In L. Weis, E. Farrar, & H. Petrie (Eds.), *Dropouts from school: Issues, dilemmas and solutions* (pp. 23–53). Albany: SUNY Press.

Frey, W. (1978). Black in-migration, white flight and the changing economic base of the city. *American Sociological Review, 44*, 425–448.

Harrison, B., & Bluestone, B. (1988). *The great u-turn*. New York: Basic Books.

Havighurst, R. (1966). *Education in metropolitan areas*. Boston: Allyn & Bacon.

Hummel, R., & Nagle, J. (1973). *Urban education in America: Problems and prospects*. New York: Oxford University Press.

Jencks, C. (1972). *Inequality*. New York: HarperCollins.

Kantor, H., & Brenzel, B. (1993). Urban education and the "truly disadvantaged": The historical roots of the contemporary crisis, 1945–1990. In M. Katz (Ed.), *The underclass debate: Views from history* (pp. 366–402). Princeton, NJ: Princeton University Press.

Kasarda, J. (1989). Urban industrial transition and the urban underclass. *Annals of the American Academy of Political and Social Science, 501*, 3–45.

Katz, M. (1971). *Class, bureaucracy and schools: The illusion of educational change in America*. New York: Praeger.

Katz, M. (1993). *The underclass debate: Views from history*. Princeton, NJ: Princeton University Press.

Katznelson, I., & Weir, M. (1985). *Schooling for all: Race, class and the democratic ideal*. New York: Basic Books.

Kennedy, M., Jung, R., & Orland, M. (1986). *Poverty, achievement and the distribution of compensatory education services*. Washington, DC: Office of Educational Research and Improvement.

Kozol, J. (1991). *Savage inequalities: Children in America's schools*. New York: Crown.

Long, L. (1988). *Migration and residential mobility in the United States*. New York: Russell Sage Foundation.

Massey, D., & Denton. N. (1993). *American apartheid: Segregation and the making of the underclass*. Cambridge, MA: Harvard University Press.

Mayer, S. (1991). How much does a high school's racial and socioeconomic mix affect graduation and teenage fertility rates? In C. Jencks & P. Peterson (Eds.), *The urban underclass* (pp. 321–341). Washington, DC: The Brookings Institution.

Mosteller, F., & Moynihan, D. (1972). *On equality of educational opportunity*. New York: Vintage.

Natriello, G. (Ed.). (1987). *School dropouts, patterns and policies*. New York: Teachers College Press.

Noyelle, T. (1987). *Beyond industrial dualism: Market and job segmentation in the new economy*. Boulder: Westview.

Noyelle, T., & Stanback, T. (1983). *The economic transition of American cities*. Totowa, NJ: Rowman and Allanheld.

O'Connor, J. (1973). *The fiscal crisis of the state*. New York: St. Martin's Press.

Pallas, A. (1980). *School dropouts in the United States*. Washington, DC: Center for Educational Statistics.

Perry, D., & Watkins, A. (1978). *The rise of the sunbelt cities*. Newbury Park, CA: Sage.

Raffel, J., Boyd, W., Briggs, V., Jr., Eubanks, E., & Fernandez, R. (1992). Policy dilemmas in urban education: Addressing the needs of poor, at-risk children. *Journal of Urban Affairs, 14*(3/4), 263–290.

Ravitch, D. (1983). *The troubled crusade: American education, 1945–1980*. New York: Basic Books.

Rusk, D. (1993). *Cities without suburbs*. Washington, DC: Woodrow Wilson Center Press.

Schrag, P. (1967). *Village school downtown: Boston schools, Boston politics*. Boston: Beacon.

Sternlieb, G., & Hughes, J. (1981). New dimensions of the urban crisis. In R. Burchell & D. Listokin (Eds.), *Cities under stress: The fiscal crises of urban America* (pp. 51–57). New Brunswick, NJ: Center for Urban Policy Research.

Verstegen, D., & Ward, J. (Eds.). (1991). *Spheres of justice in education*. New York: Harper Collins.

Wilson, W. (1987). *The truly disadvantaged*. Chicago: University of Chicago Press.

Chapter Eleven

Ecological Embeddedness of Educational Processes and Outcomes

William L. Yancey and Salvatore J. Saporito

According to Kantor and Brenzel (1993), the continued failure of inner-city schools, despite twenty-five years of federal, state, and local efforts to improve urban education, may be understood in terms of the fundamental changes that have taken place, not in schools, but in the social ecology of cities and the structure of urban labor markets. These researchers note that "by concentrating poor and minorities in the city, the postwar transformation of social space tightened the link between urban education and educational failure and intensified the educational barriers facing inner-city children" (p. 291). They argue that the larger socioeconomic context of schooling—the ecology of the community in which a school is embedded—is a principal determinant of the success of schools.

While Kantor and Brenzel emphasize the distinction between city and suburban schools, their argument can be extended to specific schools and communities within cities. The differentiation and segregation of urban neighborhoods by race, ethnicity, and socioeconomic status (Lieberson, 1980; White, 1987; Massey & Denton, 1993), coupled with the fact that schools generally draw students from relatively small geographic areas, leads us to conclude that differences in social, political, and economic characteristics observable between cities and suburbs may also be observed between local communities and schools within large urban areas such as Philadelphia.

In this chapter, we report the results of our research, which was designed to explore the relationship between the educational character of inner-city schools and the mosaic of differentiated communities in which they are embedded. We systematically explored the connection between communities and schools. We first located Philadelphia's public elementary schools in their socioeconomic and racial/ethnic contexts by identifying the specific neighborhoods from which their students are drawn. We then summarized the characteristics of the neighborhoods represented in each school and compared these summaries to the characteristics of students and to the educational climates and levels of achievement at each school. Understanding how the social composition of communities translates into the composition of schools and academic success of students is the central concern of this chapter.

The major conclusions of this investigation are relatively straightforward. Schools are different. They have different students and different cultures, and exhibit different levels of educational achievement. Much of the difference is a consequence of the communities within which schools are embedded. Schools equal more than the sum of their students, and students are more than the traits listed on their registration cards. In short, social context is critical. As Kantor and Brenzel (1993) point out, "Though growing up in a poor family increases the likelihood that a student will experience academic difficulties, increases in the proportion of low-income students in a school are associated with decreases in achievement, even after individual and family characteristics are taken into account" (p. 384). Students in schools represent several levels of social influence that include their families; structures of opportunity; and normative, evaluative, and informational systems within networks of adults and peers in the school and the community. Besides these internal influences, multiple levels of external structures are also involved. Both schools and neighborhoods are important structures that have causal efficacy in the educational process independent of individual-level processes (Rigsby, 1993).

Methods

In order to make systematic contrasts between the characteristics of students' communities and the characteristics of schools, it is necessary to obtain information describing each school's community and to integrate these data with information describing schools and students. Massive amounts of demographic data are readily available from the federal census, in which numerous characteristics of populations are provided by census tract. Additional information by census tract is available from other government agencies such as the police, welfare, and health departments.

Deciding how to define and operationalize a school's community is a critical issue in an investigation of this sort. One approach is to use data from census tracts in a school's vicinity to describe its community. We have taken a somewhat different approach. Our premise is that the areas where students actually live, not necessarily the immediate neighborhood surrounding their school, offer a more accurate reflection of a school's community. Thus, for the purposes of our investigation, it was necessary to determine where each student lives, to obtain information describing these areas, and to summarize this information for each school.

This task was made possible by what is known in Philadelphia as the Pupil Directory File (PDF). The PDF is a database that includes all students enrolled in public schools. Among other things, it identifies each student's school and the census tract in which he or she resides. With a computer matching program, data describing each student's census tract were attached to each student's record. These data were then aggregated for each school by calculating the average value of a given characteristic—for example, poverty rates—for the tracts represented in each school. Thus, if a given school draws students from several different census tracts and we are attempting to characterize the rates of poverty among children between the ages of five and seventeen years, we would multiply the poverty rates of each tract by the number of students living there. These products would then be summed for the tracts represented in this school and divided by its total number of students. The result is a weighted average of the poverty rates across the neighborhoods represented in the school being examined (see Yancey, Goldstein, & Rigsby, 1986).

After aggregating these neighborhood data, we merged them with data describing characteristics of the schools. The school information was taken from the annual reports of the School District of Philadelphia's Management Information Center, which were available for the school years 1985–86 through 1990–91. We extracted information describing the average standardized reading test scores; the rates of average daily attendance, pupil turnover, and busing and transportation assistance; and the percentage of students receiving free or reduced-price lunches (School District of Philadelphia, 1985–1990).

A Brief Description of Philadelphia

Philadelphia, one of America's oldest industrial cities, has witnessed a massive loss of manufacturing jobs since the turn of the century. Since World War II, it has undergone a wrenching change from an economy dominated by the production of manufactured goods to one dominated by business and consumer services. Jobs have increased in both the low- and high-wage sectors, but not in the moderate-wage range. Employment change in the surrounding suburban areas has been more balanced in terms of income, although there has been a decrease in manufacturing jobs in suburban areas since 1980 (see Adams et al., 1991). Subsequently, the city has faced critical fiscal crises that have resulted in the restriction of government services in several areas, including education.[1]

The Philadelphia metropolitan area exhibits the characteristic pattern of an increasing concentration of poor (defined as individuals who are, or who are members of families that are, living below the poverty line) and racial/ethnic minorities in the central city, as noted by Kantor and Brenzel (1993). Between 1960 and 1990, the proportion of the city's metropolitan area population actually living in Philadelphia declined from 46 percent to 33 percent, while the proportion of the region's poor residing in the city remained at 60 percent. The rate of poverty has declined in suburban areas while, except for a 5 percent decline between 1960 and 1970, the poverty rate in the city has not materially changed since 1960, when 17 percent of its families were identified as living below the poverty line.[2] Since 1950, the combined African-American and Latino metropolitan area's population has increased from 13 percent to 24 percent. Yet, with the exodus of the white population from the central city, the city's combined African-American and Latino population has increased from less than 20 percent in 1950 to over 45 percent in 1990.

The socioeconomic and racial/ethnic differentiation between the central city and suburban ring is replicated within the central city itself. Philadelphia, like many other major metropolitan areas, is segregated by race (Massey & Denton, 1993). Figures 11.1 and 11.2 show the distribution of the African-American and Latino populations in 1990 across the city's census tracts. The level of segregation between African Americans and whites has increased steadily since the turn of the century. It reached its all-time high in 1980 when the index of dissimilarity between African Americans and whites was .83; in 1990 it was .82. For Latinos and whites this figure decreased from .81 in 1960 to .69 in 1990.[3]

The city is also segregated by socioeconomic status. Figure 11.3 shows the distribution of poverty across the city, indicating that the poor are heavily concentrated in northern and western Philadelphia. With the exception of the city's center, which contains several relatively affluent neighborhoods, there is the familiar pattern of declining rates of poverty toward the city's periphery. A comparison of the residential locations of Philadelphians living below the poverty line with those above it for the years 1980 and 1990

**Figure 11.1. Distribution of
African-American Population in Philadelphia, 1990.**

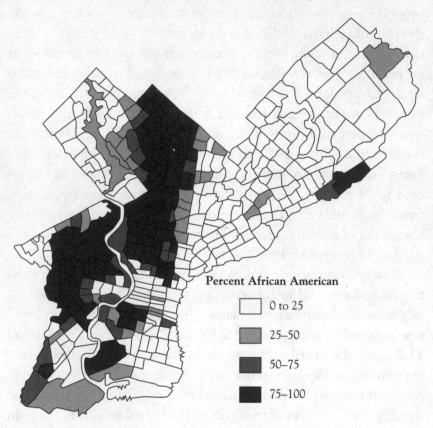

Percent African American

- 0 to 25
- 25–50
- 50–75
- 75–100

reveals that the index of dissimilarity for both years was .38. Additionally, the average poor person lived in a census tract in which 32 percent of the population was also poor.

In a recent paper, Bane and Jargowski (1991) reported that levels of concentration of the city's poor increased between 1970 and 1980. Defining a high-poverty area as a tract in which 40 percent of the population are poor, they found that in 1970, 16 percent of the city's poor lived in areas that could be so classified. By 1980, this figure rose to 31 percent—an increase of more than fifteen percentage points—indicating that the proportion of the city's population living in concentrated poverty areas nearly doubled in only

Figure 11.2. Distribution of
Latino Population in Philadelphia, 1990.

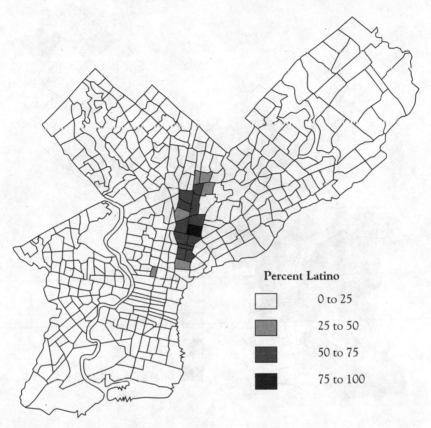

Percent Latino

- 0 to 25
- 25 to 50
- 50 to 75
- 75 to 100

ten years. There was relatively little change between 1980 and 1990, during which years 30 percent of the city's poor still lived in areas characterized by high levels of poverty. There was, however, considerable variation by race. Ten percent of poor whites lived in areas of concentrated poverty; by contrast, this figure was 33 percent for poor African Americans and 71 percent for poor Latinos.

Schools and Communities

Direct assessment of the relationships between the characteristics of schools and the communities in which they are embedded is

Figure 11.3. Distribution of Poverty in Philadelphia, 1990.

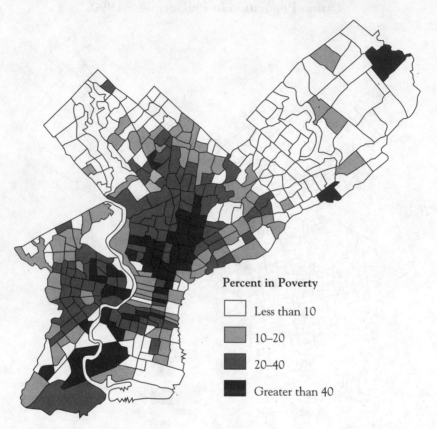

Percent in Poverty

☐ Less than 10

▨ 10–20

▨ 20–40

■ Greater than 40

limited to the examination of characteristics that are summarized for both schools and neighborhoods. In the case of Philadelphia, we have employed census information on the racial/ethnic composition and socioeconomic character of neighborhoods. We have also utilized information on the racial/ethnic composition of schools, and as a measure of the socioeconomic character of students, the percentage of students who are qualified for free or reduced-price lunches.

In spite of the expected parallels between the race and class character of the city's neighborhoods and schools, the two are not mirror images of one another. Two factors distort the reflection. The first is that all school-aged children do not attend public schools; the second is the degree to which students attend schools near their homes. Both factors vary across the city.

In 1990, only 71 percent of Philadelphia's students attended public schools; white students, particularly those from families of relatively high socioeconomic status, were more likely to attend private or parochial schools.[4] Thus, in 1990, the federal census reported that Philadelphia's school-aged population was 50.9 percent African American and 8.9 percent Latino. By contrast, 62.6 percent of the students attending public schools were African American and 9.7 percent were Latino.

The impact of varying rates of private school attendance becomes apparent when one compares the average of a given census tract characteristic for Philadelphia as a whole with its average represented in the city's public elementary schools.[5] If students attending public elementary schools were representative of the city's school-aged population, the averages would be similar. This is clearly not the case. The average percentages of African Americans and Latinos for all tracts in the city are 44.7 percent and 7.1 percent, respectively; the averages for these two groups for tracts represented by public elementary school students are 53.6 percent and 7.6 percent. Public elementary school students were also more heavily drawn from tracts with higher proportions of poor and disadvantaged populations. Thus, there are higher rates of poverty in tracts representative of public elementary school students (26.9 percent) than in the city as a whole (22.8 percent).

Schools vary in the degree to which they draw students from relatively small geographic areas. Local students may attend alternative private or parochial schools; students from outside the contiguous area may be bused to a school because of a magnet or other special program or to relieve overcrowding in a particular neighborhood school. As part of the School District of Philadelphia's voluntary desegregation plan, schools targeted for desegregation provide special programs designed to attract pupils from throughout the school district. Fourteen percent of public elementary students receive either mass transit tokens or ride yellow buses to school. In the sixty-three schools that have been desegregated or are targets for desegregation, 52 percent of students are bused.

Participation in the voluntary desegregation program is not universal. Students and their families must apply for the program and all students who apply are not accepted. While we have not obtained detailed information regarding the specific criteria used, there is evidence to indicate that the selection process is not random. A 1991 survey, representative of all nonwelfare students in Philadelphia's public schools, indicated that there was little difference in the percentages of racial/ethnic groups who used school buses or public transportation to get to school.[6] Children from lower-income families and those living in the poorest neighborhoods in the city are more likely to walk to school. By contrast, children from higher-income families, particularly those living in census tracts containing relatively large proportions of poor families, are more likely to use school buses or public transportation to get to schools located outside their neighborhoods. The outcome of this selection process is that lower-status students become concentrated in "local" schools, while higher-status students become concentrated in more "cosmopolitan schools" with other higher-status student populations.

In spite of the distortions caused by varying rates of private school attendance and travel to more distant schools, there are strong relationships between the characteristics of communities and the compositions of student populations. Thus, in the case of the racial/ethnic composition of schools and neighborhoods, for the 172 elementary schools examined here, the correlations are almost perfect, ranging from .955 to .980 for the years 1985 through 1990.[7] Slightly weaker correlations were found between the percentage of school-aged children whose family income was below the poverty line in the communities represented in schools and the percentage of students receiving free or reduced-price lunches.

Figures 11.4, 11.5, and 11.6 present scatterplots of the relationships between the racial/ethnic and economic characteristics of schools and communities in 1990. The bimodal nature of the joint distributions of the racial/ethnic compositions of neighborhoods and schools is particularly notable. Almost half the schools in the city draw students from racially/ethnically homogeneous neighborhoods and are themselves racially/ethnically homogeneous. Seventy of the schools have student populations that are more than 90 percent African American, while for fourteen schools this figure is less than 10 percent.

Although the zero-order correlations between the characteristics of schools and communities are strong, the relationships are not linear. Schools that draw students from racially/ethnically mixed neighborhoods contain higher percentages of African-American students than are expected based on the compositions of their neighborhoods. For example, there are fourteen schools with

Figure 11.4. Distribution of Poverty in Communities and Schools in Philadelphia, 1990.

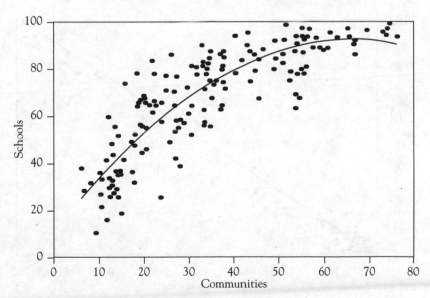

Figure 11.5. Distribution of African Americans in
Communities and Schools in Philadelphia, 1990.

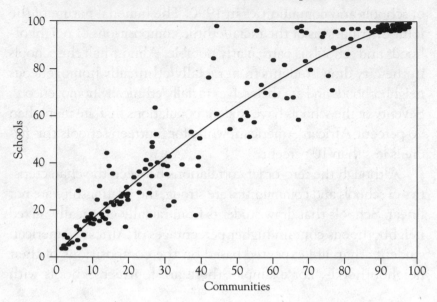

Figure 11.6. Distribution of Latinos in
Communities and Schools in Philadelphia, 1990.

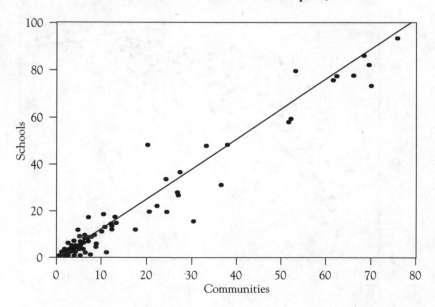

community populations between 40 percent and 60 percent African American. On average, the African-American student populations of these schools are 20 percent higher than those of their communities. For Latinos, the relationship appears to be linear; the proportion of Latino students is a direct function of the proportion of Latinos in the census tracts represented in the schools.

In the case of socioeconomic status of communities and schools, the curvilinear nature of the relationship is marked. Schools drawing students from census tracts with moderate concentrations of poverty have higher percentages of students receiving free or reduced-price lunches than expected, given the rates of poverty found in the neighborhoods from which their students are drawn.

In general, these data indicate that children living in moderate-income, racially/ethnically mixed neighborhoods are less likely to attend public schools near their homes. What accounts for the degree of concentration of Latinos, African Americans, and children from low-income families in the public schools of Philadelphia? To explore this question systematically, we have conducted three multiple regression analyses in which the characteristics of the communities represented in each school were regressed against the percentages of the schools' African-American, Latino, and low-income student populations. In addition to the percentages of the communities' populations that were African American and Latino and the percentage of the school-aged population from families identified as poor, we also included the percentage of children who attended public schools. As a measure of the socioeconomic heterogeneity of the communities represented in each school, we used the standard deviation of the average rent value of housing in the census tracts that were feeders for each school. This statistic reflects the degree to which a school draws students from economically diverse areas which, in Philadelphia, has a correlation of .557 with the percentage of students who are bused or use public transportation to travel to school. Finally, we used a measure of the degree to which the census tracts represented in each school were racially mixed but internally segregated. For example, imagine a neighborhood whose population is 50 percent African American and 50 percent white. In such an area, all white families might live on one side of the neighborhood, and all African-American families on the other. By contrast, African-American and white families may be scattered across the entire neighborhood. Both examples are racially mixed, but the first is segregated, whereas the second is integrated. Ira Goldstein (1985) has shown that racially mixed but internally segregated communities are characterized by substantial proportions of both African-American and white populations and that the incomes of both groups are relatively low.

The results of these analyses are presented in Table 11.1, which shows the standardized regression coefficients (Beta weights) for those variables found to be significantly related to the percentages of the schools' African-American, Latino, and low-income student populations in 1990.

With respect to the linear nature of the relationships shown in Table 11.1, the only factor found to be related to the percentage of Latino students was the percentages of the feeder communities'

Table 11.1. Ecological Factors Related to Racial/Ethnic Composition and Percentage of Low-Income Students of Schools (Standardized Regression Coefficients).

	Percent Latino	Percent African American	Percent Free/Reduced-Price Lunch
Percent Latino	.979	n.s.	n.s.
Percent African American	n.s.	.945	n.s.
Poverty of 5–17 year olds	n.s.	n.s.	.582
Percent Private School	n.s.	.129	n.s.
Local Segregation	n.s.	.181	.337
Heterogeneity of Feeder Area	n.s.	n.s.	−.310
R^2	.959	.945	.786

n.s. = not significant

Latino populations. This result reflects the highly concentrated nature of the Latino population in Philadelphia (see Figure 11.2). No other variables we examined were related to the concentration of Latinos in schools. Few of the children in these neighborhoods, which are uniformly poor and segregated, go to private schools. In the case of the percentage of African-American students, the results indicate that schools that draw students from areas with relatively higher rates of private school attendance and areas that are racially mixed but internally segregated contain a higher proportion of African-American students than was expected, given the racial composition of their communities. These are racially mixed areas that contain the demographic potential for the racial integration of schools, yet they are also associated with interracial conflict— that is, cross burnings, fire bombings, racially laden graffiti, and so forth (Goldstein & Yancey, 1988). The interracial tension in these communities may explain the higher rates of private school attendance by white children. At any rate, the outcome is larger concentrations of African-American students in these schools.

Characteristics of communities that are associated with concentrations of low-income students are somewhat different. First, we found that the association between rates of poverty in communities and rates of low-income students in schools, while important, was not as strong as the association between the racial/ethnic composition of communities and schools. Two additional community characteristics were found to be related to increased concentrations of low-income students: the degree of local racial/ethnic segregation and the economic heterogeneity of the schools' communities. Schools that draw students from racially mixed but segregated communities had higher proportions of low-income students, suggesting that in these communities the higher-income students were choosing to attend private schools or public schools outside the local community. The economic heterogeneity of the schools' communities complemented this finding. Schools that draw students from diverse census tracts have lower concentrations of low-income

Based on data obtained from the Philadelphia Health Department's "birth file," which summarizes information on every birth in the city, we calculated the proportion of babies who were born to teenage mothers and the proportion of mothers who received inadequate prenatal care—that is, did not see a physician before the third trimester of pregnancy—for each of the city's census tracts. The adequacy of prenatal care is an important correlate of birth weight, which, in turn, is associated with a series of developmental characteristics that are negatively related to academic success (see Institute of Medicine, 1985). The adequacy of prenatal care is strongly correlated with socioeconomic status and, in our view, reflects the community residents' access to health care. All these characteristics of the census tracts were aggregated and summarized for each school using the scheme described in the "Methods" section of this chapter. In addition, we included the standard deviation of the average rent value of housing across the tracts represented in the schools as a measure of the heterogeneity of the schools' feeder areas.[8]

Seven school-community clusters emerged from this analysis. Table 11.2 presents the average values of the characteristics used as criteria for grouping the schools into these seven school-community types. As suggested by the labels we assigned, the classification is based largely on the socioeconomic status and racial/ethnic composition of the communities represented in the schools.

We labeled the first school-community cluster, made up of forty-one schools, White Middle Class. The schools in this cluster draw students from communities with predominantly white populations that exhibit the highest rates of private school attendance and the lowest rates of poverty, teenage motherhood, and inadequate prenatal care.

The second cluster consists of a small group of six schools whose distinctive characteristic is the heterogeneity of the census tracts in their schools' feeder areas. We labeled this cluster Magnet Schools. The rates of poverty, private school attendance, teenage

Table 11.2. Characteristics of School-Community Clusters.

Cluster Labels	Number of Schools	% Poor 5–15 Years	Standard Deviation Rent	% Private School	% Latino	% African-American	% Teen Mothers	Births Inadequate Prenatal
White Middle Class	41	15.6	62.7	35.5	3.6	18.5	3.7	10.4
Magnet Schools	6	33.5	135.4	20.4	3.7	46.2	7.0	19.8
African-American Middle Class	26	22.4	56.1	16.4	2.1	77.5	7.9	15.8
White Working Class	21	31.8	28.8	27.2	9.3	15.0	6.6	16.4
African-American Working Class	33	39.7	44.3	12.0	1.4	82.6	11.0	21.5
African-American Poor	33	58.2	46.6	7.4	6.5	86.8	13.8	24.9
Latino Poor	12	62.0	18.1	11.4	57.6	2.3	12.7	23.6

motherhood, and prenatal care found in its schools are close to the average for the entire school district. These schools draw students from areas that are racially/ethnically heterogeneous, although the percentages of their communities' populations that were Latino and African American are below the average for the city as a whole.

The third cluster, labeled African-American Middle Class, comprises twenty-six schools. This cluster is distinguished from the White Middle Class group largely by the predominantly African-American populations characterizing its schools' feeder areas, although all other characteristics that reflect socioeconomic status (rates of poverty, private school attendance, teenage motherhood, and adequacy of prenatal care) indicate that this cluster is less affluent than the White Middle Class group.

The fourth cluster, labeled White Working Class, is made up of schools with student populations that are predominantly white. The communities represented in these schools exhibit rates of poverty, teenage motherhood, and inadequate prenatal care that are slightly lower than the citywide average. The schools in this cluster draw students from relatively small and homogeneous feeder areas, and in spite of the marginal economic status of their populations, lose substantial proportions of their students to private schools.

The fifth and sixth clusters are somewhat similar to one another. The schools of both clusters are made up of students from areas of the city with populations that are predominantly African American; both are characterized by relatively high rates of poverty, teenage motherhood, and inadequate prenatal care. The difference between these two clusters is in their socioeconomic status. Among the African-American Poor cluster, the average rate of poverty among school-aged children is 58 percent; 14 percent of its babies are born to teenagers, and 25 percent receive inadequate prenatal care. Among the African-American Working Class cluster, the poverty rate is 40 percent; the rates of teenage motherhood and inadequate prenatal care, 11 percent and 22 percent, respectively, are slightly lower than those of the African-American Poor cluster.

Latino Poor, the seventh cluster, is distinguished from the African-American Poor cluster largely in the percentages of its schools' populations that are Latino. Rates of poverty, teenage motherhood, and inadequate prenatal care reflect the low socioeconomic status of the communities from which these schools draw. As reflected in the small standard deviation of rent value across the census tracts represented by this cluster's students, these communities are geographically the smallest and most homogenous of the entire city.

Cluster analysis provides a means of measuring the overall similarity of each of the clusters. For each possible pair of clusters, differences between the standardized means for each criterion are squared and summed across all criteria. The square root of these squared and summed differences, known as the Euclidian Dissimilarity Coefficient (EDC), reflects the overall similarity or, conversely, dissimilarity among the clusters (SPSS, 1988). A matrix of EDCs as obtained for the seven school-community clusters is presented in Table 11.3.

Application of this procedure indicated that some of the school-community clusters are quite similar. For example, the EDC between the African-American Working Class and African-American Poor clusters is 1.58. By contrast, the EDC between the White Middle Class and Latino Poor clusters is 5.87, which indicates marked differences. In order to summarize the similarities and differences between these clusters, we plotted the distances implied by the EDCs (see Figure 11.7). However, these distances cannot be accurately represented on a two-dimensional surface; therefore, this figure represents a useful approximation. Examination of Figure 11.7 reveals the relative similarity of the three African-American clusters, located in the upper-left quadrant, opposite the two white clusters. The Magnet Schools cluster is in the upper-right quadrant, relatively close to the African-American Middle Class cluster. The Latino Poor cluster is the most distinctive and is shown here in the lower-left quadrant—a considerable distance from all other clusters.

Table 11.3. Euclidean Dissimilarity Coefficient Matrix for School-Community Clusters.

	White Middle Class	White Working Class	African-American Middle Class	Magnet Schools	African-American Working Class	African-American Poor
White Working Class	2.12					
African-American Middle Class	3.12	2.46				
Magnet Schools	3.47	3.12	2.55			
African-American Working Class	4.54	3.12	1.82	3.02		
African-American Poor	5.89	4.27	3.34	3.90	1.58	
Latino Poor	5.87	4.03	4.59	4.86	3.72	3.38

Figure 11.7. Similarity of Characteristics of School-Community Clusters.

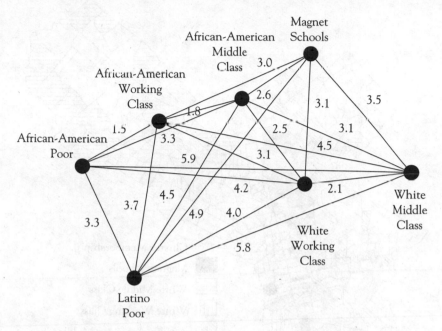

Note: Approximate distances based on Euclidean Dissimilarity Coefficients.

The geographic distribution across the city of the seven school-community clusters is shown in Figure 11.8. With the single exception of the Magnet Schools cluster, whose students reside in diverse areas and go to schools concentrated in a few tracts near the center of the city, the geographic location of these clusters reflects the ecology of the city.

In Philadelphia, the concentrations of poverty are in census tracts located in the northern and western sectors of the central city. The white working-class communities are situated predominantly in the old industrial and ethnic areas of southern and near northeastern Philadelphia, while the African-American population is concentrated in the northern and western sections of the city. The Latino population is concentrated in a relatively narrow strip that separates the African-American population from the working-class

Figure 11.8. School-Community Clusters in Philadelphia.

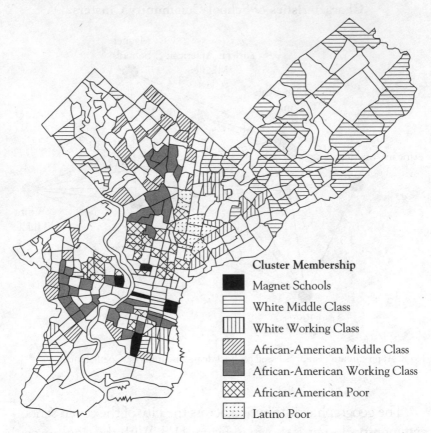

Cluster Membership

◼ Magnet Schools

▤ White Middle Class

▥ White Working Class

▨ African-American Middle Class

▩ African-American Working Class

⬚ African-American Poor

⋮ Latino Poor

white areas of Kensington and Port Richmond in near northeastern Philadelphia. Correspondingly, the Latino and African-American poor school-community clusters are concentrated in northern and western Philadelphia. The schools that make up the African-American working class cluster are also located in the northern and western areas of the city, but are situated further from its center, while schools in the African-American Middle Class cluster are positioned in the northern and western edges of the city. The White Working Class schools are fixed in the southern and northeastern areas of the city, which corresponds to the location of the concentration of industrial white working-class communities. The higher-status white schools are spread across the predominantly white middle-class areas of the far northern sections of the city.

Community Ecology, Educational Climates, and Outcomes

Next we examined the relationships between the characteristics of neighborhoods in which schools are embedded, their educational climates, and the academic success of students. To explore this issue, we used data from the school district's Management Information Center, which summarizes the characteristics of schools and students. The averages of four characteristics of the schools represented in each of the school-community clusters are presented in Table 11.4: the percentage of students who are bused to a given school, the rate of turnover of student populations during the academic year, the average daily attendance, and the average scores that students obtained on standardized reading tests.

Rates of turnover, the percentage of students bused, and average daily attendance are directly related to reading test scores. There are multiple interpretations of each of these characteristics. Student turnover not only has a detrimental impact on teachers' ability to develop a coherent argument over an academic year, but it also reflects the residential and perhaps economic stability of students' families. Attendance, obviously, reflects the presence of students in classrooms where instruction takes place; it may also, however, reflect the degree to which families support and monitor students' schooling. Busing in Philadelphia is largely voluntary; filling out busing application forms and actual travel to school requires additional investments of time by both families and students. To some degree, eligibility for busing depends on students' academic records; as we have noted, with the exception of those who are bused to relieve overcrowding, the more successful students seem to make up the majority of those bused. Additionally, in order to enhance the success of the busing program, the school district provides

Table 11.4. Characteristics of Students and Schools by School-Community Cluster.

	Number of Schools	Percent Bused	Turnover	Average Daily Attendance	Average Reading Test Scores
White Middle Class	41	32.5	11.0	91.7	55.8
Magnet Schools	6	38.6	10.7	92.2	54.2
African-American Middle Class	26	12.2	14.2	92.2	43.4
White Working Class	21	8.8	15.4	90.0	41.2
African-American Working Class	33	3.6	14.6	90.5	35.9
African-American Poor	33	2.6	15.8	90.0	34.1
Latino Poor	12	2.4	19.6	89.5	28.9
Explained Variance		51.2	15.9	24.3	62.1

specialized programs designed to attract pupils from throughout its feeder areas to certain schools. Finally, in our view, average reading scores are an indicator of how effective a given school has been in educating its students.

These characteristics vary considerably by the nature of the school-community cluster in which they are embedded. About a third of the students attending schools included in the White Middle Class cluster and almost 40 percent of those in the Magnet schools cluster are bused to school. About 10 percent of students attending schools in the African-American Middle Class and White Working Class clusters and less than 5 percent of those attending schools in the African-American Working Class and Latino and African-American Poor clusters take buses to school.

A relatively clear pattern of increasing rates of student turnover and declining rates of daily attendance becomes apparent as one examines these clusters. Schools that draw students from the city's poorest neighborhoods have the least stable student populations and the poorest attendance records. Examination of the average reading test scores of each of these groups of schools also reveals a distinct pattern. Reading scores rise as one moves across these categories, beginning from the two poor minority clusters, to the working class clusters, and finally to the higher-status clusters.

Analyses of variance of these measures of the academic climate of the schools across school-community clusters indicates that differences are statistically significant beyond the .001 level. Cluster memberships account for 51 percent of the variance in the percentage of students who are bused, 16 percent in rate of student turnover, 24 percent in attendance, and 62 percent in average reading scores.

Figure 11.9 summarizes the similarities and differences in academic climates between school-community clusters.[9] Again, we have plotted the distances implied by the EDCs which, as noted earlier, cannot be accurately represented on a two-dimensional surface. Examination of Figure 11.9 reveals the relative similarity of the academic climates of the Magnet Schools and White Middle Class clusters, which appear in the upper-right quadrant. The African-American Middle Class cluster is positioned in the middle of the graph. The academic climates of schools in this cluster are slightly more similar to those of the Magnet Schools and White Middle Class clusters than those of the four lower-status clusters. The academic climates of the White and African-American Working Class and African-American Poor clusters are quite similar to one another, although clearly distinct from the others. Finally, the Latino Poor cluster is found in the lower-left quadrant, also reflective of its distinctive character.

Another method of examining the relationship between the characteristics of the communities in which schools are embedded

Figure 11.9. Similarity of Characteristics of Academic Climates.

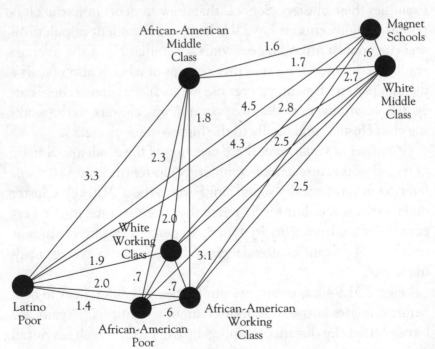

Note: Approximate distances based on Euclidean Dissimilarity Coefficients.

and their educational climates is to compare dissimilarities in school-community clusters (see Table 11.3 and Figure 11.7) with dissimilarities in academic climates. The correlation between the EDCs of the educational climates and EDCs of school-community clusters is .558, which indicates that the differences in the nature of the communities in which schools are embedded are directly related to differences in their academic climates. There are three exceptions to this general pattern. One centers around the fact that schools in the White Middle Class cluster are embedded in communities that are quite different from those of the schools in the Magnet Schools cluster, yet these two groups of schools appear to be quite similar in their educational climates: both have high rates of busing and attendance, low rates of student turnover, and high average reading scores.

The other exceptions are found by comparing the White Working Class cluster to the African-American Working Class and African-American Poor clusters. Despite their sharp differences in nature, the rates of busing, turnover, attendance, and reading scores observed in these three clusters are quite similar. The racial/ethnic segregation of the city apparently has the effect of creating distinctive communities which, in these cases, does not have a major impact on differentiating the academic climates in schools. Though distinct, these clusters share similar socioeconomic characteristics: all three are characterized by racial/ethnic and class segregation; all three are poor; all three are oppressed. Unfortunately, but certainly not surprisingly, their educational outcomes are also similar—all three have unhealthy school climates and low achievement levels.

If we remove these three exceptions, the correlation between the dissimilarities of school-community clusters and academic climates increases to .696. We believe the evidence is clear—the character of the neighborhoods in which schools are embedded is associated with educational character and outcomes. Additionally, the differences in educational climate observed between schools is closely associated with differences in the nature of the communities in which the schools are embedded. Simply put, the larger context in which schooling takes place is a critical component to our understanding of educational processes.

Conclusions

The conclusions of this research are relatively straightforward and can be expressed in terms of at least two ecologies. First, what takes place in schools (in particular, their success in teaching students) is directly affected by the character of the communities from which students are drawn. The contrasts that have previously been drawn between a city and its suburbs may also be drawn among inner-city schools. These schools are differentiated, largely as a consequence of the differentiation of urban areas into communities divided by socioeconomic status, race, and ethnicity. Although we cannot be certain, we suspect similar patterns of differentiation of neighborhoods and schools can be found in other large cities.

Second, the continued development of the urban system (Noyelle & Stanback, 1984), the economic transformation of the metropolitan area (Adams et al., 1991), and the suburbanization of employment and selected populations set the parameters within which the differentiation of Philadelphia's neighborhoods has taken place. There are also social processes at work in the larger community (for example, the placement of students in private schools) that distort the reflection between schools and their neighborhoods. The higher levels of socioeconomic segregation found in Philadelphia's schools than in its neighborhoods appears to be an unanticipated consequence of public policies designed to integrate public schools racially and ethnically, and to overcome private attitudes and family/student choices. The result is an exacerbation of poverty and its academic consequences for schools serving the city's children. The ecology of educational processes must go beyond an analysis of the relationships between specific neighborhoods and their schools; the nature of these relationships is profoundly affected by the larger political economy of the city.

The implications of our analysis of the relationships between schools and communities have a dual nature. First, to the extent that what takes place in schools is determined by the contexts within which schools are embedded, school-community policies must be directed toward reducing the inequalities and differentiation of urban communities. Second, as a society, we must learn that the realm of educational policy extends beyond matters traditionally associated only with teachers, classrooms, school-community relations, or school administrators. Policies concerning unemployment, the location of manufacturing centers, family income, access to medical service, racial/ethnic discrimination, and intergroup conflict are also, in effect, educational policies.

We do not maintain that schools are helpless institutions that passively adapt to external processes. Rather, this analysis of schools and communities in Philadelphia indicates that there are seven distinct school-community clusters in the city, and that, to the extent communities and schools are different, school services and curricula will need to take these differences into account to be effective.

Awareness of the processes and factors that may impede a school's ability to succeed is a prerequisite to combatting them. The methods we have used provide a means for urban school district administrators to identify schools whose children face specific problems. Thus, for example, the methodologies of this analysis provide the means of identifying schools whose communities and families do not have adequate access to health services—as indicated by very high rates of children being born with inadequate prenatal care. Students from these communities may require health services, just as some require meals. The information regarding rates of teenage motherhood provides a means by which school districts may identify schools and students who would be helped by family planning, sex education, birth control, and special programs for teenage mothers. Similar information may be obtained from other government agencies charged with dealing with issues such as lead poisoning, drug addiction, crime, and interracial conflict. Geocoding and aggregating such information to specific schools makes it possible to identify which schools and students require which special services.

Notes

1. The School District of Philadelphia is dependent on city government for financial support. School board members are appointed by the mayor, rather than elected, and the school district does not have autonomous taxing authority.

2. Poverty level data were not included in the 1960 census, although subsequent estimates define the average 1959 poverty level for a family of four at $2,973 (U.S. Bureau of the Census, 1989, p. 453). Our estimates of proportions of families living below the poverty line are based on the percentage of families with 1959 total incomes of less than $3,000.

3. The index of dissimilarity reflects the difference in the distribution of two groups across a series of nominal categories. In the case of residential segregation it reflects the difference in the percentage distributions of two racial/ethnic groups across census tracts. One interpretation of this index is that it reflects the proportion of either group that would have to move from census tracts in which they are overrepresented to tracts in which they are underrepresented in order to balance the two distributions. Thus, an index of dissimilarity comparison of African Americans and whites living in Philadelphia in 1990 reveals that 82 percent of whites would have had to change census tracts in order to achieve racial integration. For details of calculation methods, see Taeuber and Taeuber (1965).

4. This finding is based on an analysis of the 1990 Public Use

Micro Sample (U.S. Bureau of Census, 1990). Within the city of Philadelphia, there was a strong relationship between family income and private school attendance, except among African-American students living in predominantly white areas. In suburban areas, while 25 percent of children attended private schools, racial/ethnic differences in private school attendance were small, though statistically significant, and the effect of family income on private school attendance was not statistically significant.

5. To determine the citywide average, we weighted the data according to the number of children between the ages of five and seventeen years. Elementary school averages were weighted by the number of public school students living in each tract.

6. These results are based on a secondary analysis of these data, and are not given in the original report of this research (Yancey & Goldstein, 1991).

7. The following are the zero-order correlations between the racial/ethnic and socioeconomic characteristics of neighborhoods and students:

	Percent African American	Percent Latino	Percent Low Income*
1990	.963	.980	.826
1989	.963	.974	.822
1988	.961	.972	.831
1987	.959	.970	.855
1986	.956	.964	.860
1985	.955	.961	.861

*Percentage of school-age population below poverty line and percentage of students receiving free or reduced-price lunch.

8. We have used the SPSS-X (SPSS, 1988) cluster analysis program. The method of clustering is based on the squared Euclidean Distances in which the more homogeneous groups are combined using complete linkages (total differences between smaller clusters). Each of the criteria used was first standardized. Thus, all criteria were given equal weight in the clustering process.

9. These Euclidean Dissimilarity Coefficients of educational climate are based on the percentages of students who are bused, rates of turnover and attendance, and average reading scores.

	African- American Poor	White Middle Class	White Working Class	African- American Middle Class	Magnet Schools	African- American Working Class
White Working Class	2.98					
African- American Middle Class	2.15	2.00				
Magnet Schools	.63	3.47	2.36			
African- American Working Class	3.18	.81	1.77	3.55		
African- American Poor	3.65	.83	2.30	4.04	.62	
Latino Poor	4.78	1.94	3.36	5.13	1.99	1.42

References

Adams, C., Bartelt, D., Elesh, D., Goldstein, I., Kleniewski, N., & Yancey, W. L. (1991). *Philadelphia: Neighborhoods, division and conflict in a postindustrial city.* Philadelphia: Temple University Press.

Bane, M. J., & Jargowski, P. (1991). Ghetto poverty in the United States: 1970–1980. In C. Jencks & P. E. Peterson (Eds.), *The urban underclass* (pp. 235–273). Washington, DC: The Brookings Institution.

Goldstein, I. (1985). *The wrong side of the tracts: A study of residential segregation in Philadelphia, 1930–1980*. Philadelphia: Temple University, Department of Sociology.

Goldstein, I., & Yancey, W. L. (1988). Neighborhood disputes and intergroup tension events in Philadelphia: 1986–1988. *The state of intergroup harmony—1988*. Philadelphia: Philadelphia Commission on Human Relations.

Institute of Medicine. (1985). *Preventing low birth weight*. Washington, DC: Author.

Kantor, H., & Brenzel, B. (1993). Urban education and the "truly disadvantaged": The historical roots of the contemporary crisis, 1945–1990. In M. Katz (Ed.), *The underclass debate: Views from history* (pp. 366–402). Princeton, NJ: Princeton University Press.

Lieberson, S. (1980). *A piece of the pie: Black and white immigrants since 1880*. Berkeley: University of California Press.

Massey, D. S., & Denton, N. A. (1993). *American apartheid: Segregation and the making of the underclass*. Cambridge, MA: Harvard University Press.

Noyelle, T. J., & Stanback, T. M. (1984). *The economic transformation of American cities*. Totowa, NJ: Rowman and Allanheld.

Rigsby, L. C. (1993). *Toward an articulation of research traditions in the sociology of education*. Unpublished manuscript. Philadelphia: Temple University Center on Education in the Inner Cities.

School District of Philadelphia, Office of Research and Evaluation. (1985–1986; 1986–1987; 1987–1988; 1988–1989; 1989–1990; 1990–1991). *Superintendent's Management Information Center*. Philadelphia: Author.

SPSS Inc. (1988). *SPSS-X user's guide*. Chicago: Author.

Taeuber, K. L., & Taeuber, A. F. (1965). *Negroes in cities: Residential segregation and neighborhood change*. Chicago: Atheneum.

U.S. Bureau of the Census. (1989). *Statistical abstract of the United States* (109th ed.). Washington, DC: U.S. Government Printing Office.

U.S. Bureau of the Census. (1990). *Census of population and housing: Pennsylvania. Public use micro sample: Five percent micro sample*. Washington, DC: U.S. Government Printing Office.

White, M. J. (1987). *American neighborhoods and residential differentiation*. New York: Russell Sage Foundation.

Yancey, W. L., Goldstein, I., & Rigsby, L. C. (1986). *The ecology of educational outcomes*. Philadelphia: Institute for Public Policy Studies, Temple University.

Yancey, W. L., & Goldstein, I. (1991). *A socio-economic study of public schools in Philadelphia*. Philadelphia: Institute for Public Policy Studies, Temple University.

Chapter Twelve

The Complex World of an Embedded Institution

Schools and Their Constituent Publics

Alan Peshkin

Twenty years ago, when I set out to study the midwestern village of Mansfield, I knew little about the embeddedness of schools, in villages or elsewhere. The rural people of Mansfield, their lives, and their high school, were another world to me. I was a city boy; I had ridden a street car to school and never imagined or thought about the interrelationships of communities and schools. I had spent my high school years happily cocooned in my adolescent preoccupations and, as well, in my neighborhood. I had not thought of school as part of the neighborhood; my concerns were just the good things of family and friends, streets, and parks.

In Mansfield I saw joined for the first time the equivalent of my neighborhood and my high school, linked in a relationship that would shape my thinking and research for the next twenty years. What I learned I placed in my book's subtitle, *Schooling and the Survival of Community* (Peshkin, 1978). What I further understood I captured in the word *fit*, by which I meant that Mansfield High School was a school that fit its community—its *host* community, to be more precise, because that word conveys a sense of how communities relate to the schools that serve their children.

To speak of schools as contributing to the survival of their communities was to go beyond my prior conceptions of schooling. Before Mansfield, I thought that schools promoted the well-being of individuals—not always as well as I liked or in ways that I liked—

but this outcome seemed self-evident and thus needed no elaboration. I also believed that schools promoted the well-being of the nation, an outcome that related to citizenship and its attendant rights and responsibilities.

Individual well-being is palpable, continual, and salient because it is personal. The story of my life, of our lives, is the story of this benefit. National well-being is abstract, intermittent, distant; it is easily overlooked in the pursuit of personal benefit. Given this limited awareness of the functions of schooling, I was surprised to learn these facts about stable, rural, agricultural Mansfield: it routinely elected farmers and natives as school board members, rather than those who by profession and education might seem better qualified to outside observers. The leadership of farmers and natives assured that educators would be employed who needed no introduction or socialization to educational and community life in Mansfield. Just by being themselves these teachers would be fitting instructors for Mansfield's youth.

The result of school board guidance in basically homogeneous Mansfield was a school that graduated students suited for life in Mansfield. They returned easily and comfortably to village life, their values strikingly similar to those of their parents, and their affection for Mansfield's sense of community calculated to sustain a status quo of stable, nurturant, unalienated people. The beauty of this status quo is blemished primarily by external perspectives, that is, by the yardsticks held up by non-Mansfielders who—unimpressed by the contributions of Mansfield High School to Mansfield—could see what "finer things" Mansfield youth were not attaining. Such outsiders would not find virtue in the good fit of Mansfield's school and community.

Without calculation or plan, the people of Mansfield had fashioned a school that belonged in Mansfield; if it would not suit anyone anywhere else, Mansfielders did not believe it had to. The presumption of this degree of autonomy is the result of our national tradition of local control and local financing, but also of the school's location in a state (Illinois) whose standards, relatively speaking, do not require reorientation of the essential characteristics of a school that have been defined by its host community. Mansfield High School was a community school, a creature of Mansfield's subculture, and a perpetuator of that subculture. To be sure, the school attended to individual, personal well-being and also to national well-being, in the usual ways of political socialization. If asked, educators and parents could readily endorse both orientations. A community orientation, though not formally articulated, was supported by the conduct and decisions of persons at all levels of association with the school, from teachers to administrators, board members to parents.

Bethany Baptist Academy

After Mansfield, I studied Bethany Baptist Academy (Peshkin, 1985), another high school in Illinois, established by the pastor of the conservative Bethany Baptist Church. It differed from Mansfield High School in that it was private; its students were self-selected; its community was a subgroup of believers associated primarily with Bethany Baptist Church; it was subject to minimal state regulations relating to health and safety; its budget was derived from student fees; and both its raison d'être and daily operating procedure were drawn from scripture. To work at Bethany Baptist Academy in any capacity one had to be a born-again Christian and an active participant in a fundamentalist church. All employees had to pass this test.

Though a member of a national Christian education association, Bethany Baptist Academy was quite autonomous in shaping its curriculum. It was constrained, if at all, more by the academic requirements of the non-Christian colleges its students might attend than by any organizational or governmental requirements. Reacting to perceptions of godlessness, immorality, and secular humanism in the public school, the many Bethany Baptist Academies of America are the schools that doctrine built for its own survival.

For all their differences, Bethany Baptist Academy and Mansfield High School were community-maintenance institutions. In both settings, a sociocultural homogeneity prevailed that established clear mandates for their educators. Mansfield's secular ethos, formed from its village, rural, agricultural nature, basically overshadowed other subcultural variations relating to class, religion, or occupation. Bethany's sacred ethos, formed from its view of scripture, absolutely overshadowed all other conditions of individual variation. Mansfield High School's success rested on the election of the "right" school board members and, thereafter, the selection of the "right" educators. Bethany Baptist Academy's success rested on the absolutism of doctrine and the voluntary concordance on the nature and implications of this doctrine among those associated with the school.

Riverview High School

Riverview High School, a multicultural school in a blue-collar city of 40,000 in California, was the setting of my next study (Peshkin, 1991). To contrast the homogeneity of Mansfield and Bethany, I searched for a more culturally complex site. I found it in ethnically stratified Riverview, where waves of immigration brought in Sicilians, who, with other Europeans, today constitute 33 percent of Riverview High School's student population. African Americans make up another 33 percent; Mexicans, 22 percent, and Filipinos and other Asians, 12 percent. These groups had come to stay; they were not succeeding each other, so the community's ethnic character was reasonably stable and assured.

For most of this century, ethnic slights and injustices had been incorporated into the routine practices of Riverview's white-dominated city council, school board, and educational establishment. This situation began to change after the assassination of Martin Luther King, Jr., in 1968. In Riverview, as elsewhere, ethnic organizations became defenders of their people. After twelve years of vigilance and intervention, "their people" had been transformed into "our people." The white dominance had changed, moderated, reformed. Ethnic organizations continued to exist, but they became significantly less vigilant and intervening. An ethnic peace prevailed that allowed educators at Riverview High School to concentrate on its central purpose: providing an education that would enable students to "make it" in the dominant society. The fairness of school policy and practice and the traces of ethnicity in the school's curriculum sufficiently satisfied and quieted community adults. They accepted the school's universalist orientation, one that looked past the subcultural differences of its students to focus on their common interest in post–high school jobs and further education.

Riverview High School was the scene of several operative interests that differentiated it from Mansfield and Bethany. Ethnic interest groups are an example. At least for one period (1968–1980), these groups were constituents at odds with one another; believing they all could not win, they sought to optimize their own interests. Mansfield and Bethany had no such local interest groups. Moreover, California's state office of education is actively present in the life of its schools, with initiatives that carry significant implications for their conduct. State financial regulations delimited the extent of local taxation, thereby making school districts more dependent on the state. This, too, distinguishes Riverview from Mansfield. Finally, Riverview High School had many students whose interests and aptitudes, divergent by conventional standards, made them candidates for alternatives to the academic mainstream. Accordingly, educators at the school were attuned to learning about and introducing nonstandard instructional options. Neither Mansfield High School nor Bethany Baptist Academy had this need.

Mansfield graduates were attracted to positions in agriculture, the area's single most important occupation, and to office and factory jobs in nearby cities. Bethany Baptist Academy was, in fact, a vocational school. It socialized students to believe that the highest callings they could pursue were in full-time Christian service as preachers, evangelists, missionaries, workers in Christian schools, and workers in the Christian media. Riverview responded to another reality: almost a third of its 1,600 students were from families on welfare, less than 20 percent of its students attended college, and the relatively well-paying jobs of their working parents were in smokestack industries that declined annually. The point is that the different vocational circumstances and career orientations of students motivate their schools to relate to different postgraduate markets of opportunity.

Prep High School

By studying Prep High School in New Mexico,[1] I learned about a private, nonboarding institution whose graduates routinely went to college. The school's funding derived from high tuition fees and a large endowment; it was controlled by an appointed board of trustees whose members selected and then gave substantial authority to the school's top administrator, its headmaster. At one time, the primary attributes of Prep's students were their wealth and academic success. Now that a large fund offers student aid, their primary attribute is academic success.

Bethany Baptist Academy associated with a network of doctrinally appropriate (that is, Christian) institutions—a Christian honor society, a credit union, pedagogical journals, and annual meetings. Prep associated with a network of private school-oriented institutions. Both affiliations were parallel to a comparable network with which public schools associated. Whereas all three types of schools may draw on some common academic journals and academic fads, each has differences that reflect and are reinforced by the singularities of their respective host communities and professional associations. The distinguishing feature of Prep is its linkage to higher education, a fact of consequence to students—first, in getting admitted to the "right" college, and second, in doing well there.

Indian High School

Each of the four schools mentioned so far has a particular host community: Mansfield High School and Riverview High School belong to the sociopolitical entities of, respectively, Mansfield and Riverview; Bethany Baptist Academy belongs to the doctrinal entity of Bethany Baptist Church; and Prep High School belongs to the personal aspirational entity of parents who chose Prep High as the most promising means to assure their children's occupational futures. Indian High School, also located in New Mexico, has still another variant of host community. It belongs to the ethnic entity composed of the tribes from which most of its students are drawn. Together these schools reveal at least four different types of community publics.

Indian High is a private boarding school for Indian[2] children, operated fully by Indian leadership. Since it is funded by the federal government through the Bureau of Indian Affairs, and since its wish to be accredited obliges it to conform to state requirements, it has a nexus to both federal and state agencies, but also to its own professional and political organizations. The latter arise from the considerable political interests of Indians in establishing and defending their territorial and institutional rights.

American Schools for American Children

All five of these high schools are American schools for American children. Each is similar in terms of what is taught, played, and enjoyed. Each differs in terms of who is considered qualified to be an educator, what is construed as the acceptable cognitive and affective thrust of the education they offer, and what purposes schooling should be instrumental in serving. Each is a legal institution that complies with the stipulations of its state. Each school responds to congeries of publics—some by necessity, such as school boards and taxpayers; some by choice, such as professional associations and researchers.

Notwithstanding their many publics, the schools manage to fashion an experience that fundamentally satisfies their client users. Nationalizing forces—in such forms as textbooks, SAT and ACT examinations, teacher education programs, and professional organizations—conduce to creating the common forms and, thereby, the impression of a national education system. In general, however, the students in the five study schools could not readily or comfortably transfer from their own school to any of the others. The issue is not with either the necessity or the desirability of interschool transferability, but with the price at which local distinctiveness is sustained, given the nation's concern for the commonweal. Underlying a school's local distinctiveness is its status quo, the result of its history, tradition, inertia, resistance, habits, policies, and practices. Many who entertain change in schools see in them a tabula rasa, not a status quo. This status quo is the product of local constituent interests, albeit never exclusively.

Another issue of concern is what is excluded from the school experience by a good school-community fit—what is not learned, not experienced, not felt, not understood, because it is deemed unfitting. My interest ultimately is in what I imagine to be true: the interminable waves of messages that engulf schools from a myriad of near and distant constituencies compel them to fashion coping mechanisms to hold back this torrent. Otherwise they risk being overrun and overloaded by more possibilities for change, for more accommodations of one sort or another, than they could ever manage to absorb. As a result, they develop dispositions to protect themselves from both good and bad ideas more often than they develop the skills to carefully scrutinize and select promising prospects for change. The resulting conservatism may be good for sustaining their community fit, but not for educational growth, and not for managing the strikingly complex task of shaping a school that is attuned to the interests of community and society, and to the roles of students as citizens of each polity.

During the years in which I researched these five schools in relation to their host communities, I could not escape the general clamor of voices that addressed the problems and fate of all schools. The words of education presidents and governors, blue ribbon committees, commissions, polls, and so on ad infinitum overflow and saturate our minds. If much of what we hear is moot, there remains a most serious matter to consider: our schools are embedded in the assessments and prescriptions of numerous constituent publics who assume that they are entitled—no less!—to address issues of schooling. Schools are thus tugged in every direction, and they are accused of a multitude of misdeeds in relation to their proximity to or distance from the desired goals of their tugging publics.

I explore embeddedness in order to clarify the complexity of circumstances within which schools operate. These circumstances indicate the general nature of the ties to local and nonlocal publics; the tangle of often competing interests that center their benefit-seeking advocacy on schools; and the resulting difficulty faced by those who hope to reform schools or to ally with schools for some problem-solving endeavor.

A Multiplicity of Constituent Publics

The plethora of constituent voices that have an impact on schools arise from our commitment to democracy and our sense that it sanctions both the hearing and the honoring of the voice of the people. This plethora also arises from two other circumstances. First, though considered a profession, teaching lacks the authority accorded by outsiders to other professions. To be sure, no profession is assumed to have perfect mastery, but no profession more than teaching enjoys this assumption to such a limited degree. Consequently, everyone may feel entitled to speak out on the subject of schooling.

Second, the disposition to speak out is reinforced by our tradition of local control. People generally believe their local schools belong to them; precious beings—their children—attend them. A refrain with considerable currency is, who knows better than parents what is good for children? Indeed, a problem generated by the multiplicity of constituent publics is whose sense of "better" will prevail, given uncertain, ambiguous authority?

These strands supporting the right to speak out originate in the traditions of this country; we take them for granted. Other strands relate to expertise—the rights that training and experience confer on educators. Still others spring from law—the rights that are specified for citizens, legislators, and school board members.

With or without explicit reference to one of these strands, each person may arrogate to himself or herself the right to shape, define, influence, or criticize the local, state, or nation's schools. As a result, resolving whom our schools should serve, in what ways, and by what means, is as simple as defining the nature of responsibility and authority in American society—which is to say, less ironically, that our schools are set in an intricately complex web of near and distant, single and multipurpose, overt and covert, formal and informal interests and advocacies. All constituents invest in a conception of their well-being; none is disinterested. All may presume rights, hold expectations, tender prescriptions. As well, all can vote, though their voting extends to different zones of influence, with different consequences. Compare the possible outcomes of voting for local-, state-, and federal-level officials; of voting, on the one hand, for school board members, and on the other, for governor or president of the United States. School boards hire superintendents who may set the educational tone of an entire school district; presidents hire secretaries of education who may set the educational tone of the entire nation.

Table 12.1 presents a summary perspective of educational constituents. It builds on the fact that individuals and groups have a particular type of relationship to schools based on the nature of

Table 12.1. The Nature of Educational Constituents.

Type of Constituent Interest in Schools	Basis of Constituent Interest in Schools	Examples of Constituents
Professional	Expertise	Educators
Civic	Law	Citizens
Legislative/Executive/ Judicial	Law	Legislators, governors, school board members, judges
Custodial	Tradition	Organizations, media, interest groups
Beneficiary	Law and tradition	Students, business, military, religious and ethnic subgroups, community, state, nation

their interests in a certain school, a set of schools, or all schools.[3] To base relationships on one type of interest does not preclude relationships based on another. The same person, for example, can have interests as a teacher (professional), a taxpayer (civic), a part-time graduate school student (beneficiary), and a teachers' union officer (custodial).

The general interest that locates a person or group within one of these five constituent types does not stamp all members of the constituency with the same outlook. Clearly, each constituency contains a range of possible competing and complementary manifestations of the general interest. For example, teachers and administrators are subtypes of professional constituents, but they do not necessarily share common views about the particulars of schooling, either within or across subtypes. This same qualification holds for the persons and groups within all five constituent categories. Indeed, constituents may find their allies for a particular educational cause in their own subtype or in the many other subtypes located in any of the constituencies. For different causes, different configurations of allies emerge.

The interest of any type or subtype of constituent assumes a range of forms in the life of the constituent. Consider the place of schools in the life of students—who are present by dint of law; of parents—who may be deeply concerned onlookers; of educators— who can be moved by the motivations of their own careers; and of nonparent citizens—who calculate the financial costs of what occurs in schools. The point is that as constituents perceive their interests, so do they relate to schools, expressing their concerns in large and small ways, occasionally or continuously, their involvement central or peripheral to their self-identity, their outlook narrowly or broadly focused on schools.

Interest, in short, covers a vast expanse of behavioral possibilities. Some of the possibilities remain latent until activated by an event that triggers constituent perception of a disagreeable difference. Such differences arise when constituents perceive a discrepancy between some current school practice or proposed reform and their own interests. They thus conclude that what is being proposed or done is harmful, not good enough, or too costly.

A final distinction among the interests of each type of constituent places the beneficiary type in a class by itself. The other four, in one way or another, act on the schools, some from the inside, others from the outside. Beneficiaries, receiving some good from the schools, acquire this good through the work of one or several of the other constituents. Simply stated, constituents try to influence educators, voters, legislators, or governors, who by virtue of their special relationship to schools can possibly affect what goes on in them. Their interest is in who receives what benefits at what cost.

The Professional Constituent

The professional constituent is grounded in expertise, the outcome of special training and experience. This expertise is the domain of those whose work focuses on one classroom in a single school (classroom teachers); all the classrooms in a single school (building principals); all the schools in a locality (school district administrators); or some curricular aspect of all the schools in a locality (school district curriculum specialists). Further, it is the domain of state and national educators, encompassing those whose work focuses on some aspects of the schools in a state (specialists in finance or curriculum, for example); on all aspects of a state's schools (the state superintendent of instruction); or on aspects of schools nationwide (educators working for the federal government in one of its several agencies). The work of professors of education ranges across the same spectrum, from the local classroom to the nation's schools, varying with the applied and theoretical nature of their professional work.

This partial rendering of the focal points of professional interests should serve to suggest the multiplicity of constituents drawing on expertise to relate to schooling. Unlike most other constituent types, the professionals have a daily, abiding interest in schools. Schools are the fixed scene of their work, the source of their continual well-being, sense of self, and security. The fate of professionals is tied directly and immediately to the fate of schools.

The Civic Constituent

The civic interest is the most ubiquitous because it contains all persons of legal age who are entitled to vote. Their interest is as lay public, contrasting with the professional tie of the educator and the official tie of the legislative/executive/judicial type. Civic actions, defined by law, include one voluntary aspect—voting—one involuntary aspect—taxpaying—and one combined case—that of the bond issue, whereby constituents are invited to vote for or against a tax rate or a project with financial implications. Voting for bond issues is optional; if they pass, paying for them is not.

The Legislative/Executive/Judicial Constituent

Among the numerically smallest but most powerful of the constituent groups is the legislative/executive/judicial type. Together, these constituents are legally authorized to make and interpret laws and to allocate money, with implications for the policies and practices of all schools in a state or the nation; of all schools of a certain type (for example, nonpublic); or for a particular aspect of all schools (for example, vocational or special education). Executive constituents are elected (sometimes appointed) persons who are empowered to make policy or financial decisions that affect educational practice. Governors and presidents have executive interests, as do school board members.

Like the professionals, the school board members' interest in the schools is not intermittent or episodic, rather, it endures as long as they retain their board membership. This is not true either for legislators (except those on standing committees that deal with education) or for those who work in an executive position. Their positions entail responsibilities broader than education; nonetheless, they have the largest official platform from which to make pronouncements about education.

The Custodial Constituent

All professional and civic constituents are served by constituents with a custodial interest, who constitute the fourth type of association with schooling. Custodians derive their warrant for association with education from tradition. They serve a guardian function on behalf of two subsets of constituents. The first subset comprises lay and professional persons with direct contact to a particular

school district—educators, parents, and school board members—
and professional persons who work in educational agencies (state,
federal, and so forth) or in colleges and universities. The custodial
service is promoted by organizations such as the Parent-Teacher
Association and the American Federation of Teachers. These organizations not only seek to ensure the immediate functional interests of their group, but also may take initiatives that address the
broadest questions about what education should be. Their charge
is to foster the interests of the group they were established to serve.
Each level of an organization—local, state, national—can attend
to the group's interests as they emerge at that level, often with help
from other levels. Organizations created to serve professionals by
school level (early childhood teachers) or by discipline (mathe-
matics teachers) also should be included within the custodial type
because they not only address pedagogical practices but also protect
their constituents' work by lobbying persons in the legislative/exec-
utive/judicial category.

The second subset is composed of all persons living within an
area as small as a rural school district or as large as the nation. For
this subset, the guardian function is that assumed by the media on
behalf of some interest for which it has taken up the cudgels. Constituents may initiate contact with the media on behalf of a cause,
or the media itself may do the initiating. While the media are no
more without a point of view than are other constituents, their
interests are not necessarily defined a priori by attachment to any
particular level, type, or outcome of education, or to any particular
group. More than reporting the news, the media are self-styled
watchdogs.

The Beneficiary Constituent

To grasp the extent of embeddedness of U.S. schools, it is essential
to understand the permeability of the boundaries within which
most schools operate. Does anyone feel constrained from speaking

out about or advocating the enactment of anything related to schooling? Are there any closed, sacred domains where constituents fear to tread? If the voices in nationally appointed blue ribbon committee reports garner more attention in the media and in scholarly journals and meetings, the less-anointed are quick to pronounce their own views. Moreover, it is uncertain whose voices actually count most when it comes to what educators do in their classrooms and schools. Much as schools might wish that they were less open to constituent scrutiny and proclamation, they appear to be open to the concerns and influence of wishful constituent publics.

As beneficiaries of the outcomes of schooling, individuals and groups come together to form the fifth and final constituency. Beneficiaries benefit; at the most general level, this is what is shared by those included in this category. To delineate benefits, however, is to differentiate the many types of persons who look to or routinely get benefits from schools. Students are the most fundamental beneficiaries. To be sure, students and their parents naturally center their notion of benefit on the student-child: What is good for him or her? And, at times, what is good for the family?

This narrow conception skirts the social functions of schooling, captured in the anthropologist's concept of cultural transmission, which relates to group survival and well-being. This function is most clearly perceptible in Mansfield, whose students learned to participate in maintaining the local community. Most broadly considered, the school's social function addresses the well-being of society. A good citizen embodies the exigencies of this function, for the benefit of all.

Societal benefits follow the impact of schools on students: first, students change or benefit in some way, then society benefits. For example, students learn what facilitates their becoming good workers, skilled in a trade, craft, or profession. They benefit from their work, as does their employer and, thereafter, the nation. This chain of benefits is, for many constituents, the connection between themselves and schooling.

Between benefits construed for students, on the one hand, and for the nation, on the other, is an infinite variety, limited only by what benefits can be imagined as the consequences of schooling. For the sake of providing some specificity to the array of possibilities, I have categorized constituent beneficiaries as follows:

- *Individual* (students and their families)
- *Civic* (the local, state, and national community)
- *Professional* (educators)
- *Ethnic* (Italians, Mexicans, Native Americans, and so forth)
- *Doctrinal* (including special interest and religious groups)
- *Occupational* (electricians, accountants, secretaries, and so forth)
- *Institutional* (business and industry, for example, R.J.R. Nabisco, Inland Steel, and RCA)

Schools are unsurpassed in the magnitude and variety of expectations held for them. The hoped-for benefits from schooling are so highly valued that their pursuit has spawned, and will continue to spawn, endless pedagogical variations at the combined hands of beneficiaries and professionals seeking educational means that best suit their purposes. These variations arise within both the public and the private school sectors. A list including urban magnet schools, schools taught in mountains or deserts, Waldorf schools, and elite boarding schools merely hints at the array of available forms that schools can assume.

The range and number of educational variations proliferates in response to the seemingly infinite capacity of constituents to construe academic forms that would better promote their benefits. The number of under-beneficiaries also increases. These are usually poor, minority students who often do not seek or receive benefits from schooling much beyond basic literacy and numeracy. They are the dropouts and the dropped out, the resisters and the refusers of school norms, whose putative deficiency of will and ability mark them as losers in schooling's game of benefits. This sad fact may motivate all five types of constituents to redress what is "wrong" with these relative nonbenefiters.

It is a problem for locality, state, and nation when constituent conceptions of benefits sharply differ and engender conflict. This is the case with school districts rocked by controversy over the acceptability of reading certain textbooks, performing a particular play, or including religious symbols on school-sanctioned occasions. A more persistent and exasperating problem occurs when some beneficiaries—the poor and the ethnic minority students—hold too minimal a conception of benefits to conflict with anyone else's. Such at-risk persons make those who actively seek schooling's benefits feel at risk when they do not avail themselves of the instrumental possibilities of our schools.

Though schools promise benefits of unassailable value, no one can verify what educational forms conduce to what benefits; furthermore, the nature and priority of the values underlying the benefits are controversial. Moreover, given the additive nature of school change, whereby new aspects more usually join rather than replace old aspects, schools may be overchallenged to accommodate the claims on their practices by a multitude of benefit seekers. Pressed to respond, educators learn a pedagogical tokenism designed to placate and satisfy, without doing injury to their pedagogical status quo. Over time, as educators repeat this type of response to externally induced change, they polish the wit and skill essential to deflect constituent pressure and to hold fast to the security of their educational routines. While schools may be importuned by benefit-seeking constituents, the latter's pursuits, however earnest, will fly or flounder depending on the willingness of the internal educational publics (students, educators, parents, school board members) to countenance what any constituent, internal or external, desires.

Impacts of Embeddedness at Riverview High School

The five high schools I studied are beholden to their host communities' aspirations, decisions, and financing—that is, they are subject to the manifestations of their several constituencies. On the local level, embeddedness influences what schools do now (the sustaining impact), what they should not do (the constraining impact), what they should do better (the ameliorating impact), and what they should do that is not currently done (the reforming impact). Beyond this level, embeddedness and the possible forms of its impact are engendered by constituent publics at state, regional,[4] and national levels. Though I discuss them separately, the four levels intertwine. In the following example, I characterize the nature of the embeddedness extant in all schools by extended discussion of the case in Riverview High School.

Constituent activity takes the expected forms in Riverview. The school's educators, its professionals, not only meet their classroom, building, and district obligations to teach and meet with other educators; they also attach themselves to nonlocal professionals as they pursue degrees, take courses, participate in workshops, and attend conferences. At any given time, an extensive, nonlocal, professional network encompasses the work of Riverview's educators. This network is fashioned by the interests of individual educators who see opportunity—for degrees or for professional growth—in some form of external professional contact. It is also shaped by the school district's central leadership, as when ethnic turmoil recently rocked the community and professionals were invited in to organize problem-solving workshops.

The local civic constituency votes on a regular basis to decide who will sit on Riverview's school board, a decision that determines the composition of this constituent group. On occasion, the civic public engages in a recall activity, which allows citizens to undo earlier decisions. Riverview was moved to a recall at the height of community distress in the early 1970s over a school board seen as insensitive to the interests of its nonwhite citizens. The recall vote, which failed, so mobilized the community that at the next regular election a new majority was forged. The orientation of the school board has remained changed to this day.

Given California's recourse to propositions to determine educational policy, Riverview's schools are influenced by statewide voter decisions relating to finance, curriculum, and language use. Indeed, there seems to be no limit to the school-related propositions that the state's civic constituency is invited to consider.

In California, a combination of energetic leadership in the state office of education and the frequent use of statewide education propositions acts to diminish, though not abolish, the options available to local communities for shaping their schools as community-maintenance institutions. Mansfield, Bethany, and Prep high schools were notably successful in reflecting the values of, and thereby perpetuating, their local communities of, respectively, place, doctrine, and personal aspiration. To some extent, the choice of whom to hire and fire retains for all localities the community-maintenance function.

A tension exists, however, between locally and nonlocally defined interests—the former directed to the good fit between community sentiment and school practice, the latter to the forms of achievement argued as good, say, for international economic competition or for national racial understanding. If such forms of achievement are not embodied in legislative decree, then schools may opt to ignore them. If such forms of educational achievement are embodied in legislative decree but do not square with the interests of local constituents, then the decrees risk subversion by educators and learners unwilling or unable to commit themselves to change.

At the state level, a legislature and governor are enabled by law to create policy that significantly shapes the school life of students and educators. During my research in Riverview, the high school was responding to a state mandate designed to make schools more academic. Riverview educators interpreted the mandate to mean it should increase academic requirements and thereby orient the curriculum more to the needs of college- and university-bound students. In a school whose students typically do not go to colleges or universities, this orientation is a significant departure from its usual, more vocationally oriented curricular practices. At the time of my study in Riverview, no constituents had felt a grievous discrepancy between their interests in a vocationally oriented curriculum and the increased academic requirements sufficient to motivate a reaction.

Of all the ways that school boards can affect schools, Riverview's school board acts on behalf of the community's constituent interests. As the focal point for districtwide decision making, school board meetings are attended by representatives from other constituencies. Years after the ethnic turmoil subsided, persons from minority ethnic group organizations monitor the meetings, believing that a watched school board behaves better than one not watched. Members of Riverview's teachers' union also attend the meetings, and are thus able to report to its own leadership how its interests are faring, and to consider the need for a response. Similarly, a reporter from the local newspaper observes each meeting, attuned to the possibilities of what might interest the paper's reader constituents. At the local level, custodial interest focuses on the school board. Its regular monthly meetings provide a public arena for all who want to scrutinize the compressed picture of school life that is enacted at such meetings, and also for all who want to exercise their right to influence school conduct.

In the event that custodial organizations or interest groups conclude that a sustaining, constraining, ameliorating, or reforming impact is needed, they call, write, or appear personally to express their interest. Educators, on behalf of their own interests, and school board members, on behalf of everyone's interests, entertain the petitions of the custodial group. This tripartite interaction became a regular feature in the 1970s because of ethnic groups' pressure for a curricular relevance that would place their people fairly in the instructional materials and practices of their children's classrooms. As often happens when ethnic or religious group interests are provoked, the same issues also are played out elsewhere in the state and nation. The result is a possible intensification of constituent concern and enhanced awareness of educational alternatives for what can and ought to be done.

Schools have a legion of beneficiary constituents. In Riverview, when the issue of ethnic curricular relevance stirred passions, a group of white parents rejoined with pressure to emphasize "the basics" and patriotism. Groups with some sense of distinct identity sought recognition in the school district's ethnic calendar of heroes and important historic occasions. Getting one's fair share of the benefits became the order of the day. Federal monies made possible the building of library collections and the hiring of full-time specialists to promote ethnic interests. The availability in Riverview of state and federal money represents the success of some sets of constituents to reach the keepers of the purse strings.

Local businesses in and around Riverview benefit from the high school's work-study program, which enables students to spend part of each day at work in an out-of-school job. Special regional vocational programs, available to students from all nearby school districts, provide training for jobs in nearby shops and factories. In these programs, special populations get access to jobs with training that are not available in Riverview, to the benefit of both students and employers. The military benefits by its access to schools for the purpose of administering tests and recruiting for some branch of the armed forces.

Given that the interests of Riverview's constituents basically are satisfied within the region of its county, the school and its users (students and their families) are not ordinarily attuned to constituent forces much beyond the region. In contrast, Prep High School's graduates not only attended colleges and universities outside New Mexico, but they also sought jobs all over the country, their special experience at Prep High turning them toward career and lifestyle opportunities available, so they thought, only in more sophisticated places.

Beneficiaries troop expectantly through the schools: students seek access to jobs, careers, and further education; all levels of polity seek enlightened voters and responsible citizens; business and industry seek effective workers; and religious groups seek schools that are safe by their doctrinal lights. For better and worse, Riverview High School and all its kin attract new constituents who see in schools an opportunity for some interest to be promoted, for some benefit to be gained. Accordingly, we have seen the impact of past and present interest in safe driving, safe sex, and safe thought on driver education, sex education, and censorship. We have also seen the interest in better bodies, better workers, better thinkers, and better shoppers that has resulted in physical education, computer education, training in higher-order thinking skills, and consumer education. Benefit seekers may succeed in the passage of legislation that compels schools to offer interest-satisfying instruction, thereby contributing to the shaping of schools, piece by piece. Beneficiaries with an interest in the whole of school life do not abound.

Conclusions

Every person in this country, visitor or resident, citizen or alien, benefits from schooling, at least at the most fundamental level of school-learned and school-reinforced knowledge, skills, and affect that contribute to civility and personal and occupational efficacy. Beyond this fundamental level, where matters of value and goodness become moot, people may play their professional, civic, legislative/executive/judicial, custodial, or beneficiary roles with ever-increasing degrees of concern, energy, and determination. As the degrees scale upward, so too do constituent clamor and consciousness of their stake in schooling and of how this stake may be affected by, for example, a change in amount and distribution of funding, a change in teaching methods or content of instruction, or a change in a school's relationship to out-of-school agencies. Furthermore, constituents may heighten their efforts to affect educational policy and practice by one or more of their possible activities: voting, legislating, lobbying, advocating, informing, protecting, resisting, or researching.

Schools are embedded institutions. They are susceptible to the flux generated by those constituents inside the school and in its host community, as well as by those located outside. The flux is a compound of electoral, legislative, judicial, and executive decisions, and also of the individual and group urgings, recommendations, and lobbying of a matrix of multilayered, multivalued constituents. For different reasons, they feel entitled to express their preferences and to shape what goes on in schools. Accordingly, schools also are contested institutions.

Rather than be surprised or dismayed by this contestedness, constituents bent on changing schools, or on collaborating with them, should strive to understand the results of an embeddedness that derives naturally from a complex of concerns, desires, and benefits. All of these elements fuel constituent interests that impinge on the lives of learners and educators. Quiet times for schools may be preceded and followed by times of raging debate, and all points in between. Given the diversity of this country, constituent interests always will be more or less at odds, some conflicts ultimately unresolvable (because they incorporate antithetical first principles), others subject to settlement or compromise (because they occur in a local school district where the necessity of working out some form of modus vivendi eventually becomes unavoidable). Schools may be both mired in and buoyed up by this embeddedness. In itself neither negative nor positive, embeddedness always is a fact to be reckoned with.

As long as constituent interests and their extant pedagogical implications go uncontested, schools remain quiet; the status quo is taken as the proper order of things. If contested, interests become stakes, and stakeholders learn the boundaries of their interests, where they clash with those of others, and the extent of their own tenacity to hold fast to their own.

Interests invest constituents in some dimension of schooling that usually is well short of the whole educational life of learners, educators, or schools. The partial nature of most constituent interest in schooling means, obviously, that most attend only to one aspect of school life. Attending to more than one aspect takes constituents beyond their interest and, often, well beyond their expertise.

Some constituents may be interested in a whole unit of schooling: district superintendents may be interested in their entire district, state superintendents and governors in their entire state, and congressional legislators, the president of the United States, and philosophers of education in the entire nation's schools. Those who speak and act at a whole-unit level are not necessarily accepted by other constituents. Furthermore, such an encompassing degree of interest is daunting and most difficult to sustain; many who operate at this level are in ad hoc groups, such as blue ribbon committees charged with preparing a state-of-the-schools report. They do their work and go home, since the overarching vision they may have developed is not likely built on and sustained for subsequent whole-unit undertakings.

If most constituents have partial interests and those with overall interests operate at untenably graspable levels of complexity, then it is the partial interests that are most forcibly and cogently argued. Moreover, most professionals gain their expertise in some aspect of the educational whole. Partiality and all that it connotes is a likely outcome; another is that at best we have very few constituents who become skilled in working at the level of whole units, where the need is for consummate statesmanship. Small wonder that schooling suffers from a dearth of constituents capable of taking a long, broad overview.

At all levels of education—district, state, region, or nation—we pay a price for not comprehending the embeddedness of schools. The price is incurred for not appreciating the extent of constituents always ready to propose reforms (a new organizational structure, a new technology, a new conception of middle school science), or, to the contrary, to resist on any grounds what anyone proposes. Failing to grasp this fact, the reformers bump into the harsh reality of oppositional interests, even when proposing reforms with unimpeachably sterling qualities, and the resisters denigrate the motives and efforts of those perceived as trespassers on the terrain of their professional comfort. Not to imagine whose interests may be threatened or served by a particular reform is to forego the opportunity to become informed about what and who must change if change is to succeed (Lippitt, Watson, & Westley, 1958); sooner or later, failure is the probable outcome.

Schools are not readily available for change. Their necessity for accomplishing a communal or societal good engenders hope that springs eternal: knowing that we need schools to attain some good, we naively assume their availability for that good. By such naiveté, constituents for reform court failure for otherwise sound ideas. This hope may be particularly nourished when constituents want to use schools not for their subcultural transmission function, as in the rural, Christian, and prep schools I researched, but for their problem-solving function—that is, for the problems students are presumed to bring to school that interfere with their benefiting from education, as in the multiethnic and Indian schools I studied. In such schools, students enter with perceived deficiencies of language, attention, interest, health, and family support. The schools, including many that poor and minority children attend, may reach inside to create academic options deemed suitable for nonmainstream children, and outside to work with community organizations in the belief that schools alone cannot remedy the deficiencies that impede children's success. Such causes are inarguably worthy. Their progress, however, may falter at the roadblocks set by constituents inside and outside the school who conceive the intent and practice of schools in other terms. If the cause is worthy while the knowledge of institutional embeddedness is lacking, the cause may collapse.

With schools embedded in layers of constituent interests, educators may become awash in a sea of words. They can be immobilized by this flood; they can ignore it. When they cannot ignore the portion of it that bears an official imprimatur, they may learn to resist and subvert it. Older educators can respond with the learned cynicism of "This, too, shall pass." Some local educators may be offended by the perceived arrogance of noneducator constituents as well as by educator constituents—geographically and otherwise removed from their sociocultural community—who deign to extend claims and plans based on "alien" interests and benefits.

There can be no stemming the verbal floodtide; it accompanies America's tradition of democracy. Shutting down debate, discouraging voice, does not square with our sense of constituent prerogatives. At our best as a nation, we fight to give voice to those who have been mute. At our best as individuals, we try to resist the constituent interest within us that seeks only what is good for our own children. This conclusion is easiest to sustain when it does not relate to the relatively scarce benefits of status, authority, money, and power. The best of us may draw the line at egalitarianism in the realm of such valued benefits.

If the floodtide waxes and wanes and the substance of the particular interests varies over time, it remains a constant in American society. Those who have daily, enduring, or official ties to schools must become students of their embeddedness. They must comprehend how embeddedness operates, the fact of its protean complexity, and that constituent stakes can take the form of self-serving interest or enlightened self-interest, but seldom disinterest. Too much is at stake in schools for their resources to be squandered in the course of reform efforts that ignore the legitimacy and potentially creative confusion of a multitude of constituent interests and pressures.

Given the considerable attention paid to schools in the last several decades, educators may feel stuck to a hot seat of over-concern, over-expectation, and over-promise. Excess does not breed comfort. Everyone wants schools to do good, if not to undo bad. Schools are everyone's pet panacea. This is the downside, but likewise the upside. In this excess there is a ferment, a dynamism, that not only puts schools on a hot seat, but also stimulates newly participant constituents—for example, professors, philanthropists, foundations, corporations, and communities—by means of new money, ideas, and needs. For educators to gain more than they lose from this ferment and to see more opportunity than misery in constituent hyperactivity, perhaps they, their custodial organizations, and their mentors and masters in schools of education and state departments of education need training beyond pedagogy and its allied fields of study. Perhaps they need training that helps them understand the magnitude and meaning of institutional embeddedness and how to find opportunity in its profusion of constituent voices.

And for urban-community constituents to successfully incorporate schools as allies in the cause of their community, participants from both school and community must collaborate in long- and short-term activity. Most particularly, those publics outside the school who wish to reshape schools for the sake of some new and worthy ends must appreciate what the educator public inside the school always knows: each fall, schools open for another year of educating children as teachers themselves were taught, and as they, as prospective teachers, learned to educate. Their disposition to carry on with the tasks of schooling in conventional ways is anchored in self and in educational, local, and national history and tradition.

Grant the best of circumstances: good plans and good people in the community and in the schools to reorient the schools to effectively respond to community needs. If a due awareness of the implications of institutional embeddedness is not wed to the good plans and people, I am pessimistic about the prospects of their success.

Most fundamentally, for schools to be agents of integrated services to children, school and community constituents must ask: What and who needs to be changed for such a change to occur and be sustained over time? Who and what is included in the unit of change, beyond the school, for the proposed reorienting of school practice to succeed? What resources of time, space, energy, opportunity, and so forth are needed in the short, mid, and long term? Is the continuity of wise leadership available to direct the process of change?

I raise these questions not to discourage those who would undertake change, but once again and finally to be cautionary: because schools are embedded institutions, they are not readily available for change. Clearly, for the reorientation of schools to be instrumental in the new ways invited by inner-city communities, more is needed than good hearts, good goals, and good people agreeing that serious problems must be resolved. What more is needed cannot be contained in a formula or a list of steps to follow. Each collectivity that embarks on change plans involving schools can begin with general understandings about schools, but then must proceed by taking account of the particularities of their constituent publics.

Notes

My thanks to Maryann Peshkin, Philip Zodhiates, Sue McGinty, and Elliot Eisner for their helpful comments.

1. Since I recently completed the data collection for the study of Prep High School and Indian High School, I have no books to cite.
2. In several years of contact with Indian High School, I seldom heard Indians refer to themselves as Native Americans. I use their term for themselves.
3. Others have written well and usefully on the embeddedness of American schools. See especially Chapter Four of Wirt and Kirst (1989). They provide an excellent overview and analysis of the practice of interest groups. See also Cohen (1978),

who focuses on the reform of the political relationship between schools and interested groups.

4. I do not elaborate on the many regional agencies that focus on education, such as accrediting associations, research professionals, and others whose locus of interest includes more than one state but fewer than fifty.

References

Cohen, D. K. (1978). Reforming school politics. *Harvard Education Review*, 48(4), 429–447.

Lippitt, R., Watson, J., & Westley, B. (1958). *The dynamics of planned change*. Orlando, FL: Harcourt Brace Jovanovich.

Peshkin, A. (1978). *Growing up American: Schooling and the survival of community*. Chicago: University of Chicago Press.

Peshkin, A. (1985). *God's choice: The total world of a fundamentalist Christian school and community*. Chicago: University of Chicago Press.

Peshkin, A. (1991). *The color of strangers, the color of friends: The play of ethnicity in school and community*. Chicago: University of Chicago Press.

Wirt, F. M., & Kirst, M. (1989). *Schools in conflict*. Berkeley, CA: McCutchan.

Chapter Thirteen

Commentary

Breaking the Cycle of Causation

Samuel F. Redding

The chapters by Bartelt (Chapter Ten) and by Yancey and Saporito (Chapter Eleven) both explore a theoretical model described as the "ecology of education." By this the authors mean that a school is best understood by considering its embeddedness in various levels of systems, or ecologies. Four systemic levels are outlined in these chapters:

1. The national patterns of family migration that result from shifts in macroeconomic factors

2. The particular urban area, including race and social-class segregation found in neighborhoods and school attendance

3. The more dynamic system of incentives, public policies, and personal preferences that cause some students to attend private rather than public schools and/or elect busing to attend schools outside their neighborhoods, and some teachers to use seniority privileges to choose to teach in particular schools

4. The school itself

The promise of this line of inquiry lies in the potential to break a vicious cycle of causation that has tied education theorists in a knot of circular argumentation for a quarter of a century. Bartelt and Yancey and Saporito state the paradox well: differences in social/familial factors are reflected in differential educational attainment, and differences in educational attainment (due to the credentialing power of schooling as well as the acquisition of knowledge and skills) affect social/familial situations. The central question is whether schools can effectively break this discouraging cycle or whether they must merely reflect and perpetuate the socioeconomic ecology in which they are embedded. A secondary question, not explored here, is whether the credentialing function of schooling actually exacerbates the cycle of poverty and low academic attainment more than is warranted by the substantive deficiency in students' knowledge and skills.

Macroeconomic Trends

The macroeconomic trends of cities during the last few decades have been in the direction of decentralization (the spread of cities' populations into broad, suburbanized, metropolitan areas) and from manufacturing to service-oriented bases of employment. Center cities are experiencing population decreases and the loss of jobs; the jobs they retain are increasingly in the service sector, which features a greater dichotomy of wages (that is, high-paying, skilled jobs and low-paying, nonskilled jobs) than did manufacturing, which provided a substantial base of middle-income employment. Poor people become poorly educated and remain in areas in which the number of jobs is declining and, increasingly, the only jobs available to unskilled (poorly educated) workers are in the low-paying end of the service sector.

A city's position in the national system of cities determines the extent to which it suffers or benefits from macroeconomic trends. Northern cities were most industrialized and have suffered most from the shift away from industrialization. Western and Sun Belt cities need not carry a deteriorating industrial base into a new era; they benefit from an influx of the most mobile families pursuing the best jobs in the expanding economic sectors. Interestingly, within a category of cities, increased job opportunities tend to result in more racial and socioeconomic segregation.

In a northern city such as Philadelphia, public schools have higher proportions of minority and poor children than does the city. The schools, however, are less racially segregated than the city. White and higher-income families are more inclined than low-income families to send their children to private schools, thus increasing the percentage of poor and minority students in the public schools. Experienced teachers also choose to teach in the same schools that children who are bused choose to attend. Lower-status children, regardless of race, are likely to walk to a local school, while higher-status children are likely to ride buses to a more cosmopolitan school. Thus, public schools are less racially segregated than the city but more segregated by socioeconomic status.

Socioeconomic status, then, is a more important determinant of educational climate than racial/ethnic composition. Yancey and Saporito (Chapter Eleven this volume) define educational climate in terms of four measures: (1) years of experience of teachers, (2) average daily attendance, (3) percentage of students bused, and (4) rate of student turnover. But what is the relationship between educational climates, as defined by these four factors, and student academic performance, as measured by standardized achievement tests? Faculty experience is not a significant predictor of achievement when the other three measures of educational climate are controlled. Experienced teachers merely use their seniority privilege to gravitate to schools where achievement is already superior. Student turnover is also problematic because, when controlled for racial composition, it loses any predictive connection to achievement.

What remains, then, is an argument that academic achievement is higher in schools with higher percentages of bused students (who tend to be from the relatively higher-income families in their neighborhoods) and higher average daily attendance. This raises basic questions: Is achievement primarily a function of the family or of the school? Is it the initiative of parents who request busing and already possess a level of commitment to and involvement in their children's education that will in other ways contribute to higher achievement, or does their selection of what they perceive as a better school simply result in their children's receiving a better education from a better school?

While the schools with more experienced teachers, higher average daily attendance, less turnover, and higher percentages of bused students produce higher achievement test scores, individual students who attend the classes of more experienced teachers, exhibit lower mobility and higher attendance, and elect busing do not, themselves, achieve higher test scores than their counterparts in the same school. Indeed, teaching experience, attendance, low turnover, and bused students are all indicators of a positive school climate—one that attracts teachers and students and that keeps them in class. The school must be doing something right to attract teachers and students in the first place. Or perhaps the school began with a base of high-achieving students enabling it to attract experienced teachers and students whose families take the initiative to bus their children. Both Bartelt and Yancey and Saporito would suggest the latter explanation. The socioeconomic community affects the character of its student population which, in turn, affects the educational climate of the school (stability, attendance, faculty experience, bused students) and also achievement. Simply put, student achievement is directly linked to the socioeconomic status of the community in which a school is embedded and of the students themselves.

Do bused students perform better in the target schools than they would have in the neighborhood schools? How do we control for the factors of family choice and initiative in making this determination? What is it that families with higher socioeconomic status possess that enables their children to perform better in school? Is it the same thing that enables the families to attain higher socioeconomic status? If it is an identifiable set of parental attitudes and behaviors, how can a school reach out to its community to encourage the proliferation of these attitudes and behaviors? If it is social capital, how can the school engender social capital? If it is a richness of experience, how does the school provide that experience?

In asking these questions, we first assume that the school is the appropriate institution for altering the attitudes and behaviors of the community in which it is embedded. If the school is not the appropriate institution, how does it ally itself with the institutions that are better suited for changing communities? Integration of services in a school-community relationship may provide a framework for building and influencing communities in ways that ultimately contribute to academic learning. This will happen, however, only if changing community and family attitudes and behaviors is seen as an objective of service integration.

Schools Embedded in Communities

Alan Peshkin (Chapter Twelve) addresses the subtleties of community and provides a bridge from both Bartelt's and Yancey and Saporito's focus on the connection between community/family variables and school performance to a consideration of the possibilities of shaping communities and influencing family behaviors. He begins with a wonderfully crafted narrative that describes his first contemplation of the concept of community in relation to schooling. He then moves in to a multilayered taxonomy of schools and their constituents, of communities and their components.

The complexity of Peshkin's logically structured analysis conveys the dynamic nature of social organization, both formal and informal. He does not fall into simplistic categorization, viewing people, for example, as solely teachers or parents or students. Rather, he calls attention to the bracing reality that a teacher may also be a parent, a taxpayer may also be an educator, a Methodist may also be a school board member, and so forth. Schools are embedded in a dynamic, chaotic, complex array of communities, all of which lay claim to its soul as a rightful privilege of democracy.

While cheerfully celebrating the variegated richness of democratic society, Peshkin acknowledges that schools are beset by a deafening cacophony of constituent voices. Educators are singularly subject to criticism from every parent, priest, and publican because they lack a "protective bulwark of technical mastery" (Peshkin, Chapter Twelve this volume). Everyone has gone to school, so everyone feels free, compelled in fact, to comment on the practices of educators and the conditions of schooling.

While democratic society arranges itself into infinitely complex subgroupings that overlap and are in constant motion, schools retain broad similarities that defy the diversity of the students and communities they serve. Public schools, especially, evince a stupefying sameness underneath the idiosyncracies of their mascots and team colors. Schools, whether in rural Mansfield or suburban Riverview, are very much alike in their structure, their routing, and their internal culture.

Throughout most of American history, some families maintained a tug-of-war with schools. Compared to the value of their children's work, the value of education was ephemeral. Farm families needed children to plant and harvest; shopkeepers needed children to stock shelves; urban families needed children to bring home cash from the many odd jobs inherent to city life. When children were in school, they were able neither to help at home nor earn income outside the home. To many families, the value of children's labor was greater than the value of education. In the past generation, however, the value of education has become almost universally recognized. Poor families have little use of their children's labor and, in fact, find in school a temporary relief from the burdens of child rearing. The job market demands a threshold of education, compulsory education laws require school attendance, and mass culture (including mass media) trumpets the necessity of education to a satisfactory lifestyle.

If education is universally valued, why then do some families, as Bartelt and Yancey and Saporito relate, complete paperwork to get their children accepted to schools outside the neighborhood and arise early in the morning to place their children on buses, while other families send their children off to the neighborhood school thinking little of an alternative? The difference is not in the value families place on education but in their attitudes and behaviors in navigating through the seas of their everyday worlds. Whether born into the communities of Mansfield or Riverview, the congregation of Bethany, the tribe of Indian High School, or the social stratum of Prep High School, a child is born a doctor or a lawyer or a teacher or a president in the secret heart of his or her mother or father. Americans value education and its fruits, but environments have a way of obscuring and mitigating values—some of the environments that sustain parents' lives are also filled with cold realities that wear away at their dreams. Yet, miraculously, every year in every class that graduates from Mansfield or Riverview or Bethany or Indian High, some young person will go on to be a doctor, and another a lawyer, and another a teacher, and another will become president of something. In the poorest of schools, some children succeed; in the best of schools, some children fail.

A lesson to be drawn from Alan Peshkin's chapter may be that while democracy spawns many voices, the voices of parents and teachers must close their ears to the clamoring constituents and multilayered ecologies, and whisper to one another their dreams for their own children and students. A school community can be too broadly defined, muddying the mix with too many competing but distant interests so that the result is a compromised blandness, one more school that is in too many ways like all other schools. Or a school community can be appropriately defined to include only those who hold dreams for children they can call by name, thus fueling the value for education and encouraging behaviors that benefit children.

Bartelt and Yancey and Saporito force the reader to confront the question: What do rich people have that makes their dreams come true? Is it resources, personal characteristics, social capital, or linguistic vitality? Or is it simply money? In fact, the "rich" in Bartelt's and Yancey and Saporito's studies are not rich by an absolute standard; they are only of higher income than those in their own neighborhoods who opt for neighborhood schools. By absolute standards, many of the families who choose to bus their children to schools are poor. Peshkin forges beyond simple distinctions of social class to examine the multitude of loyalties, affiliations, and attachments found among constituents of a school community. Some families are temporarily poor—graduate students with small children, unemployed managers, masses of people in the throes of economic depression. This type of poverty, however, is not likely to result in low academic attainment because these families retain histories of autonomy; they will make tough choices, postpone gratification, and behave in ways that ultimately benefit their children. Other families are locked into multigenerational poverty, retaining little memory of a world that is within their control, holding little hope for a better tomorrow, and possessing few habits of life that foster their children's academic success. Yet they value education and dream of their children's success in school.

If service integration is to succeed, it must proceed in ways that encourage family autonomy, choice, and perceived linkage between the value of education, the behaviors that encourage academic success, and the educational outcomes that lead to a better life. If, on the other hand, service integration means bringing more of the smothering welfare mentality to the people left behind in the neighborhood schools their more assertive friends have fled, the children of the poor will not be served. What children of the poor need most are schools worth choosing and parents with the opportunity and inclination to make the choice.

Chapter Fourteen

Commentary

Collaboration and Family Empowerment as Strategies to Achieve Comprehensive Services

Don Davies

Families, communities, and schools hold shared and overlapping responsibility for the healthy development and the social and academic success of all children. The nature and quality of the connections among the multiple institutions in every child's world are of major importance to the child's successful development. Children and their families do not experience their lives in neatly compartmentalized ways, but the policies that support educational and human services at all levels reinforce fragmentation and reduce the chances that children and their families will get the help they need.

In this commentary I argue that comprehensiveness should be a primary policy goal, to be sought in order to address the problem of fragmentation, and that collaboration and family empowerment are key strategies to achieve comprehensiveness.

This argument comes in the midst of a floodtide of policy activity about family-school-community relationships in the United States. Much of this activity, which began in the mid-1980s, bears directly or indirectly on the primary theme of this volume—integrating education and other human services.

The strongest and most numerous waves have been and will probably continue to be at the state level, where there is a multitude of new legislated mandates, regulations, and programs. Many of these developments were reported and analyzed in two reports (Davies, Burch, & Palanki, 1993b; Palanki & Burch, 1992) of the

Center on Families, Communities, Schools, and Children's Learning (referred to in this chapter as the Center). New state initiatives are reported almost every day.

There have also been significant new federal streams as well, accompanied by a multitude of eddies of local initiatives not directly tied to federal and state policies, and a great many ripples created by the private sector through foundations, advocacy groups, research centers, and special commissions.

To continue the metaphor, the tide is running unevenly from community to community, state to state, and across federal agencies. The nature of these developments and their real and potential impact has hardly begun to be felt by most frontline practitioners and administrators. Additionally, there is little more than anecdotal evidence to date concerning what the effects have been on the ultimate beneficiaries—children and their families.

Why is there such a surge of policy activity in this arena? The large gap between growing social, educational, and economic needs and society's response to these needs is the most obvious starting point for an answer. The needs grew just as local, state, and federal programs were being cut back or expanding slower than the demands for service. Service providers were constrained by lack of money and also by the arduous task of changing policies and traditional practices to meet new conditions and the needs of new constituents.

The growing needs and the slowness of government institutions and schools and other service providers to change their traditional ways produced high levels of concern on the part of business leaders and economists about the connections between these conditions and the nation's declining productivity and competitiveness with the developed countries of Asia and Europe. Corporate leaders became active in educational reform efforts.

Concerns also grew about the threat posed by the gap between need and institutional response to the nation's aspirations for social justice and equal opportunity for all people. Major advocacy groups increased their visible efforts and captured the attention of some policymakers.

Research and policy work also began to have some impact in the arena of family, school, and community. Several examples can be cited: (1) the High Scope studies showed the lasting positive effects of good early childhood programs that combined education, health, and family interventions (Raney & Campbell, 1987; Weikart, 1989); (2) James Comer's success in increasing achievement in several New Haven, Connecticut, schools called attention to the importance of the whole child, and linked emotional, physical, social, and intellectual development (Comer, 1980); (3) a growing body of research showed a positive relationship between student achievement and parent engagement in children's learning (Epstein, 1982; Henderson, 1987); and (4) many studies confirmed the connection between good health care and nutrition from prenatal through infant and toddler stages on children's later physical, social, and academic success (Zigler & Freedman, 1987).

Many policymakers became interested in greater government and agency efficiency as one answer to the need-response gap and paid attention to proposals for "reinventing government" (Osborne & Gaebler, 1992), examining interagency coordination, privatizing some services, decentralizing and reducing the size and control of central bureaucracies, and so forth. A search for efficiency as an antidote to limited resources led some state policymakers to consider various approaches to coordination among education and other state agencies, "reinventing" the service integration idea that had received a great deal of attention in the 1960s and 1970s (for example, the federally funded Model Cities program and Elliott Richardson's services integration task force and pilot projects).

As the broader school restructuring and reform movement gathered steam in the late 1980s in a number of states and cities, some efforts were made to incorporate parents and community representatives into restructured mechanisms for school planning and governance. The traditional advisory committee was often employed, despite the accumulated evidence bespeaking the token nature of most such devices. Parent participation in decision making and governance was given slight attention in developing policies, except in the important cases of the Illinois legislation that formed parent-dominated local school councils in every Chicago school, and the Kentucky Education Reform Act.

In my view, the impetus for policy change has come largely from the elites and from policymakers themselves, with little evidence of grassroots or consumer demand, as was present in significant ways in the 1960s antipoverty and civil rights movements. Families or, to use Eric Eisenberg's phrase, "end users" have not been involved much in the initiation, planning, or execution of the new policies.

The origins and present directions of the flood of policy activity designed to promote family and community involvement make me fearful that there may ultimately be little direct benefit to these end users, particularly those who are poor.

When the Center was created in 1990, we were determined to examine policy activity with a critical lens and be especially concerned about the perspective of families. We developed a multiyear policy project to do just that.

A Multiyear Project

During the first year of our work we traced state and policy developments in six areas related to family-school-community collaboration: (1) interventions for infants and toddlers, (2) family support, (3) coordination of health and human services with education, (4) parent choice, (5) school restructuring, and (6) Chapter 1 of the elementary and secondary education legislation. As we assessed policy activity in these areas, we applied several criteria: flexibility, intensity, continuity, universality, participation, coordination, and comprehensiveness. We noted substantial but uneven state activity and concluded that fragmentation was still characteristic of the system. We called on federal, state, and local policymakers to coordinate policies that sought to bring parents, communities, and schools together to enhance children's development (Palanki & Burch, 1992).

In the second year of our effort, we examined in some detail federal and state policy activity and local implementation in four areas: (1) service integration, (2) transition from preschool to kindergarten, (3) parent involvement in decision making, and (4) services for migrant and homeless children. Most federal and state policy activity continues to be highly categorical, targeted at specific populations, and bound by specific funding earmarks and limits. A highly compartmentalized, fragmented federalist policy system (or nonsystem) continues to be a major obstacle to making services and programs for children and families more comprehensive across broader categories of need, topics, and participants; fragmentation continues to be the reality between local, state, and federal levels and among the branches and executive units within each level. This naturally results in disjointedness at the service-delivery level—multiple local, state, federal, and privately funded agencies serve the same clients with overlapping (or sometimes conflicting) services, or fail to serve children or families at all because they do not fall within the correct "birthday window" or income requirement.

While we confirmed the inadequacies of the policy system, we also found a number of promising comprehensive projects and programs (Davies, Burch, & Palanki, 1993b). In the third and fourth years of the project, we gathered data about some of these promising programs that appear to be achieving some success in providing more comprehensive services to children and families, using strategies of collaboration and family empowerment. Our goal was to learn how some local administrators and frontline workers have learned to function within the existing fragmented system to serve their clients better and to take advantage of openings that make greater collaboration and family empowerment possible.

Policy Goal: Comprehensiveness

Through our analysis we have identified *comprehensiveness* as one approach policymakers or service providers are trying to address the problem of fragmentation in educational and social programs. This term denotes the pulling together of programs on the basis of the needs of children and families, as well as recognizing the interconnections between problems and developing varied strategies in order to resolve them (Davies, Burch, & Palanki, 1993b). Comprehensive programs and/or services demonstrate most or all of the following characteristics:

- They attend to the needs of the "whole child," which are multiple and interrelated and include physical, emotional, social, academic, and moral development.
- They recognize the needs of the families in which children are embedded, as children's and families' needs are connected.
- They are inclusive, not inflexibly bound by categories of participant characteristics.
- They allow for coordination with other programs.
- They provide for continuity across age levels.
- They allow for intensity of service that can be geared to level and nature of need.
- They are accessible to those who need the services, including those who are most distressed.

My reflection on our policy analysis to date and review of the other chapters in this volume encourage me to assert that the policies that foster programs with these characteristics will be more likely to "fit" the needs of children and families, even though I recognize that much more research and evaluation is needed to understand how these general characteristics work in practice and with what outcomes.

Strategy: Collaboration

While many strategies are being used to move toward comprehensiveness, I believe collaboration is critical if any significant degree of comprehensiveness is to be achieved in practice. According to Charles Bruner (1991), collaboration is a process by which goals can be reached that cannot be achieved by acting singly. Bruner views collaboration as a means to an end, not an end in itself; the primary end, I would assert, should be the responsiveness of comprehensive services and policies to family needs.

Bruner differentiates among levels of collaboration along a useful framework. His first level is primarily administrative at local and state levels and is what some analysts would call "coordination." The second level focuses on joint efforts of service providers from different agencies working together, not simply formal interagency arrangements. Examples of this type of collaboration include a partnership between a teacher and parent to support a child's need to improve math skills, or between a school counselor and public health nurse to connect a mother with a psychological counselor.

At the third level, frontline workers in a single agency are vested with the ability to use discretion in providing services; for example, a school principal might use funds from an education program to offer workshops on child nutrition to teenage parents. They are also given opportunities to participate in agency planning and decision making; for example, teachers and/or social workers are invited to sit on a program policy board. This level of collaboration introduces what my colleagues and I call "empowerment" of frontline staff.

Collaboration as Empowerment

In Bruner's fourth level, the concept of empowerment is extended to families—the end users or beneficiaries of programs and services. At this level, frontline workers—teachers, social workers, public health nurses, youth center counselors, and so forth—work with family members to determine family needs, set goals, and work toward greater family autonomy and self-direction.

This type of collaboration also empowers families. It enhances their capacity to get and use information; take action on their own interests and problems; meet their obligations to their children and communities; contribute to and influence policies and decisions affecting them; and function independently and effectively as community residents, workers, and citizens in a democratic society (Davies, Burch, & Palanki, 1993b). Empowerment is a vital part of collaboration and a means to comprehensiveness. More important, it is a core value of democracy—the right of those affected by the decisions of governments and institutions to influence those decisions.

Bruner's model helps make clear that the strategies of collaboration and empowerment are interlocking. Collaborative strategies should provide central roles for end users. In turn, empowerment strategies will help families become more effective as collaborators, with more to bring to the partnerships that are forged.

Looking for Examples

There are several initiatives in which policymakers and service providers are seeking greater utilization of comprehensive approaches. The Kentucky statewide school reform program, the New Jersey Good Starts Program, the Even Start Program, and the School-Based Integrated Services Program in Dade and Broward Counties, Florida, are four examples of initiatives that have moved toward the framework of comprehensiveness (Davies, Burch, & Palanki, 1993b).

We have found, however, very few examples of collaborative initiatives that have been able to achieve high levels of family empowerment. The scarcity of illustrations of worker-family collaboration is a reflection of the strong traditions of top-down planning and decision making in education and the human services fields, from the levels of federal to state, state to city or town, city or town to individual school or agency, school or agency to front-line worker, and, finally, professional to parent or client.

Parent Involvement in Decision Making

Scores of federal and state policies require or encourage involving family members in decision making at the state or local level, usually through advisory committees, policy boards, or task forces. These requirements seldom seem to acknowledge what has been learned over many years about how such participation can be made useful and why it is often so meaningless.

The participatory policies are often duplicative, vague in terms of function, and not well connected across state and local levels and categorical programs. For example, a parent of a child participating in a decision-making council in Head Start or a special education program is unlikely to be offered the same kinds of opportunity and support once the child moves into Chapter 1 or regular education classrooms.

Few states reported working to build a coordinated statewide system of parent or community collaboration that extends from local programs up through statewide planning committees. There are numerous examples of building-level efforts to involve parents in advisory or decision-making roles, but few instances of family involvement in state-level planning and policymaking boards. It is as though the assumption is being made that families need not be involved in decisions that affect large numbers of children.

There are a few examples of federal and state policies that encourage well-designed participatory mechanisms, provide for coordination across programs and continuity across ages of children, and, most important, appear to produce positive results in local practice. California's work to encourage state-to-local and state-federal coherence in parent participation requirements is one such example. Other examples include Denver's Family Opportunity Program, the Dade and Broward Counties School-Based Integrated Services Program, and the Head Start demonstration projects.

Policy Design to Support Family Empowerment

Empowerment must go well beyond opportunities for participation in decision making, policymaking, or advisory groups. My colleagues and I propose some elements of policy design that support strategies of collaboration and family empowerment in local programs. These elements are not exhaustive, but are intended to point to concrete steps that policymakers can consider:

1. *The family as agenda setter and partner in collaboration.* As agenda setters and partners in collaboration, families can play many different roles, including (1) assessors of the needs and strengths of family, school, and community; (2) designers of and decision makers in programs; (3) implementers of programs in paid and voluntary roles; and (4) evaluators of program outcomes.

2. *Multiple access points to service.* Providing comprehensive services to families with differing and overlapping needs requires multiple access points to services, such as community centers, schools, and/or churches. Providing multiple access points includes many strategies, from co-location of services to referral networks.

3. *Broadly representative advisory or policy boards.* Representatives of all or most of the agencies affected in planning and implementation should be included in project councils, boards, or task forces to foster a collaborative spirit. To involve families effectively on advisory and policy boards will require clear specification of purposes and functions, as well as authority on budget, personnel, and program; provision of staff assistance; and opportunities for training. In addition, such boards need to develop creative approaches to accommodate diverse families and their needs (for example, proxies or surrogates for migrants or homeless families and interpreters for board members with limited English proficiency might need to be arranged).

4. *Opportunities for training parents to assume less traditional functions*. Training for parents to assume less traditional positions (for example, home visitors, facilitators, parent center coordinators) should be an important part of a strategy to empower families. This component should include counseling and opportunities for continuing education—from high school completion to community college to bachelor's and graduate degree programs.

5. *Individuals serving as advocates for families*. Collaboration at the worker-family partnership level can be encouraged by providing people who explicitly serve as family advocates. These individuals help make families feel more at ease working with professionals, increasing the likelihood that they will volunteer their input.

6. *Funding of community organizations*. New types of collaborative initiatives designed around the concept of family empowerment can be encouraged by allowing community-based organizations to apply directly for funds. These organizations often have more credible access to the most isolated or alienated members of a community than schools or social agencies.

7. *Special support services*. Special consideration of the needs of low-income and immigrant families, single parents, and those who live in hard-to-access areas or are homeless is needed to support collaboration at the worker-family partnership level. Examples of special support identified in the policy review include provision of transportation, translation and interpretation, baby-sitting, and child care.

8. *Collaborative evaluation mechanisms*. The policy review revealed evidence of only limited attention to and funding for special study and evaluation. Much of the emphasis in evaluation has been placed on single programs or projects. There is obviously a need to know much more about what works, under what conditions, and for what purposes, and for studies that examine outcomes across levels and program lines.

There are few reports indicating that families, the end users, are included in planning and carrying out studies and evaluations. The Center's Parent-Teacher Action Research Project is one important example (Davies, Burch, & Palanki, 1993a). In this project, which encompasses eight school sites in seven cities and rural areas, teams of parents, teachers, and community members have proposed, implemented, and studied various interventions to promote family-school-community partnerships. These partnerships have successfully involved parents as home visitors and/or program monitors. In short, family members and teachers have become both implementers and researchers.

To work with these elements, staff of the Institute for Responsive Education (IRE) have received funding from the Danforth Foundation, the MacArthur Foundation, and the Pew Charitable Trusts, to demonstrate in several additional field sites how poor families and frontline school and agency staff can together produce a program of family support and human services that will enhance children's academic and social success. The school sites were selected on a competitive basis from among members of IRE's League of Schools Reaching Out, an international network of approximately eighty schools working toward comprehensive programs of family-school-community collaboration.

This project, known as the Responsive Schools Project, has found a special niche in its from-the-bottom-up, consumer-driven approach. The project will seek to learn how to strengthen the capacity of poor families to shape and use programs of integrated human services, working in partnership with teachers, school specialists, and health and human services providers. Family empowerment is both our method and our intended outcome.

A Final Comment

Consumer demand can be a spur to policies for promoting comprehensive services with increased collaboration and family empowerment. Increased demand will allow end users—or the organizations representing them—seeking to influence policymakers an opportunity to press for policies that provide more comprehensive services.

The recent reorganization of public schools in Chicago provides an opportunity to test the proposition that parents with decision-making power will press for such policies as integrated services or for other forms of family-school-community partnership.

I believe that service delivery policies and practices are likely to be fragmented and unsatisfactory unless the role of families in shaping the services available to them is central. My rationale for this emphasis is a based on a now old but powerful idea, well articulated by Audrey Cohen (1978): "[To] agree that this [is] a noble goal toward which we should strive is not enough. It is necessary to specify how the ideal can be translated into achievable action. . . . The goal of citizen participation and the role of the client as an effective integrating agent are one and the same" (p. 4). Learning how to make the concept of family empowerment a reality must be an important part of the next stage in the development of integrated services and family-school-community collaboration if they are to take root and have a lasting and positive impact on families and communities.

References

Bruner, C. (1991). *Thinking collaboratively: Ten questions and answers to help policy makers to improve children's services*. Washington, DC: Education and Human Services Collaboration.

Cohen, A. (1978). *The citizen as the integrating agent: Production in the human services*. Washington, DC: Project Share, Department of Health, Education, and Welfare.

Comer, J. P. (1980). *School power: Implications of an intervention process*. New York: The Free Press.

Davies, D., Burch, P., & Palanki, A. (1993a). *Getting started: Action research in family school-community partnerships* (Report no. 17). Baltimore, MD: Center on Families, Communities, Schools and Children's Learning, Johns Hopkins University.

Davies, D., Burch, P., & Palanki, A. (1993b). *Fitting policy to family needs: Delivering comprehensive services through collaboration and family empowerment* (Report no. 21). Baltimore, MD: Center on Families, Communities, Schools, and Children's Learning, Johns Hopkins University.

Epstein, J. L. (1982). *Student reactions to teacher practices of parent involvement*

(Report P-21). Baltimore, MD: Johns Hopkins University Center for Research on Elementary and Middle Schools.

Henderson, A. (1987). *The evidence continues to grow: Parent involvement improves student achievement.* Columbia, MD: National Committee for Citizens in Education.

Osborne, D., & Gaebler, T. (1992). *Reinventing government: How the entrepreneurial spirit is transforming the public sector.* Reading, MA: Addison-Wesley.

Palanki, A., & Burch, P. (1992, January). *Mapping the policy landscape: What federal and state governments are doing to promote family-school-community partnerships* (Report no. 7, with D. Davies). Baltimore, MD: Center on Families, Communities, Schools, and Children's Learning, Johns Hopkins University.

Raney, C., & Campbell, A. (1987). The Carolina Abecedarian Project: An educational experiment concerning human malleability. In J. Gallagher & C. Raney (Eds.), *The malleability of children.* Baltimore, MD: Paul H. Brookes.

Weikart, D. P. (1989, June). *Quality preschool programs: A long-term social investment* (Occasional paper 5). New York: Ford Foundation Project on Social Welfare and the American Future.

Zigler, E., & Freedman, J. (1987). Head Start: A pioneer of family support. In D. Powell, S. L. Kagan, B. Weissbourd, & E. F. Zigler (Eds.), *America's family support programs: Perspectives and prospects* (pp. 57–76). New Haven, CT: Yale University Press.

Part Four

Lessons from Existing Programs

Chapter Fifteen

The Effectiveness of Collaborative School-Linked Services

Margaret C. Wang, Geneva D. Haertel,
and Herbert J. Walberg

Across the United States, innovative school-linked health and human services programs are being implemented to provide assistance to children and youth in high-risk contexts. These programs reach out to families beset by urgent problems including poverty, teenage pregnancy, single parenthood, substance abuse, limited health care, and inadequate and unaffordable housing (Levy & Copple, 1989). These problems place children at risk of school failure and, by necessity, place schools at the nexus of interconnected social problems.

For many years private and public community agencies have provided psychological, financial, medical, and job training assistance to individuals and families in at-risk circumstances. These individual agencies, however, often have heavy caseloads and limited resources, and are isolated from other service providers (Chang, Gardner, Watahara, Brown, & Robles, 1991). Increasingly, educators have cautioned that schools alone cannot respond to all these problems (Council of Chief State School Officers, 1989). Kirst (1991a) argues that more systematic social policies must be developed. Schools, according to Kirst, can no longer rely on their own school boards and property taxes to guarantee the well-being of students. The creation of interagency collaborative health and human services programs can provide a high-quality response to the problems faced by students in at-risk contexts. These collaborative programs would be linked to schools and other service agencies to prevent the overburdening of schools or any single agency.

Interagency collaborative programs reach out to those at greatest risk and mobilize resources to reduce and prevent school dropout, substance abuse, juvenile delinquency, teen pregnancy, and other forms of modern morbidity. Nearly all school-linked programs develop mechanisms for effective communication, coordinated service delivery, and mobilization of resources of communities.

Most of these innovative collaborative programs, although enthusiastically embraced, have not provided evidence of replicable, long-term, beneficial effects on students. The lack of empirical information documenting the near- and long-term impact of these innovations is a source of concern. Schorr and Schorr (1988) conclude that: "Many Americans have soured on throwing money at human problems that seem only to get worse. They are not hard-hearted, but don't want to be soft-headed either" (p. xvii). Increasingly, policymakers recognize the high cost of social programs that are not evaluated for their immediate, intermediate, and long-term effects. In addition, evaluators often only assess the impact of narrowly defined services and fail to assess the combined effects of multifocus interventions. Policymakers, school practitioners, and service delivery agencies do not have adequate information about program features and the implementation of innovative programs. This chapter presents a first attempt at establishing an empirical database documenting the relative effects of collaborative school-linked services serving children and their families in at-risk contexts.

A Chronology of Collaborative School-Linked Services

Since the 1890s, improving the plight of poor children and youth has been a goal of the U.S. public school system (Tyack, 1992). During the past century, social reformers advocated schools as the coordinating organizations that could orchestrate community services and remedy a wide range of social ills. Tyack (1992) documents historically the waxing and waning popularity of collaborative programs to meet the needs of students and their families. He finds that the past century has demonstrated that school reform, including the provision of health and human services, typically occurs from the top down, with advice from the community being ignored and programs intended for the poor frequently rooted in the wealthiest communities.

Reformers in the 1890s campaigned for medical and dental examinations, school lunches, summer academic programs, recreational activities, and school-based child welfare officers. Many of the health-oriented programs were based on a philosophy of improving the human capital of the nation's children and ensuring equal educational opportunity for them. However, reformers were not convinced of the capacity of parents, especially immigrant parents, to provide for all their children's needs. Sadly, social reformers rarely sought input from parents as they designed and implemented these new services. Tyack (1992) notes that although parents recognized the value of the health and medical services provided, some parents found these programs intrusive and sometimes fought the reforms to preserve their own authority and ethnic, religious, or community values.

Reactions to the programs varied. Conservatives expressed concern that the school's academic mission would be diluted. Progressive educators lauded the new services and believed that without them students would drop out of school. Financial officers were apprehensive about identifying sources of money to support the new services. Despite these varied reactions, collaborative school-linked services were entrenched in our nation's public schools by the end of the 1930s.

During the Great Depression, there was an increase in budgets and staffs for school-based services, especially health services (Tyack, 1992). By 1940, almost all cities with populations more than 30,000 had some form of public health service (70 percent run by the schools, 20 percent by health departments, and 10 percent by a collaboration of both). Other services, such as lunches and mental health, did not enjoy such sustained commitment. During the late 1940s, school lunches became the norm, despite conservative fears of excessive state control.

During the 1960s, education was viewed as a vanguard against poverty, and funding for school-based social services was increased. The collaborative programs established after World War II involved a greater degree of community participation. The enlarged role of the community, however, sometimes spawned conflicts among community groups, school officials, and service agencies. Despite these difficulties, Lyndon Johnson's "War on Poverty" had reached millions of children by 1970, and collaborative programs had found a niche in public schools. Collaborative programs received support from influential community groups, did not clash with prevailing instructional approaches, and met some of the needs of poor children.

Collaborative programs were transformed as they became established in the public schools (Tyack, 1992). In an attempt to address truancy, for example, some school social workers became part of the schools' bureaucracy. This change represented a shifting of goals among school social workers. Some social workers began to employ models from community mental health agencies, while others began to work with more privileged clients. To ensure the political viability of new social services, legislators often generalized such programs. Thus, although services were delivered best in wealthy communities with large property tax bases, the children of both the wealthy and the poor became recipients of collaborative interagency services.

From the late 1960s to the early 1980s, the role of the schools shifted toward producing students who could succeed in a competitive global marketplace. This shift, combined with significant budget cutbacks, reduced some of the social services provided earlier. Despite the reduction in services, the nonteaching staff remained sizable. Teachers accounted for 70 percent of all school employees in 1950, but only 52 percent by 1986, indicating that schools had become multipurpose institutions that looked beyond the academic performance of their students (Tyack, 1992).

Schools have become the location of choice for collaborative programs. Larson, Gomby, Shiono, Lewit, and Behrman (1992) argued that schools are enduring institutions that play a critical role in the life of communities. With this history (Tyack, 1992), they can deliver services to children and their families in a nonstigmatizing manner.

Not everyone views collaborative school-linked services as a panacea. In the controversial book *Losing Ground*, Charles Murray (1986) argued that government services, including school-linked programs, produce long-term negative consequences for recipients. He maintained, for example, that school-based health clinics contribute to the increase in the number of unmarried pregnant teenagers. Murray cautioned policymakers of the unintended effects that may emerge as government services proliferate.

Solutions other than collaborative school-linked programs have been proposed to reduce risk factors. Kirst (1991b) identified the use of vouchers, tax credits, a negative income tax, and less costly approaches (such as traditional parental care for children) to ameliorate the myriad social ills surrounding students in at-risk contexts.

The Status of Collaborative School-Linked Services

In *Within Our Reach: Breaking the Cycle of Disadvantage*, Schorr and Schorr (1988) gathered, over the course of twenty years, information from researchers, practitioners, administrators, and public policy analysts supporting the efficacy of collaborative programs. They identified risks that affect the lives of children, including premature birth; poor health and nutrition; child abuse; teenage pregnancy; delinquency; family stress; academic failure; persistent poverty;

inaccessible social and health services; and inadequate housing, medical treatment, and schools. They argued that these risks require a societal response, not simply a response from the affected child or family.

The authors held that there is plenty of information available on both risk factors and effective interventions to guide action. They identified three principles that capture the role and function of collaborations in breaking the cycle of disadvantage: (1) a call for intensive, comprehensive services that address the need of the "whole" child and the community; (2) a recognition that the family should be supported, not displaced, by other social institutions; and (3) a shift in efforts from remediation to early intervention and eventually to prevention. They are two of many advocates calling for collaborative integrated services to supplement the schools' role in society (see Behrman, 1992; Chang et al., 1991; Hodgkinson, 1989; Melaville & Blank, 1991; Morrill & Gerry, 1991; National Commission on Children, 1991).

Levy and Copple (1989) documented the groundswell of state-level efforts to develop collaborative integrated services from 1975 to 1989. They record that in that fourteen-year period, fifteen written agreements were prepared; twenty interagency commissions were formed to coordinate state and local agencies; eighty-eight committees, commissions, and task forces were convened; and sixty-three collaborative programs and projects were implemented. The twenty-fourth annual Gallup poll provided further evidence of the popularity of collaborative integrated services: 77 percent of adults favored using schools as centers to provide health and social welfare services by various government agencies ("Public in Poll," 1992).

Rationale for Collaborative School-Linked Services

Three features of collaborative programs have been identified: joint development of an agreement on common goals and objectives, shared responsibility for the attainment of goals, and shared work to attain goals using the collaborators' expertise (Bruner, 1991). Morrill (1992) asserted that collaboration requires concerted action, not just communication, among committed partners. In this chapter, collaboration is defined as the process of achieving a goal that could not be attained efficiently by an individual or organization acting alone.

Data on the incidence and costs of children's problems show an increase in some problems, such as delinquency and the need for foster care; other problems, such as dropout and teenage pregnancy rates, though decreasing, require higher benefit expenditures and result in reduced student productivity (Larson et al., 1992). Such evidence supports the need for systemic responses to these problems. Melaville and Blank (1991) characterized the current system of organized services for children as crisis oriented, compartmentalized, disconnected, and decontextualized.

Instrumentalism and incrementalism are dominant political beliefs evidenced in policy toward at-risk children (Kirst & Kelley, 1992). Instrumentalism justifies social interventions by the economic or social returns they produce; as such, it becomes useful for society to invest in school-linked services as a method for meeting the needs of underprivileged families. Incrementalism justifies social interventions only in cases of extreme parental and familial dysfunction. These political beliefs support the use of collaborative school-linked services as a strategy to meet the complex needs of children and their families.

Key Features of Collaborative School-Linked Programs

Collaborative school-linked services can help guarantee the educational accomplishment of children (Wang, Haertel, & Walberg, 1993) by providing access to medical, psychological, and economic resources that are necessary—but not sufficient—conditions for academic success. Many types of collaborative school-linked programs have been targeted toward the needs of students in at-risk contexts

(Levy & Shepardson, 1992; Wang, 1990). Within GOALS 2000, the educational reform package supported by the Clinton administration, a number of projects include schools as centers of community services (U.S. Department of Education, 1993). Current collaborative programs include those directed at parents of young children, teenage parents, pregnant teenagers, dropouts, homeless children, and alcohol and drug abusers.

There is no single model for collaborative school-linked services (Levy & Shepardson, 1992); rather, new programs emerge out of the needs of children and families in local communities. Collaborative school-linked services can be described in terms of their goals, the services offered, the location of services, and the service providers. Another key feature of school-linked programs is whether they provide services alone, curriculum and instruction, or both.

Curriculum-based programs provide knowledge to recipients. Dropout programs, for example, may provide remedial instruction in basic skills, while teenage pregnancy prevention programs may provide information on conception, contraception, and pregnancy. Other curriculum-based collaboratives include programs that teach new mothers and fathers about their children's developmental stages, supply information on the effects of drug use, or provide educational activities for preschool children. Some programs not only present information but teach new skills. One example is the drug prevention program that not only provides knowledge about the effects of drug use but also teaches refusal and coping skills.

Some collaborative school-linked programs are not curriculum based but rather extend services to targeted clientele. These types of collaborative programs may provide health and mental health care, recreation, housing, day care, substance abuse treatment, transportation to appointments, and other services. Some programs provide both curriculum and services.

Collaborators in these programs also vary. Early collaborative programs brought teachers and parents together to improve the academic achievement of children. Other such programs involve health care workers, social workers, psychologists, university researchers, business people, community volunteers, and peers.

Levels of Collaboration

Bruner (1991) identified four levels of collaboration that can occur in organizations. The first level describes interagency collaboration at the administrative level, often at top managerial levels in state and local governments. This level of collaboration often results in the creation of task forces, coordinating councils, changes in staff organization, or incentives and job evaluation systems to promote interagency collaboration. The second level of collaboration involves giving incentives to service delivery workers for working jointly with staff in other agencies. The third level of collaboration involves changes within a single agency. At this level, service workers are encouraged to help clients by going beyond procedures and rigidly applied rules. Supervisors are encouraged to interact collegially with service workers and handle individual cases in ways that promote a balance of responsibility and authority. The fourth level of collaboration exists between the client or family and service workers, in which they work jointly to identify needs and set goals in order to increase the self-sufficiency of the client.

Identifying Current Programs

This chapter summarizes evidence presented in forty-four sources describing one or more collaborative school-linked programs. The literature search, selection of criteria, and coding procedures are described below.

The Literature Search

A search was made of practitioner and research journals in education, public health, public policy, and social services. A key article, "Evaluation of School-Linked Services" (Gomby & Larson, 1992), identified sixteen current collaborative programs. In addition, a search of the Educational Resource Information Clearinghouse (ERIC) and the 1992 annual conference program of the American Educational Research Association (AERA) was conducted and relevant papers were secured. Finally, forty-five different organizations were contacted, including state and local agencies as well as project staffs. These efforts resulted in the identification of fugitive documents that were available only from the agency sources and not yet available in libraries.

Selection of Sources

A few basic criteria were used for the selection of sources for this study. All sources had to present results from programs involving school-based collaboration. In any single program, the school could be involved as the provider of academic services, the central location where families access social and health services, or the goal of the program (as in readiness programs that prepare children for success in school). The programs selected involved students from preschool to high school. Collaboration or integration among institutions and agencies was a primary aspect of programs selected. All the programs were designed to impact the lives of children or their families; were implemented in the past decade; and contained an outcome-based evaluation or some measurement of short-term, intermediate, or long-term results. Some evaluations contained process or implementation data, but process data were not required for a study or evaluation to be included.

Coding Procedures

The types of sources selected included narrative reviews, interventions, program evaluations, meta-analyses, and correlational studies. All were published since 1983. Ten features were coded for each source: (1) type of source (for example, narrative review, program evaluation); (2) sample size, referring to the total number of clients or program sites (for meta-analyses and quantitative syntheses, the sample size refers to the number of studies analyzed); (3) at-risk contexts served by each program; (4) program goals; (5) outcomes; (6) collaborators or partners in the program; (7) type of evidence reported (that is, numerical—including frequencies, percentages, means, and standard deviations; statistical—including hypothesis and significance testing; or qualitative—including anecdotes, client statements, or administrator perceptions); (8) data collection tools (such as school records, interviews, performance tests, achievement tests); (9) nature of cost data (that is, none, minimal, and cost-effectiveness or cost-benefit analysis); and (10) curriculum-based versus services orientation or both.

The forty-four sources identified were then divided into six categories: parent education and school readiness; teen pregnancy prevention and parenting; dropout prevention; chemical dependency and prevention; integrated services (programs designed to integrate services from a variety of different agencies and address multiple risk factors); and parent involvement. A list of bibliographic citations for each of the forty-four sources synthesized is available from the Temple University Center for Research in Human Development and Education.[1]

Key Features of Six Program Areas

The forty-four sources for the present review were organized under six program areas. For each area, the at-risk context, goals, collaborators, and curriculum-based versus service orientation are reported in Table 15.1.

At-Risk Contexts

Many of the collaborative school-linked programs are targeted for urban, low-achieving, and economically and socially disadvantaged

Table 15.1. Key Features of Six Program Areas.

Program Area	At-Risk Context	Goals	Collaborators	Curriculum Versus Service Orientation
Parent Education and School Readiness (8 sources; 18 programs reviewed)	Uneducated, low-income families with young children often in urban areas; teenage parents.	Parental competencies; family literacy; children's academic achievement; provision of health and social services.	Social and healthcare workers, schools, private foundations.	Both—(a) curriculum includes child development, child-rearing practices, and parental self-help; (b) services include home visits by nurses and social workers, transportation to appointments, counseling, health screening, access to resource centers.
Teen Pregnancy Prevention and Parenting (5 sources; 7 programs reviewed)	First-time, unmarried, low-income, pregnant teenagers; a few designed for ethnic minorities in urban areas.	Pregnancy prevention: provide information about birth control, sex, and pregnancy in order to prevent pregnancy; provide contraceptives. Teenage parenting: provide knowledge about pregnancy, birth control, child development, and parenting skills; promote completion of mother's high school education; promote employability and job skills for mothers.	Schools, home nurses, Planned Parenthood; other health and human service agencies; obstetricians, midwives, pediatricians, and nutritionists; university medical schools.	Pregnancy prevention programs: Both—(a) curriculum includes information on birth control, sexuality, and family life education; (b) services include counseling, medical exams, and contraceptives. Teenage parenting: Both—(a) curriculum includes information on birth control, sexuality, child care, and health education, prenatal care, job training; (b) services include prenatal care, transit to appointments, nurse home visitations, parenting programs.

Dropout Prevention (8 sources; 25 programs reviewed)	High school students often in urban areas, with history of high absenteeism and course failure; also students not able to conform to school expectations; sometimes students involved in criminal activity, chemical dependency, or teenage pregnancy.	Increase student attendance; reduce dropping out; identify and contact truant students; increase students' academic performance; increase probability of students' attending college or entering job market.	Schools; parents; juvenile justice departments; businesses; social services; and occasionally universities and colleges.	Both—(a) curriculum includes remedial basic skills and vocational education programs; (b) services include counseling, mentoring, health services, phone calls for absenteeism, preparation for GED, and coordination of Job Training Partnerships Act.
Chemical Dependency Abuse and Prevention (8 sources; 171 programs reviewed)	All students; some designed especially for urban minorities; Native Americans and children of alcoholics.	Reduce consumption of alcohol and drugs; increase knowledge about alcohol and drugs; promote coping skills against pressure to abuse substances; teach responsible drinking habits; develop self-esteem.	Peers; schools; community and social agencies; media; counselors; health care workers; police and businesses.	Both—(a) curriculum includes information on alcohol and drugs; social and decision-making skills; (b) services include peer and other counseling, alcohol- and drug-free activities, and support groups.
Integrated Services (6 sources; 6 programs reviewed)	Wide range urban and rural students; delinquent children; children from dysfunctional families; urban minorities; low-achieving youth.	Coordinate services (often coordinating services is an intermediate goal toward ends such as lowering dropout rates); often a single program encompasses multiple goals.	Schools; universities; businesses; state and local governments; foundations and non-profit agencies; health and mental health care providers; community and religious institutions; parents; peers.	Both—(a) curriculum develops a variety of knowledge and skills; (b) services include vocational counseling, health care, health and mental health services, and case management.
Parent Involvement (8 sources; over 240 programs reviewed)	Families of children from preschool to high school; frequently, urban, economically, and socially disadvantaged families.	Foster greater parental concern for children's educational achievement; improve academic achievement; encourage greater parent involvement in children's education; create more intellectually stimulating home environment; foster close family relationships.	Schools; parents; mental health providers; businesses; media; universities.	Primarily curriculum—parenting skills; child development information.

children and youth and their families. However, the Dropout Prevention, Teen Pregnancy, and Chemical Dependency program areas are targeted for all students.

Goals

Parent Education and School Readiness, Teen Pregnancy Prevention and Parenting, Dropout Prevention, and Parent Involvement programs all focus resources on improving students' academic achievement. In addition, many of these programs have goals that focus on parental competencies, family literacy, and child development and the provision of mental health and health services. Selected programs such as Teen Pregnancy and Chemical Dependency have particular goals associated with the program's special emphasis (for example, providing information on birth control, or about alcohol and drugs).

Collaborators

Across all program areas, the most typical collaborators include schools, families, and social and health care workers. A supportive but less central role has been played by universities, private foundations, religious institutions, the media, law enforcement agencies, and the business community. In the area of Chemical Dependency Abuse and Prevention, peers have played a key role in modeling refusal and coping skills, and in distributing current information on alcohol and drug abuse and prevention.

Curriculum Versus Service Orientation

In most collaborative school-linked programs, both curriculum and services are offered as part of the programmatic intervention. Parent Involvement programs are the exception, relying primarily on curricular interventions. The curriculum presented in most collaborative programs provides knowledge and new skills in the program's area of emphasis. Services most typically involve health care, transportation to appointments, and counseling.

Effectiveness of Collaborative School-Linked Programs

Each of the forty-four sources identified in the literature search was categorized into one of the six program areas, coded, and its outcomes analyzed. A total of 176 outcomes were identified and examined across the six program areas. Of these, 140 (or 80 percent) indicated that the interventions produced positive results; 29 (or 16 percent) reported no evidence of change; and 7 (or 4 percent) indicated that the interventions produced negative results. These counts provide information only on the direction of the outcomes, not the magnitude of the program effects. Thus, both small, insignificant improvements and large, statistically significant effects are all counted as positive results, regardless of the size of the improvements. Nevertheless, these overwhelmingly positive results point to the success of programs that promote collaborative school-linked services. The total number of outcomes and percentage of positive outcomes within each program are presented in Table 15.2. The percentage of positive outcomes ranged from 95 percent in Integrated Services to 68 percent in Parent Involvement programs. Even 68 percent is strong testimony to the efficacy of collaborative school-linked programs.

Effects on Program Participants' Cognition, Affect, and Behavior

The five types of outcomes commonly utilized in the research studies and evaluations of these collaborative school-linked programs are attendance; achievement test scores, grade point average, and academic grades; reduced behavior problems; self-esteem; and dropout rates.

In parent education and school readiness programs, positive out-

Table 15.2. Positive Outcomes by Program Area.

Program Area	Total Number of Outcomes	Number of Positive Outcomes
Parent education and school readiness	48	38 (79 percent)
Teen pregnancy prevention and parenting	6	5 (83 percent)
Dropout prevention	36	26 (72 percent)
Chemical dependency abuse and prevention	27	21 (78 percent)
Integrated services	37	35 (95 percent)
Parent involvement	22	15 (68 percent)

comes were reported for attendance ($n=2$), academic performance ($n=6$), reduced behavior problems ($n=5$), self-esteem ($n=2$), and dropout rates ($n=1$). No negative outcomes were reported.

Results for teen pregnancy prevention and parenting programs were very sparse. Although these programs attended, appropriately so, to reductions in pregnancy rates and increased knowledge of sexuality and child-rearing practices, they did not report the impact of their programs on most of the other common outcomes. They reported a positive outcome only on dropout rates ($n=1$). No negative outcomes were reported.

Dropout prevention programs reported a positive impact of their programs on three of the outcomes: attendance ($n=6$), academic performance ($n=7$), and self-esteem ($n=5$). One negative outcome was reported (academic performance: $n=1$).

Chemical dependency abuse and prevention programs also reported positive outcomes for attendance ($n=2$), academic performance ($n=2$), reduced behavior problems ($n=2$), and self-esteem ($n=1$). However, there were few instances of each type of outcome. Only one negative outcome was reported (self-esteem: $n=1$).

Studies of integrated-services programs have employed research and evaluation designs that captured student performance using a wide range of outcomes. Integrated-services programs reported positive outcomes in attendance ($n=4$), academic performance ($n=8$), reduced behavior problems ($n=6$), self-esteem ($n=2$), and dropout rates ($n=6$). One negative outcome was reported (attendance: $n=1$).

Of the five most common outcomes reported (attendance, academic performance, reduced behavior problems, self-esteem, and dropout rates), parent involvement programs have reported primarily academic outcomes. They document improved achievement outcomes ($n=6$) and attendance ($n=1$). No negative outcomes were reported.

Of all the documents measured by these collaborative programs, the most frequently examined was the academic performance of participants and the least examined was dropout rates. The total number of outcomes and percentage of positive outcomes by outcome types are presented in Table 15.3.

Attainment of Program Goals

In addition to their impact on students' cognitions, affect, and behaviors, each program was designed to attain specific goals, such as delay of first usage of drugs and alcohol, or reduction of pregnancy rates. The success of each of the program areas in attaining its particular goals is presented in Table 15.4. These results indicate that collaborative programs largely achieve the goals they set forth. The effectiveness of each program area is described below.

Table 15.3. Positive Outcomes by Outcome Types.

Type of Outcome	Total Number of Outcomes	Number of Positive Outcomes
Attendance	18	15 (83 percent)
Academic performance (achievement, grade point average, academic grades)	36	29 (81 percent)
Reduced behavior problems	17	13 (76 percent)
Self-esteem	12	10 (83 percent)
Dropouts	9	8 (89 percent)

Table 15.4. Attainment of Goals by Program Area.

Program Area	Total Number of Outcomes	Number of Positive Outcomes
Parent education and school readiness	30	22 (73 percent)
Teen pregnancy prevention and parenting	5	4 (80 percent)
Dropout prevention	11	8 (73 percent)
Chemical dependency abuse and prevention	19	14 (74 percent)
Integrated services	9	9 (100 percent)
Parent involvement	10	8 (80 percent)

Parent Education and School Readiness

Eight sources were examined in this program area. These sources reviewed results from eighteen programs. Results from the programs indicated favorable effects on maternal behaviors and mother-child interactions, whereas the effects on infant development were more modest. Program-favoring effects were also documented by an increase in community resources and parental participation in job training and employment. However, the effects on parental teaching skills were mixed; some programs were more successful than others, depending on the amount of time spent on maternal interactions and other specific behaviors. Overall, the programs demonstrated success in influencing the outcome domains closest to their emphases—for example, children's readiness for school, parenting skills, maternal development, and use of community resources. The long-term effects of these programs are more equivocal. Earlier evaluations of preschool programs have provided evidence that academic advantages fade over time but social and behavioral changes, such as incidence of grade retention, special education placement, and reduction of dropout rates, support the long-term effectiveness of parent education and school readiness programs (Lazar, Darlington, Murray, Royce, & Snipper, 1982).

Teen Pregnancy Prevention and Parenting

Five sources were identified describing results from seven collaborative programs. Results documented that clients' knowledge about pregnancy, reproduction, and birth control increased in all seven programs. One program showed evidence of participants' decreased willingness to engage in sexual activity at a young age. Generally, however, client attitudes toward the risk of additional pregnancies were not studied. Of the three programs that examined school retention of pregnant teenagers, all showed positive effects for immediate retention after the child's birth. Only one program examined the retention of mothers forty-six months after delivery. At this time, client dropout rate was comparable to that of pregnant teenagers who had not been enrolled in the program. Some increased concern about employment and decreased job turnover among the teenage parents were also documented. Two of the five programs for teenage parents that examined pregnancy rates showed a decline. Results from the two pregnancy prevention programs documented delayed age of first intercourse, decreased pregnancy rates, and increased use of birth control clinics and contraceptives.

Dropout Prevention

The overall national dropout rate has declined and, in the early 1990s, was at an all-time low (Wehlage, Rutter, Smith, Lesko, & Fernandez, 1989). In contrast, however, dropout rates in urban areas have remained high, focusing attention on the need for innovative programs in these locations. In this program area, eight sources were identified and twenty-five collaborative programs were described.

All but one of the programs increased students' attendance rates, and most increased students' grade point averages and the number of credits earned. Of the studies that examined dropout rates, a decrease was noted. Only one program assessed the longitudinal effects of a prevention program on dropout rates, and it demonstrated a continuous decrease in dropout rates. Behavioral indices across all programs revealed weak effects, including no evidence of decreased suspensions and disciplinary referrals and improved graduation rates. In addition, participating students did not have more definite graduation plans as a result of the program intervention. The study by Wehlage and colleagues (1989) explored the psychological effects of fourteen dropout prevention programs. Their results revealed modest positive effects on social bonding, sociocentric reasoning, self-esteem, locus of control, and academic self-concept.

Chemical Dependency Abuse and Prevention

Nine alcohol and drug abuse sources were reviewed. They included results from 171 programs; results from a meta-analysis contributed data from 143 research studies and evaluations.

The findings show that students' use of drugs decreases as a result of participating in chemical dependency programs. The effectiveness of these programs on alcohol use is less clear. It appears that the most effective alcohol and drug prevention programs are those that deliver knowledge about the effects of alcohol and drugs to students in combination with refusal and coping skills.

Based on results of a meta-analysis of 143 programs, Tobler (1986) documented the superiority of chemical dependency programs that involve peers as collaborators. The superior effects of peer programs reflect the special influence peers have on one another's behavior and the value of specific skills training. Peer programs are successful at modifying student behavior regardless of the drug being used. Chemical dependency programs that use peers as collaborators are likely to decrease student drug use—or at least decrease the likelihood that students will try new drugs.

Integrated Services

The six sources in the area of Integrated Services reviewed results from six collaborative programs. Outcomes measured by the programs were diverse; a few used institutional change as evidence of program success, but most relied on student outcomes including grades, attendance, attitudes, and noncompliant behavior. Other outcomes included degree of parental involvement, teacher attitudes, number of services provided to clients, and number of disciplinary and special education referrals.

Among the types of institutional change documented are linking existing institutions, holding joint planning and budgeting sessions, creating a management information system, hiring case managers, and forming business-school compacts.

Based on results presented in these programs, integrated-services programs have positive effects on students' achievement tests, grades, dropout rates, and attendance. Of utmost importance is the finding that all of the six programs show large numbers of services being provided to children and families in at-risk circumstances. A second important outcome, which is rarely reported, is the effect of these programs on teachers. In the Jewish Family and Children's Services (1991) project, teachers reported that their knowledge of child development and sense of responsibility toward the children increased with program implementation. The evaluation conducted by Philliber Research Associates (1991), moreover, suggested that children who received intensive case management exhibited higher academic achievement and better work habits despite increased absenteeism.

Parent Involvement

The eight sources reviewed in this area represent results from more than 240 parent involvement programs. Two of the eight sources were meta-analyses: Graue, Weinstein, and Walberg (1983) summarized results from 29 programs and White, Taylor, and Moss (1992) from over 200 programs. The remaining six sources reviewed included four program evaluations, one correlational research study, and one intervention study.

Results from the studies suggest that parent involvement programs have weak to moderate positive effects on improving children's academic performance. Although these programs improved parental involvement in children's education, their impact on academic achievement was mixed.

The two meta-analyses provide conflicting evidence about the effects of parent involvement programs. Graue and colleagues (1983) found that programs to improve parent involvement and home environments in elementary school have large effects on children's academic learning. On the other hand, employing results from early intervention programs for preschoolers, White and others (1992) concluded that "average effect sizes of treatment versus no-treatment studies in which parents are involved are about the same as the average effect sizes of treatment versus no-treatment studies in which parents are not involved" (p. 118). Based on these findings, they concluded that there is no basis for parent involvement programs to claim cost-effectiveness.

Evaluating Collaborative School-Linked Programs

Many studies of collaborative school-linked programs suffer from high attrition, control groups that are not comparable, and a wide range of unique outcomes, some of which are based on measures of unknown reliability and validity. Few data are reported on implementation of process. In addition, many evaluation reports do not document the magnitude of program effects nor include information on costs, making it difficult to judge the practical significance of the programs.

Often collaborative school-linked programs make use of varied (and sometimes conflicting) goals, assumptions, definitions, procedures, and analytic tools. Additionally, studies of these programs are frequently designed by teams of researchers from several disciplines and social and health care agencies that have a service delivery perspective.

Innovative programs are designed to achieve specific outcomes. Systematic evaluation of the program's implementation is central to the validation and improvement of the program. The traditional treatment/yield paradigm and classic pre- and posttest control group experimental designs, while useful from a conclusion-oriented evaluation perspective, are not sufficient in determining whether a program has been successfully implemented. Evaluations must include documentation of the following: What elements of the program need to be implemented (and at what levels) to make the program work? What are the critical features of the programs that should be observed to validate program implementation? What barriers interfere with the successful implementation of the program?

Evaluating the collaborativeness of these programs poses a major challenge. There are few direct measures of collaborativeness. Should it be measured by linkages among institutions, by the accessibility of services to clients, or by the satisfaction of the collaborators?

The evaluation of collaborative school-linked programs requires identifying a wide range of client outcomes. Evaluators should be concerned not only with process and implementation data, but also with measuring improvement in student academic achievement, school attendance, graduation rates, decreased pregnancy rates, coping skills, reduced behavioral problems, and other cognitive, affective, and behavioral outcomes. Most important, collaborative programs need to document whether their clients are able to access readily an increased number of community resources.

As with most reform efforts with broad agendas, collaborative school-linked programs are faced with many, often competing, demands. Strategic planning, responsible implementation, and, above all, practical wisdom are required as these innovative programs unfold.

Conclusions

Five conclusions are drawn from the current review of collaborative school-linked programs:

1. The challenges that face children, youth, and families in at-risk contexts are generated from a mix of cultural, economic, political, and health problems. The complexity of these conditions defies simple solutions. To solve these problems resources must be gathered from the community—public and private agencies, local and state health and human services departments, and businesses and religious institutions—and coordinated with the resources available in schools.

2. Narrow plans that reform a school's instructional program alone will not solve the problems addressed. Policymakers, practitioners, and the public must be made aware of the importance of integrating community resources with the educational resources available in schools.

3. Empirical results from current collaborative school-linked programs are positive but have to be regarded cautiously. Many of these programs have not been rigorously evaluated. Evaluation and research studies of these programs often contain inadequate descriptions of the program components, use a limited number of outcomes, have few direct measures of collaboration, do not collect process or implementation data, do not have comparable control groups, have high rates of attrition, and report few data on program costs. The studies of collaborative school-linked services that are available are those that are published. As published evaluations and studies

generally report positive findings, the results presented in this chapter may be biased in a positive direction. Further research and more rigorous evaluation are needed to arrive at general policy conclusions.

4. Better implementation data are needed to validate the effectiveness of these programs. Evaluation reports must include documentation of linkages among agencies, the changing roles of administrators in schools and service agencies as they collaborate, the changing role of staff, and the establishment of a management information system.

5. There is little communication among researchers, policy analysts, policymakers, and practitioners concerning the growing knowledge base on collaborative school-linked services. Operational strategies and tactics need to be identified to support collaborative school-linked services. These strategies should link district administrators, middle management, principals, teachers, and service delivery agencies so that key information is accessible to all collaborators.

Collaborative school-linked services are becoming a common feature of the educational reform landscape. Although the programs demonstrate positive outcomes, the results must be treated with guarded optimism until results from more rigorous evaluation and research studies are available.

Note

1. Bibliographic citations are available from Dr. Margaret C. Wang, Director, Temple University Center for Research in Human Development and Education, Ritter Hall Annex, 9th Floor, 13th Street & Cecil B. Moore Ave., Philadelphia, PA 19122.

References

Behrman, R. E. (1992). Introduction. *The Future of Children, 2*(1), 4–5.

Bruner, C. (1991). *Thinking collaboratively: Ten questions and answers to help policymakers improve children's services.* Washington, DC: Education and Human Services Consortium.

Chang, H., Gardner, S. L., Watahara, A., Brown, C. G., & Robles, R. (1991). *Fighting fragmentation: Collaborative efforts to serve children and families in California's counties.* San Francisco: California Tomorrow and the Children and Youth Policy Project, University of California, Berkeley.

Council of Chief State School Officers. (1989). *Family support, education and involvement: A guide for state action.* Washington, DC: Author.

Gomby, D. S., & Larson, C. S. (1992). Evaluation of school-linked services. *The Future of Children, 2*(1), 68–84.

Graue, N. E., Weinstein, T., & Walberg, H. J. (1983). School-based home instruction and learning: A quantitative synthesis. *Journal of Educational Research, 76*(6), 351–360.

Hodgkinson, H. L. (1989). *The same client: The demographics of education and service delivery systems.* Washington, DC: Institute for Educational Leadership/Center for Demographic Policy.

Jewish Family and Children's Services. (1991). *Schools partnership project: A successful model for improving school performance.* San Francisco: Author.

Kirst, M. W. (1991a). *Integrating children's services.* Menlo Park, CA: EdSource.

Kirst, M. W. (1991b). Toward a focused research agenda. In William T. Grant Foundation Commission on Work, Family, and Citizenship and the Institute for Educational Leadership (Eds.), *Voices from the field: 30 expert opinions on America 2000* (p. 38). Washington, DC: Editors.

Kirst, M. W., & Kelley, C. (1992). *Collaboration to improve education and children's services: Politics and policymaking.* Paper presented at School-Community Connections: Exploring Issues for Research and Practice (an invitational conference sponsored by the National Center on Education in the Inner Cities), Leesburg, VA.

Larson, D. S., Gomby, D. S., Shiono, P. H., Lewit, E. M., & Behrman, R. E. (1992). Analysis. *The Future of Children, 2*(1), 6–18.

Lazar, I., Darlington, R. B., Murray, H., Royce, J., & Snipper, A. (1982). Lasting effects of early education. *Monographs of the Society for Research in Child Development, 47.*

Levy, J. E., & Copple, C. (1989). *Joining forces: A report from the first year.* Alexandria, VA: National Association of State Boards of Education.

Levy, J. E., & Shepardson, W. (1992). Look at current school-linked service efforts. *The Future of Children, 2*(1), 44–45.

Melaville, A., & Blank, M. J. (1991). *What it takes: Structuring interagency part-nerships to connect children and families with comprehensive services.* Washington, DC: Educational and Human Services Consortium.

Morrill, W. A. (1992). Overview of service delivery to children. *The Future of Children, 2*(1), 32–43.

Morrill, W. A., & Gerry, M. H. (1991). *Integrating the delivery of services to school-aged children at risk: Toward a description of American experience and experimentation.* Paper presented at the Conference on Children and Youth at Risk (sponsored by the U.S. Department of Education and the Organization for Economic Cooperation and Development), Washington, DC.

Murray, C. (1986). *Losing ground.* New York: Basic Publishers.

National Commission on Children. (1991). *Beyond rhetoric: A new American agenda for children and families.* Washington, DC: Author.

Philliber Research Associates. (1991). *The caring communities programs: A preliminary evaluation for progress.* Accord, NY: Author.

Public in poll backs change in education. (1992, August 28). *New York Times,* pp. A9, A12.

Schorr, L., & Schorr, D. (1988). *Within our reach: Breaking the cycle of disadvantage.* New York: Anchor Books.

Tobler, N. S. (1986). Meta-analysis of 143 adolescent drug prevention programs: Quantitative outcome results of program participants compared to control of comparison group. *Journal of Drug Issues, 16,* 537–567.

Tyack, D. (1992). Health and social services in public schools: Historical perspectives. *The Future of Children, 2*(1), 19–31.

U.S. Department of Education. (1993, July). Snapshots: Communities on the move. *Community Update,* No. 4.

Wang, M. C. (1990). *Center for education in the inner cities* (Technical proposal). Philadelphia: Temple University Center for Research in Human Development and Education.

Wang, M. C., Haertel, G. D., & Walberg, H. J. (1993). Educational resilience in inner cities. In M. C. Wang & E. W. Gordon (Eds.), *Educational resilience in inner-city America: Challenges and prospects* (pp. 45–72). Hillsdale, NJ: Lawrence Erlbaum.

Wehlage, G. G., Rutter, R. A., Smith, G. A., Lesko, N., & Fernandez, R. R. (1989). *Reducing the risk: Schools as communities of support.* Philadelphia: Taylor & Francis.

White, K. R., Taylor, J. J., & Moss, V. D. (1992). Does research support claims about the benefits of involving parents in early intervention programs? *Review of Educational Research, 62*(1), 91–125.

Chapter Sixteen

The School of the Future

Implementation Issues in a School-Community Connection

Harriet H. Arvey and Alfredo Tijerina

Five years ago, planning began in Texas for a comprehensive experimental program covering the full range of proven innovations in school-community initiatives for children from birth to adolescence. Leadership was provided by Dr. Wayne Holtzman, president of the Hogg Foundation for Mental Health (hereafter the Foundation) located at the University of Texas, Austin, where Holtzman is also professor of psychology and education. He was assisted in the planning process by professional staff and advisers of the Foundation.

Foundation planners envisioned an experimental "school of the future" that would emphasize longitudinal evaluation of children's development, teaching and learning activities, community renewal, and family growth and development (Holtzman, 1992a). The importance of allocating time and resources sufficient to assure successful implementation of the key components was considered, as well as the need to gather baseline data for systematic study of changes in children and families. Planners believed a project of this nature should be adequately documented, analyzed, and interpreted for replication and that the essential features of what is now known as the School of the Future would have to be recognized and accepted by all stakeholders.

Dr. Holtzman and Foundation staff spent months in Austin, Dallas, Houston, and San Antonio (the cities selected to participate in the project), meeting with school district administrators and community leaders to develop and promote the School of the

Future concept and to gain local support. The success of their efforts was in large part due to the reputation of Dr. Holtzman and the Foundation's history of generous support for numerous locally developed programs across Texas. Further, the Foundation was known for providing continuing support programs by using its influence to broker ongoing funding from state agencies and other foundations. The Foundation supported program evaluation through additional funding and by linking research fellows and senior faculty from the University of Texas to local programs, a component that also contributed to the warm reception it received across the state.

Sites consisting of one or two feeder elementary schools and one middle school were selected in each of the participating cities. The Foundation provided initial grants of $50,000 per year per site for five years, committed in the spring of 1990; an additional $200,000 per year was set aside to provide technical assistance and evaluation support to each site.

The long-term goal of the School of the Future project as articulated by the Foundation was to enrich and enhance the lives of children in the four communities. Education and physical and mental health were all expected to be positively affected by the project over time. The Foundation envisioned that these outcomes would be accomplished through the development of a long-term partnership among local human services agencies, public school systems, teachers, parents, and the community. Each school district was invited to develop a proposal that included specific objectives, a budget, and a plan of work, and to secure necessary school board support.

Each of the districts hired a social worker as the coordinator responsible for the following:

1. Working with school administrators and teachers
2. Establishing links among school district personnel, local agencies, and other potential resources for the school's children and their families

3. Developing parent education, job training, and support programs that encourage parents to become involved

4. Identifying major concerns and needs of the students and their families

5. Creating an awareness of the program among school personnel, members of the community, and providers of services and funding

Each selected school was located in a low-income, minority neighborhood. In Austin, slightly less than 50 percent of the students in the project's one elementary and one middle school were Latino, 25 percent were African American, and 25 percent were white. In Houston, the two elementary schools and one middle school were located in low-income, predominantly Latino neighborhoods but had a significant number of African-American students. The middle school and one elementary school in the San Antonio project were in a heavily Latino neighborhood containing the oldest public housing project in the country. The two elementary schools in Dallas were located in a former shopping center that had been converted into a school. Together with the nearby middle school, this multipurpose facility served a predominantly poor, African-American neighborhood. During their first year of operation, the four projects developed in ways that were consistent with the social, cultural, and ethnic characteristics of each neighborhood (Holtzman, 1992b).

Research and Evaluation Plan

From the inception of the project, School of the Future planners at the Foundation considered the critical ethical questions relating to the evaluation design and its implementation. Dr. Scott Keir, a sociologist with the Foundation, was appointed to direct the evaluation. Five doctoral candidates from the University of Texas were appointed as research fellows to help with data collection and analysis. A group of evaluation experts from the University of Texas faculty were recruited and assigned to specific sites as advisers. In addition, each city had an evaluation adviser recruited from a local university or research institute. The evaluation team was further enhanced by the inclusion of the executive staff of the Foundation. The complete team of staff and advisers met frequently during the design phase and continued to meet every few months to review progress. Finally, a separate group of researchers handled the qualitative analysis from a historical perspective. As a result, the Foundation-supported evaluation teams from each site were made up of four or five members, whereas the teams assembled to oversee the program development and implementation consisted of one coordinator supported by the Foundation and administrators from the school district and community agencies who voluntarily associated themselves with the program.

The purposes of the evaluation were to assist in planning, to inform key decision makers, and to develop a blueprint for replication. The evaluation took the form of a nonrandomized experimental control group with a pre- and posttreatment design. Data were collected from all schools participating in the project, as well as from comparison schools matched demographically with the experimental schools. The plan called for cross-site as well as within-site comparison. Data collection procedures were standardized so that similarities and differences could be analyzed both across and within sites between project and comparison schools. Evaluation planners decided that repeated assessment of the same students as well as cross-sectional analyses of each grade level would be done over at least a five-year period (Culler & Keir, 1992).

Both short- and long-term outcomes were expected. Short-term changes were expected in school climate, parental involvement, and school-community relationships. Long-term changes were expected in the students themselves in mental and physical health and academic achievement.

One-hour-long key informant surveys were administered to a sample of approximately twenty teachers, parents, administrators, and community leaders at each site. Students were surveyed with three instruments during a single classroom period to provide baseline data. These included:

- Achenbach's Youth Self-Report, which measures the student's mental and physical health, including aggressive behavior, popularity, depression, delinquent behavior, somatic complaints, thought disorders, and identity problems (Achenbach, 1991a).

- The National Education Longitudinal Study of 1988 (NELS:88), which has been used extensively by the Center for Education Statistics of the U.S. Department of Education to survey students on various school issues (National Center for Education Statistics, 1988). The School Life section of NELS:88 measures how students feel about their school, their teachers, and their classmates and provides information on students' perceptions of school climate.

- The Self-Perception Profile for Adolescents, also known as Harter's Perceived Competencies Scales (Harter, 1982, 1985). The three most relevant subscales of the instrument were used—Scholastic Competence, Social Acceptance, and General Self-Worth. These short scales measure students' feelings about their academic abilities, social relationships, and general happiness in life. Each teacher was assisted in the administration of the survey by one graduate research associate. The survey was administered in the fall of 1991 to all sixth- and seventh-grade students at both participating and comparison schools. Data collection for students in the eighth grade began during the fall of 1993.

- Achenbach's Teacher Report Form (TRF), another version of the Child Behavior Checklist offered by Achenbach (Achenbach, 1991b). This instrument was used to gather data on children in kindergarten through fifth grade, who would not be able to complete the self-report version. (The Harter subscales and the School Life section of NELS:88 are not appropriate for younger children.) Early in the fall of 1992, the TRF was used in both the experimental and the comparison schools to collect information from teachers on all children in the lower grades. Teachers were compensated for their time in supplying the information.

A great deal of data were collected from the school districts' computer files. Demographic variables such as ethnicity and socioeconomic status were included along with academic indicators such as grades, standardized test scores, and attendance rates. With assistance from the research and evaluation departments at each of the school districts, data on more than fifty variables were transferred to the Foundation's computer data files. In addition to the student-level information, aggregate-level data on the schools and the districts were also collected. The district-level data make possible a comparison between School of the Future students and other students in the same school district. Additional data were gathered at some sites through other research efforts, particularly in Houston.

Obviously, a number of evaluation problems and issues emerged as Foundation staff began to work with the four different school districts. Fortunately, Houston Independent School District's research department had extensive experience conducting program evaluations and offered their assistance.

Process Evaluation

In addition to the evaluation just described, a separate process evaluation was designed to explore and document the sociological, political, and organizational realities that underlie the process of education and social service reforms in urban areas (Ellmer & Lein, 1992). The inclusion of Dr. Laura Lein, professor of anthropology, University of Texas, and her cadre of research assistants was seen as beneficial by many involved in the School of the Future, both as local program staff and as members of the Foundation's research team. Employing an ethnographic research approach to explore the meaning and process of organizational change from the perspective of participants at all levels, Dr. Lein and other researchers gave voice to the children and families involved in the implementation.

The process evaluation involved a revision and analysis of all records and correspondence related to the project as well as in-depth interviews with persons identified as pivotal to the development and/or evaluation of the project. The interviews were designed to elicit a detailed chronology of project events as experienced by different individuals. An open-ended systematic interview schedule was developed and adapted to reflect the level of involvement of each informant and the level of project development. Within each interview, a critical incident approach was taken to elicit specific illustrative examples of each point in significant detail. In addition to the interview reports, comparison site profiles were developed. The profiles and a summary of the report on the Houston program are included later in the chapter.

Houston's School of the Future

Serving 197,000 students in 240 schools, the Houston Independent School District (HISD) is the largest school district in Texas and the fifth largest in the United States. It is Houston's largest employer, with approximately 20,000 employees, more than 11,000 of whom are teachers. For many years HISD's predominant minority group was African American. The district did not desegregate until 1970 and was under court order until 1986. For many years the Latino population was relatively small (12 percent) and Latinos were not recognized as a protected class until 1975, when HISD included them as a separate ethnic group in its desegregation plan. Since the mid 1970s, the number of Latinos migrating to Houston has increased steadily. The ethnic composition of HISD today is 46.5 percent Latino, 37.1 percent African American, 13.6 percent white, and 2.8 percent Asian or other. Obviously, great social changes have occurred, and neighborhoods and schools in Houston, as in other U.S. cities, have changed with them. More than 85 percent of the district's elementary-school-age students receive free or reduced-price lunches. Social services and health care providers are seriously overburdened and are not accessible to a large portion of families who need them most.

School districts in Texas are independent taxing entities and enjoy a relatively positive relationship with other state agencies and community-based organizations because they are not in direct competition for the same pool of funds. This positive relationship existed in Houston, and the concept of school-community collaboration was not new. In fact, since 1987–88, the district has been in partnership with the Family Service Center (FSC) of Houston, a nonprofit counseling and educational service center, to provide counseling and social services free of charge to students and their families at Hogg Middle School. The Foundation funded this program for its initial three years, and because of its success along with other school-community collaborations developed to augment the program, the Foundation asked HISD to make Hogg Middle School the focus of the School of the Future Project. The district and FSC had gladly complied and two elementary feeder schools, Brock and Memorial, were identified to complete the neighborhood focus. The student characteristics of the three Houston schools that participated in the study are presented in Table 16.1.

Objectives

Houston School of the Future planners defined three broad objectives that would need to be met before the realization of the project's

**Table 16.1. Student Characteristics
of the Three Participating Schools.**

	Hogg Middle School	Brock Elementary	Memorial Elementary
Number of Students	1,065	307	419
Grades	6–8	Pre-K–6	Pre-K–5
Ethnicity			
% Black	7	30	3
% Hispanic	89	69	93
% White	3	1	4
% Other	<1	<1	<1
Economic			
% Free Lunch Program	68	95	82
% Reduced-Price Lunch Program	7	4	8
Special Population			
% in Special Education	17	13	3
% in Limited English Program	41	40	54
% Attendance	92.5	95.3	87.2

Source: Office of Research and Evaluation, Houston Independent School District. (1991). *HISD District and School Profiles, 1990–91.* Houston: Author.

goals: (1) to increase and improve the quality of parental involvement at each school, (2) to obtain needed resources, and (3) to coordinate resources so that service delivery occurs in a smooth and naturalistic manner. Houston planners believed that the success of the School of the Future endeavor was dependent on the amount of ownership assumed by the neighborhood parents. Since many of these parents were uncomfortable at the school, worked ten to fourteen hours per day, and were single parents rearing several children, involving them would need to be well thought out. Basic resources such as health care, recreational facilities, and social services were lacking in these schools and neighborhoods. In one school, the physical space to involve parents, volunteers, and other services during the school day was limited. The planners felt that these and other problems must be overcome and that any new services that were implemented should not become an extra bureaucratic layer for families to negotiate or for school personnel to administer. They maintained that services should complement and be integrated with the existing ecology of the schools and neighborhoods.

In its earlier relationship with the FSC, the school district had opted to designate FSC as the fiscal agent, an important component of the proposal developed jointly by the FSC and the Houston Independent School District. The proposal, built on the experiences of the two agencies, delineated a shared set of beliefs that were viewed as essential to a successful family, school, and community partnership:

- The family, neighborhood school, and community service resources available to serve the developmental needs of children must come together as a working system if they are to be responsive and effective.

- The problems and issues confronting developmental success for children and families of the neighborhood are complex, requiring innovative approaches and multiple educational, health, and human services.

- The resources of the family, school, and community will work as a fully functioning system only if all components of the system are involved in identifying issues and solving problems.

- The involvement of families, school personnel, and a variety of community service professionals and volunteers will take place only to the extent that each believes he or she belongs to a working "partnership" (a relationship involving close cooperation between parties having specified and joint rights and responsibilities), with the expressed purpose of facilitating change.

- The neighborhood and school are the philosophical and practical focus for this partnership, ever cognizant that the school cannot succeed alone.

- The predominance of a growing Latino population in the neighborhood and school dictates indigenous participation in the partnership, including a preference for bilingual, bicultural capacity in project coordination.

- Training for school and community service resource personnel in the principles of family dynamics and the practices of healthy family functioning is an essential component for long-term system development.

- The infrastructure of the project must be minimally formal and maximally flexible.

To aid in this flexibility, the FSC agreed to continue as the grant recipient and fiscal manager of the project at the Houston site. As fiscal manager, it provided easy access to funding, thus avoiding the bureaucracy and problems inherent in the administration of a large school district (Crean & Arvey, 1992).

Organization

The Houston School of the Future project was guided through the knowledge, advice, and involvement of the project coordinator, the partnership council, and the partnership council's executive committee. The project coordinator was crucial to the development of the School of the Future. Qualifications for this position included the following: (1) knowledge and experience in working with individuals, groups, and community organizations; (2) knowledge of community service resources; (3) knowledge and understanding of the importance of advocacy in promoting community systems change; (4) knowledge and understanding of the Latino population, its culture, and its community (with bilingual capability preferred); and (5) understanding of and commitment to the necessity of changing traditional approaches to public education and family-school-community resource integration.

The project coordinator was responsible for bringing together the various services at each school as well as for keeping records for research and monitoring the project. A bilingual Latino social worker served as coordinator and brought to the program an extensive knowledge of community organization and development. He had broad experience working with the Houston schools in various capacities, including direct services, planning, and administration. The coordinator oriented each school's principals, staff, and parents to the concept of the program and organized a parent council at each school that was involved in the governance of the project. He then helped secure needed business and community "partners" for each school.

A number of public and private service agencies came together in Houston in various capacities to aid in the developmental process and to provide representatives to Houston's partnership council. Others on the council were drawn from the parents and school staff.

Governance of the School of the Future in Houston rested with the executive committee of the partnership council. Among their responsibilities were defining local objectives for the project, procuring needed resources and partners, and overseeing the activities of the project coordinator. The executive committee had twelve members from the partnership council, representing parents, key service providers, school and educational personnel, and the private sector. A designated administrator from the school district served as chair of the executive committee while a representative from the FSC served as vice chair. The principals from each of the three schools served on the committee along with a parent member. The project coordinator was an ex-officio member of the executive committee.

Needs Assessment, Surveys, and Baseline Data

An essential part of the evaluation information was results of needs assessments and surveys as well as baseline data collected at the beginning of the project. The data collection procedure, explained below, was designed to elicit information from all participants in the experiment.

Family Assessment Interviews

Early on, the project coordinator identified and interviewed forty-five adults from thirty families who were already receiving services from the Hogg Middle School Counseling Program. The demographics of the families were striking. None of the adults interviewed had permanent employment; the average income of these families was less than $12,000 per year; less than 10 percent of the parents spoke English; half the families were headed by single parents. Furthermore, more than half the families interviewed had at least four school-aged children.

Through family assessment interviews, families receiving Hogg Middle School counseling services (n = 45) identified some of their most serious family- and school-related problems:

Family

- Ninety-one percent of the families reported experiencing difficulties in meeting basic needs.
- Eighty-seven percent indicated that alcohol and/or substance abuse was a serious problem in their households.
- Eighty-two percent said that abuse and emotional deprivation were negative influences in their homes.
- Sixty-four percent reported the presence of child abuse or neglect in their households.
- Forty-two percent cited ongoing family conflict as a serious problem; 38 percent claimed either to have witnessed or been the object of homicidal threats by other family members.

School

- Eighty-two percent indicated that their children frequently cut school or classes.
- Sixty-four percent reported that their children had experienced academic failure.
- These families also reported that their children experienced a variety of school-socialization problems: peer conflict (69 percent), gang-related or other antisocial behaviors (64 percent), and general discipline problems (62 percent).

Although conducted with a nonrandom sample, the family assessment interviews revealed the multifaceted nature of the problems these families faced. Family-centered problems, no doubt, contributed to the academic problems of individual students; the school found itself forced to deal with the negative manifestations (for example, peer conflict, discipline problems, and so forth) of these difficult home environments. In short, destructive home environments have negatively impacted the educational environments of the school.

Youth Risk Behavior Survey of Fifth- and Eighth-Grade Students

An important decision of the Houston planners was the recommendation to the Foundation that Dr. Guy Parcel, head of the Houston Center for Health Promotion, serve as the location evaluation expert. Dr. Parcel is internationally recognized for his work in sex education and health promotion programs focused on reducing risk behaviors in youth. Because health needs were a great concern to the families in the participating schools, and because the development of health services was viewed as a critical component of the project, the planners thought that the addition of Dr. Parcel would bring a needed health promotion emphasis as

well as possible grant opportunities in this area. Dr. Parcel's promotion of the program's research possibilities for graduate students
in public health from the University of Texas helped to realize these
expectations.

In the fall of 1991, Dr. Parcel's students in the graduate program
of the School of Public Health at the University of Texas administered the Center for Disease Control's Youth Risk Behavior Survey
to eighth graders at Hogg Middle School. The survey collected data
on five priority health-risk behaviors: (1) behaviors that result in
intentional and unintentional injuries; (2) drug and alcohol use;
(3) tobacco use; (4) sexual behaviors that result in human immun-
odeficiency virus (HIV) infection, other sexually transmitted diseases, and unintended pregnancy; and (5) diet behaviors and
physical activity. Of a possible 293 students, 239 (128 girls and 111
boys) completed the survey. The results presented cause for concern. Especially relevant were these findings:

- Thirty percent of eighth graders indicated that they had handled some form of weapon in the thirty days prior to taking
  the survey. Of these, knives were the most used weapon (30
  percent), followed by guns (9 percent).

- Fifty-nine percent had been in a physical fight within the past
  twelve months, and 8 percent had been in six or more fights
  in that time period. Seven percent of the fights were with
  more than one person, possibly indicating some form of gang
  activity.

- Roughly 27 percent had considered suicide in the past year,
  with 20 percent having made at least one behavioral suicide
  attempt.

- In the thirty days prior to the survey's administration, 46 percent had had at least one alcoholic drink. Five percent of
  those who drank, however, had had at least one drink on
  twenty or more of those thirty days.

- Twenty-two percent had tried or used marijuana, 9 percent had tried or used cocaine, and 11 percent had tried or used other illegal drugs.
- Thirty-eight percent had had sexual intercourse, and 62 percent indicated they had had multiple partners. Thirty-three percent reported using no birth control method.
- Four percent reported contracting some form of a sexually transmitted disease.
- Ten students reported getting pregnant or getting someone pregnant while another five were unsure whether pregnancy had occurred.

A modified version of the survey was given to fifth graders at Brock and Memorial elementary schools. The survey collected data on household demographics and drug, alcohol, and tobacco use. Of a possible 121 students, 109 (63 boys and 46 girls) completed the survey. Some of the more pertinent results follow:

- Fifty-five percent of children's households had six or more people; 10 percent had three or fewer people.
- Sixty-three percent of the fifth graders had had more than a sip of alcohol; 24 percent claimed they had drunk alcohol five or more times.
- Sixty-one percent had never smoked more than a puff of a cigarette, 16 percent had smoked more than a puff five or more times, and 49 percent had friends who smoke.
- Fifteen percent reported having used marijuana and 8 percent reported having used it five or more times. Ten percent reported having four or more friends who used marijuana.
- Fifty-five percent reported having witnessed a drug transaction in their neighborhood and 9 percent of those transactions involved a family member. Forty-eight percent had seen someone smoking crack cocaine and 8 percent of those students had been asked to sell crack cocaine.

Results from these surveys were used to target intervention strategies. Such data have provided the needed documentation to obtain grants and other available resources.

Key Informant Survey Results

Twenty key informant surveys were conducted by Hugh Crean, a psychology doctoral candidate and Foundation research fellow, in the fall of 1990 at the three schools participating in the Houston School of the Future project: Hogg Middle School, and two of its feeder schools, Memorial and Brock. Participants in these surveys were administrators, teachers, parents, counselors, and the chief executive officer (CEO) and project director of the FSC. A situation unique to the Houston site was that the schools were located in three distinct neighborhoods, making coordination more difficult. At the beginning of the project, each of these schools had a new principal who was committed to the project and became quite active in obtaining needed resources for the respective schools. This commitment resulted in similar enthusiasm and support from the teaching staff at each of the schools. A brief summary of the surveys for each school is presented here.

Hogg Middle School. Hogg Middle School serves grades six through eight. Its student population has increased significantly over the past several years. In 1990, there were approximately 1,100 students in the school, 89 percent of whom were Latino. Three-quarters of these children qualified for the federal free or reduced-price lunch programs and more than 30 percent were from single-parent homes. Half the children were over age for their assigned grade.

Hogg Middle School already had a variety of counseling and tutoring programs before the School of the Future project began. Many additional programs had recently been implemented. For example, engineers from the Shell-Western Corporation sponsored the school's Gulf Coast Alliance for Minorities in Education Program, with approximately twenty-five volunteer engineers helping eighth-grade students in math and science projects. Each volunteer also became a mentor for a student and assisted in developing a plan for the student's future in high school and beyond. Another mentor program available to many students at Hogg was Leadership 2000. Twenty-five predominantly Latino lawyers spoke with different groups of students about their own experiences in working to become successful. Many of the lawyers came from backgrounds similar to those of the students at Hogg Middle School, a few having grown up in the same neighborhood. These volunteers provided students individual career planning.

The FSC counseling program had become an integral part of the school. The two counselors in the program provided students and their families a variety of programs and services dealing with substance abuse, child abuse, school dropout, teen pregnancy, and suicide. Furthermore, they linked families with other community agencies and programs when appropriate. A number of teachers commented not only on the effectiveness of the counselors with the students and families, but also on how easy and natural it was to refer students to the program and to interact with the counselors.

Another positive development at the school was the hiring of a Latino principal and more bilingual teachers. While the percentage was growing, the school's teaching staff was still only 8 percent Latino. In a school whose students were 89 percent Latino, the hiring of more Latino staff was urgently needed as it improved communication between teachers, students, and parents.

A major issue as the School of the Future started in Houston was the community's perception of the school. Racial tensions, gang activity, and drug problems were all perceived to be "running rampant." Much of this reputation stemmed from an incident that had occurred five years earlier. Middle school students and students from a nearby high school gathered to watch a fight between a high school student and one of the older middle school students. The groups provoked each other with racial insults. Violence broke out.

Police were eventually called in to break up the altercation, which made local news. Although no such incident had occurred since, this memory continued to linger in the community.

The negative community image was a primary concern for the principal and many of the project staff. It affected the student body because many parents subsequently elected to send their children to magnet schools or private schools rather than to Hogg, even though many of these children expressed a desire to go to Hogg to be with their friends. The situation improved as the principal targeted the community's perception as an immediate concern. For example, the guidance counselors visited and presented information about the middle school to the fifth-grade classes of its thirteen elementary feeder schools. Although the counselors found that rumors of the aforementioned incident still existed, they were no longer badly exaggerated. Most of the students at the thirteen schools reported hearing good things about the middle school, particularly regarding its academic program and the social services offered.

An example of the effectiveness of these presentations was evident in a later interview with a teacher at Brock, a feeder school for Hogg. The teacher told of a family that was debating whether to have their daughter attend one of Houston's magnet schools or Hogg. The student and her parents were so impressed by the guidance counselors' presentation that she and her family immediately decided that Hogg was the best choice. Nevertheless, many families continued to send their children to other schools without considering all the available options at Hogg.

The principal and staff felt that merely getting parents into the school could influence this perception. A first step was to make parents more comfortable about visiting Hogg. Many staff members felt that more positive incentives were needed for parents to visit the school. One teacher discussed creating a "jazzercise" class for parents and teachers, allowing for more informal and natural interaction. The staff believed that if parents felt at home in the school, a stronger parent-teacher organization could be formed.

A critical need in the Hogg neighborhood and, in fact, in all three participating schools was the need for more activities for children; there were no organized places for them to play other than the school yard. Organized activities for children were almost nonexistent. Students were out of school by 3:15 P.M. and were left unsupervised while the parents worked until 5:00 or 6:00 P.M. most evenings.

Another concern common to all three schools was the families' sole reliance on the school nurse for medical care. There were no accessible medical clinics or other health care providers in these neighborhoods; the nearest clinic was a twenty-minute drive away. Because of triage, families often waited hours at the clinic before being seen for routine care. In addition, many families were intimidated by the clinics because they were not legal residents of this country and feared that legal action might be taken against them.

Memorial Elementary School. Memorial Elementary, built in the 1920s, had a student population of just over 400. Planned renovations over the next six months would bring another 100 children to the school. Although the school is adjacent to a major city park, its student population comes from an extremely poor neighborhood isolated from the park by a major thoroughfare. More than half the students at Memorial were home alone or with siblings at some point during the day.

There was a good mix of experience among the teachers at Memorial, four or five having been there for more than fifteen years while three or four were in their first year of teaching. The concept of teachers working as a team was fundamental to Memorial's view of education. Communication was open and teachers had input into all educational issues; they were not afraid to ask for advice or to give or receive constructive criticism.

Although poor, the neighborhood was stable; most families had lived there for more than ten years. The teachers at Memorial were familiar with the neighborhood and its families, a situation that facilitated school-home interactions. Many teachers had been to the students' homes. If a phone was available in the home, teachers called parents regularly to keep them informed of their child's progress. The teachers' involvement in their students' home life allowed them to be more sensitive to the many needs of these children.

Since health and human services were virtually nonexistent in the neighborhood, many families relied on teachers as consultants for a number of services. For example, some teachers filled out tax returns for families while others developed a form letter for families to use as proof of residence. The teachers were aware of their role as social service brokers and the school accepted responsibility for assisting these families. They also shared many of the same fears experienced by the families in dealing with the large centralized bureaucracies of Houston.

Organized parent involvement at Memorial was practically nonexistent. An active and committed parent-teacher organization (PTO) was seen by many of the teaching staff as the most pressing need at Memorial. The previous year, the active PTO consisted of one person who worked alone to organize and run the "organization." When this person became employed at the school and was no longer able to continue in her role as president, the PTO vanished. Given the amount of communication that occurred between the school and the home, the teachers at Memorial were unsure why the school was unable to organize a PTO, but they were determined to succeed.

Resources at Memorial had been quite limited. IBM, which had several volunteers active in providing math and science training, was the only school-business partner involved with the school prior to the School of the Future project. The company also provided cash incentives to the school for classroom materials and had donated a number of IBM personal computers. A severe lack of space at the school was also problematic, constraining the amount of volunteer involvement that could occur during the school day.

In fact, four of the six interviews conducted as part of the key informant strategy were held either in the hallways or in the cafeteria, which was also used for overflow classes.

Despite such difficulties, Memorial's academic program was sound, finishing fifteenth out of ninety schools in the HISD on the latest standardized testing—an excellent accomplishment given the school's socioeconomic makeup and the difficulties with language experienced by many of the students.

Brock Elementary School. Brock Elementary School has 307 students in kindergarten through sixth grade. Its neighborhood is highly transitional. As recently as ten years ago, African Americans were the predominant population; during this study, however, the neighborhood was 70 percent Latino. Located on one of Houston's major thoroughfares, Brock, with its neighboring small businesses and run-down cantinas, struggles with the everyday problems of life in a high-crime area where, of late, drive-by shootings have become disturbingly common.

The school was often described as "the nicest building in the neighborhood." It is relatively new and has adequate physical resources. The children and families of the neighborhood rely on the school grounds for recreation; other than the school playground, there are no accessible play areas for children. More structured recreation is badly needed. The only organized sports in the area are sponsored by the YMCA located two miles away. One teacher pointed out that children in this neighborhood are forced to wait until middle school before starting Little League or other athletics, by which time the level of play has become too competitive for youngsters just starting organized sports. Boys and girls interested in the arts also must wait until middle school and then go to a magnet school to get the advanced training they desire.

Two-thirds of the young and enthusiastic teaching staff at Brock had fewer than three years of teaching experience. Staff morale was high. The teachers were impressed with one another's focus on social problems and awareness of the needs of their students. A number also commented favorably on the staff's detailed knowledge of the informal networks in the neighborhood and the limited resources available to families.

Brock had a number of business partners prior to the beginning of the School of the Future project. They included volunteers from Apple Computer, Southwestern Bell Telephone, and Winsted, McGuide, Sechrest, and Minnik, a local law firm. Representatives from such companies, as well as teachers and parents, make up Brock's Private Sector Initiative Council that had provided the school with a cash grant of $1,500 to sponsor parental involvement activities the previous year. These companies also provided a variety of mentoring and tutoring programs. For example, lawyers tutored students in the social sciences and sponsored a yearly "mock court" experience. These partners continued to be active in the school. In addition, St. Joseph's Multi-Ethnic Cultural Association (MECA) sponsored an after-school and summer arts program for students. This organization also provided artists, writers, and actors who volunteered one morning per week with interested students. In the spring of 1991, the actor in residence worked with students in producing a play for the parents.

As with Memorial and Hogg schools, staff at Brock believed that parental involvement in school governance was critical to the success of the school. Brock parents felt better about being in the school as a result of the "Parents as Partners" program and the Chapter 1 Morning Meetings. The Parents as Partners program was devised specifically for attracting parents into the school. Using the $1,500 grant from the Private Sector Initiative Council, the staff sponsored bimonthly evening meetings at the school for parents and teachers. Each meeting covered a different topic suggested by the parents, providing a forum for speakers from different agencies to discuss their programs or ideas. Dinner was served at the school and child care was provided by volunteer teachers who also furnished various forms of organized entertainment. From eighty to one hundred families came to each meeting. A core group of fourth-grade parents who can serve as future PTO leaders were identified by their participation in this program.

Parents were brought closer to the activities of the school through the Chapter 1 Morning Meetings. These monthly meetings were coordinated by the Chapter 1 counselor and focused on basic parenting skills. The program took a developmental approach, dealing with the capabilities of children at different life stages. Speakers from local human service agencies were brought in to discuss free or low-cost services that were available. Starting with only four mothers in January 1991, the group had sixteen mothers and two fathers by May. Although Brock Elementary had done reasonably well in developing these programs, more parent involvement was needed.

Demographics, Achenbach Youth Self-Report, and School Climate Results for Hogg Middle School

To establish the baseline data presented below, Foundation researchers used the Achenbach Youth Self-Report to survey 523 students from Hogg and from a sample of six additional middle schools throughout Texas during the 1991–92 school year. Demographics of the sampled schools are presented in Table 16.2; this table displays the students' ethnic background, gender, grade placement, and language used at home and at school.

Mental health information was also obtained from students completing the Achenbach Youth Self-Report (YSR). The YSR is designed to obtain reports from eleven- through eighteen-year-olds about their own competencies and problems. Because of time constraints, only behavior problem scores were obtained in the School of the Future evaluation. Students complete the YSR by rating themselves from 0 to 2 (0 = not true; 1 = somewhat true; and 2 = very true and often true) on a variety of behaviors (for example, crying, stealing, irritability) that they may have experienced in the past two months. The 102 items constitute nine syndrome scores and

Table 16.2. Comparison of Hogg Middle School Students with State Middle School Students Who Responded to the Achenbach Youth Self-Report.

Background Information	Hogg Middle School (%)	State Middle Schools (%)
Ethnic background		
Latino	89*	70
African American	6	15
White	4	14
Asian	0	2
Gender		
Male	46	45
Female	54	55
Grade level		
Sixth	45	49
Seventh	55	51
Language spoken at home		
Only Spanish	33	11
Mostly Spanish	17	6
Spanish and English	34	44
Mostly English	4	9
Only English	12	28
Other	0	2
Language spoken at school		
Only Spanish	6	2
Mostly Spanish	1	1
Spanish and English	50	28
Mostly English	17	19
Only English	26	49
Other	0	1

*Percentages have been rounded and may not add up to 100.

three broad band scores (an internalizing score, an externalizing score, and a total problem score).

As shown, the syndrome scales—withdrawn, somatic complaints, and anxious/depressed—were grouped under the *internalizing* heading. The internalizing score was derived by summing these syndrome scores (minus the score on one item that is used on both the withdrawn and anxious/depressed syndrome scales). The syndrome scales designated as delinquent behavior and aggressive behavior were grouped under the heading *externalizing*; the score for this category was derived by summing these two subscales. The third broad band, total problem score, was obtained by summing all the behavior problem items, omitting items 2 (Allergy), 4 (Asthma), and 16 socially desirable items. Tables 16.3 and 16.4 present a comparison of the students at Hogg Middle School with other students sampled across Texas and the Achenbach's normed sample.

The data indicated a significant need for mental health services at the middle school level. The means for the youth surveyed in Texas fall closer to the Achenbach referred sample's means than for the nonreferred group; the nonreferred group was not currently receiving mental health services nor had its members ever been referred for services. The referred group was a clinical sample of

Table 16.3. Achenbach's Youth Self-Report Form for Males, Including Hogg, Statewide, and Achenbach's Normed Sample of Middle School Students.

	Hogg Middle School Mean	Statewide Other Middle Schools Mean	Achenbach's Normed Sample Mean (Referred Group)	Significance Level
Withdrawn	4.5	4.2	4.8	NS
Somatic complaints	4.4	4.3	3.6	NS
Anxious/depressed	7.4	7.5	8.2	NS
Social problems	4.7	4.5	4.1	NS
Thought problems	3.6	3.7	3.5	NS
Attention problems	5.7	5.9	6.7	NS
Delinquent behavior	4.9	4.9	5.4	NS
Aggressive behavior	10.0	10.9	11.8	$p<.05$
Self-destructive	3.8	3.9	3.9	NS
Internalizing	15.8	15.6	16.1	NS
Externalizing	15.0	15.8	17.3	NS
Total problem score	51.9	53.0	54.9	NS

NS=not significant at .05

Table 16.4. Achenbach's Youth Self-Report Form for Females, Including Hogg, Statewide, and Achenbach's Normed Sample of Middle School Students.

	Hogg Middle School Mean	Statewide Other Middle Schools Mean	Achenbach's Normed Sample Mean (Referred Group)	Significance Level
Withdrawn	5.0	4.9	5.9	NS
Somatic complaints	5.8	5.6	5.0	NS
Anxious/depressed	9.5	9.6	11.4	NS
Social problems	4.3	4.3	4.2	NS
Thought problems	3.9	3.9	3.9	NS
Attention problems	5.5	6.0	7.1	$p<.05$
Delinquent behavior	3.9	4.1	5.4	NS
Aggressive behavior	9.6	10.7	12.3	$p<.01$
Internalizing	19.8	19.5	21.5	NS
Externalizing	13.5	14.8	17.7	$p<.05$
Total problem score	55.1	56.6	63.4	NS

NS=not significant at .05

children who received mental health services. These participants were being treated in settings such as child guidance clinics, university child psychiatric clinics, community mental health centers, private practices, and inpatient facilities.

However, one should be aware that the Achenbach samples were a nationally representative sample of youth aged eleven to eighteen while the Texas sample was limited to middle school-aged youth (ranging in age from 11 to 16 with an average age of 12.38). A major sampling difference was that 70 percent of the national sample were white and 70 percent of the Texas sample were Latino. The Texas sample was all from low socioeconomic status (SES) backgrounds while only 21 percent of the Achenbach sample had lower SES backgrounds.

Generally, the Hogg Middle School sample fell very close to the mean of the remaining schools. The only differences found were on the aggressive behavior subscale for boys and on the attention problems, aggressive behavior, and externalizing problems for girls (since aggressive behavior is one of the two subscales included in the externalizing score, the differences found in externalizing may be expected). In all instances, the Hogg sample looks slightly better than the sample of other School of the Future comparison sites across the state.

Finally, Hogg Middle School students differed from other state middle schools in being less likely to believe that discipline in their school is fair (64 percent versus 69 percent). Consistent with this view, Hogg Middle School students were more likely to report that rules were too strict (69 percent versus 62 percent) and less likely to report that "there is real school spirit" (61 percent versus 75 percent).

Accomplishments of First-Year Implementation in the Houston Project

Throughout the first year of the program, the program coordinator, executive council members, and principals worked to attract services, partners, and funding. The major thrust was to (1) increase counseling services, parent involvement, parent education, and parent training activities; (2) provide more substance-use prevention and counseling; and (3) develop after-school and enrichment activities. Emphasis was placed on attracting services and partners that had bilingual, bicultural capabilities and commitment. During the first year, major accomplishments were evidenced:

- In each of the three schools, a parent council was established to facilitate communication between the school staff and neighborhood families. Parent councils met several times throughout the school year and provided input to the project coordinator and the executive committee.

- Selected parents received training from the United Way on how to use Houston's Help Line. Parents were instructed about use of a variety of human service resources and how to disseminate information to the neighborhood families.

- More than two hundred students and their families received counseling from the FSC's Hogg Counseling Project. The counseling services dealt with substance abuse, child abuse, school dropout, teen pregnancy, and suicide. Families were referred to other community agencies and programs when appropriate.

- A Girl Scout Activity Center was started at Memorial Elementary. Nearly fifty girls participated in the program at no cost to themselves or their parents.

- A part-time clinical psychology intern assisted Memorial Elementary by providing counseling services to more than thirty-five parents and their children. A direct outgrowth of this service was Laurelwood Psychiatric Hospital's offering of Latino therapists to conduct family support classes at Memorial Elementary in the second year.

- MECA expanded from Brock and Hogg to include Memorial Elementary in its provision of arts and cultural programs. MECA wrote a grant proposal to fund counseling services for youth at Hogg Middle School who were in danger of leaving school and becoming involved in Houston's drug culture.

- Houston foundations gave over $20,000 to the project for providing other needed resources at the schools.

- Kick Drugs Out of America, a program developed by film star Chuck Norris that focuses on keeping students off drugs while also teaching them karate skills, was planned to begin at the Hogg Middle School during the second year.

- The HISD increased the ancillary staffing at both elementary schools to provide each with a full-time nurse and half-time counselor.

After the second year of operation, optimism and enthusiasm concerning the School of the Future prevailed in the schools.

Involving parents in a governing role was a slow, energy-consuming process; therefore, the executive committee of the School of the Future's partnership council recommended that emphasis in the second year be directed to further developing and supporting the school-based parent councils. The executive council hoped to step back and assume a more traditional role as a policy and review board while continuing its commitment to strengthening networks and developing grant proposals for additional funding. The school district was considering offering accelerated academic programs at the three schools, additional counseling services, and student assistance programs aimed at preventing substance abuse and improving the school climate.

Accomplishments of Second-Year Implementation in the Houston Project

Second-year strategies and refined objectives, particularly a recommitment to increase parent participation, were developed at a planning retreat held in June 1991. The United Way, which hosted the retreat, provided a consultant in management assistance who was also an expert in Latino community-based social services to facilitate the review and planning process. Participants were teams of parents, teachers, principals, and community partners representing each school, as well as Foundation staff and executive council members. The goal was to continue the development of stronger ties between parents, the school, and the community.

A great deal of discussion centered on the difficulty of involving parents because of language, cultural, and economic factors. In spite of a $20 stipend provided to parents to cover the cost of babysitters or transportation, only three attended the planning meeting.

The second year of operation was successful in increasing the number of partners who provided direct services to students and families, significantly increasing parent participation. Among the activities related to the goals of the program were these:

- A local foundation provided funding to hire three parents as Parent Volunteer Coordinators.
- MECA was awarded a grant to train teachers, parents, and volunteers on the latest techniques for working with support systems and at-risk families.
- More than 100 parents from the two elementary schools participated in parent education classes coordinated by the school counselor.
- Private Sector Initiatives of Houston expanded their Parents as Partners Program to include both elementary schools— Memorial and Brock—providing family night meetings with dinner and speakers.
- The ASPIRA Foundation provided funding for family counseling and leadership development for ten Hogg Middle School youth and their families.
- Houston Achievement Place developed and implemented an alternative to the suspension program for Hogg Middle School students.
- The Houston Children's Museum sponsored an overnight activity at the Museum for elementary students from both schools.
- The Texas Council for Alcohol and Drug Abuse provided funding to train staff, parents, and volunteers in drug resistance education and referral sources.
- The Kick Drugs Out of America martial arts program involved 150 sixth-grade students daily and continued through the summer.
- Weekly parent meetings were sponsored by the Houston Police Department and focused on prevention of inhalant abuse, a major problem with students in the neighborhood.
- Volunteers from Parents Anonymous provided parenting classes for both elementary schools.

- The Mental Health Association's "WHO" Program made presentations to both elementary schools on child abuse and made referrals for entire families as needed.

- The San Jacinto Girl Scouts expanded their activity at project schools by offering an adolescent curriculum on decision making for life at the middle school and Daisy's Scouting Program was added at Memorial.

- Cypress Point Hospital, Latino Services, provided a therapist to work as a consultant with the parent education program at all schools.

- Each elementary school held health fairs targeting families and their needs. Nearly 300 families participated and received some form of assistance or information.

- The Metropolitan Organization (TMO), a coalition of churches organized for public service in area communities, held several workshops on community responsibility and neighborhood action; these involved parents from project schools. TMO continues to work with a local food store to develop education scholarships for eighth graders. An in-school store providing incentives for students is being planned by this group.

- Catholic Charities' Project Learn expanded English as a Second Language classes for parents to all three sites.

- Accelerated education programs were implemented by the school district in all three sites.

- MECA increased activities in the three schools. The program introduced mariachi, ballet, and folkloric dancing classes in both elementary schools, and continued classes in drama, painting, and sculpture. A summer creative arts program supplemented activities for children near the Brock and Hogg system. More than 450 children, parents, and teachers participated.

- More than 250 students and their families were served by the FSC Counseling Center at Hogg Middle School. Two social work interns from the University of Houston joined the staff to co-lead a group and to work at the elementary schools with fifty children and their families.

- Several groups were studying problems affecting urban Latino families in the three schools. The Center for Health Promotion and Development and the University of Texas School of Public Health provided technical assistance and identified issues that affect family functioning and student health-related problems. The National Center on Education in the Inner Cities at Temple University (Philadelphia, Pennsylvania) provided access to research and national trends in effective teaching and improved education of inner-city youth. The U.S. Department of Education's Southwest Educational Lab in Austin provided networking opportunities as a means of tapping into state education programs and funding opportunities. Relations with the U.S. Department of Education and the Department of Health and Human Services have been established to formalize strategies whereby services integration can occur as part of the America 2000 program.

- The School of the Future applied for funding from the Texas Commission on Alcohol and Drug Abuse to fund a prevention program for the School of the Future sites.

Implementation Issues

This section examines some of the issues that arise in initiating, organizing, and implementing a school-community collaboration. The examples in this section were drawn from discussions with key partners (HISD, FSC, MECA) in Houston; Foundation staff; and an anthropology doctoral candidate from the University of Texas. Discussion of the issues is structured around the five features identified by the Foundation as essential for a School of the Future.

Integration of Services

The integration of a broad spectrum of health and human services targeted to the needs of students and families continues to be a key element in school-community collaborative efforts. However, many schools such as those in Houston were too crowded to offer physical accommodations for social service providers. Federally mandated Chapter 1 and special education programs required separate classroom areas and brought additional support staff who needed offices at site schools. Recent Texas reforms lowering the pupil/teacher ratios and mandating programs for three- and four-year-old children who are disadvantaged have further contributed to crowding in many inner-city schools. As the federal Chapter 1 initiative and state reforms targeted disadvantaged, minority language, or at-risk children, schools that served them were continually pressured to accommodate more programs and more staff.

A related issue was the integration of services. The School of the Future program funds one coordinator who must work with three different schools and faculties, as well as various parent groups and partners. In Houston, neither elementary school was large enough to qualify for the assignment of an assistant principal, and one school counselor was shared between the two schools. As is often the case, the job of integrating services and resources fell to the school principal, whose primary responsibility was the educational program.

Further hampering the integration of services was the manner in which services developed in or became available to schools. Regardless of planning, partnerships do not develop in an orderly fashion, with one service gap after another being filled by a community partner/provider. When a potential provider offers service, it is difficult to ask that person or agency to wait until more pressing needs are filled. Based on the needs survey and data from key informant surveys, Houston planners targeted areas of need such as English classes, after-school programs, parent training, and substance-abuse prevention and drug-related education and referral. The planners then actively solicited partners who could provide these services.

Parent and Teacher Involvement

Involvement of parents and teachers in program activities was viewed as an essential feature in most school-community collaborations. Often teachers were the most stable members of these initiatives, especially those who had taught in the same school for long periods. Building principals, in contrast, were often replaced every few years, as has been the case in Houston. Teachers, therefore, emerged as critical to the success or failure of any school-based initiative. The process of data gathering, particularly the key informant survey, provided the greatest opportunity to explain the program to teachers and to develop their support and ownership. On reflection, teacher input should be more systematically sought by the executive council and Foundation planners. Teacher representation on the council from each school would help adjust the focus more evenly between social service needs and learning needs.

The highly complex issue of parent involvement has proved to be the most challenging aspect of the project. The planning process indicated that many parents viewed the school as a source of help and school staff as experts in dealing with legal issues, written forms, and language. However, getting these same parents in the door for activities was another matter. Even more difficult was asking them to assume leadership roles in the school. At first, the most obvious obstacle appeared to be that many of the parents do not speak English. However, as the program developed, we came to view cultural differences as far more significant in determining participation, and these cultural differences were not anticipated, even by the Latino staff involved in the planning.

Most of the families were Mexican American, with a few new Central-American immigrant groups, primarily Salvadoran. However, the difficulty in increasing participation appears to be consistent across groups. We learned a great deal from the parent member of the executive council, a neighborhood Mexican-American woman who had not finished high school and had only in the last few years become active in her children's education. This woman taught us that parents had no indication of what was expected. There were strong cultural norms that made it difficult for a woman to feel comfortable in a leadership role outside the home. Almost everything involved in the program—the language, organization, procedures, goals, objectives, priorities, planning, motions, and consensus—was beyond the language and experience of these parents. Even when schools provided baby-sitters and stipends for child care or transportation, women did not participate.

Involving the fathers was more difficult. Fathers, regardless of ethnicity, traditionally viewed the school and the church as the territory of the mother. Also, most of these fathers worked several jobs and did not have regular employment. These men, like their wives, often had no experience in a U.S. school and had only a few years of regular schooling themselves.

When funds were donated by a local foundation to pay the salaries of parent volunteer coordinators, one for each school, project staff felt sure there would be droves of applicants. The job market was not good in Houston, the wage offered was well above minimum, the hours were flexible and geared to the needs of the employee, and the job description was written by the project coordinator who had a great sense of the cultural barriers. Yet, the positions are still not filled. On reflection, staff have determined that the job title was too intimidating and not easily understood. Further, describing the position on paper was not conducive to recruiting neighborhood parents, as they did not visualize themselves as the person described. Another incident that really exposed differences in the expectations of planners and the experience of the people affected was the first partnership luncheon. Confusion resulted because many parents, including the parent representative, a woman actively involved in her children's school and a perceived leader among parents, had never before attended a "luncheon" and were understandably apprehensive.

Involvement of Organizations

Involvement of many organizations, both public and private, as partners was a feature almost too easily accomplished in urban school-community collaborations. In reality, there were too many partners from the very beginning. Collaborations by definition are inclusive rather than exclusive. They seek to connect groups with common interests in the welfare of families in particular communities. Poor urban neighborhoods were the arena for a multitude of public and private social service agencies and were the target of corporate volunteer activities. In Houston, more than 3,000 school-business partnerships had been established in 240 schools. In addition, numerous churches, small businesses, and grassroots community development entities saw themselves as natural stakeholders in the outcomes of reform efforts.

The real implementation issue here was to coordinate these groups, give each an opportunity for participation that matched its mission and interests, and create some appearance of organization, a rational whole from the sum of the parts. A very real challenge was to acknowledge the efforts and interests of the groups while directing their energies in ways that would move the program further toward its defined objectives.

The School of the Future evaluation process, including needs assessments, was critical to this process in Houston. For the planners and executive council, the same issues continued to emerge as a result of the systematic evaluations. The very fact that these issues were repetitive assisted partners to internalize findings, develop a common language, and reinforce commitment to a specific set of objectives.

Companion issues that always surface in collaborations involving public agencies are eligibility and funding. Texas and Houston were no different from other states and cities in that each public entity had its own criteria for service and its own bureaucratic structure. Services for Spanish-speaking clients, many of whom were illegal immigrants, were not easily provided by public agencies. These agencies had long-established civil service employment structures and limited, specified funding streams. Bilingual professional staff were not available and intake procedures were overwhelming. Historically, there have been a number of efforts in Houston to integrate services and simplify eligibility requirements, but, unfortunately, most have been thwarted at the state level and subsequently evaporated at the local level.

Helping agency partners find common ground has been one of the activities of the coordinator. He has found it necessary to help potential partners understand the purpose of agencies and how each can fit within the School of the Future structure. As an example, he facilitated a successful alliance between an agency that had traditionally served African-American youth and the predominantly Latino middle school. Houston Achievement Place (HAP) was a residential program located in the Hogg neighborhood whose leadership and clientele were predominantly African American. HAP developed an after-school program at a neighborhood park for local youth but Latino parents were reluctant to allow their children to participate. The project coordinator arranged visits to the park by the middle school principal, who soon became an advocate for the HAP program. HAP leaders agreed to come to Hogg to conduct an ongoing support group for students with truancy problems. HAP counselors and FSC counselors co-led groups at Hogg. Training in cultural issues was provided to HAP staff and HAP recruited Latino employees for their program. Finally, visits to the program were arranged for the parents. As a result, School of the Future students and parents began benefiting from a free program that includes daily basketball, volleyball, pool, snacks, arts and crafts, parent training, and social service support.

Commitment of Administrators

A strong commitment to the project by superintendents, principals, and other school administrators was the fourth essential feature of this initiative. Committed leadership was essential to the success of this school-community partnership, particularly when it involved the coordination of a growing number of partners and programs. The school district administrator assigned to develop the program had been instrumental in preparing the 1986 proposal to the Foundation for the FSC Counseling Center at Hogg Middle School. She had a strong interest in the successful expansion of those services and was willing to expend the time necessary to develop the program.

The CEO of the FSC was recruited from another state and was selected for his success at fund-raising and promoting innovative community-based programming. The fact that the district administrator and the FSC executive shared a common vision and both were willing to make this program a priority was probably critical to its reception and success in the greater community. Both of these individuals have continued to devote a great deal of time to the program and both loyally attend many meetings on its behalf. Also, both have worked constantly to bring additional resources and funding to the program. A third key leader has been the executive council member from the United Way. Like the CEO of the FSC and the district administrator, she has brokered other services to augment the program. It is easy for early enthusiasm to wane and for new projects to distract people in demanding positions; however, these three key players have remained constant and have continued to commit significant time and energy to the program.

Participation in Evaluation

A willingness to participate in the evaluation of the project was the final essential feature considered key to the success of the program. The following discussion on evaluation issues in the Austin sites was extracted from the program history written by Michael Duke, a graduate student in anthropology at the University of Texas.

The manner by which the program should be evaluated was a subject of considerable discussion. While the cross-site evaluations envisioned by the Foundation (annual mental health surveys, the process evaluation) were accepted by the Austin Schools with little or no controversy, the ways in which the project as a phenomenological entity should be evaluated was a subject of great interest. In measuring the success of the program, a particular concern of the Foundation was ascertaining the number of outside programs and funding sources available to the community that were the direct result of the School of the Future program.

However, there was a rather strong belief by at least some people at the sites that the Foundation's emphasis on qualitative and quantitative evaluations so early in the program relied on an outdated model (world-as-laboratory). This group believed that documenting the progress of the program from their perspective should involve looking at the phenomenology rather than discrete effect. In other words, rather than seeing School of the Future as a direct agent for change, the Houston planners visualized the program as a catalyst for improving mental health in the community. Further, certain planners felt that the program should not worry so much about taking credit, that if the project was successful in acting as a catalyst for improving mental health in the community it would accomplish its objectives. In the words of one key informant, the ultimate success of the program will happen when programs don't come from the coordinators but from the parents (Duke, 1991).

Parental-Student Consent for the Youth Self-Report. An important part of the evaluation was the administration of the YSR, and an essential issue addressed prior to its use was that of consent—specifically, whether parental permission should be obtained through active or passive consent. Active consent required a child to produce a signed permission form in order to take the survey. Passive consent, in contrast, required the student to submit the signed form only if the parents did **not** wish for their child to participate. Much of the discussion focused on the positive and negative features of each approach. Active consent allows parents to be directly involved in decisions concerning their children's education. As some were quick to point out, however, relying on active consent tends to decrease dramatically the rate of participation, and too few respondents could have potentially negated the scientific validity of the survey. In the end, Houston followed the recommendation of the Foundation's Evaluation Director and used a passive consent form.

The administration of the survey posed its own set of challenges. The principal of Hogg Middle School did not wish to use valuable class time to administer the survey. Instead, a questionnaire was administered in homeroom during a two-day period. This two-part administration resulted in a number of incomplete responses. That is, if a student was absent during either of these two days, the survey was only half completed and thus of little value.

Another concern was acquiring student consent prior to the administration of the survey, which sometimes proved challenging. The script that the proctor was to read before handing out the questionnaire was quite specific in its insistence that student compliance was voluntary. However, after the coordinator read the script aloud to the class that he was proctoring, all the students more or less spontaneously decided not to participate. This placed the coordinator in an awkward position. On the one hand, he wanted to respect the wishes of the students; on the other, he was obliged to maximize the level of participation in the school. Thus, the coordinator was forced to skirt the spirit of the introductory script to a certain extent, pointing out to the students that their actions would make them the only class in the school to refuse to participate. Ultimately, all but two students consented.

Spanish Translation of Youth Self-Report. Another issue was that the survey's Spanish translation proved to be highly unsatisfactory. Although only a handful of students opted for the Spanish version, there was significant confusion among students and bilingual proctors alike as to the specific meaning of particular questions. The linguistic confusion arose largely because the translation had been written for the Latino communities in the northeastern United States, which were predominantly Puerto Rican and Dominican. The translation was then assumed to be normative for all Spanish speakers. However, the differences in dialect and vocabulary between northeastern Latinos and the Latinos of Mexican and Central-American descent who dominate Houston's Spanish-speaking population caused significant confusion, even among the bilingual proctors. Unfortunately, since the translation carried a copyright, it could not be "retranslated" into a more understandable form.

An additional problem with the translation was the length of the Spanish version compared to the English version: the English version was four pages long, the Spanish version was twelve. While written English generally tends to be more concise than Spanish, linguistic differences alone cannot explain the discrepancy between the length of the two surveys. Rather, the translation—for whatever reason—elaborated on the questions to a much greater degree than did its English-language counterpart. Because of these discrepancies, the coordinators and others were concerned that the Spanish-speaking students would be unable to complete the survey within the allotted time.

Further, at least one bilingual teacher administering the survey felt uncomfortable asking fairly blunt questions on sexuality in Spanish, although she did not find it to be particularly embarrassing in English. For her, formal, noncolloquial Spanish did not readily lend itself to sexual discourse without falling back on euphemistic language.

Conflicts in Scheduling the Youth Self-Report. In the comparison school, the scheduled survey dates had to be postponed because a school district survey was to be administered at that time. The new school superintendent was very interested in site-based management, and the district's survey was designed to be administered to parents, teachers, and students, in order to ascertain their awareness of their particular school's governing bodies, the services that it offers, and so on. This ambitious survey was announced to the schools with very little forewarning. School administrators first became aware of the district's plans in the middle of the fall semester and were expected to have the surveys completed by the end of the calendar year.

In addition to the problem of rescheduling the YSR survey, the district's questionnaire added to the considerable glut of surveys administered in the two middle schools during that semester. Besides the Achenbach and the district surveys, the Youth Risk Behavior Survey was administered throughout HISD. This survey, which was originally developed by the Centers for Disease Control, was designed to be administered in varying forms to older elementary students as well as those in middle schools. The survey elicited students' attitudes toward drug use, family and school issues, and depression. In addition, the Foundation's research associate for the Houston site had planned to administer his own teacher survey to collect data for his doctoral dissertation.

The rescheduling of the YSR survey at the comparison site was not the end of School of the Future's troubles, however. The school's administration was decidedly lukewarm about the survey. This ambivalence was reflected by the principal's refusal to allow the survey to be completed in individual classrooms, preferring instead that it be administered to larger groups. As a result, the YSR was given in the school auditorium to approximately three hundred students at a time. This arrangement created difficulties for the proctors from the Foundation and the University of Texas School of Public Health as they tried to answer students' questions while attempting to keep them from sharing their responses. Despite these handicaps, the survey in both schools yielded data that was statistically significant (Duke, 1991).

Contribution of Graduate Students and Researchers. An important contribution to the participants' understanding of the program was a side product of the evaluation process. Foundation researchers and the graduate students from the School of Public Health in Houston spent a lot of time with teachers. Listening to teachers and discussing with them the program, the children, and the problems facing these children daily helped to break down the teachers' biases and suspicions regarding the "true motives" of evaluation. The evaluation staff felt that trust was built over time and that the frequency with which they were in the building contributed to making data gathering more routine and easier.

Conclusion

Despite setbacks or difficulties, considerable and steady progress has been made toward meeting the project's goals. Increases in parent involvement at the schools and some parent leadership were evident, while more neighborhood businesses and agencies became involved during the project's tenure than had participated earlier. The school staff also noted changes in the parents' self-esteem as evidenced by their increased participation and presence at school functions. There have been steady increases in after-school activities and recreational opportunities for children. The level of commitment from the Foundation, school administration, and FSC as well as executive council members has not waned. In Houston, all partners were encouraged by the realization of increased health services through the school-based clinic that serves children from Hogg middle school and Brock and Memorial elementary schools.

Last, participants in this unique school-community initiative believe they have learned a great deal about the delicate nature of involving parents as key players—a component without which any such undertaking is doomed to failure (Crean & Arvey, 1992).

References

Achenbach, T. M. (1991a). *Manual for the youth self-report and 1991 profile*. Burlington, VT: University of Vermont Department of Psychiatry.

Achenbach, T. M. (1991b). *Manual for the teacher's report form and 1991 profile*. Burlington, VT: University of Vermont Department of Psychiatry.

Crean, H. F., & Arvey, H. (1992). A declaration of beliefs and visions: Houston's school of the future. In W. H. Holtzman (Ed.), *School of the future* (pp. 97–114). Austin, TX: American Psychological Association and the Hogg Foundation for Mental Health.

Culler, R., & Keir, S. (1992). Outcome evaluation: Plans for a five-year longitudinal study across sites. In W. H. Holtzman (Ed.), *School of the future* (pp. 31–43). Austin, TX: American Psychological Association and the Hogg Foundation for Mental Health.

Duke, M. (1991). *The school of the future: A program history*. Unpublished manuscript. University of Texas; Department of Anthropology.

Ellmer, R., & Lein, L. (1992). Process evaluation: Exploring the realities behind education and social service reforms. In W. H. Holtzman (Ed.), *School of the future* (pp. 19–30). Austin, TX: American Psychological Association and the Hogg Foundation for Mental Health.

Harter, S. (1982). The perceived competence scale for children. *Child Development, 53*(1), 87–97.

Harter, S. (1985). *Manual for the self-perception profile for children: Revision of the perceived competence scale for children*. Denver, CO: University of Denver Department of Developmental Psychology.

Holtzman, W. H. (1992a). Community renewal, family preservation, and child development through the school of the future. In W. H. Holtzman (Ed.), *School of the future* (pp. 3–18). Austin, TX: American Psychological Association and the Hogg Foundation for Mental Health.

Holtzman, W. H. (Ed.). (1992b). *School of the future*. Austin, TX: American Psychological Association and the Hogg Foundation for Mental Health.

Meyerhoff, M. K., & White, B. L. (1986). New parents as teachers. *Educational Leadership, 44*(3), 42–46.

National Center for Education Statistics. (1988). National education longitudinal study of 1988. Washington, DC: U.S. Department of Education.

Research and Evaluation Department, Houston Independent School District. (1991). *HISD district and school profiles, 1990–91*. Houston, TX: Author.

Chapter 17

Slipping Through the Cracks

The Education of Homeless Children

Roslyn Arlin Mickelson, Maria Grace Yon,
and Iris Carlton-LaNey

Current debates about the quality of American education invariably overlook the population of students who experience the greatest educational inequities: the children of homeless families. According to the National Coalition for the Homeless (1990), between 500,000 and 750,000 children in the United States are homeless. Most do not attend school regularly and 43 percent do not attend at all. Historically, homeless children did not attend school because of state and local enrollment restrictions. In some school districts, school attendance was blocked for children who had no proof of residency status, age, or immunization and health records. Besides system factors that complicate school attendance, homeless children often do not attend for more social structural reasons. While some are victims of radical downward mobility from the middle class, the majority of them come from families already on the margins of the economy. They are disproportionately from racial and ethnic minority families, especially in inner cities. Their parents are often exhausted from trying to supply the daily necessities of food, clothing, and shelter. Homeless children often refuse to attend school because they are embarrassed about their living situation, their inadequate clothing, their poor hygiene, and the lack of school supplies. Due to gaps in their previous education, malnourishment, and lack of adequate rest, homeless children often do not perform well even when they attend school.

In response to some of the school system barriers, Congress passed the Stewart B. McKinney Homeless Assistance Act in 1987. The educational provisions of the McKinney Act are based on the assumption that all homeless children have a right to a free, appropriate education. This legislation allocated $4.6 million to help educate homeless children and prohibited schools from using permanent residency requirements to exclude children from attending school. Further, the act stipulated that rules regarding guardianship must be waived for homeless students living with foster parents or relatives other than their legal guardians. The McKinney Act was amended in 1991 to ensure that homeless children are educated in the least restrictive environment.

Despite the provisions of the McKinney Act, the vast majority of large urban areas across the nation ignore the specific educational needs of homeless youth (Yon, 1995). One exception is A Child's Place: A Transitional School for Homeless Children in Charlotte, North Carolina. It is one of only a handful of schools in the nation that specifically targets the educational needs of this population. A Child's Place (ACP) is more than a transitional classroom for homeless youth. It is an interagency collaborative attempt to serve poor families and children in an inner-city setting.

In response to the growing numbers of homeless children and families with multiple needs, educators and policymakers have become increasingly sensitized to the necessity of collaborative approaches—that is, the necessity of connecting education to other services (Dunkle & Usdan, 1993). As Kirst and Kelley (Chapter Two this volume) suggest, the collaborative service movement is an attempt to address the problems of children in a coherent and comprehensive manner. A Child's Place is a realization of such efforts in Charlotte, North Carolina.

This chapter reports the findings from a case study of A Child's Place. The chapter goals are to describe the history and politics of this interagency collaborative effort, to identify ACP's strengths and weaknesses, and to report policy implications from the study.

Although no national public policy currently exists for long-range solutions, it is important to identify the successful strategies local communities presently employ to provide crisis-oriented, short-range services and programs to homeless families. Whereas thoughtful, streamlined collaborative efforts among schools and community agencies may provide certain important short-term services to poor, at-risk youth and their families, the authors hasten to point out that the larger structural issues of increasing poverty in an era of shrinking social services and resources remain.

A Child's Place in Context

In the past several years, families with children have joined the ranks of the homeless in significant numbers. These families now constitute more than a third of the homeless population and are rapidly growing (Melnick & Williams, 1987). Based on available data, estimates are that 500,000 to 750,000 children nationally have no homes (Dobbin, 1987; Martin, 1987; National Coalition for the Homeless, 1990). They live in shelters, motels, cars, or on the streets of America (U.S. Department of Education, 1990).

The problems confronted by homeless families and children have significant and profound effects. These difficulties are related to shelter and family cohesion, physical health, psychosocial development, mental health, and their children's schooling (Bassuk, Rubin, & Lauriat, 1986; Brandon, Newton, Harmon, & Behber, 1991; Kozol, 1988). Homelessness undermines family stability; and family instability, of course, increases homelessness. Both, in turn, lead to fragmentation and potentially destructive dependency on social service agencies. The impact of homelessness compounds the original difficulties faced by the family and frustrates their attempts to cope with them.

Although homeless shelters offer refuge to many families, life in the shelters is at a minimum extremely stressful. Many shelters do not permit intact families to live together. Adult men reside in one location; adult women and their children remain together in a different facility. There is a lack of physical and emotional space. Living quarters are generally cramped and families have little to no privacy. The atmosphere in the shelter is generally volatile, and it is not uncommon for mothers to argue with one another, most often about the behavior of one another's children. Homeless mothers rarely have time for themselves because many spend twenty-four hours a day with their children. They are severely stressed and have little time or energy to respond to the stress and increased neediness of their youngsters. To a large degree, these children must fend for themselves. This situation sets up a cycle that is harmful to the mother-child interaction (Boxhill & Beatty, 1990).

Homeless children, more than their peers, suffer from poor health and a variety of physical illnesses—often as a result of inadequate diets, unhealthy living conditions, stress, and improper personal hygiene. Health problems are compounded by the tendency of their parents to let illnesses and ailments go untreated (Waxman & Reyes, 1987).

Emotional and socialization problems are common consequences of homelessness. These children are found to rate higher than their peers in shyness, dependent behavior, aggression, attention deficiencies, withdrawal and demanding behavior, stress level, anxiety, and depression. Homeless children also suffer from significantly lower self-esteem (Waxman & Reyes, 1987). Mothers report that their children's behavior deteriorated after the family became homeless. The children became provocative and hard to control. Many children feel too unsafe to trust adults or to express their feelings openly. Instead, they become shy and withdrawn.

Homeless children who have experienced the loss of a primary caretaker are often reluctant to become involved with another potentially disrupted relationship, even with peers (Bassuk, Rubin, & Lauriat, 1986). Siblings often turn to each other for nurturance and protection or identify with the nurturant mother and try to replace her (Boxhill & Beatty, 1990). Regressive behavior is commonly observed among preschoolers. Young children become more introverted and withdrawn, reflecting their current level of over-whelming stress as well as their enormous need for nurturance and protection.

Until very recently, there has been little scholarly research on the education of homeless children. The few existing studies have found that homeless children of school age encounter major difficulties in obtaining schooling. The Center for Law and Education (1987) found that homeless children are denied access to their previous schools when their shelters are outside of that school's boundaries. Students are also denied school transportation, special needs classes, and other services. Another report found additional problems of irregular attendance, failing and below-grade performance, and a high percentage of need for special education classes among homeless students. Forty-three percent of these children had already repeated a grade (Waxman & Reyes, 1987).

Historical Precedents for Community Action

Charlotte is a rapidly growing Sunbelt community with a population in its greater metropolitan area of over 1,100,000 people. Approximately 32 percent of the population is African American, 65 percent is white, and the remaining 3 percent is Asian and Latino. Charlotte is noted for the spirit of volunteerism and its active religious community, characterized by a great deal of interfaith cooperation. Unlike many other Southern cities, the history of race relations in Charlotte is not marred by the violence for which cities like Selma or Birmingham are noted. In fact, that history in this community is best characterized by the way the community approached desegregation of its schools.

The story of Charlotte's school desegregation really begins with the desegregation of its lunch counters in the mid-1960s. Legend has it—and there is substantial evidence to support this claim (Gailliard, 1988; Piedmont Airlines, 1985)—that the civic leadership, including government officials and the heads of major corporations and businesses located in the city, cast their eyes northward to Greensboro, saw the social unrest surrounding the historic lunch counter sit-ins, and concluded that desegregation of public accommodations was inevitable. These civic leaders reasoned that it would be in the community's best long-term interests if they could control the process and thereby avoid negative headlines and possible violence. Shortly thereafter, Charlotte desegregated its public accommodations; a group of prominent white businessmen invited a group of prominent African-American businessmen to a very visible, public luncheon at a downtown restaurant.

Almost a decade after it desegregated its public accommodations, the city faced a similar challenge with its school system. In 1971 the Supreme Court upheld the decision of Judge James B. McMillan who ruled in *Swann v. Charlotte-Mecklenburg* that busing was a proper and legitimate remedy for official school segregation. Once again the enlightened business, religious, and civic leaders forged a consensus among the warring factions and crafted a solution—this time to desegregate the schools. The ways in which this was accomplished led to continued racial and social peace as well as economic prosperity for the city, and Charlotte's reputation as a good place to live, work, and relocate a business remained untainted. Economic growth and development continued throughout the last two decades. This history of community action regarding school desegregation foreshadowed the actions of the community on behalf of homeless children in the 1990s.

Growth of Homelessness

North Carolina ranks as one of the more popular states in the nation for corporate relocation. Although wages are relatively low, the area's unemployment rates were half to one-third the national average throughout the 1980s. Sunbelt growth and relatively higher unemployment rates elsewhere around the country attract people to Charlotte; at the same time, the low unemployment rates make

the labor market difficult to penetrate. These circumstances contribute to the growth of homelessness in Charlotte. Another exac-
erbating factor is low wages. One county official reported that many
of the men in the homeless shelter were employed full-time in the
bustling construction industry but make too little money to spend
on rent and support their families back home in rural Kentucky.
The homeless men's shelters thus become de facto low-income
housing. Similarly, St. Peter's Soup Kitchen at a local church provides noonday meals to the hungry who often include these same
construction workers. A Salvation Army staff member stated:

> I've seen the population [of the Salvation Army Shelter] change.
> There were no children a few years ago. It was only a night time
> facility. The single women would immediately go out and find work.
> Now on an average night one third of the people who stay here are
> children. In the summer one half of the people who stay here are
> children. We went from no children six years ago to almost 500 chil-
> dren staying here in one year's time. Between 30 percent to 40 per-
> cent of moms are drug addicted [cocaine and crack]. The population
> has changed which means all our solutions have to change drasti-
> cally. . . . they stay here instead of two or three weeks, they may stay
> here for two or three months. Now I have to worry about day care
> while the moms are in [drug] treatment or at work.

The interconnection among rural unemployment, low wages
despite rapid economic growth, family disintegration, spousal and
substance abuse, and urban homelessness is starkly illustrated by the
situation in Charlotte. The intersection of these forces in Charlotte
is emblematic of the larger urban crisis facing this nation.

Homelessness and Community Resources

As the crisis in the political economy of the country deepens, more
and more families are forced into homelessness at the same time that
the disintegration of the "safety net" accelerates. Drugs, alcohol,

family violence, and loss of jobs all contribute to increasing numbers of homeless families. A number of social service agencies in Charlotte attempt to deal with homeless people. Public social services available include food stamps, aid to families with dependent children (AFDC), Medicaid, public housing, mental health services, therapeutic day care, screening for the developmentally delayed, and an array of health services through the health department. Traditional programs like food stamps have special expeditious arrangements to provide food for homeless individuals and families.

A number of private local services and programs in Charlotte help public agencies to meet the crisis needs of the homeless. The Salvation Army provides emergency shelter for women and children. Charlotte Emergency Housing or Plaza Place also house homeless families. The George Shinn Men's Shelter serves homeless men, many of whom have wives and children in the Salvation Army Shelter. Rebound Christian Rehabilitation Center is a ninety-day residential program for homeless adult males with chemical dependence. The Metrolina Food Bank, Loaves and Fishes, and St. Peter's Soup Kitchen along with numerous churches provide food for this population. Travelers Aid Society of Charlotte, Inc., provides crisis intervention to the homeless and the potentially homeless who are not residents of Mecklenburg County or surrounding areas. They have recently instituted a Family Resettlement Program that provides intensive case management services to families who are trying to relocate in the county. Crisis Clothing Ministry and Good Will Industries provide clothing. Day care for young homeless children is available at the Rainbow Room located at Plaza Place. The Salvation Army is currently working toward licensure of a day care facility for their residents. To ensure that residents are aware of and referred to appropriate agencies, these private organizations have an established brokering and referral system that works well within the confines of its limited funding sources. A Child's Place is part of this network of private and public agencies that collaborate to serve the needs of homeless children and their families.

Despite the rapid increase in homeless people in Charlotte during the past decade, before A Child's Place was founded, the Charlotte-Mecklenburg school system did not have any specific programs for homeless children who attended school or outreach programs to find and enroll those who slipped through the cracks. In Charlotte, then, there are numerous public and private social service agencies that attempt, individually and collaboratively, to serve the complex needs of homeless people. It is in this social landscape that ACP grew.

A Description of the Program

A Child's Place is a nonprofit organization located in the heart of the commercial center of downtown Charlotte, North Carolina. In 1990–91, the second year of its operation, ACP served 68 homeless children from 43 families; in 1991–92, its third year, 124 children from 79 families; and in 1992–93, its fourth year, 148 children from 101 families. Since it opened its doors, A Child's Place has served approximately 500 children from 200 families. According to the executive director, the kindergarten-through-sixth-grade transitional school is a joint effort between Charlotte-Mecklenburg Schools (CMS) and private social service agencies in Charlotte whose mission is (1) to locate homeless children and assist them in receiving appropriate education; (2) to act as an advocate for the families of these children as they progress toward economic, social, and emotional stability; and (3) to educate the larger Charlotte community regarding homelessness. A Child's Place attempts to meet these goals through on-site schooling (in its two classrooms) and social service agency efforts and the coordination of communitywide social services to homeless children and their families.

A Child's Place opened in the fall of 1989 largely through the efforts of three professionals working with social service agencies in Charlotte; these individuals realized that the educational needs of children living in facilities for the homeless were not being met. Although in 1987 the Stewart B. McKinney Act made states responsible for the free, appropriate education of homeless children, the Charlotte-Mecklenburg Schools, like most other districts across the nation, had not addressed the myriad problems of homeless students as of 1989 (U.S. Department of Education, 1990). According to a survey of ninety-six urban school systems in large cities, Yon (1995) found that 48 percent of the school systems had made no plans for the education of homeless children and that 43 percent had not received any funding for this purpose. Furthermore, only 45 percent of districts had designated a coordinator for homeless students. Several of the investigator's surveys were returned uncompleted because the district "had no homeless children."

When plans for A Child's Place were proposed in the late 1980s as a school for homeless children, the school system, county social service agencies, and the general public eventually responded favorably. The school became a program of the Charlotte-Mecklenburg Schools, and for administrative purposes was designated part of a nearby school so that its principal could also lead A Child's Place. A downtown church provided space and a board of directors of approximately twenty people was formed. Its members were drawn from the business community; human services; the clergy; the educational, medical, and legal professions; and the public at large. Funding beyond school district support came from grants and fundraising activities. Currently, professional staff consists of a full-time teacher and teaching assistants, and the administrative oversight of the principal of the school in which the program is housed. An executive director, a family advocate (social worker), and a secretary complete the ACP social service agency staff.

Most students who attend A Child's Place live in shelters or motels for the homeless located in and around the downtown. Table 17.1 shows the housing arrangements of the children who attended ACP during the 1991–92 school year. Some families double-up with extended kin or friends. A few families live in their vans or cars. Students are transported to and from school on Charlotte-Mecklenburg school buses. Students who enroll in A Child's Place are

**Table 17.1 Temporary Housing of
A Child's Place Students, 1991–1992 (N = 124).**

Housing Resource	Number of Families	Number of Children
Salvation Army Women's Shelter	37	62
Charlotte Emergency Housing	11	15
Battered Women's Shelter	13	17
Comfort Inn (downtown)	4	9
Downtown Motor Inn	2	2
Uptown Motor Inn	2	4
Budget Inn	2	4
Other motels	4	5
Doubled-up with friends and/or relatives	4	6
	Percent Families	Percent Children
Total in shelters	77	76
Total in motels	18	19
Total doubled-up	5	5

Source: Family Advocate's Report, 1992.

given medical, dental, and eye exams and needed services. On enrollment, students and their siblings are invited to the clothing closet where they can choose from new or clean, good-quality used clothing. New underwear and shoes are provided for children. Each child is given a back pack with school supplies and toothbrushes and paste.

Attendance on any given day ranges from approximately ten to thirty elementary school students. On rare occasions, children are turned away because of a lack of space. For a variety of reasons, secondary school children attend regular junior and senior high schools and do not receive services from A Child's Place. Students remain at A Child's Place an average of eighteen days (Family Advocate's Report, 1991). When students leave the program because their families have found housing and some form of stability, most enroll in the local school where a school social worker is assigned to them.

Occasionally, a child will remain in ACP despite the family's move to new housing if the family advocate determines that the environment or family continues to be unstable. Effective communication between the new school and ACP is rare once students leave. Consequently, the academic and social progress of former ACP students is difficult to ascertain. Table 17.2 presents a demographic profile of students.

Table 17.2 Demographic Profile of A Child's Place Students, 1991–1992 (N = 124).

Characteristics	Number	Percent
Age		
5	23	20
6	18	15
7	18	15
8	17	14
9	15	12
10	11	9
11	14	11
12	2	2
13	1	1
Race		
White	30	24
Black	83	67
Hispanic	1	1
Asian	4	3
Other	6	5
Gender		
Male	74	60
Female	50	40
Residence of Family Before Homeless		
Charlotte-Mecklenburg County	53	67
North Carolina	4	5
Out of State	22	28

Source: Family Advocate's Report, 1992.

A Child's Place was housed in a downtown church for its first three years, moving to nearby Irwin Avenue Open Elementary School in 1992. During its first two years, ACP had been attached administratively to another nearby school, switching to Irwin after a turnover in administration. Prior to its relocation, ACP maintained regular contact with Irwin. To strengthen this connection, professional staff and students began each school day with breakfast at Irwin and were then transported to the nearby church site. ACP students often ate lunch and attended special programs at Irwin as well, traveling there and back by school bus. A Child's Place operated on a normal school calendar. Efforts were made to place every child in after-school care and summer programs to ensure that they were cared for and received enrichment that might not otherwise be provided to them.

When A Child's Place was located in the church, students were separated into two classrooms joined by a door.[1] After the relocation to Irwin, the two classes were housed in a very large room separated by room partitions. The kindergarten through third grade students worked with the teacher as a whole class, in small groups, or independently. The teaching assistant worked with the fourth through sixth graders in the other classroom under the supervision of the teacher. This division of labor was reversed every other day and continued after the move to the school site. A volunteer program staffed by community members provided additional classroom assistance daily. The volunteers assisted with tutoring, small group instruction, and supervision. Other volunteers known as "lunch buddies" acted as role models and friends; each one worked with a specific child whom the volunteer met with weekly. Breakfast and lunch were catered by school district vans that delivered hot meals to the church daily. A group of volunteers provided nutritious snacks before the day's end, sometimes the last food children ate before the next day's breakfast at Irwin. The younger students were also provided ample rest time in the afternoon. They went on field trips and engaged in enrichment activities such as attending plays and concerts as part of the curriculum. Reading at home was highly encouraged and books were sent home daily in children's backpacks.

Irwin Avenue Open Elementary School is a popular magnet school often sought by parents from diverse class and race/ethnic backgrounds because of its reputation for excellence, open education, and tolerance of students from varying backgrounds. Irwin's principal has served as ACP's administrator for the past year. As of this writing, the effects of ACP's move from the church to the school can be tentatively assessed. According to ACP staff, the operation of the program is much more efficient for several reasons. First, children do not spend time on school buses riding between the church and Irwin for meals, programs, and other activities. Second, the clothing closet is located in a private area between the two classrooms so children and staff can readily access supplies without disrupting instruction as was previously the case when the clothing closet was located on a different floor in the church. Third, the classrooms and offices are not separated from the rest of the school by locked doors. Now ACP students eat with other Irwin students, choosing which of four lunch periods they wish to take. ACP students participate in recess and other recreational activities along with Irwin students. The instructional component of ACP continued as before. Study buddy and lunch buddy volunteers have returned. Students are more able to participate in age-appropriate groups, although a few ACP students are mainstreamed into the regular Irwin classroom. This is possible because the unique emotional, physical, familial, safety, and educational needs of homeless children, which prompted the creation of a "transitional classroom," continue regardless of the physical location of the program. The full effects of the move have yet to be determined.

In the 1992–93 school year an auxiliary component of ACP began in two additional elementary schools with populations at risk for homelessness, or significant numbers of homeless children in classrooms. ACP Resource Rooms provided a part-time social worker, clothing, school supplies, hygiene products for children, and information about homelessness for teachers and other school personnel at the two schools.

Research Questions

Because of its interagency nature and its target population, A Child's Place offers a unique opportunity to explore a number of questions concerning education and social service delivery for poor children and their families, specifically:

1. What is the nature of ACP's interagency collaborative model?
2. What are the strengths of ACP's interagency collaborative model for meeting the educational (and other social) needs of highly stressed youths like homeless children?
3. What are the limitations or weaknesses of ACP's model for meeting the educational (and other social) needs of highly stressed youths such as homeless children?
4. What are the larger societal forces that (a) contribute to the growing number of homeless children and families, and (b) facilitate and/or inhibit the capacity of A Child's Place to serve its children?

Data and Methods

The data presented in this chapter are drawn from a case study of A Child's Place conducted by the three authors over a period of several years (1990–1993). All three were members of the board of A Child's Place. Initial involvement in research for all three authors began with their assignment to the board's research committee. The nature of their involvement as participant observers, then, is structural. As scholars with appointments in social work, sociology, and education, they bring complementary perspectives to this enterprise.

The data collected consist of field observations, interviews with key informants, and content analysis of documents. Field observations were conducted during all ACP board meetings, in several board retreats, and in the hallways, offices, and classrooms from 1990 to 1992. During the spring semester of the 1991–92 school year, the authors observed intensively in the ACP classrooms and took field notes. In-depth, semistructured interviews were conducted with volunteers, ACP's professional education staff (past and present principals, the previous teacher, teaching assistant), school district personnel in charge of ACP, ACP's social work staff (present executive director and child advocate), the social work staff of several agencies that collaborate with ACP, other board members, and a variety of school district personnel. All field notes and interviews along with minutes and other documents were transcribed and jointly analyzed by the authors. Analysis followed conventions of qualitative data analysis discussed by Miles and Huberman (1984), Spradley (1980), and Yin (1984). Data from observations, interviews, and documents were triangulated to identify findings, draw conclusions, and make interpretations.

Findings

The leitmotif which characterizes the history of A Child's Place is a search for an organizational identity. Throughout the three distinct phases in the life of ACP, participants have struggled to define the interagency collaboration as a school with a social service component, as a social service agency with an educational component, or both. Some of this ambiguity may have resulted from the process by which the program came into existence, which Estelle Richman (1992) characterized as "Ready, fire, aim!" Not until the school's third year did a clear definition of ACP's mission and goals emerge, and flowing from this resolution was greater clarity regarding the organizational structure and programmatic components.

The findings from the case study can best be understood within the framework of Barbara Gray's model of the collaborative process. She identified three phases: *problem setting*, which gives the situation an explicit form that allows stakeholders (defined as those groups and/or individuals who have a stake in the problem under consideration) to communicate about and act on it; *direction setting*, which involves reaching agreement about the issues affecting the problem domain; and *implementation*, which refers to carrying out the agreements that require action (Chapter Five this volume).

Phase I: Problem Setting

In 1988 the Executive Director of Travelers Aid began to notice increasing numbers of families arriving in Charlotte with nowhere to go. They were sent to the Uptown Men's Shelter,[2] which was not equipped for families. Women and children would huddle in a corner of the shelter; school-aged homeless children, obviously, were not attending school if they were in the shelter. During this same period social workers at various other agencies began to discuss among themselves the new and rapidly growing phenomenon of homeless families with young and school-aged children. One member of ACP's founding troika of social workers who together instigated the actions that culminated in the creation of ACP was a member of the church attended by the school system's assistant superintendent for planning and research. A second one was his neighbor. They approached him with their concern about the growing numbers of homeless children who were not in school. There was a need, the social workers claimed, for a special school or special provisions for these children. The assistant superintendent replied that he needed "the facts" before he could take the issue any further. He requested systematic data to support the claims that special services were needed for this population. Neither the school official nor the social workers invoked the McKinney Act as a justification for the proposed intervention. Almost a year passed before action was taken.

In January 1989 the ABC television show *20/20* featured Seattle's highly successful school for homeless children. An executive with a major bank, who was also a board member of the Uptown Day Shelter for men, saw the program and was deeply moved. He called the Charlotte-Mecklenburg school superintendent and asked, "Dick, what are we doing for the education of homeless children?" The superintendent promised to get right back with an answer, called his assistant superintendent for planning, and asked, "Dan, what are we doing for the education of homeless children?" The assistant superintendent promised to get right back to his superior, called one of the three social workers, and asked, "Celeste, what can we do for the education of homeless children?" A Child's Place was born then, not because human service or education professionals saw a need and began the process, but because of the intervention of one of the city's powerful business leaders who prompted various school officials to act (see Mickelson & Ray, 1994, and Ray & Mickelson, 1993, for details of this general phenomenon in Charlotte).

Phase II: Direction Setting

The first meeting for ACP was held in February 1989. School district skepticism was dissolved after officials toured the shelters and motels and found numbers of homeless children. "But why a special school? Why not mainstream the children?" asked school officials. Interviews with families and children convinced school district officials that there was a need for a special school experience for homeless youth. Social workers were cognizant of the various other needs of these children and their families (nurturance, attention, love, food, shelter, clothing, hygiene, medical and dental care, family advocacy). Once school officials were convinced of the unique needs of this population of students they told the founding three, "This is your wagon; now drive it."

The Charlotte-Mecklenburg Schools provided A Child's Place with a shared principal, a teacher, an assistant, supplies, and furniture. The three social workers had to find a location and develop a program. The bank executive found an anonymous benefactor who donated $65,000. The banker made a conference call to key corporate leaders in the area and raised additional money. A board of directors was appointed, a half-time coordinator was selected, and in the fall of 1989 ACP opened its doors on the first floor of a church in the heart of the business district and near the shelters and low-budget motels.

The first year of operation (1989–90) was marked by a lack of clarity of purpose and inadequate communication among the school district, professional educators (the shared principal, teacher, assistant), the board, and the social service providers (school social worker, part-time program coordinator) who worked at ACP. The board was very fluid in membership and in function as people jockeyed for position and tried to define who did what for whom in ACP. The pediatrician and child advocate who became the third board president remembered the initial period as marked by confusion, as board members sought to define their role and the nature of the program:

> So, we [the board] had a few meetings talking about, what are we? Are we a super PTA? Are we an advisory group or are we a community agency in partnership? I remember people thought it was okay to be an advisory group but don't ask us to pay $50,000. If we're going to be like [a] support group that provides some goodies for the students, that's fine. But then our budget should be, we shouldn't be hiring a director [coordinator, later executive director] full time and paying this huge salary for this social worker. That's the school system's business. I didn't care either way, which ever it went, but it just seemed to me that you had to go one way or the other.

Moreover, the board initially did not function as a policy board but rather took on administrative tasks, actions that confused the issue even further. For example, the first principal recalled:

The first year I was president of the board and was the part-time administrator. There were real problems in terms of the organizational chart. Who was in charge of what and who was supervising whom? And who could take orders from whom and the issue of what is in the best interests of the kids got lost somewhere in the shuffle, while we dealt with "I told the teacher to do this and she wouldn't do it" and that kind of stuff. It was really unfortunate. A line was drawn and we all took sides and it was forevermore a battle and every time I came down there I had to be the mediator. We had some concerns but it really became a personality issue. And it was a unique situation. You had an alliance between a school system of 2000 people and a nonprofit board and in the fledgling year people were trying to decide which jurisdiction . . . trying to make a collaboration. I think the board hadn't yet philosophically decided whether the program needed to stand on its own, be a part of the school system, stand on its own with agencies . . .

At the same time, the collaboration between ACP's staff and the larger social service community was strong and increasingly efficient. Social workers within the program and in other agencies all reported high levels of coordination, collaboration, and cooperation. The family advocate commented that "compared to what I worked with for a short time in [another city], I personally have found that the interagency cooperation is greater here than what we experienced in [another city]."

The executive director of another agency that houses homeless women and their children concurred with this assessment of interagency collaboration among social service providers: "The agencies do well. We have a great network. I don't know if it is indicative of the size of the city that it works so well, but it works amazingly well here in comparison to [a large northern city]."

The spring prior to the first year of ACP's operation, several teachers, teachers' aides, and school social workers applied for the positions. The person selected as teacher was a stern disciplinarian who believed that her role was part of her "ministry," that it was God's will that she teach these homeless children. She also believed that the children needed to be taught that there are consequences for their actions because the reason they were homeless was that "their parents had never learned that lesson." The teacher's assistant was also a minister and shared many of these convictions. The school social worker's conception of her role was relatively narrow (that is, she did not include family advocacy as part of her responsibilities). All three professionals saw ACP as a school with an auxiliary social service component that provided clothing, and some other limited services to the children and their families. They were answerable to their principal who was also the president of the board of directors. The part-time coordinator functioned as a conduit for social services but was not active in planning, fund-raising, or policy development. No one had a clear idea of the complexity of the problems associated with educating homeless children or the variety of social service agencies that must be involved collaboratively to provide for the needs of these children and their families.

The second year (academic year 1990–91) began with the selection of a full-time coordinator. She entered the position with the notion that her job was to define the program, develop it, raise money—in other words, to act as an executive director. The teacher, assistant, social worker, and principal viewed her role as more of a service assistant. There was no coordination; instead there was open conflict. For example, the new coordinator developed an elaborate volunteer program and then informed the teacher that on such and such a day the volunteers would arrive at these times. The teacher, described by several informants as a "prima donna," said, "No, they cannot come into the classroom because they will be disruptive." Many observers believe this response reflected her desire to maintain authority and autonomy more than a concern for instructional help since volunteers are sorely needed. The founding social workers were troubled by the wild and chaotic activities, the conflict between the new coordinator and the teacher, and the apparent movement of ACP toward being a school—an entirely different direction from their original vision of an agency with a public school component. To every criticism or directive from the board and/or the coordinator, the education professionals responded: "Well, this is how we do it in CMS [Charlotte-Mecklenburg Schools]." By the middle of the second year, it was clear that the originating social workers, the coordinator, and the professional staff still had diverse and conflicting conceptions of what A Child's Place was.

This period was marked by conflict over personnel and the nebulous organizational structure of ACP. Because the coordinator was relatively powerless and received very mixed messages from the social service agency staff, the three founding social workers, and the school professionals, friction continued among the key personnel. By December, 1990 ACP's program and operation were teetering on the edge of an abyss. In the winter of 1991, the board fired the coordinator, and two of the original founding social workers took over as interim co-executive directors. The board's firing of the new coordinator after only five months was a critical move because it forced them to draw up an organizational chart and to make a formal choice: Was ACP a school or an agency? These were essential decisions if similar problems were to be prevented in the future (see Figures 17.1 and 17.2).

Figure 17.1 presents a post hoc representation of the organizational structure of ACP through the period of the coordinator's firing. Figure 17.2 represents an alternative model devised by the executive committee of the board as an option to adopt in order to avoid future conflicts. Figure 17.1 supposedly represented a "school with a social service component" option while Figure 17.2 supposedly offered a "social service agency with an educational component" alternative. Both figures appear as they were presented to the ACP board for deliberation.

Figure 17.2 was adopted. This indicated the board's conception of ACP as an agency with a formal agreement with the CMS, that

Figure 17.1. Original Organizational Chart for A Child's Place.

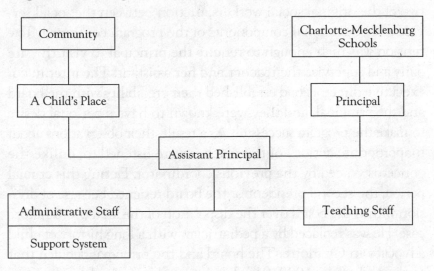

Figure 17.2. Adopted A Child's Place Organizational Chart.

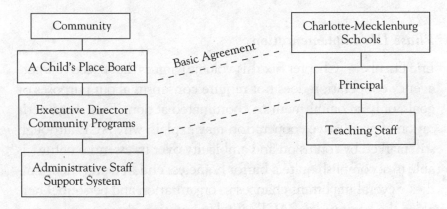

an executive director would manage and direct the program based on the board's policies, and that all instructional matters would be the responsibility of the principal. Both Figures 17.1 and 17.2 reflect the desire of the board for interagency collaboration as well as the confusion surrounding the nature of such efforts. There was, and still is, little relationship between actual day-to-day operations and either figure.

Although the coordinator was replaced on an interim basis by two of the original social workers, friction between the social service and educational components of the program continued. The tension was high enough to require the principal to visit the site daily and supervise the teacher and her assistant. The interim co-executive directors had established their credibility with the board and the principal, and they were known to have a personal desire to make the program successful. As a result, their observations about inappropriate actions of the teacher were listened to, unlike the concerns voiced by the previous coordinator. During this crucial period, the second president of the board resigned because of division within the board over the disposition of the fired coordinator's case. He was replaced by a pediatrician with a long history of child advocacy in Charlotte. The board and the principal decided that at the end of the 1990–91 school year, the original teacher and assistant would be replaced.

Phase III: Implementation

Eric Eisenberg (Chapter Six this volume) argues that effective interagency cooperation does not require consensus about purposes or goals, only a commitment to coordinated action. This characterization of productive cooperation may explain why ACP, although still marked by confusion and ambiguity over its essential nature, is able to accomplish quite a bit for homeless children and their families. Several important changes in organization and personnel heralded the beginning of ACP's implementation phase.

In the summer of 1991 a new executive director came to A Child's Place. She was experienced in collaborative social agency service for homeless people. According to several informants, under her guidance, ACP came together as an agency with a school component; according to others it was a transitional school that met the complex needs of homeless children and their families. Regardless of the continuing battle over definitions, there was a consensus that under the new executive director's leadership ACP blossomed. She acted as an effective liaison between the board, CMS, and social service agencies. The new teacher and assistant who were hired proved to be far better suited to work with homeless children than their predecessors had been. Because the board narrowly defined social work, its members changed the title of the social worker to "family advocate," which to them connoted continuous and concerted advocacy. A social worker with a master's degree and experience with homeless families was hired in that position. But once she was hired, the family advocate broadened the focus of social work well beyond what is typically associated with school social work tasks. The new team (executive director, teacher, assistant, family advocate) worked collaboratively in planning, execution, and follow-through; the ACP program had found its direction.

While a formal consensus had been reached by the professional and teaching staffs and the board as how best to operate ACP (and it was working well through this writing), the two camps nonetheless continued informally to define it differently. The professional educators continued to see it as a school with a social service component and the social work staff saw it as an agency with an education component. Even though those involved agreed to disagree as to what ACP was, the program worked well because all shared a vision of what needed to be done for the children and their families, and brought their joint commitment to coordinated action.

During ACP's third year (1991–92) the board finally drafted a mission statement and more clearly defined the role of the board as fund-raising rather than policy formation.[3] Confusion remained, however, about the identity and role of A Child's Place. Even under the leadership of a strong president and new executive director, an issue arose in 1991–92 that again brought to the foreground all the conflicts and tensions, confusion, and turf battles that had characterized the struggle to define ACP over the previous three years. This was the battle over moving the program from the church site to a local elementary school. The controversy centered once again on the question of definition: Was this an agency with a school component or a school with a social service component? Major questions discussed during board meetings were these: How will the move to Irwin Avenue affect the identity of ACP as a program? Is the move too soon for ACP considering the recent turmoil over personnel? Will the school system take control of ACP? The board decided, in consultation with the executive director and the educators, that in the best interests of the children the ACP classrooms should become part of Irwin Avenue Open Elementary School.

The move took place prior to the beginning of the 1992–93 school year. But the very nature of the discussion attempting to balance the interests of ACP as an organization against the interests of the children in the program is remarkable. It was not the case that board members were more interested in preserving the agency than in serving the children; rather, they firmly believed the children's needs would be better served with ACP remaining as a quasi-independent and physically separate entity than by merging into Irwin Avenue Open Elementary School. The significance of this debate lies in what it reveals about the perhaps inevitable tensions and difficulties over turf and goals which arise even in the best of interagency collaborations.

By ACP's fourth year (1992–93), the program's formal direction as an agency with an educational component became clearer, yet there was still uncertainty. The CMS system also is a member of the interagency collaboration, but its involvement is limited to allowing the use of a public school building and providing instructional staff, transportation, a liaison with ACP staff, and limited funding for supplies. The liaison's role and relationship to ACP have yet to be determined.

Figure 17.3 shows an unofficial revised organizational chart developed by the executive director of A Child's Place. This chart was drawn to present her perception of ACP's actual operating structure. She developed it for inclusion in a grant proposal. Recall

Figure 17.3. Unofficially Revised Organizational Chart.

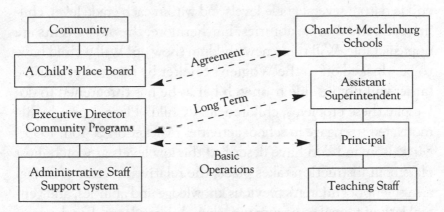

that the organizational chart officially adopted is the one shown in Figure 17.2. The existence of the revised chart was discovered by one of the researchers during a telephone conversation with the executive director for the purpose of clarifying the differences between the charts shown in Figures 17.1 and 17.2. Intrigued by the discovery, the researcher (who was also at that time a member of the board) asked, "Will you be presenting this at a board meeting?" To this question the executive director replied, "Oh, I'm glad you reminded me." It was never brought to the board's attention.

Summary

An assessment of ACP's success is problematic. A Child's Place provides a safe, secure place for homeless children. It structures their lives, provides food, clothing, acceptance, and medical and dental care. It cannot, however, meet all their needs.

Serving the Educational Needs of Homeless Children

The educational experiences of students in this transitional classroom are minimal. To be fair, any description of teaching and learning at ACP must be placed in context: in any classroom there are children from several grade levels and within each grade level, children of quite diverse abilities. Furthermore, the day's events are unpredictable. Will three new children show up? Will a child have to be whisked off to the Women's Shelter by taxi so her abusive father will not be able to snatch her as he has threatened to do? Despite these problems, children at A Child's Place appear highly motivated to engage in school activities (Mickelson & Yon, 1995). Mickelson and Yon have described the low levels at which most classroom instruction takes place, the relative absence of formal assessment of children's previous knowledge and abilities, and general lack of formal assessment of what children learn. For the most part, children do individual assignments in a variety of workbooks and handouts, or read to themselves. When volunteers are present, they help with these activities.

Serving the Needs of Homeless Families

The social service program that ACP provides for the children's families is stronger and more consistent than its educational program for homeless students. A major reason for the strong service program is the high levels of collaboration among social service agencies. ACP facilitates family resettlement, serves as a broker, and fosters parental support and a sense of community. These services give structure and normalcy to one part of parents' lives. A number of parents were surveyed at the end of the 1993 school year and indicated that they were highly satisfied with the services they and their children received at ACP (Yon & Sebastien-Kadie, 1994). Participants were twenty-seven homeless parents of fifty-four school-age children. Half of the children attended ACP; the other half were in regular public schools. Only two parents were displeased with ACP. One felt it was in a "bad neighborhood," and the other felt her child belonged in a regular classroom because her child was older than the other children. Parents found the professional staff to be informative, helpful, and caring. They reported overwhelmingly that their children had positive experiences at ACP and seemed to find ACP a haven in a time of crisis.

Slipping Through the Cracks

Despite these important successes, the educational component of services for homeless children allows students to slip through the cracks for several reasons. Most homeless children are not in either ACP or a regular school; if they are in a regular classroom there are rarely provisions for meeting their unique needs. During the 1992–93 academic year, ACP resource rooms (with a part-time social worker, clothing, school supplies) were established at two of the sixty elementary schools in the district. Even those who attend school in ACP's transitional classroom receive minimal instruction. Once children leave ACP, there is little to no follow-up in most cases. The family advocate described the difficulties she encountered:

> I've got families that I lose and don't have any idea where they go. One of my big efforts this year is to increase and develop and perfect the follow-up effort. Over the summer I developed just a really basic follow-up system that allows me to flip up on the computer a letter, a survey, something to keep the client in touch after they've left here. Last year that happened kind of sporadically and I saw people on the street as often as anything. I kept up with them through the school—phone calls to teachers. But I want it to be much more definite this year. Much more definite follow-up plans. At the end of school last year I had the majority of families who were enrolled during that time just bolt from the shelters when school was out. And I mean I have records in the file right now waiting for someone from another school to request them. And I don't know where these families are. They just disappeared and they left the shelters without any forwarding address.

The professional staff and board are presently discussing whether to hire another social worker (with a B.S.W. degree) to do the daily crisis intervention and school enrollment-related work with new children. This would free the current family advocate (who has a M.S.W. degree) to do case management including much needed follow-up. There is a consensus among board and staff that at present, there is too much work for one social worker to do.

The authors believe that homeless children and their families slip through the cracks—at least in Charlotte—for several reasons:

1. The creation and design of ACP has been compared to "building a plane while flying it." The problems identified required immediate solutions. Before the program opened, no one realized the extent of or the complexity of homeless children's needs. Initially, people looked only at the intersection of homelessness and education. Because the problems were multiple and complex, the solutions needed to be as well. But initially, the program focused primarily on education. With any social problem there is a causal chain. Intervention in one link in the chain may ignore the other.

2. Initially, no one clearly defined ACP's identity. Consequently there was enormous ambiguity for several years within the program, making interagency collaboration difficult.

3. The governments of the city of Charlotte and Mecklenburg County were not fully supportive of the individual agencies involved in the collaborative venture. There was no infrastructure that linked private and public services. Elected officials tended not to understand either the problems of homeless families or the services available. In 1993, however, a countywide effort to link and coordinate services for children was initiated by several child advocates. The extent to which the Children's Network will assist homeless youth remains unclear.

4. The school system's approach to homeless children can be described at best as benign neglect and at worst as obstructionist. The Charlotte-Mecklenburg Schools have never been proactive about educating homeless children. During the last two years the superintendent initiated a number of important and controversial reforms, to improve teaching, learning, and curricula, but none address the unique needs of homeless students. Moreover, the executive director and board president of ACP had to wait for six months for an appointment to talk with the superintendent about the program. At that, they were given only three hours' notice before seeing him.

5. The business elite in Charlotte have always played an important role in shaping the city's business climate and public image. As mentioned earlier, these leaders are very concerned with the city's image. For example, in the spring of 1993, the NCAA Regional Basketball Competition was held in Charlotte. The weekend before the games many homeless people were removed from streets and under freeways in order to spruce up the appearance of the city for its expected visitors. It is possible that the relative neglect of homeless children by private and public officials is a conscious effort to downplay the presence of homelessness in this community.

Policy Implications

The magnitude of homelessness and its accompanying human misery and social dislocations call for a coherent national strategy to address the problems. No such policy exists. The growing number of families with multiple needs requires interagency collaborative solutions. A national policy would address employment and industrial planning, housing, family and child welfare, health, and education. Homelessness as a social phenomenon is a consequence of this complexity of issues and is inseparable from a host of chronic social dislocations that can be addressed only by a national domestic policy.

Homeless people, however, have specific needs. The efforts of the National Coalition for the Homeless have been instrumental in getting limited legislation enacted to address some of the many needs of this population. One specific area that has been addressed is the educational needs of homeless youth. The Stewart B. McKinney Act of 1987 was an important step, but the 1987 allocation of $32 million was far too little to impact the problem seriously (Curran & Renzetti, 1990; Karger & Stoesz, 1990). The difficulties of providing education for homeless children in Charlotte illustrate that despite the existence of the act, and a generous, volunteer community—perhaps the best of circumstances—homeless children fall through the cracks.

Policies to address the problems of this group must be crisis oriented and concrete. Simply, they must provide housing that is safe and affordable. Housing programs must be appropriately funded, coherent, and clearly focused. The authors agree with those who argue that housing is both a necessity and a right, and that market forces ought not to dominate the allocation of this resource. They support the National Low Income Housing Coalition's eight-point housing program that includes the following: (1) an income-based housing payment entitlement program; (2) expanded production and preservation programs for needs not met by housing payments; (3) guaranteed fair access to housing; (4) progressive and redistributive tax and spending policies; (5) greater reliance on community-based nonprofit organizations; (6) retention of the existing housing stock; (7) less expensive and more accessible housing credit; and (8) a reduction in displaced residents caused by private or governmental actions (Dolbeare, 1983, pp. 50–51).

A key educational policy suggested by this study concerns the monitoring and enforcing of existing laws. The McKinney Act is often ignored. The history of ACP suggests that legislation without a compliance component is often useless. School districts across the nation are not monitored to see whether, in fact, they meet the educational needs of homeless students. In Charlotte, all the pressure to address the education of homeless youth came from outside the school system, suggesting that any educational policies for at-risk youth ought to include both carrots and sticks to ensure compliance.

This case study suggests another educational policy: the need to incorporate collaborative or integrated services in all school restructuring. As Kirst and Kelley (Chapter Two this volume) note, school-linked services are not the fringes of the educational restructuring movement. We concur with their view that school-linked services must be viewed as essential rather than peripheral to reform efforts. Given the current massive restructuring of the Charlotte-Mecklenburg School system, an integrated-services approach should be interwoven throughout reforms.

One could argue that the typical linear arrangement of learning in schools is inherently in conflict with the lives of homeless children in at least two ways. First, because most homeless children have had a high rate of absenteeism, there may be major gaps in their school learning. Second, many minority and poor students have great difficulty adapting to mainstream schools whose organization, curricula, and pedagogy often conflict with the cultural capital, lived experiences, attitudes, and behaviors the children acquired in their homes and communities. From this perspective, perhaps the most promising, powerful, and liberating practice for the education of homeless children may be that of whole language. Whole language is a socially critical, holistic approach to everyday problems and literacy. The philosophy that guides practice in whole language classrooms is one that attempts to empower students, that challenges social stratification, and promotes an egalitarian social order (for a detailed discussion of whole language see Edelsky, 1991).

Conclusion

While the nature of the interagency collaboration among the various public and private agencies and the school system is often problematic, it is clear that the community of Charlotte is on the forefront of such efforts to provide education and services for homeless children and their families. Yet, despite this success, ACP remains one small bandage on the oozing sores of social dislocations caused by the restructuring and downsizing of American firms, deindustrialization of American cities, and internationalization of industry and capital from the first to the third world. The absence of a systematic, long-range, national domestic policy, the failure to infuse interagency collaborations into most educational restructuring efforts, plus the corruption and neglect by federal actors who have responsibility for the meager programs that currently exist (HUD, for instance) indicate that the devastation of homelessness for millions of people is likely to continue. ACP cannot address these problems; difficulties of this magnitude require genuine systematic changes in societal infrastructure.

As Jean Anyon (1993) incisively observed, providing social services and schooling for homeless children is akin to cleaning the air on one side of a screen door. Until long-term solutions are found for the crisis in the U.S. political economy, increasing numbers of at-risk children will slip through the cracks even of successful programs like A Child's Place.

Notes

1. The entire area occupied by ACP was physically separated from two other children's programs on the same building level. Several of the informants interviewed for this study suggested that aside from security reasons, the programs may have been separated because the affluent parents of children who at-

tended the church's preschool and the community school for the arts wanted to segregate their children from the poorer ones attending ACP.

2. Civic and business leaders waged a campaign to change the name of the central city to "uptown" rather than "downtown" because of the former's more positive connotation.

3. For example, when their term expired in June 1993, the three authors of this chapter were not invited by the executive committee of the board to serve an additional term, largely because of their weak fund-raising records during the previous three-year term. Their vacant seats have been filled by high-profile, wealthy business leaders from the community.

References

Anyon, J. (1993, April). *Class, race and urban school reform: A case study of theoretical analysis*. Paper presented at the annual meeting of the American Educational Research Association, Atlanta, GA.

Bassuk, E. L., & Gallagher, E. M. (1990). The impact of homelessness on children. In N. A. Boxhill (Ed.), *Homeless children: The watchers and the waiters* (pp. 19–33). Binghamton, NY: Hawthorn Press.

Bassuk, E. L., Rubin, L., & Lauriat, A. (1986). Characteristics of sheltered homeless families. *American Journal of Public Health*, 76(9), 1097–1101.

Boxhill, N., & Beatty, A. (1990). *Mother child interaction among homeless women and their children in a public night shelter in Atlanta*. Atlanta, GA: Child and Youth Services.

Brandon, P. R., Newton, B. J., Harmon, J. W., & Bebber, D. G. (1991, April). *A study of the educational problems of homeless children*. Paper presented at the annual meeting of the American Educational Research Association, Chicago, IL.

Center for Law and Education. (1987, April). *Education problems of homeless children and suggested legislative language changes*. Washington, DC: Author.

Curran, D. J., & Renzetti, C. M. (1990). *Social problems*. Boston, MA: Allyn & Bacon.

Dobbin, M. (1987, August). The children of the homeless. *U.S. News and World Report*, pp. 20–21.

Dolbeare, C. N. (1983). The low-income housing crisis. In C. Hartman (Ed.), *America's housing crisis* (pp. 50–51). London: Routledge and Kegan Paul.

Dunkle, M., & Usdan, M. (1993, March 3). Putting people first means connecting education to other services. *Education Week*, p. 44.

Edelsky, C. (1991). *With literacy and justice for all. Rethinking the social language and education*. Philadelphia: Falmer Press.

Family Advocate's Report. (1991). *A Child's Place: A transitional school for homeless children*. Charlotte, NC: Author.

Family Advocate's Report. (1992). *A Child's Place: A transitional school for homeless children*. Charlotte, NC: Author.

Gailliard, F. (1988). *The dream long deferred*. Chapel Hill, NC: University of North Carolina Press.

Karger, H. J., & Stoesz, D. (1990). *American social welfare policy*. New York: Longman.

Kozol, J. (1988). *Rachel and her children*. New York: Fawcett.

Martin, M. (1987, September). *Homeless families* (Unpublished manuscript). In M. Martin (Chair), Proceedings of the Annual Meeting of the Profession, National Association of Social Workers, New Orleans, LA.

Melnick, V. L., & Williams, C. S. (1987). *Children and families without homes*. Washington, DC: Center for Applied Research and Urban Policy.

Mickelson, R. A., & Ray, C. A. (1994). Fear of falling from grace: The middle class, downward mobility and school desegregation. *Research in Sociology of Education and Socialization, 10*, 207–238.

Mickelson, R. A., & Yon, M. G. (1995). The motivation of homeless children. *International Journal of Social Education, 2*, 16–34.

Miles, M. B., & Huberman, A. M. (1984). *Qualitative data analysis*. Newbury Park, CA: Sage.

National Coalition for the Homeless. (1990). *Homelessness in America: A summary*. Washington, DC: Author.

Piedmont Airlines. (1985, March). Charlotte: City on the move. *PACE Inflight Magazine*, p. 13.

Ray, C. A., & Mickelson, R. A. (1993). Restructuring students for restructured work. *Sociology of Education, 64*, 1–23.

Richman, E. (1992, October). Untitled commentary presented at School-Community Connections: Exploring Issues for Research and Practice (an invitational conference sponsored by the National Center on Education in the Inner Cities), Leesburg, VA.

Spradley, J. P. (1980). *Participant observation*. Troy, MO: Holt, Rinehart & Winston.

U.S. Department of Education. (1990). *Report to Congress on final reports submitted by states in accordance with section 724(b)(3) of the Stewart B. McKinney Homeless Assistance Act*. Washington, DC: U.S. Government Printing Office.

Waxman, L. D., & Reyes, L. M. (1987). *A status report on homeless families in America's cities*. Washington, DC: U.S. Conference of Mayors.

Yin, R. K. (1984). *Case study research*. Newbury Park, CA: Sage.

Yon, M. (1995). Education of homeless children in the United States. *Equity and Excellence in Education, 28*, 31–43.

Yon, M., & Sebastien-Kadie, M. (1994, Fall/Winter). Homeless parents and the education of their children. *The School Community Journal*, 67–77.

Chapter Eighteen

An Evaluation of Family Support and Integrated Services in Six Elementary Schools

Lawrence J. Dolan

In recent years, evidence has increased that public schools need additional support if they are to remove the barriers that hinder them from effectively educating all children. Local, state, and national policy groups regularly report the need for better coordination of human services with schools that should serve as the hub for service delivery. Among the most effective presentations of this position have been reports from the National Association of State Boards of Education (Levy & Copple, 1989), the Educational and Human Services Consortium (Melaville & Blank, 1991), the Center for the Future of Children (Behrman, 1992), and the joint report of the U.S. Department of Education and the U.S. Department of Health and Human Services (Melaville & Blank, 1993).

Building on this convincing rationale for school-linked human services is a growing array of programs that have been implemented in schools around the country (Dolan, 1992). Many of these reputable programs, such as the School Development Program (Comer, 1988) and the New Jersey School-Based Youth Services (New Jersey Department of Human Services, 1990), reflect many of the principles characteristic of "effective" programs. These characteristics include a focus on families, a balance of preventive as well as crisis-response activities, and a comprehensive and flexible set of services.

However, relatively few programs have a rigorous evaluation plan in place to assess implementation or effectiveness of a program for children and their families. Most programs rest on political viability and values that are often not informed by evaluation studies (Dolan, 1992; Gomby & Larson, 1992). Given the relative infancy of school-based family support and integrated-services programs, this lack of attention to formal evaluation might reflect a stage of program development that is more concerned with activity development than outcome assessment. Both users and observers suggest that these programs do have face value and make a difference to the participants. Often, limited starting resources have constrained evaluation. However, models of family support and service integration are now moving out of the prototype stage of development and are being considered for replication across the country. Careful evaluations of program processes and outcomes are critical to informed judgments on expanding programs and optimizing conditions for program impact.

The limited number of evaluations of school-based family support and integrated-services programs results in part from the extraordinary difficulties that evaluators encounter. Most program staff resist evaluation of their program since it can divert resources from service delivery. Often they feel that the program will not be treated fairly since it has not had sufficient time to measurably affect the children and families involved. In addition to this resistance, evaluators often find poor records, no meaningful contrast samples, little information on the nonusers of the services, and a lack of consistency in program adaptation from site to site. Finally, most family support and integrated-services programs are embedded in a much larger context of school reform, with multiple and overlapping intervention strategies. This redundancy of services is often considered a strength when the goal is to create a safety net for children and their families. However, this same redundancy causes difficulty for evaluators who need to pinpoint the relative effectiveness of specific components.

In light of this need to evaluate school-linked services, we examine a family support and service-integration program that is part of a larger elementary school reform effort called Success for

All (Slavin, Madden, Karweit, Dolan, & Wasik, 1992). Success for All was started in one elementary school in Baltimore during the 1987–88 school year and has been implemented in more than eighty elementary schools throughout the United States. Three of these schools in Baltimore, each representing a different degree of program implementation, were selected by the author for a study of the consequences of varying family support and integrated-service programs. The three Success for All schools were matched with three comparable contrast schools with regard to Chapter 1 status, racial composition, and achievement patterns as of the 1988–89 school year. Presented here are a brief description of Success for All and of the family support and integrated-service model, and the results from a process and outcome study that was conducted to address the effectiveness of this component of the model.

The Success for All Model

The basic approach to designing a program to ensure success for all children begins with two essential principles: prevention and immediate, intensive intervention. The Success for All program aims to prevent learning problems by providing children with the best available classroom programs and by engaging their parents in support of their school success. When learning problems do appear, corrective interventions must be immediate, intensive, and minimally disruptive to students' progress in the regular program. That is, students receive help early, when their problems are small. With an intensive and effective treatment of learning difficulties, students can catch up with their classmates and can profit from their regular classroom instruction. Instead of letting students fall behind to the point that they need special or remedial education or are retained in grade, students in Success for All are given the help they need to keep up with their classmates.

The components of Success for All are as follows (additional details can be found in Slavin et al., 1992):

Tutors. In grades one to three, specially trained certified teachers work one-to-one with any students who are falling behind their class-mates in reading. First-grade students are the priority for tutoring.

Reading Program. During reading periods, students are regrouped across grade lines for ninety minutes so that each reading class contains students at one reading level. This clustering eliminates the need for reading groups within the class and increases the amount of direct instruction time for students. Also, use of tutors as teachers during reading time reduces the size of most reading classes. The reading program in kindergarten and first grade emphasizes language skills, auditory discrimination, and sound blending, and uses engaging, phonetically regular minibooks that students read to one another in pairs. At the second- through fifth-grade levels, students use school- or district-selected reading materials, basals, and trade books. The program emphasizes cooperative learning activities built around partner reading, identification of characters, settings, problem solutions in narratives, story summarization, writing, and direct instruction in reading comprehension skills. At all levels, students read books of their choice for twenty minutes each evening as homework; classroom libraries are developed for this purpose.

Preschool and Kindergarten. A half-day preschool is provided for all eligible children. The program emphasizes language development, readiness, and positive self-concept. A full-day kindergarten program continues the emphasis on language, using children's literature and big books as well as thematically related activities. Early reading activities focusing on oral and written composition, activities promoting the development of print and math concepts, and alphabet games are added in the full-day program. Peabody Language Development Kits are used to provide additional language experience.

Cooperative Learning. Cooperative learning drives the Success for All curriculum. Students work together in partnerships and teams, helping one another to become strategic learners. Emphasis is placed on equal opportunities for success, individual accountability, common goals, and rewards.

Eight-Week Assessments. Students in grades 1–5 are assessed every eight weeks to determine whether they are making adequate progress in reading. This information is used to assign students to tutoring, to suggest alternative teaching strategies in the regular classroom, and to make changes in reading group placement, family support interventions, or other means of meeting students' needs. The school facilitator coordinates this process with active involvement of teachers in grade-level teams.

Facilitator. A full-time facilitator works with teachers in each Success for All school to help them implement the reading program. In addition, the facilitator coordinates eight-week assessments, assists the Family Support Team, facilitates staff support teams, plans and implements staff development, and helps all teachers make certain that every child is making adequate progress.

The results of Success for All have been extremely positive. Effect sizes (ES) for the students in the lowest 25 percent of their classes at pretest averaged +1.3 for students in schools with adequate tutoring resources. By the third grade, the Success for All low achievers still far outperformed matched control students (ES = +1.07). Effects were also very positive for students in general, averaging ES = +.55 at the end of first grade and ES = +.46 at the end of third grade. In addition, the program reduced retention from near 11 percent to near zero and cut special education placements in half.

The Family Support and Integrated-Service Model

The goal of Success for All is to have every child succeed. We know, however, that some students cannot benefit from improved instruction alone because of serious family, behavioral, or attendance problems. In order to better meet the needs of these students, Success for All schools have developed Family Support Teams. These teams form a third layer of intervention behind classroom instruction and one-on-one tutoring to help children at risk of falling into academic trouble. Students receive an automatic review by the team if they are not making progress in spite of the classroom and tutorial support. By concentrating on referrals due to poor academic progress, the scope of the team is more focused than other service-integration and family support models.

A Family Support Team comprises a cross-section of the school's resource personnel: guidance counselor, social worker, parent liaison, administrator, and facilitator or master teacher. In some sites, staff from social services and the health department also are part of the team. The composition and mandate of the Family Support Teams are contingent on the available personnel at each school. In schools with fully funded plans, money is designated to hire a full-time social worker and attendance monitor. The social worker not only provides on-site clinical services but also coordinates the activities of the Family Support Team. Schools with modified plans utilize existing personnel to participate on the team. In all cases, the administration's participation on the Family Support Team has proved to be crucial for effective schoolwide implementation.

Most teams meet on a weekly basis. In the meetings, the team determines schoolwide programs and develops action plans to meet the needs of students deferred because of academic difficulty. Depending on the needs of the school, Family Support Teams address issues of attendance, intervention with individual students, parent involvement, and service integration between school and community agencies. (For more details, see Haxby, 1993.)

Attendance. One of the main activities of the Family Support Team is to coordinate attendance activities for the school. If a school has an attendance problem, the team generally institutes one of two attendance intervention plans. In each plan, the team develops attendance monitoring strategies, provides effective intervention for attendance problems, and implements schoolwide absence prevention problems. Attendance concerns receive priority, particularly in the beginning of the school year, until stable and favorable patterns of attendance are established.

School-Based Intervention. A major task of the team is to develop action plans to address the needs of any child who is not progressing due to family, behavioral, or attendance problems. The goal is to reduce special education referrals by identifying students and intervening early. Referrals can be made by teachers, administrators, or parents; the Success for All facilitator screens these referrals first to make sure that tutoring or fundamental classroom management strategies cannot solve the problem. Once cases are screened, the team discusses each case and plans an approach to remedy the situation. The team works to produce a multifaceted approach to address the problem. Frequently, the team works with the parent to create a home-based family reward system or classroom behavior modification plan. A parent liaison may make home visits to address attendance problems, and the facilitator and teacher may develop classroom strategies to increase the child's motivation. A guidance counselor may work with a family to develop parenting skills or with a child to improve the child's self-esteem. The team frequently uses the services of local agencies; if a child needs glasses or a family home needs heat, it is the team's responsibility to make sure that community services are provided. Once they develop an action plan for a case, the team chooses one of its members to be a case manager. This case manager ensures that the plan is coordinated and implemented. The team reviews every case on a regular basis until the problem is resolved.

Parent Involvement Programs. Parent involvement is a key component of student success in the Success for All program. Parents are not only invited to school or involved in tasks that support students and teachers but are also included in developing programs to enhance student achievement. Family Support Teams create school advisory boards composed of parents, administration, and faculty to make policy decisions and recommendations. Some teams include parents in disciplinary policy committees that rewrite and review schools' discipline codes.

Other teams work with parents on specific school projects. For example, one school has worked with parents to create an after-school homework room. One common activity is to provide parenting skills workshops at school. Motivating parents to support the curriculum at home is another critical parent involvement activity. In addition, in parent workshops, parents are taught at-home activities that enhance classroom instruction. All these projects have been designed to meet student needs and to support parents as positive contributors to the educational development of their children.

Service Integration Between School and Community Agencies. Many students who have educational difficulties have problems that require services from a range of community agencies. Yet families are often unable to access these services. Also, families frequently are more willing to use services that are convenient and in a familiar location. Therefore, depending on the needs of a particular school, Family Support Teams need to be aware of community resources and in some cases explore community linkages for school-based services. For example, Family Support Teams might investigate providing some community health and mental services at the school. One Success for All site has a public health nurse-practitioner and part-time pediatrician who provide on-site medical care; another school is connected with a family counseling agency that provides some school-based services. Other examples of on-site services in Success for All schools include school-aged child care, family literacy and job training programs, and mental health counseling. Some linkages can be formed with agencies that provide some sort of concrete service such as food, clothing, shelter, or heat. Some schools have worked with community agencies to create a food distribution center and a clothing and shoe bank on the school's premises. The team works with parents to identify needed services and then establishes a link with local agencies to make community services more accessible.

Obviously, the activities of the Family Support Teams vary depending on available staff, student and family needs, and community investment in the school. All teams must ensure that the needs of children having difficulty are being met, that school attendance programs are working, and that parents are encouraged to participate in school. Other activities depend on the time constraints of the team.

The multifaceted role of the Family Support Team is crucial in addressing the needs of students who are at the highest risk of school failure. An effective team not only attempts to meet the needs of at-risk students but also creates a schoolwide climate that fosters parent involvement and a proactive approach to the complex problems faced by many students and families in Success for All schools.

School restructuring efforts are expanding to cater to the provisions of federal support for disadvantaged children, the mandates of the special education community, and pressure for funding equalization. In addition, the growing consensus that schools need to reach out to the families and communities they serve and form partnerships with other human services also must be addressed in school restructuring efforts. A program of activities, as seen in the Success for All model, does not occur overnight; making and maintaining meaningful links to other agencies take time and a tremendous amount of energy if the institutional and territorial barriers to collaboration are to be overcome.

Developing rigorous yet relevant evaluation designs that attempt to measure the impact of such family support programs is pivotal. Clearly, good descriptive information about who gets served, what services are received, and whether the problems were alleviated is the first step in such an evaluation. Attempts to tease out the value added by a family support strategy above and beyond the academic model, although difficult, are currently being studied. As Success for All evolves and expands to additional sites, it is likely that success for at-risk students will come only as a result of a comprehensive and coordinated set of strategies. One key element of such a model will surely be family support that provides a proactive and multifaceted approach to addressing the needs of at-risk children.

The Design of the Study

The first phase of the evaluation of family support and integrated services involved six schools from the Baltimore City Public Schools. In three of the schools (SFA1, SFA2, SFA3), the Success for All model had been in place from fall 1988 through spring 1992. The other three schools (C1, C2, C3) were considered good contrast sites because of their Chapter 1 status, percentage of mobility, racial composition, and previous standardized achievement test scores. All sites were designated as schoolwide Chapter 1 sites by the district; during the 1988–89 school year, 30 of 124 elementary schools in the district received federal money for Chapter 1 programs. The six schools are in the most severely disadvantaged neighborhoods in Baltimore. More than 95 percent of the students in all six schools were African American. Table 18.1 presents selected characteristics of the six schools.

The only school characteristic that was different between the Success for All and the contrast schools was the number of students in the schools. This could potentially confound the analyses of certain data (for example, the number of referrals to special education) and should be taken into consideration when the data are interpreted. Mobility rates ranged from 16 percent to 25 percent. Most of the mobility in Baltimore is within the district, often the result of housing difficulties. Baseline achievement data are discussed in the "Results" section.

Table 18.1. School Characteristics.

	SFA1	SFA2	SFA3	C1	C2	C3
Number of Students	438	557	453	723	750	806
Percent Free/Reduced Price Lunch	89	81	91	95	94	86
Percent for Chapter 1 Eligible	70	64	66	64	71	64
Percent Mobility	20	16	19	25	17	21

Two types of data were obtained during the 1990–91 and 1991–92 academic years. The first type consisted of school-based records and central office data on pupil information and standardized achievement. The main data from records and computer files were collected from the year prior to introduction of the Success for All program and from the 1991–92 academic year, three years after the start of Success for All. The following data were obtained:

- 1987–88 average daily attendance percentage for each school
- 1991–92 average daily attendance percentage for each school
- 1987–88 retention percentage, percentage of students who were forced to repeat a grade (number retentions/number of students)
- 1991–92 retention percentage (number retentions/number of students)
- 1987–88 percentage of students in special education
- 1991–92 percentage of students in special education
- 1991–92 ratio of special education referrals to eventual placements
- 1987–88 percentage of third graders above grade level in reading (reading total score on the California Achievement Test)
- 1991–92 percentage of third graders above grade level in reading (reading total score on the Comprehensive Test of Basic Skills

The only problematic data in the above set were the special education referral data, as school-based records of initial referrals that were reviewed needed to be confirmed by central office records. Considerable effort was required to obtain the 1991–92 referral data. The data from 1988–89 for special education referrals were considered too invalid to be utilized in the analyses.

The next set of indices relate to processes of the family support and integrated-service program at each of the sites. These data were obtained through school records and verified by interviews with school and agency staff members. In some cases, minutes of meetings and logs of activities were kept by school staff. Data on these variables were collected during the 1990–91 school year, the second of the three years of the Success for All program under investigation. These data include the following:

- The number of referrals to the school-based team that were not special education related
- The number of long-term (more than one month) interventions initiated by the school team
- The number of workshops held for parents during the school year
- The number of full-time equivalent staff who serve on the school-based team
- The number of full-time-equivalent staff from outside agencies (social services, health, and so forth) who work primarily at the school
- The number of outside agencies that have active involvement with the school

In addition to the examination of school-based records, interviews were held with five members of the school or agency staff, five parents of fifth-grade students, and five fifth-grade students in fall 1990 and spring 1991 regarding a number of issues pertaining to family support and integrated services. A total of ninety interviews were conducted (fifteen at each school). Among the issues addressed were these:

- Levels and types of services available in and outside the school

- Ways in which service integration occurs at the school
- Barriers to access of services and recommended strategies to reduce these barriers
- The process of initiating new service options
- Types of services delivered (prevention versus crisis-response services)
- Management issues of providing family support of integrated services
- The importance of location for service delivery
- Ways in which decision making is shared
- Ways in which schools and agencies evaluate their effectiveness
- Perceptions of effectiveness by different members of the school community (staff, parents, and students)

The data collected were used to answer a number of basic questions regarding the Success for All sites compared to their contrast sites on issues relating to family support and integrated services. Over time, are there differences in the schools with regard to attendance, retention, special education referral and placement, and academic achievement? Clearly, if differences do emerge, it will be difficult to pinpoint a causal relationship, since the family support and integrated-services programs represent only one component of the school program.

How these schools differ on some of the measures equated with family support and integrated services were evaluated with a second set of questions: Do teams meet? Who attends? Are students referred? Do students receive interventions with appropriate follow-up? Are there ample opportunities for parents? Are other agencies linked with the school and in what form are they linked? Even though a family support model is described in Success for All, schools will most likely function quite differently depending on the staff involved, the identified needs of the community, and the history of family support and integrated services in the community. The contrast schools had no special training or attention; however, they also have mechanisms in place to manage student and family issues. Differences between the Success for All and contrast samples on issues of delivery of family support and integrated services are noted.

Descriptions of the Six Elementary Schools

As noted, the Success for All schools were matched with schools that were comparable on selected demographic characteristics. The six schools are described in the following sections.

Success for All Site 1 (SFA1)

SFA1 is a PK–5 Elementary School serving 438 students. The school receives schoolwide Chapter 1 funds plus approximately $400,000 per year from a private foundation to implement Success for All. This additional money supports six tutors and a number of Family Support Team staff. The Family Support Team consists of the school principal, an instructional facilitator, a parent liaison, a guidance counselor, an attendance monitor, and a school social worker. The team meets biweekly. The outside agencies involved with the school are a local university hospital, Boys Club, a family literacy program supported by the Office of Economic Development, and a community organization that assists with food distribution. Interviews with Family Support Team members suggest that many children and families are served but little collaboration exists among team members. The majority of the team members point to this lack of collaboration as a significant problem.

Success for All Site 2 (SFA2)

SFA2 is a PK–5 Elementary School serving 557 students. The school receives schoolwide Chapter 1 support plus district discretionary funds to support the Success for All program. This additional money supports three tutors, an instructional facilitator, and a full-time school social worker. The Family Support Team, led by the school social worker, includes a public health nurse, a half-time counselor, an academic facilitator, a parent liaison, and a Department of Social Services (DSS) social worker. The DSS provided the services of a social worker to work on-site with attendance problems. The school was also the site for a school health clinic staffed by a full-time nurse-practitioner and part-time pediatrician. The Family Support Team met on a weekly basis, with the school social worker acting as the case manager of referrals. Interviews suggest high levels of collaborative activity within the Family Support Team.

Success for All Site 3 (SFA3)

Unlike SFA1 and SFA2, SFA3, which serves 453 students from PK–5, implemented SFA solely with schoolwide Chapter 1 support. As a result, it had fewer tutors (three) and no additional support for staff on the Family Support Team. The Family Support Team consisted of the school principal, academic facilitator, a half-time counselor, a behavioral adjustment teacher, a parent liaison, two parents, and two teachers. This team also met biweekly. Although the team mentioned some local agencies (health clinic, community mental health center) and reported high levels of collaboration, there is little evidence that other agencies were actively involved with the school.

Contrast Site 1 (C1)

This K–5 Chapter 1 school (in which more than 75 percent of the student population is eligible to receive Chapter 1 services) serves 723 students. A pupil services team consisting of a full-time counselor, an attendance monitor, a school psychologist (one day per week), a parent liaison, and the school principal met on a biweekly basis. The group served mainly to screen children for special education. No involvement from outside agencies was reported on site; however, a comprehensive community center (job training, health care, adult literacy, day care, family counseling) was available nearby. The team referred many families to the center for assistance, but little follow-up was noted on the referrals. Most felt fortunate to have this comprehensive facility close at hand because little was available to students or their families on site.

Contrast Site 2 (C2)

This schoolwide Chapter 1 site serves 750 students in what many believe to be the most disadvantaged neighborhood in the city. Other than a special screening committee, no group met to discuss students and their families. A guidance counselor, one half-time school social worker, a parent liaison, and one half-time public health nurse were on site. Although the team never met formally, informal networking took place. The social worker kept records on children she served. A mentoring program was in place through an outside business, and a local university provided some mental health counseling one day per week. All who were involved reported little communication among these professionals.

Contrast Site 3 (C3)

This schoolwide Chapter 1 site serves 806 PK–5 students. Despite the principal's receptivity to outside organizations in the school and the school's history of previous relationships, there was little current evidence of agency involvement with the exception of a local community organization that ran a family literacy program for thirty-three parents. Physical health screening and referrals were routinely done by a community health clinic located three blocks away. A pupil services group met on a biweekly basis but was attended only by the assistant principal, a parent liaison, and a half-time counselor. This group discussed each child's case prior to a special education referral but was limited in its ability to handle a large number of referrals. Contacts with the staff of agencies previously involved with the school suggest that they received little support from school administration and did not feel included in school affairs. Most of these agencies had been the initiators of their involvement with the school.

Results

The first set of results focuses on change in school-level outcome variables. Table 18.2 presents the data for attendance, retention, special education placements, referral/placement ratio for special education, and third-grade students' performance on standardized reading achievement. With the exception of the special education referral/placement data, the data presented are from the 1987–88 academic year, the year prior to Success for All implementation (SFA2 started some elements of the program in 1987–88), and for 1991–92, the last year data were gathered on these variables.

With the exception of reading achievement, only school-level data were reported since grade-level data were not uniformly available for all schools. We were unable to access student- or family-level data on more sensitive measures of family support and integrated-services outcomes. Neither the data on affective or social characteristics of students or families nor the resources to collect this type of data independent of the school system were available. At best, the variables in Table 18.2 can be considered proxy indicators of more sensitive measures. Without additional intervening measures, the ability of this study to imply causality is severely limited.

Attendance, one school-level outcome variable, is typically addressed by the Family Support Team with programs for chronically absent children, a good monitoring system, and incentives for positive attendance patterns. The contrast schools show little

Table 18.2. Indicators of Effectiveness of Family Support Team.

	SFA1	SFA2	SFA3	C1	C2	C3
1987–88 % Attendance	87	86	89	89	87	91
1991–92 % Attendance	93	89	93	88	90	91
1987–88 % Retention	11	12	07	10	13	06
1991–92 % Retention	01	01	03	08	12	05
1987–88 % Special Education	16	12	12	09	10	13
1991–92 % Special Education	12	07	07	08	09	12
1991–92 Referral/ Placement Ratio	.78	.82	.80	.57	.63	.55
1987–88 % 3rd Graders Above Grade	23	35	30	25	30	27
1991–92 % 3rd Graders Above Grade	42	52	39	27	33	25

change in attendance over the three years, while Success for All schools improved marginally (3 to 6 percentage points), although they did not meet the 95 percent criterion set as an attendance standard.

Retention–having a student repeat a grade—has traditionally been the intervention of choice in many urban schools. The 1987–88 retention rates hovered around 10 percent in all six schools. Over the course of intervention, the Success for All schools show dramatic declines in the retention rates, basically eliminating retention with the exception of the most needy cases. This reduction comes in part from the cross-grade regrouping for reading, typically the major factor in predicting which students will be retained. It is important to note that beyond the obvious affective implications of reduction in retention, other data, such as special education and achievement results, should be interpreted with the realization that the cohort sample is not biased by eliminating retentions from the analyses.

A goal of Success for All's family support and integrated-service program was to keep special education "special," to give children as much help and assistance as needed, and to avoid unnecessary special education referrals and placements. In other studies (Slavin et al., 1992), Success for All has led to the reductions of referrals labeled "learning disability." In the Baltimore schools in this study, some special education rates were as high as 16 percent of the student population. While contrast school data were stable over the three years, Success for All sites had a reduction in special education placements of approximately 5 percentage points. Most of the students who were in special education in 1987–88 remained in special education or moved to another school over the course of this study. The reduction occurred in the number of new students to special education. Many of these students received extended services from the Family Support Teams and other service providers.

During the 1991–92 school year we studied the degree of accuracy of referrals made to the special education review committees. This ratio of referrals to placements reflects whether teachers are using the special education system to dump students with any sort of problem (inaccurate referrals) or are first trying other options (tutoring, Family Support Team, community agencies) for these students and then referring only those who seem unable to benefit from the regular classroom, even with assistance. All students who are referred must undergo extensive assessments that are expensive to the school district; therefore, it is important that referrals not be made lightly. Success for All schools had much higher referral to placement ratios than did the contrast sites, indicating that most referrals were made appropriately.

Success for All's position on family support and integrated services is to remove the barriers to school learning. Therefore, the essential outcome to investigate is student achievement, even with the realization that many factors are involved in accounting for the variance in achievement. The variable studied was the number of third graders who met expectations in standardized reading performance. Many of the resources of the program target kindergarten through third grade reading, and many of the students assessed during the 1991–92 school year had been a part of the Success for All programs since first grade. The results point to significant gains in the number of students reaching grade-level expectations in two of the three Success for All schools, whereas the contrast schools maintain a stable pattern of performance. After three years the majority of Success for All schools still fall below grade level, in spite of the large gains noted from the 1987–88 school year.

The next set of results focuses on characteristics of the Family Support Teams in the Success for All schools and the comparable student service teams in the contrast schools. These pupil service teams are supposed to serve as an immediate step for students prior to a referral to special education. In the middle year of this study, 1991–92, data on the teams were collected.

Table 18.3 presents the characteristics of the school teams. The first variable is the number of documented student referrals to the team from any source (team member, administrator, teacher, parents, and so forth). To qualify as a referral, the case had to be on the formal agenda of the team meeting and discussed with the entire team. These were not considered special education referrals at the point of discussion, although many eventually did need review by the school-based special education committee. The three Success for All teams were busy throughout the school year as they had many more referrals than the contrast sites. SFA1 and SFA2 had more referrals than SFA3, perhaps due to the additional family support and agency staff.

The next variable was the number of long-term interventions completed by the teams. A long-term intervention was defined as one in which the student's involvement with the team lasted more

**Table 18.3. Characteristics of
the Family Support Team 1990–91.**

	SFA1	SFA2	SFA3	C1	C2	C3
Referrals/ Not Special Education	126	120	72	38	51	49
Long-Term Interventions	78	56	23	10	21	15
Number of Parent Workshops	26	30	15	10	12	12
Number of Full-time Equivalent Staff Family Support	4.5	4.5	1.5	1.5	2	1.5
Number of Full-time Equivalent Staff Outside Agencies	0.5	2.5	0	0	0.5	0.2
Number of Outside Agencies	5	7	3	3	3	2

than one month. These interventions were evaluated by analyses of case records kept by the team. Again SFA1 (78) and SFA2 (56) had substantially more long-term interventions with students than SFA3 (23). The contrast sites had considerably fewer long-term interventions (10, 21, and 15, respectively) even though the contrast sites were also considerably larger schools.

Assessing the amount of parent involvement through such indices as number of visits or number of volunteer services was difficult, although Success for All schools provided almost twice the number of opportunities for formal parent workshops than the other schools. The planning of parental involvement activities was the direct responsibility of the Family Support Teams in Success for All schools. The average attendance at Success for All workshops was 33.5 parents while the contrast sites averaged 19.5.

Success for All schools had more staff devoted to family support and service linkage activities. SFA1 and SFA2 each had a ratio of 4.5 to 1 staff members compared to the other four schools. The presence of outside agency staff at the school was only greater at SFA2, the school that had 2.5 full-time-equivalent staff from other agencies on site. Finally, SFA1 and SFA2 had more formal linkages to other community agencies than did the other four schools. SFA3 was more similar to the contrast schools in this regard.

Again these variables are only proxies for the actual services and quality of these services that the children and their families receive. The schools that had additional resources and more linkages to outside agencies had more children referred, provided longer interventions for the children, and had more parents involved with the school. The speculation is that these services were an important factor in the school differences noted in Table 18.2.

In the interviews, staff were asked questions relating to the level of service integration in the school. Eight characteristics of service integration were addressed:

- *Joint Planning*: Were outside agencies involved in school planning activities?

- *On-Site Services*: Did any agency routinely deliver services at the school location?

- *Share Records*: Did agencies share records of students with each other?

- *Share Funding*: Did agencies share funding sources to deliver school-based services?

- *Team Meetings*: Did agency staff attend school team meetings or did school staff attend outside agency meetings on a routine basis?

- *Share Case Manager*: Did a case manager coordinate activities across school and outside agencies?

- *Progress Reports to Teams*: Were regular progress reports on school and agency activity reported to the school team?

- *Formal Referral Mechanisms*: Were there formal referral mechanisms to community agencies?

Table 18.4 presents the level of integration at each of the six schools. A relative weight for level of integration was assigned to each school on the basis of interview responses. In order for a school to be checked for a given characteristic, more than two respondents had to indicate that the characteristic existed at their school. This analysis is not to imply that all these characteristics are of equal value. The most common characteristics were the provision of on-site services (4), team meetings (4), and referral mechanisms (4). Least common were the sharing of records (1) and the sharing of funds (0). Success for All sites place a strong emphasis on bringing in outside services that could assist them in removing barriers to student learning. The data in Table 18.4 suggest that many of the processes that could lead to better integration of services exist at a higher level in the Success for All schools than in the comparison schools.

The interviews, although limited in number, resulted in a number of other findings:

• Fewer barriers to services for students were mentioned for the Success for All schools. However, parents from all schools men-

Table 18.4. Level of Service Integration.

	SFA1	SFA2	SFA3	C1	C2	C3
Do Joint Planning		x		x		
Have On-Site Services	x	x	x		x	x
Share Records		x				
Share Funding						
Have Team Meetings	x	x	x			x
Share Case Manager	x	x				
Make Progress Reports to Team	x	x	x			
Have Referral Mechanisms to Other Agencies	x	x	x	x		
Level of Integration	5	7	4	2	1	2

tioned many reasons for their not being able to utilize school-based services, such as transportation, child care, other responsibilities, and issues of confidentiality.

• Schools that had services delivered on site were not more likely to have higher reported levels of service integration than schools that had good connections to community agencies that delivered services in locations away from the school.

• With regard to the history of agency involvement with the school, it appears that schools were basically reactive to agency or third-party requests to become involved in the schools. Schools were not the initiators. The building principal seemed to define the agency's role, if any, in the school.

• Neither the school nor the agencies showed evidence of any program evaluation efforts to examine whether their services were implemented as planned or affected students and their families in a meaningful way.

• In spite of a model that stresses prevention, the Success for All schools responded mostly to the acute care of children and families in crisis. The majority of time at the team meetings was still devoted to crisis-response issues rather than preventive activity, showing little difference from the contrast sites in this respect.

• The one school (SFA2) that had a case manager coordinating the Family Support Team had the highest level of satisfaction with the team of any of the schools.

• Even within the Success for All schools, the Family Support Team and their activities varied widely from site to site. The teams adapt to the needs of the students and their families and the conditions of their communities. These adaptations should not be considered implementation failures but rather appropriate responses to the needs of the students and their families. This variation among teams is distinct from the more prescribed focus of the academic curriculum and instruction intervention of Success for All.

Conclusion

The purpose of this study was to describe different variations in the delivery of family support and integrated services within six elementary schools in the Baltimore Public School system. Of particular interest was whether the Family Support Teams in the three Success for All schools made a difference in the lives of the students and their families when compared to contrast samples. In general, some impact was noted on the available proxy variables, yet the evaluation must be presented in the context of some difficult evaluation concerns. The primary limitations were the lack of additional data from community records, the inability to tease out the effects of the Family Support Teams from other components of the Success for All model, and the lack of follow-up data at the student level with which to assess the long-term impact of the interventions. To some degree, the partitioning of components to understand impact is not as critical a concern since the most successful interventions that focus on at-risk students have built-in layers of interventions that often overlap with each other. Redundancy is considered a strength for programs that aim to prevent students from falling between the cracks, particularly at the earlier grades.

Another central finding of this work is the tremendous variety of family support and integrated-service models that were investigated. Even though the sample of six schools is relatively small, each school seemed to have a unique adaptation, even within the Success for All schools. Outside agencies and schools formed different relationships with each other in historical patterns, community needs, resources, leadership styles, and amount of outside intervention. To some extent, the only common features were the two goals of family support and integrated services. The actual strategies were more like adaptations to a wide range of context conditions. This factor should be important to consider as a growing number of school reform initiatives place family support and service integration high on their lists of priorities for educational reform.

References

Behrman, R. E. (1992). *The future of children: School-linked services*. Los Altos, CA: Center for the Future of Children, the David and Lucile Packard Foundation.

Comer, J. (1988). Educating poor minority children. *Scientific American, 259*(5), 42–48.

Dolan, L. J. (1992). *Models for integrating human services into the school*. Baltimore, MD: Johns Hopkins University, Center for Research on Effective Schooling for Disadvantaged Students.

Gomby, D. S., & Larson, C. S. (1992). Evaluation of school-linked services. In R. E. Behrman (Ed.), *The future of children: School-linked services* (pp. 68–84). Los Altos, CA: Center for the Future of Children, the David and Lucile Packard Foundation.

Haxby, B. (1993). *The Family Support Team manual*. Baltimore, MD: Johns Hopkins University, Center for Research on Effective Schooling for Disadvantaged Students.

Levy, J., & Copple, C. (1989). *Joining forces: A report from the first year*. Alexandria, VA: National Association of State School Boards of Education.

Melaville, A. L., & Blank, M. J. (1991). *What it takes: Structuring interagency partnerships to connect children and families with comprehensive services*. Washington, DC: Education and Human Services Consortium.

Melaville, A. L., & Blank, M. J. (1993). *Together we can: A guide for crafting a pro-family system of education and human services*. Washington, DC: U.S. Department of Education and U.S. Department of Human Services.

New Jersey Department of Human Services. (1990). *The school-based youth service program*. Trenton, NJ: New Jersey Department of Human Services.

Slavin, R. E., Madden, N. A., Karweit, N. L., Dolan, L. J., & Wasik, B. A. (1992). *Success for all: A relentless approach to prevention and early intervention in elementary schools*. Arlington, VA: Educational Research Service.

Chapter Nineteen

Commentary

Lessons Learned About Integrating Services

Andrea Zetlin

There seems to be a consensus that a distinct population of children are failing in school. The same consensus holds that solving the problem of how best to educate these children will require a broad group of professionals, agencies, and parents working together to test new ideas and practices and bring about positive change in school success rates. To a large extent, this sentiment echoes what James Comer (1987) said so elegantly: that we cannot separate the academic from social and emotional development in children, and we need to incorporate all the resources of the school (including parents and the community) into a common blend of care and education.

A popular strategy for strengthening family-school-community connections is through the school-based, integrated-service models described in this book. Unfortunately, many of these programs have been given names such as "School of the Future," "New Futures Initiative," "Schools of the 21st Century," and so forth, when the reality is that there is an urgency to implement these programs on a large scale today.

These programs (which I refer to as extended school programs) must go beyond teaching and learning activities to include family growth and development as a primary aim. As Wayne Holtzman notes in Chapter Four of this volume, these kinds of programs must have at least five essential characteristics: (1) a strong administrative commitment to the project; (2) the involvement of parents and teachers in the program activities; (3) the integration of a broad array of health and human services; (4) the involvement of both public and private organizations; and (5) a long-term commitment to the project that acknowledges the necessity of evaluation and the feedback of information into the program so that change takes place when dictated by evaluation results.

As emphasized in previous chapters, the road leading to development and implementation of these extended school concepts can be rocky, but the journey has begun with model programs such as those in Texas, North Carolina, and Baltimore, and a number in California. I am associated with one in East Los Angeles at the Murchison Street School. A great deal can be learned from these fledgling efforts, especially when the program developers are willing to share candidly the kinds of hurdles and roadblocks that have impeded their progress, as Roslyn Mickelson and her colleagues did with their description of A Child's Place (Chapter Seventeen this volume). It is this type of detailed description, of both the program development and the evaluation of how programs progress, that can forewarn others of stumbling blocks (of which there are many).

Several authors in this volume have referred to extended school program developers as pioneers navigating unexplored territories. Even though the extended school concept is almost one hundred years old, the term *unexplored* is justified. This is because the ever-growing populations most in need of extended school services (homeless children, inner-city-ravaged children, children of diverse immigrant groups) present multifaceted needs and challenges on a scale not previously encountered—and at a time of diminishing resources. In short, building support for and maintaining a collaborative venture to serve children effectively is, mildly put, a daunting task. For those attempting to meet this challenge, the collaborative initiatives (successes and failures alike) described in this book contain valuable first-hand experience and information, summarized here into seven general "lessons."

Quality leadership is essential. A top-level catalyst, champion, convener, facilitator is needed—someone who recognizes and acknowledges that the current delivery of education, health, and human services is not meeting the needs of at least some of the target population. This catalyst must have the vision and authority to facilitate interagency collaboration. The Murchison Street School initiative, for example, started as a grassroots project. In the beginning, there were very fragile relationships between the school and agencies as negotiations proceeded. Once Healthy Start funding was received, the initiative became more credible. It is now less vulnerable to the kinds of little problems that would have killed it in its initial stages.

The commitment of the parties involved to fostering parent participation in planning and implementation must be honored. We have to ask ourselves if we are truly prepared for parents' full participation. We must be willing to relinquish some of our power as administrators, researchers, and program developers. We have to listen to them, and make changes and organize our programs around their input. We must also make a commitment to help them feel comfortable, teach them how to be involved, and most important, make them feel like valued associates.

At the Murchison Street School, we had to be mentors for parents and guide them through the process of how to access the formal system of delivery. We had to teach them how to do needs assessments, how to respond to questionnaires, how to begin to ask each other questions, how to inform us of the needs of the community, how to develop a list of potential service providers and weigh the pros and cons of each service-providing agency, and finally, how to access these agencies. This is a very exhausting process but one that has tremendous payoff. Before a parent center was developed at the school, parents could be seen in droves walking their children to school, leaving, and coming back in the afternoon to take them home without ever entering the building. One year after the parent center opened, large numbers of parents were attending programs *that they proposed,* such as English as a Second Language (ESL) classes, parenting workshops, and arts and crafts programs. Today, they regularly assist in the development of instructional materials for the classroom, they sponsor grade-level and schoolwide activities, and they also regularly present the principal with a list of their agenda items.

Policies and practices must be culturally compatible with the school-community population. Too often, planners of extended school programs think cultural compatibility means translating letters or ensuring that a translator is present at parent meetings. At the Murchison Street School, we try to integrate cultural awareness into every possible aspect of our mission. This means being cognizant of families' daily realities. For example, when we have ESL classes for parents, we let them bring their children. They don't have child care; they don't have money to pay for baby-sitting. We even provide toys for the children to play with while the parents learn. It is a wonderful model for the children, and it makes the parents feel comfortable.

Long-term commitments to program development must be made. Planners, supporters, and other participants must accept the reality that the sorts of outcome data society will applaud may not become available for five or seven or ten years. Further, it is vital that key financial and political supporters have realistic expectations for success as well, both in terms of goals and the time needed to achieve them. This kind of long-term commitment includes a willingness to persevere as issues of leadership and basic philosophy are worked out, as was related in the description of A Child's Place (Chapter Seventeen). For A Child's Place, the debate continues over whether the facility should be "a school with a social service component" or "a social service agency with an education component." As part of a long-term commitment, participants must also accept the dynamic nature of program development; necessary changes will have to occur as evaluation warrants.

Basic logistics must not be overlooked. Attention to the "nuts and bolts" aspect of collaborative undertakings is vital. This includes matters as basic as securing adequate physical space to providing training and cross-training so that participants from different backgrounds learn to negotiate their new roles and responsibilities. Obviously, the need for additional funding to support operating costs cannot be overstated. Ideally, a venture is not dependent on grant money; realistically, however, many projects must rely on grants for their initial funding. Because of this, it is absolutely vital that initiatives have center coordinators with talents for acquiring supplementary funding and overseeing financial activities as well as attending to case management, interagency networking, troubleshooting, operations management, and so forth. Placing too many of these responsibilities on school principals is both unfair and ineffective.

Models should vary according to needs, goals, and limitations. Models must be developed to address the local needs and concerns of schools, particularly those with large immigrant, highly transient, and/or homeless populations. Such schools have very distinct needs; thus programs focused around them will assume different configurations. Parents of children in these schools are plagued to different degrees by inadequate child care, after-school care, and job training. For a given school, the attraction of gang affiliation might be a pressing concern; in another, a shortage of bilingual programs might be an issue. Many of these schools struggle with a mixture of high dropout and teenage pregnancy rates. It is crucial, as Margaret Wang, Geneva Haertel, and Herbert Walberg underscored in Chapter Fifteen, that a detailed evaluation of available models be conducted to yield a much-needed knowledge base on how to provide school-linked service integration that is both feasible and cost effective.

Integrated-service initiatives must develop partnerships with local universities. In forging partnerships with universities, integrated-service initiatives receive the technical assistance needed for both program development and evaluation. For these partnerships to be successful, universities must build collaboration skills into undergraduate and graduate training programs for social service workers and educators alike. Additionally, integrated-service sites should be used as training bases so that students get experience working with educators and service workers from related fields.

The desire of educators to be responsive to the needs of children and families is evident. There are hundreds, possibly thousands, of schools across the United States that have demonstrated this dedication and interest. Many observers and researchers believe that educators who are committed to addressing the needs of children and families can propose creative solutions and overcome numerous obstacles to quality education and services for all. I believe this is true; it is evidenced in the initiatives described in this volume.

It is important that educators in general, and those involved with integrated-services initiatives in particular, remain focused on proceeding with the goal of fundamentally changing the way education and social services are provided. These initiatives must involve families and must occur deep within the structures of organizations and schools so that they are manifested in more than simply add-on programs. In short, we must make significant changes in the ways schools and collaborating agencies do business if we are to foster real inter-community connections to enable the successful achievement of children in schools.

References

Comer, J. P. (1987). New Haven's school-community connection. *Educational Leadership, 44*(6), 13–16.

Name Index

Subject Index